Personnel
Selection

FOUNDATIONS FOR ORGANIZATIONAL SCIENCE
A Sage Publications Series

Series Editor

David Whetten, *Brigham Young University*

Editors

Peter J. Frost, *University of British Columbia*
Anne S. Huff, *University of Colorado* and *Cranfield University* (UK)
Benjamin Schneider, *University of Maryland*
M. Susan Taylor, *University of Maryland*
Andrew Van de Ven, *University of Minnesota*

The FOUNDATIONS FOR ORGANIZATIONAL SCIENCE series supports the development of students, faculty, and prospective organizational science professionals through the publication of texts authored by leading organizational scientists. Each volume provides a highly personal, hands-on introduction to a core topic or theory and challenges the reader to explore promising avenues for future theory development and empirical application.

Books in This Series

Neal Schmitt
David Chan

Personnel Selection
A Theoretical Approach

Foundations for
Organizational
Science
A Sage Publications Series

SAGE Publications
International Educational and Professional Publisher
Thousand Oaks   London   New Delhi

For information:

SAGE Publications, Inc.
2455 Teller Road
Thousand Oaks, California 91320
E-mail: order@sagepub.com

SAGE Publications Ltd.
6 Bonhill Street
London EC2A 4PU
United Kingdom

SAGE Publications India Pvt. Ltd.
M-32 Market
Greater Kailash I
New Delhi 110 048 India

Printed in the United States of America

Library of Congress Cataloging-in-Publication Data

Schmitt, Neal.
    Personnel selection: A theoretical approach / by Neal Schmitt
and David Chan.
    p. cm. -- (Foundations of organizational science)
    Includes bibliographical references and index.
    ISBN 0-7619-0985-0 (cloth: acid-free paper)
    ISBN 0-7619-0986-9 (pbk.: acid-free paper)
    1. Employee selection. 2. Employee
selection--Research--Methodology. I. Chan, David, Ph. D. II. Title.
III. Series.
    HF5549.5.S38 S32 1998
    658.3'112--ddc21   98-25336

98 99 00 01 02 03 10 9 8 7 6 5 4 3 2 1

Acquiring Editor:	Marquita Flemming
Production Editor:	Diana E. Axelsen
Editorial Assistant:	Lynn Miyata
Typesetter/Designer:	Rose Tylak

Contents

Introduction to the Series

The title of this series, **Foundations for Organizational Science** (FOS), denotes a distinctive focus. FOS books are educational aids for mastering the core theories, essential tools, and emerging perspectives that constitute the field of organizational science (broadly defined to include organizational behavior, organizational theory, human resource management, and business strategy). The primary objective of this series is to support ongoing professional development among established scholars.

The series was born out of many long conversations among several colleagues, including Peter Frost, Anne Huff, Rick Mowday, Ben Schneider, Susan Taylor, and Andy Van de Ven, over a number of years. From those discussions, we concluded that there has been a major gap in our professional literature, as characterized by the following comment: "If I, or one of my students, want to learn about population ecology, diversification strategies, group dynamics, or personnel selection, we are pretty much limited to academic journal articles or books that are written either for content experts or practitioners. Wouldn't it be wonderful to have access to the teaching notes from a course taught by a master teacher of this topic?"

The plans for compiling a set of learning materials focusing on professional development emerged from our extended discussions of common experiences and observations, including the following:

1. While serving as editors of journals, program organizers for professional association meetings, and mentors for new faculty members, we have observed wide variance in theoretical knowledge and tool proficiency in our field. To the extent that this outcome reflects available learning opportunities, we hope that this series will help "level the playing field."

2. We have all "taught" in doctoral and junior faculty consortia prior to our professional meetings and have been struck by how often the participants comment, "I wish that the rest of the meetings [paper sessions and symposia] were as informative." Such observations got us thinking—Are our doctoral courses more like paper sessions or doctoral consortia? What type of course would constitute a learning experience analogous to attending a doctoral consortium? What materials would we need to teach such a course? We hope that the books in this series have the "touch and feel" of a doctoral consortium workshop.

3. We all have had some exposure to the emerging "virtual university" in which faculty and students in major doctoral programs share their distinctive competencies, either through periodic jointly sponsored seminars or through distance learning technology, and we would like to see these opportunities diffused more broadly. We hope that reading our authors' accounts will be the next best thing to observing them in action.

4. We see some of the master scholars in our field reaching the later stages of their careers, and we would like to "bottle" their experience and insight for future generations. Therefore, this series is an attempt to disseminate "best practices" across space and time.

To address these objectives, we ask authors in this series to pass along their "craft knowledge" to students and faculty beyond the boundaries of their local institutions by writing from the perspective of seasoned teachers and mentors. Specifically, we encourage them to invite readers into their classrooms (to gain an understanding of the past, present, and future of scholarship in particular areas from the perspective of their firsthand experience), as well as into their offices and hallway conversations (to gain insights into the subtleties and nuances of exemplary professional practice).

By explicitly focusing on an introductory doctoral seminar setting, we encourage our authors to address the interests and needs of nonexpert students and colleagues who are looking for answers to questions such as the following: Why is this topic important? How did it originate and how has it evolved? How is it different from related topics? What do we actually know about this topic? How does one effectively communicate this information to students and practitioners? What are the methodological pitfalls and conceptual dead ends that should be avoided? What are the most/least promising opportunities for theory development and empirical study in this area? What questions/situations/phenomena are not well suited for this theory or tool?

What is the most interesting work in progress? What are the most critical gaps in our current understanding that need to be addressed during the next 5 years?

We are pleased to share our dream with you, and we encourage your suggestions for how these books can better satisfy your learning needs—as a newcomer to the field preparing for prelims or developing a research proposal, or as an established scholar seeking to broaden your knowledge and proficiency.

DAVID A. WHETTEN
SERIES EDITOR

Acknowledgments

We very much appreciate the helpful guidance of M. Susan Taylor during the planning of this book. She provided a good sense of the objectives of the **Foundations for Organizational Science** series as well as comments on the content of what we planned to address in the book. We also acknowledge our colleagues at Michigan State University who provided the intellectual stimulation and, in some cases, the ideas that are presented in this book. Marcy Schafer transformed the usual botched word processing files into a finished product that greatly facilitated the production process. Susan Taylor provided useful commentary and suggestions on each of the chapters in the first version of this book. In addition, we received and incorporated commentary from Wally Borman, Ed Levine, Ben Schneider, Lois Tetrick, and Sheldon Zedeck. We also appreciate the support of family members (Kara and Krista), who continue to tolerate strange work hours, and the institutions (Michigan State University and National University of Singapore) that supported our efforts. Finally, we thank the people at Sage, particularly Marquita Flemming, who produced the product you are now reading.

 **1** Personnel Selection Research

Importance, Research
Designs, and Examples

Personnel selection research has been conducted for most of the
20th century (for early examples, see Scott, 1911). This research
has followed the general paradigm outlined in Figure 1.1. The job for
which individuals will be chosen is examined to determine what tasks
and responsibilities will be required. This specification of the domain
of job tasks is followed by the generation of hypotheses concerning
the knowledge, skills, abilities, and other characteristics (KSAOs)
required of individuals who must perform these tasks. Specification
of the tasks and KSAOs leads to the development of measures of both
job performance variables and predictor variables and evaluation of
the hypotheses about ability-performance relationships proposed
during the job analysis phase of the project. Assuming some confirmation of these hypotheses, various steps are taken to implement the
selection procedures and to assess their practical costs and benefits in
an organizational context.

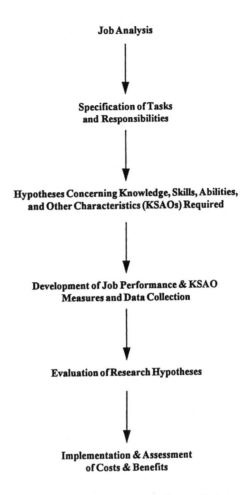

Figure 1.1. Traditional Personnel Selection Research Paradigm

This basic paradigm appropriately underlies good personnel selection or staffing research. We assume that there are individual differences in the knowledge, skills, abilities, and other characteristics that workers bring to jobs, and that these individual differences manifest themselves in job performance. Our job is to uncover and understand the nature of the relationships between these KSAO-job performance individual differences. This effort is challenging, important, and exciting. All organizations are concerned with the "human capital" that they are capable of attracting and retaining. Moreover, most organizational and research personnel point to the increasing importance of human capabilities in organizational success. A recent survey of supervisors in one of the "Big Three" automotive companies indicated that they believe that levels of all personal characteristics and abilities needed to perform entry-level jobs will increase in the coming years. In the process of describing and measuring individual differences, we must learn about many different jobs. A partial list of the jobs we personally have studied includes clerical/technical staff, emergency telephone operators, police personnel, school principals, meat processing workers, skilled tradespeople in an automotive manufacturing facility, and furniture makers. Discovering what performance represents in each of these different jobs and what makes some individuals effective and motivated contributors to their organizations and others not so effective is always different and always interesting. In the process, we must learn how organizations work and how decisions are made in organizations so that our interventions can have the intended impacts on the quality of the workforce. We must also be concerned about the reactions of the people assessed using the materials we develop, because these reactions may influence their subsequent interaction with the organization, shape public reaction to the organization, or determine the motivation and performance levels of those who are selected. In all these efforts, we are seeking to discover what is general (and unique) about the nature of individual differences in KSAOs and job performance and the relationships between measures of these two sets of constructs. In this book, we hope to communicate how human resource practitioners and researchers address these issues and to provide examples that will enrich abstract models such as the one described above.

Job Performance Defined

The basic objective of personnel selection research is to evaluate a hypothesis or theory of work performance. However, performance per se is rarely defined by selection researchers, or, in summarizing selection research, authors have ignored the fact that performance has been operationally defined in a great many different ways. Campbell,

McCloy, Oppler, and Sager (1993) define work performance as employee-controlled behavior that is relevant to organizational goals. Inherent in this definition, and explicit in their discussion, are some other notions about performance. First, performance is multidimensional. That is, there is no one single performance variable, but different types of work behavior relevant to organizations in most contexts. We will discuss these types of work behavior in more detail in Chapter 3. Second, performance is behavior, not necessarily results. For example, a salesclerk may treat a disgruntled customer in the most courteous manner possible, but because of company policy he or she may be unable to satisfy the customer and thus becomes the subject of a customer complaint. Or an employee may engage in unsafe behavior while operating a forklift, but because no other equipment or people are present, no accident occurs. In both instances, the result (a customer complaint and the lack of an accident) is *not* performance, but the result of some behavior. It is the behavior that should be of interest to selection researchers. It also must be behavior that is under the control of the employee. The forklift operator may back into a wall as a function of a faulty brake system. He or she may press the brake (work performance), but still hit the wall (result).

One reason selection researchers have not considered the performance construct seriously is that they have too often accepted organizational clients' archived definitions of performance (e.g., pieces produced or sold, number of accidents). Such indices are presumably relevant to an organization's goals, but they are, at best, only indirectly related to employee work behavior or performance. This may be because the organization's goals are inconsistent with the requirements of the jobs as articulated to job incumbents, but more often it may be the case that the organization, environment, or technology involved places constraints on an employee such that her or his behavior does not translate into the desired organizational outcome. A simple example is the case of a worker who does not have the equipment or raw material necessary to perform his or her job. Without the right resources, the worker's capabilities and willingness to perform are irrelevant. One of the major tasks of the job analyst (see Chapters 2 and 3) is to document the required work behavior as a means of developing an operational definition or measure of work performance.

As stated above, a basic assumption of those doing selection research is that individuals differ in the capabilities (KSAOs) required to do various jobs. Hence, the scientific source of the discipline of personnel selection research lies in the psychology of individual differences and ability measurement. We will discuss this scientific base in parts of Chapters 2 through 6.

Evidence Regarding
Ability-Performance Relationships

Because of practical constraints and the availability of a large existing body of knowledge on a set of ability-performance relationships, various bodies of evidence might be used to assess the validity of proposed procedures and to support their use. One form of evidence consists of documentation showing that those who developed the selection procedures exercised care in specifying the job domain and carefully matching test tasks to this job domain, so that the end result is a selection procedure consisting of tasks that are a reasonable representation of the job domain. The second type of evidence is found in studies in which performance on the selection procedures is correlated with measures of job performance. The third type of evidence is based on the nature of the hypothesized ability-performance relationship of interest and the similarity between this situation and the existing body of literature. When a great deal of evidence exists regarding the ability-performance relationship and the measures of the required ability, then such measures ought to be useful and defensible in new situations. These three types of evidence are often referred to as content, criterion-related, and construct validity in the selection area, but there is an increasing recognition that all are aspects of concern about the accuracy of inferences derived about job performance on the basis of a test score. Over time, and cumulatively across many studies and situations, it is desirable to collect all three types of evidence. No one type of evidence is primary; rather, the quality of the evidence, whatever its nature, is most important. Perhaps because of the relatively standard process by which evidence is accumulated by those developing and validating selection procedures, the field of personnel selection is generally viewed as employing an empirical atheoretical process. In some instances (e.g., the development of empirically scored biodata forms), this has been true. However, it is usually true (even in biodata research) that selection researchers form theories of job performance, are aware of theoretical research on individual differences when developing or selecting testing procedures, and either explicitly or implicitly form and test theories of ability-performance relationships in their applied research. It is one of our purposes in this book to highlight those theories and to indicate what we know about ability-performance relationships. A second purpose will be to suggest and encourage additional theoretical development in this area of organizational science.

Practical Importance of Selection

These theoretical issues and the continuing attention selection and work performance have received from researchers attest to the importance of personnel selection to organizations, but it is not difficult to document the financial importance of selection also. Statistics from the U.S. Department of Labor suggest that more than 8 million new jobs were created during the first 3½ years of the Clinton administration. Most of these new jobs, plus all the job changes that occurred during these years, were filled using some means of selection. Terpstra and Rozell (1993) have documented that companies that use the practices we will describe in this book—such as conducting validation studies, using structured interviews, and administering tests—have higher levels of annual profit, profit growth, and overall performance. The relationship between these practices and organizational performance has been shown to be especially strong in the service and financial sectors, two sectors of the U.S. economy that have been growing most rapidly. Organizations have recognized the importance of selection at least implicitly, in that they report spending more money on selection than on any other aspect of human resource management. Recent direct attempts to assess the utility of valid selection programs have produced very large monetary figures (Boudreau, 1991; Cascio, 1987b).

The amounts invested in selection procedure development and use are also large. In the first example provided later in this chapter, the development and validation costs associated with the project were about $1.5 million. At least three full-time people are employed to administer this program, and well over 250 senior-level employees have been trained to do panel interviews and actually are so employed a minimum of 2 weeks a year. In a survey conducted more than 10 years ago involving individual assessments (Ryan & Sackett, 1987), the respondents indicated that the average assessment cost between $265 and $723, depending on the position. It is common to find estimates of the per candidate cost in the use of assessment centers to evaluate managerial talent in the thousands of dollars. Nor are such expenditures limited to higher-level management positions. Toyota (USA) hires about 3,000 factory employees annually in Georgetown, Kentucky. Each employee hired invests at least 18 hours in a selection process that includes an exam on general knowledge, a test of attitudes toward work, an interpersonal skills assessment, a manufacturing exercise designed to provide a realistic preview of the job's assembly work, an extensive personal interview, and a physical exam. These investments are large, but it is also true that the organization may be making a multimillion-dollar investment in each hired person. An automobile worker may earn a $40,000 annual salary. If this person is hired at age 20, and counting pension and spousal benefits, the organization could easily be paying this individual this amount of money or more, adjusted for inflation, for the next 75 years.

Legislative and judicial pressures have increased the costs and impacts of selection decisions. Equal employment law and court cases, and more recently the Americans with Disabilities Act, have imposed additional burdens on employers to engage in fair employment practices and to be able to show that their practices are indeed job relevant. In one recent case involving the selection of entry-level police personnel, the county spent more than $700,000 to recruit candidates to take its selection tests. Most of this recruitment effort was directed at obtaining a demographically diverse set of applicants as a means of avoiding continuous litigation. Accommodations to allow individuals with handicaps to compete fairly for jobs for which they are qualified almost always cost additional funds, either in equipment or in personnel. The development of fair procedures is important for avoiding costly litigation, but, at least on a societal level, it ensures the maximum use of contributions from all members of society. If the U.S. economy is to compete internationally, we cannot refuse to use the talents of members of minority groups or exclude half our population from participation on the grounds of sex. Equality in employment opportunities for women has been seen as central to a vibrant economy by people as different as Mao Tse-tung in early 20th century China and Eleanor Roosevelt in World War II.

Organization of This Book

In this first chapter, we will provide four different examples of the development and validation of selection procedures. These examples differ in many ways, including the jobs studied, the KSAOs thought to be most relevant, the types of procedures developed to assess important job-relevant KSAOs, and the ways in which evidence was gathered to support the use of these procedures. In each case, however, significant use is made of existing theory and research on the prediction of individual differences in work performance. We use these four examples to illustrate something of the diversity of challenges faced by organizations in selecting personnel; we will also refer to them (as well as other studies) throughout the book as illustrations of particular problems or strengths. We suggest that you may want to review the examples again after reading the remainder of the book. We believe that you will have a much greater understanding at that point of what was done, the issues that needed to be addressed, and what research still needs to be done. Of course, we would expect that a similar increase in understanding will occur when you examine other reports of selection research.

In conducting selection research, the first step is almost always some form of job analysis. This job analysis forms the basis of a theory of work performance for the job in question. In Chapter 2, we describe the means by which job analyses are conducted. Conducting a job analysis from scratch in each new instance is tedious, time-consuming, and expensive. Most important, job analyses often re-create what is already known from analyses of similar jobs conducted in other organizations. Hence, psychologists have formed some general theories of work performance that are reflected in standardized job analysis instruments (Harvey, 1991; McCormick, Jeanneret, & Mecham, 1972), methods of rating job requirements (Fine & Wiley, 1974), and more formal delineations of the nature of work (Campbell et al., 1993). We discuss these general theories of work in Chapter 3.

The theories of work performance lead directly to hypotheses about the nature of the human characteristics necessary to accomplish work tasks. In Chapter 5, we describe the nature of the various individual difference variables that seem to influence work outcomes. This discussion includes information on the common methods of measuring these characteristics and the particular theoretical assumptions underlying the use of these instruments, as well as the problems peculiar to each instrument. Personnel selection researchers have used an incredible array of procedures, including paper-and-pencil measures of ability, interviews, biodata, personality tests, and job samples. We describe each of these procedures, with an emphasis on the nature of the theoretical constructs best assessed using these techniques.

Just as specific theories of job performance have led to more general theories of work performance, so too have specific measures of human abilities led to theories or taxonomies of human abilities. In Chapter 4, we describe a variety of such theories, including Thurstone's (1938) notion about primary mental abilities, Spearman's g (1904, 1927), Guilford's (1967) structure of intellect model, Sternberg's (1979) ideas about the nature of intelligence, and Fleishman's (Fleishman & Quaintance, 1984; Fleishman & Reilly, 1992b) and Carroll's (1993) taxonomies of human abilities. In the last section of Chapter 4, we discuss attempts to combine the research on abilities and the nature of work into theories of ability-performance relationships (Borman, White, Pulakos, & Oppler, 1991) or joint taxonomies of ability and the nature of work (Burke & Pearlman, 1988). In the past two decades, the use of meta-analysis (i.e., the analysis of the results of a combination of studies) to aggregate data across a large number of studies has enabled researchers in the personnel selection area to say with great confidence that particular ability-performance relationships will generalize across a wide variety of work situations. In Chapter 5, we review many of these meta-analyses and present a summary of the results of tests of the major hypotheses that have been of interest to personnel selection researchers. In addition, we make some recommendations as to which of these relationships or others should be investigated further to enhance the information available regarding the role of individual differences at work.

It is also true that personnel selection research involves a great many technical issues that must be resolved if we hope to derive generalizable rules that describe ability-performance relationships. Anyone who attempts to read the selection literature will know that the researchers make extensive use of correlation and regression analysis and, most recently, meta-analysis. They are also concerned with the dimensionality of the constructs they measure, hence they use exploratory and confirmatory factor analysis. Personnel selection researchers are also concerned about the research designs they are capable of using in applied situations and the implications these design issues have for the assessment of their theories of ability-performance relationships, hence they are concerned about the nature of range restriction, unreliability, and the power associated with tests of their hypotheses and the confidence with which they can make estimates of effect sizes. We address these issues directly in Chapter 6 and at other points in the book as they are relevant to the proper interpretation of a body of literature. For the most part, we avoid the discussion of data analysis techniques or issues when those procedures are general and likely to be taught or used in other social science research (e.g., regression and correlation analyses). When a technique is likely to be unique or most frequently used in individual difference or selection research (e.g., correction for restriction of range), we describe the analytic procedure and discuss its use in detail.

Like any other organizational intervention, the introduction of selection procedures raises a host of implementation issues. Consistent scoring and consistent use of test scores are obviously important if an organization is to recognize the potential of its investment in the development of those tests. In addition, the benefits of selection are dependent on their compatibility with other human resource systems, such as compensation, recruitment, and training. More broadly, societal and legal pressures (e.g., the concerns raised by equal employment opportunity legislation and the Americans with Disabilities Act) affect the manner in which selection procedures are used and their impacts on an organization's workforce. Finally, applicant reactions to selection procedures and the recent concern with organizational justice issues also concern organizations as they establish procedures to hire personnel. All of the issues addressed in Chapter 7 are practical, but they do set up boundary conditions with respect to the impacts that identifiable and measurable ability-performance relationships can have on organizations. In all cases, our emphasis in discussing these practical concerns is on the assumptions and theoretical hypotheses suggested when we consider these "boundary" conditions.

The nature of work is changing rapidly. In a recent issue of *Fortune,* one writer asserted that jobs as traditionally constituted no longer exist (Bridges, 1994). People cannot expect to train for a single occupation or job; rather, they must be ready to move from one job or task to another as specific projects require a different mix or level of skills. In addition, technological change in many areas requires that we all learn new ways of accomplishing our work on a continuous basis. This demand for continuous learning almost certainly has implications for the skills and personalities of the individuals recruited and selected into those jobs. Organizations have downsized and outsourced many of their functions over the past two decades, so that now many people are self-employed, employed in consulting firms, or telecommunicating as a means of doing their work. All of these forms of work are likely to require a new independence on the part of workers and may require different modes of communication and coordination of work. The service industry continues to grow, often at the expense of manufacturing. Many more of us are required to work with foreign companies or with parts of our parent firms that are located in other countries, which means that many more of us will need to interact effectively with individuals who speak languages different from ours and who are familiar with different cultures. Some of us may have to work in different parts of the world. In Chapter 8, we discuss the implications of these changes for the types of abilities that will be required of workers in different situations and, again, the types of research data that will best provide answers to the questions that will arise as a function of these changes.

In the final chapter, we summarize the major research questions raised in other chapters of the book and try to indicate the nature of the programs of research that might best answer these questions.

The planned outline of this book follows the steps in a traditional criterion-related selection study (see Figure 1.1), which also represents the normal way in which investigators in various applied social science disciplines conduct their research. We begin with theory and hypothesis development (i.e., job analysis—Chapters 2 and 3), develop and evaluate measures of the variables of interest (i.e., predictor and criterion measurement—Chapters 3, 4, and 5), collect data and evaluate our hypotheses (Chapter 6), and then assess the practical implications and the potential to implement research findings in some real-world context (Chapter 7) and the degree to which they will generalize to new circumstances (Chapter 8). Finally, we assess the need to evaluate questions generated by the research study just conducted (Chapter 9).

Examples of Selection Research

In an attempt to describe clearly the natures of the various kinds of personnel selection research, the problems of doing such research, and the challenges associated with discovering the nature of KSAO-performance relationships, we provide in the remainder of this chapter four very different examples of such research. Example 1 is a description of a study designed to develop procedures to select investigative agents in a large federal agency. This study represents a nearly textbook example of a criterion-related validation study, with attendant strengths and weaknesses. Example 2 comes from another large federal agency that wanted to use a multiaptitude test battery to select applicants into a large number of agency jobs. In this situation, a combination of strategies, including criterion-related validation, analysis of ability requirements, and job clustering, allowed for the selection of specific ability measures for each job and recommendations with respect to the extent to which the results of initial validation studies on a small subset of jobs would generalize to other jobs in the agency. Example 3 is a description of the development of a selection system for a very small city department in which the defense of the procedures developed was that they were a representative sample from the domain of tasks the job incumbents were expected to perform. Example 4 describes the selection of a single individual for a high-level executive position in a large firm. In this case, a job analysis was performed and, on the basis of this information and a psychologist's understanding of the position and the type of person the corporation believed it needed in this position, the required KSAOs were generated. The psychologist then used his understanding of the literature regarding these KSAOs to select and devise a series of measurements that allowed him to make a recommendation about the suitability of prospective applicants for this position.

It is our hope that by providing these examples at the outset, we are giving you a basis for thinking about the issues raised throughout the remainder of the book. As we have noted, we believe that your understanding of each of these cases should be greatly enhanced by your reading of the remainder of this text. We encourage you to reexamine these examples after you have read the entire book.

Example 1: Development and Criterion-Related Validation of Procedures in a Large Investigative Agency

Our first example of selection research involved the development and validation (i.e., collection of evidence that the inferences about job performance made concerning scores on the selection procedures are accurate) of procedures designed to select entry-level investigators for a large federal agency. These personnel were all college graduates, and many had specialized degrees (e.g., law, MBAs in finance and accounting). The total selection process included tests of physical ability and a background check as well as the procedures described below. Annually, about 300 of 10,000 applicants were selected to attend a 6-month training academy.

The project began with group interviews, in which the job tasks and KSAOs were generated. The interviews were followed by a survey of a larger group of incumbents and supervisors, who were asked to rate the tasks and KSAOs on several dimensions to ascertain their relative importance and the appropriateness of including them in the selection procedures. The 10 major task categories that defined the work of these agents were as follows: (a) recording information and developing written materials; (b) making oral presentations and testifying; (c) gathering information and evidence; (d) reviewing and analyzing information; (e) planning, coordinating, and organizing work and people; (f) monitoring, controlling, and attending to detail on the job; (g) working in dangerous situations; (h) developing constructive relationships with others; (i) demonstrating effort and initiative; and (j) maintaining a positive image. The required KSAOs are listed along the left side of Table 1.1; the selection procedures designed to assess each of the major KSAO dimensions are listed along the top of that table. Details regarding the methods used to derive this information about job activities and the required KSAOs are provided in Chapters 2 and 3.

Some of the procedures in this study were developed as relatively direct samples of job behavior (i.e., the interview simulation and written simulations), hence they were considered content valid, or

Table 1.1   KSAO by Selection Procedure Matrix

KSAO Dimension	Selection Procedures					
	Cognitive Ability	Personality/ Biodata	Situational Judgment	Structured Interview	Interview Simulation	Written Simulation
Ability to write effectively	X					X
Ability to organize, plan, and prioritize		X	X	X	X	X
Ability to communicate orally				X	X	
Ability to relate to others effectively		X	X	X	X	
Ability to maintain a positive image		X	X	X		
Ability to attend to detail	X					X
Ability to evaluate information	X	X	X	X	X	X
Initiative and motivation		X	X	X		
Ability to adapt to changing situations		X	X	X		
Physical requirements		X		X		

NOTE: X indicates that this test procedure was designed to measure a KSAO dimension.

directly representative of job tasks. The link between the work done on the job and the nature of the remaining tests was not easy to make, hence a concurrent (i.e., predictor and criterion data were collected from job incumbents) criterion-related validation study was conducted. In a criterion-related study, evidence is gathered to show that test scores and job performance measures are related. The criteria, or measures of job performance, used in this study were a 117-item job knowledge test and supervisory ratings made on 10 behaviorally anchored rating scales (one for each of the major task dimensions listed in Table 1.1). An example of one of these scales is shown in Figure 1.2. These 10 scales were combined to form two major performance dimensions (Core Investigative Proficiency and Effort and Professionalism) based on the relationships between ratings on the scales.

Seven different types of predictors were constructed to assess the KSAO dimensions. The job analysis indicated the importance of writing, information analysis and evaluation, judgment, and decision-

Gathering Information and Evidence

Obtaining information and evidence by conducting research, surveillance, interviews/interrogations, and possibly working undercover; verifying the accuracy of information; following up on leads; and, handling evidence properly to ensure its admissibility in court.

1	2	3	4	5	6	7
Unsatisfactory			Fulfills Expectations			Exceptional

Unsatisfactory

Agents at this level often fail to investigate or superficially investigate important sources of information. They collect information that is frequently incomplete, inaccurate, or irrelevant. They sometimes fail to verify the accuracy of information, resulting in "wild goose chases" and wasted resources. They may use improper evidence handling procedures, yielding evidence that is inadmissible in court.

PERFORMANCE EXAMPLES:

a. While interviewing a job applicant, this SA failed to ask questions regarding discrepancies in information provided on various application documents. As a result, the case was declined for prosecution by the AUSA and many manhours were wasted.

Fulfills Expectations

Agents at this level investigate obvious and standard sources of information efficiently and effectively, and they typically verify the accuracy of information. They collect the information/evidence necessary to develop prosecutable cases but they may not develop highly significant or complex cases. They properly process evidence and maintain the chain of custody.

PERFORMANCE EXAMPLES:

a. During a drug investigation, this agent conducted a search of a residence, located drugs, and sent them to the lab. The subject was convicted of drug possession.

b. This SA corroborated information received from an informant by tapping independent sources. As a result, the affidavit withstood a suppression hearing.

Exceptional

Agents at this level diligently and compulsively investigate atypical as well as standard sources of information. Due to their thoroughness and investigative skill, the information/evidence they obtain often leads to the development of highly complex and significant cases. These agents verify the accuracy of all information, carefully double checking and cross checking records, sources, etc. Their exceptional interview and interrogation skills result in gathering high quality information. They handle evidence flawlessly.

PERFORMANCE EXAMPLES:

a. When working on a drug case, this SA had eight defendants who were suspected of being involved in a drug conspiracy but none of whom were cooperating. The agent meticulously gathered evidence at the suspected leader's house. Fingerprints of the main subject were found on a couple key pieces of evidence. As a result, the leader pled guilty, and the arrest followed.

b. During an investigation that involved the seizure of several vehicles, this agent researched the identity of numerous other co-defendants and was thus able to obtain a complete list of all vehicles subject to seizure. Several other co-defendants were apprehended and additional vehicles seized.

Figure 1.2. Example of a Behaviorally Anchored Rating Scale Used to Assess Agent's Performance

making abilities, which we tried to assess using six subtests of the Air
Force Officer Qualifying Test. These 25-item subtests included measures of math knowledge, data interpretation, arithmetic reasoning,
verbal analogies, word knowledge, and reading comprehension. A
measure of the Big Five personality constructs (Digman, 1990) was
used; in particular, we felt that the conscientiousness, extraversion,
and agreeableness measures were reflected in the relating effectively
to others, adaptation, and initiative and motivation KSAO dimensions
recognized as important in the job analysis. Biodata scales were developed to measure the same constructs as well as the ability to organize,
plan, and prioritize; the ability to maintain a positive image; the ability
to attend to detail; the ability to evaluate information; and the ability
to meet physical requirements dimensions. A situational judgment
test—in which examinees were presented with situations like those
they would be likely to encounter on the job and then asked to select
from among three to five courses of action—was developed to assess
examinees' approaches to dealing with others and their abilities to
plan and organize effectively, evaluate information, maintain a positive image, demonstrate initiative, and adapt to new situations. A
structured interview was designed to assess examinees' interpersonal
skills, oral communication skills, and experience in dealing with situations involving the need to plan and organize effectively, evaluate
information, maintain a positive image, and exercise initiative, motivation, and adaptability, as well as their willingness to maintain their
physical ability. The interview was administered by a three-person
panel of carefully trained evaluators and scored using standardized
guidelines. A role-play exercise (i.e., the interview simulation) was also
administered by the members of the interview panel. The examinee
was required to play the role of a private investigator and interview
two individuals who were involved in or had information about a
bribery. Because job incumbents did a great deal of interviewing as
part of their job, this exercise very closely mirrored actual job tasks
(see Table 1.1 for the actual dimensions assessed). Because the agents
were often required to organize and compose written summaries of
complex sets of data, information, and events, a written simulation
was developed to assess the examinees' abilities in this area. Each
applicant was required to review a set of written materials and write
a recommendation based on facts presented in the materials. Each

written simulation was scored by two carefully trained evaluators who used standardized scoring instructions and rating scales.

Test data were collected from 467 actual agents, and performance ratings were collected from their supervisors, who received training with respect to the avoidance of common rating errors and an explanation of the project and their role in determining a positive outcome in the validation project. Interrater reliability of the ratings was determined through correlation of the supervisor performance ratings with ratings performed by substitute supervisors for 349 of the research participants. These reliabilities were .53 and .50 for the two major performance dimensions. The test data and the performance data were correlated as estimates of the criterion-related validity of the predictors. These correlations are displayed in Table 1.2. The numbers in italics in this table reflect tests of hypothesized ability-performance relationships. The correlations indicate that the cognitive ability measures were predictive of job knowledge and performance on the Core Investigative Proficiency dimension. The personality measures were unrelated to any of the three criteria, and only two of the biodata measures (initiative and motivation and an empirically derived scale called Biomax) were related to the two performance measures. The interview was the best predictor of the two performance dimensions. The interview simulation, the situational judgment test, and the written simulations were also related to the performance criteria. It should also be pointed out that these observed correlations are underestimates of the ability-performance relationships because of the low reliability of the performance measures (reported above) and because the study included current employees whose range of scores on the predictor variables was substantially less than the range of scores in an applicant pool. This latter problem is referred to as *restriction of range*. With the availability of information on a set of applicant examinees, corrections for this problem can be made; we discuss these corrections and a correction for lack of perfect criterion reliability in Chapter 6, where we use them to correct these validity coefficients.

Theoretically, this study provided confirmation for most of the hypothesized ability-performance relationships, with the notable exception of those involving the personality measures. The evidence for two major performance dimensions is consistent with Borman and Motowidlo's (1993) notion that job performance consists of contextual and task dimensions, and to some degree with theoretical positions that came out of the Project A research (Campbell, Ford, et al., 1990). Project A was a very large study that examined a wide range of military jobs. The researchers collected data on selection procedures and multiple performance measures on a large sample of military people in an effort to evaluate these procedures. The Project A researchers believed that all jobs comprise at least three factors: core task proficiency (similar to our Core Investigative factor), demonstrated effort, and personal discipline (these two being similar to our Effort and Professionalism dimension). A single criterion-related study can provide evidence for the viability of specific hypotheses about job performance and ability; the aggregation of the results of many such studies has provided the basis for very general theories of work performance-ability relationships, as we shall demonstrate later. (For interested readers, various issues raised during this project are addressed in a series of papers: Pulakos & Schmitt, 1995, 1996; Pulakos, Schmitt, & Chan, 1996; Pulakos, Schmitt, Whitney, & Smith, 1996.)

Clearly, this study involved the development and evaluation of a wide variety of predictors and performance measures. The primary interest, of course, was the evaluation of the relationship between the predictors (estimates of individual differences in applicant KSAOs) and the performance measures. The process of studying the human requirements of job performance is both exciting and, at times, challenging, but, as we shall see, human resource professionals have been able to contribute significantly to organizationally relevant outcomes by applying their understanding of, and ability to measure, individual differences in human capabilities and motivation.

The work of human resource professionals in helping organizations identify talent does not end with the confirmation of the hypotheses evaluated in a study like the one described above. In using these tests to select future agents, it was also necessary to address several practical issues. First, given the very large number of applicants, the organization felt it was impossible to administer the interview and written simulation to all applicants. Therefore, a two-hurdle selection system was established in which portions of the cognitive ability test, the biodata test, and the situational judgment test were administered as an initial screen; those passing these tests were then interviewed and

Table 1.2 Predictor-Criterion Correlations ($Ns = 461$-467)

Predictors	Job Knowledge	Core Investigative Proficiency	Effort and Professionalism
Verbal ability[a]	.44	.19	.03
Quantitative ability[b]	.38	.22	.05
Extraversion	−.05	−.07	.02
Agreeableness	−.03	−.06	.01
Conscientiousness	−.08	.03	.07
Adaptation to changing situations[c]	−.07	−.07	.03
Physical requirements[c]	−.06	.08	−.06
Plan, organize, prioritize[c]	−.13	.06	.08
Relate to others effectively[c]	.00	.02	.04
Maintain positive image[c]	−.07	.01	−.01
Evaluate information[c]	.02	−.02	.05
Initiative and motivation[c]	.02	.13	.11
Biomax[c]	−.04	.07	.13
Situational judgment	.11	.20	.13
Structured interview	.07	.35	.36
Interview simulation	.24	.25	.23
Written simulation	.24	.22	.05

NOTE: Numbers in italics signify instances in which a significant predictor-criterion relationship was hypothesized. Correlations greater than or equal to .09 are significant, $p < .05$.
a. Verbal ability equals the sum of scores on reading comprehension, verbal analogies, and word knowledge.
b. Quantitative ability equals the sum of scores on math knowledge, arithmetic reasoning, and data interpretation.
c. Indicates a biodata measure.

took the written simulation. Because the interview simulation was largely redundant with the interview, and because there was a fear that the consistency with which the role-plays were administered could not be maintained in the field, this exercise was abandoned. The second practical problem that arose was the impact of the use of the selection procedures on the hiring rates of different demographic subgroups. Tests were weighted and passing scores chosen for both hurdles, which resulted in small differences in the hiring rates, primarily those of African American applicants as opposed to White applicants, while still allowing for the use of the test scores in a way that maximized the predicted performance outcomes. Trade-offs involved with this practical problem continue to plague employers; in Chapter 7, we present a complete discussion of this matter. The third implementation issue was a concern with how to maintain the standardization of the administration and scoring of the interview and the scoring of the written simulation. Manuals were provided and training programs for new interviewers and raters were developed and used. In addition, interviews were audiotaped and randomly checked to determine if they were administered consistently across time and interviewers.

The satisfactory resolution of such problems and the implementation of selection procedures demand that successful human resource consultants be persons with highly developed interpersonal skills and understanding of how organizations function and change. These demands, as well as the need to understand individual differences, mean that good human resource consultants must be much more than technicians. These organizational demands increase the challenge and excitement of doing selection research.

Example 2: Selection in a Large Agency With Multiple Jobs

In this example, the organization had been using an aptitude test battery with 23 different subscales (e.g., arithmetic, pattern matching, matrices, English usage, word meaning, spelling, directions, name and number checking, artificial language) as one basis upon which to select people into more than 100 different jobs. The battery had originally been constructed so as to reflect the range of cognitively oriented abilities that might be required for the performance of the full range of jobs. The organization was interested in determining whether this battery was still an adequate means of classifying employees and how it might initiate a process that would provide data regarding the validity of this test battery for the various jobs in the organization.

To do criterion-related validation studies such as the one described in the example above for these 100 jobs would constitute a very large investment of time and money. Hence, it was critical that the researchers find some approach to grouping jobs and setting priorities with respect to validation. The approach taken in this instance was to assess the level of ability requirements of all jobs, and then cluster jobs for which similar sets of abilities were considered important determinants of work performance levels. From 6 to 12 expert job incumbents from 67 different jobs were asked to evaluate the level of skill required to perform their jobs based on 18 ability dimensions derived from the

Table 1.3 Ability Dimensions Used as the Basis for Clustering Jobs

1. Oral comprehension
2. Written comprehension
3. Oral expression
4. Written expression
5. Fluency of ideas
6. Originality
7. Memorization
8. Problem sensitivity
9. Mathematical reasoning
10. Number facility
11. Deductive reasoning
12. Inductive reasoning
13. Information ordering
14. Category flexibility
15. Speed of closure
16. Flexibility of closure
17. Spatial orientation
18. Visualization

Fleishman taxonomy (Fleishman & Quaintance, 1984; Fleishman & Reilly, 1992a). The labels of these 18 ability dimensions are listed in Table 1.3, and one of the rating scales used to rate the level of ability is presented in Figure 1.3. These ratings were then used to group the 67 jobs into eight clusters. Within each cluster, the profile of ability requirements was similar; between clusters, the ability profiles were relatively dissimilar.

After clusters were identified, one job from each cluster was chosen to be the target of a criterion-related validation study. Jobs were chosen from each cluster on the basis of (a) their centrality to the cluster in which they belonged (i.e., jobs were chosen whose average ability requirement fit the cluster's ability requirements most closely); (b) their employment of a large number of people, to allow for the conduct of a validity study with as large a sample as possible; (c) the fact that the organization expected to hire a large number of people in the immediate future; and (d) the fact that the abilities identified as important to this job were those measured by tests that typically produced large subgroup differences in measured ability, hence raising concerns about discrimination and requiring that the organization be able to provide evidence that the tests were valid. Validation of these tests for jobs central to each cluster would serve as the basis for defense

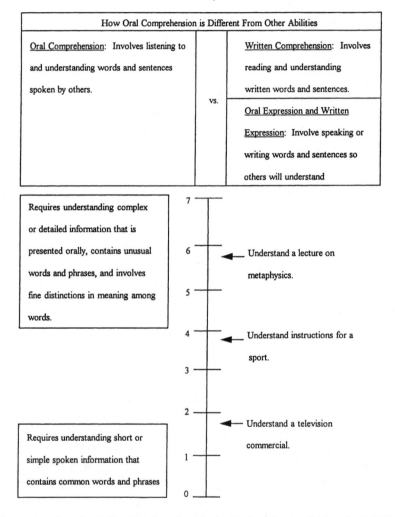

Figure 1.3. Sample Ability Requirements Scale Used to Assess the Level of Ability Required to Perform Jobs

of the same tests to select employees for other jobs in that cluster. After tests used to select employees into the core jobs were validated, the next priority would be to validate the same tests for jobs that belonged to the cluster, but that were most dissimilar to the central job. If the

Job Dimensions for Accounting Technician

1. Account and invoice processing
   Processes incoming documents for completeness and accuracy
   Computes amounts payable and ensures accurate payment based on allotted funds
2. Entitlements management
   Computes and processes "customer" entitlements
3. Records development and report generation
   Assists in the preparation of financial reports and maintains and posts manual and
   electronic records
4. Money handling
   Handles disbursements and receipts of cash and negotiable instruments properly
5. Customer service
   Serves as point of contact for inquiries on financial and accounting matters and
   provides advice and guidance to administrative, commercial, and personnel elements
6. Professional development
   Participates in training and performs progressively more difficult work for eventual
   assignment to more complicated duties and maintains knowledge, technical skills,
   and awareness of rules and laws relevant to job performance
7. Documents review
   Reviews and reconciles documents and provides fund certification as required

Figure 1.4. Performance Dimensions for One of the Target Jobs

tests were valid for these disparate jobs, then it was felt that the tests
would be valid for all jobs in the cluster. Hence, this represented a
test of the degree to which the validity of tests for one job was
transportable or generalizable to new jobs with a similar set of ability
requirements.

Validation of the tests for each major job cluster required a defensible job performance measure. Again, job experts were selected from
each of the target jobs to ascertain the major performance dimensions
for the jobs and to provide behavioral definitions of the dimensions,
along with examples of good and bad job performance on each dimension. This information was used to define the set of rated dimensions
for that job (see Figure 1.4 for an example) and the rating scales for
each dimension (see Figure 1.5 for an example).

Test data were collected from at least 100 employees in each of the
eight target jobs, and supervisory ratings were collected for the same
set of people. Table 1.4 presents the correlations among the three best
(in terms of the correlation between the test and the performance
rating) predictors for each of the eight core jobs. Clearly, there are
differences in these correlations, or validities, across jobs, which reaf-

1. ACCOUNT AND INVOICE PROCESSING

Processes incoming documents for completeness and accuracy.

Computes amounts payable and ensures accurate payment.

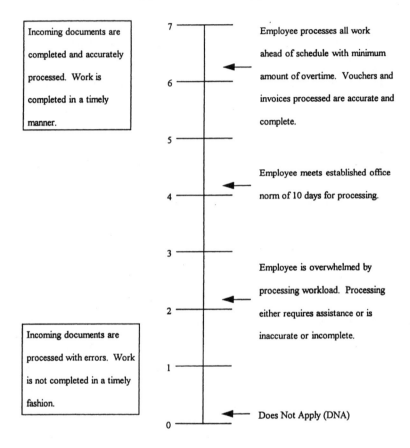

Figure 1.5. Example of a Rating Scale Used to Assess Work Performance

firms the meaningfulness of the manner in which these jobs were clustered. Performance in Job 3 is related negatively to the three tests indicated as well as to other tests in the battery. This particular job was one requiring a minimum level of the abilities measured with this aptitude battery; most incumbents were gate or building guards. On this job, high-ability people were actually performing less well as perceived by their supervisors. Performance in Job 4 is not predicted

Table 1.4   Criterion-Related Validities for Three "Best" Tests for the Eight Target
             Jobs

Job 1: $R = .44, N = 233$	**Job 2:** $R = .27, N = 150$
artificial language (.32)	English usage (.19)
English usage (.31)	word meaning (.13)
spelling (.29)	directions (.13)
Job 3: $R = .29, N = 96$	**Job 4:** $R = .17, N = 162$
pattern matching (–.19)	arithmetic (–.10)
artificial language (–.18)	pattern matching (.09)
name and number checking (–.16)	artificial language (.04)
Job 5: $R = .40, N = 126$	**Job 6:** $R = .24, N = 215$
name and number checking (.26)	directions (.17)
matrices (.24)	matrices (.16)
English usage (.18)	pattern matching (.15)
Job 7: $R = .25, N = 173$	**Job 8:** $R = .27, N = 66$
English usage (.21)	matrices (.27)
artificial language (.16)	directions (.23)
directions (.15)	pattern matching (.14)

NOTE: R refers to the multiple correlation for the total set of nine aptitude measures.

well by any of the tests in this battery, but closer examination of this group indicated that there may in fact be two groups for whom ability requirements are very different. The first group are computer programmers whose performance was not predicted; the second group were individuals who specialized in decoding messages. The latter group's performance was predicted very well (.36) by the artificial language test as well as by the matrices test (.25) and a name and number checking test (.24). The fact there are differences like these within a given job category suggests that at least in terms of the abilities needed to perform their jobs, these individuals are fairly different.

Work on this project is not yet complete. The next step will be validation work on the jobs that are least representative in terms of ability requirements within the cluster to which they have been assigned. At this point, however, the work does indicate that judgments about the ability requirements of jobs can be made successfully and used to group jobs with similar requirements. The work also has implications for theories of the structure of intelligence (see Chapter 4). In this case, as in many other instances in which aptitude test batteries have been used, the different subtests were moderately correlated (median r was about .40). The fact that aptitude tests are correlated in this fashion has led some researchers to maintain that there is simply

one main factor of intelligence underlying performance on all aptitude tests (e.g., Ree & Earles, 1991, 1992, 1993). If it were the case that
one general factor underlies performance on all the subtests in test
batteries, then no attempt to classify persons into jobs that are
uniquely suited to their capabilities would be possible, as appears to
be the case in this example. However, it should be noted that no
analyses of the type conducted by Ree and his colleagues were presented on these data.

Finally, this project did produce a body of evidence that dem-
onstrates that the test battery was valid for several jobs with large
numbers of job incumbents in this organization. Other work not
described here was also done to revise tests in which some items
appeared obsolescent and to remove some tests that no longer seemed
to index abilities relevant to any job. Although this project applies the
same general steps as outlined at the beginning of this chapter, there
is a great deal of reliance on the documentation that groups of jobs
require similar aptitudes and that validation results will generalize
across these groups of jobs. The number and variety of jobs for which
aptitude tests were selected and validated constituted the majority in
this effort. This complete project was described in a symposium
presented at the 11th Annual Conference of the Society for Industrial
and Organizational Psychology (Baughman & Mumford, 1996;
Costanza & Threlfall, 1996; Haucke & Stone, 1996).

Example 3: Selection of Emergency
Telephone Operators in a Small City

Our third example of selection research represents a very different
situation. A small city wanted to devise methods that would better help
officials to select emergency telephone operators for the city's 911
system. The total number of job incumbents in this situation was
between 32 and 40 at any given time, and only 5 to 10 persons were
hired per year, though a relatively large number (60-70) of individuals
often applied when civil service examinations were offered. In addition to the difference in numbers, this example is one in which the
only line of evidence for the validity of the tests lies in the test
construction process itself. Traditionally, this evidence has been
referred to as *content validity*; tests are developed to be as direct a
representation of the job tasks as possible.

Job analysis was a key element in this project. The process involved five steps. First, the researchers met with supervisors, who briefed them on the nature of the job; the researchers then observed and listened to workers on the job during two different occasions and reviewed various training and procedure manuals. The next two steps, task generation and KSAO generation, were carried out with the help of small groups of experienced job incumbents. In these group interviews, 78 task statements and 54 KSAOs were generated.

Two questionnaires were then constructed to evaluate the importance of the tasks and KSAOs to the performance of the job. The task rating questionnaire asked experienced workers to evaluate each task on a 7-point scale in terms of (a) the relative time spent performing the task compared with all other tasks, (b) the relative difficulty of doing the task correctly compared with all other tasks, and (c) the criticality of the task as judged by the degree to which incorrect performance results in negative consequences. The ratings of 10 job incumbents were combined, and task importance values (Levine, 1983) were computed for each task using the following formula:

Task Importance Value = Time Spent + (Difficulty × Criticality).

Using this equation to compute importance values means that a task must be both difficult and critical to be considered important. Frequent performance of a task would add to its importance. KSAOs were rated by nine workers on three different dimensions: (a) the necessity for newly hired workers to possess the KSAO (yes or no), (b) the extent to which trouble is likely if the KSAO is ignored in selection (rated on a scale of 1 to 7), and (c) the extent to which the KSAO distinguishes between superior and average workers (rated on a scale of 1 to 7). Interrater reliability and agreement indices were computed and considered satisfactory. The major task categories are displayed across the top of Table 1.5, and the major KSAO dimensions are presented in Table 1.6.

For development of selection instruments, those KSAOs that were rated by a clear majority as necessary for new workers and that received a high rating for trouble likely when ignored in selection were considered important selection criteria. Both the KSAOs and the task statements played a role in the construction of selection tests. Each test devised centered on the measurement of two or more KSAO

Table 1.5 Summary of Content Validity Judgments

	CBO	CBO	CBO	Major Task Dimension Dispatcher	Dispatcher	Dispatcher	Dispatcher	LEIN
	Collect information and process; ask questions; speak clearly and calmly	Analyze information; type requests; transmit requests	Miscellaneous duties (e.g., typing reports, record keeping)	Transmit requests; dispatch units; coordinate units; transmit information	Monitor units and emergencies; know location of units; provide information and backup; ask for information	Enter information about call and action	Coordinate requests across jurisdictions	Respond to requests; transmit information; type records; file information
Oral directions	.75	1.00	.50	-.50	-.05	.25	-1.00	-.25
Monitoring	.00	.00	-.25	.00	1.00	-.50	-1.00	-.25
Spelling	.25	.25	.50	-.25	-.75	.25	-1.00	.25
Typing	.25	1.00	.75	-.75	-1.00	.00	-.75	.75
Phone call (written)	1.00	.50	.00	-.25	-.25	.00	-.75	.25
Phone call (oral)	1.00	.50	-.50	.75	.25	-1.00	-.75	-.50
Interview	.46	.53	-.82	-.10	-.12	-.78	-.75	-.60

NOTE: CBO (complaint board operator), dispatcher, and LEIN operator are the three different positions occupied by the police technician. Workers rotated among these positions. In the content validity questionnaire, all major task dimensions were described in much more complete fashion.

Table 1.6 Critical KSAO Dimensions and Examples

Communication skills

    Ability to speak on the telephone in a clearly understandable manner

    Ability to control conversations in order to acquire information needed to respond
        to emergencies

Emotional control

    Ability to withstand pressure of attending to several emergencies at once and of
        constant monitoring of activities

    Ability to remain calm even in emergency situations when a caller is hysterical or
        upset

    Ability to control emotions in emergency to gather and transmit appropriate
        information

    Ability to handle emergencies consecutively in an orderly, efficient manner

Judgment

    Ability to judge what constitutes an emergency and requires immediate attention

    Ability to distinguish when to use common sense versus when to follow procedure
        strictly

    Ability to ask for help when needed

    Ability to ask pertinent questions to make quick assessment and direct help in
        emergency situations

Cooperativeness

    Ability to work as part of a team

    Ability to work with various types of people who differ in lifestyles and work habits

    Willingness to help coworkers

    Ability to take criticism and correction of work

Memory

    Ability to retain information on several situations at once

    Ability to pay attention and remember details of situations

    Ability to recall information from short notes about phone calls

    Ability to concentrate and attend to information

Clerical/technical skills

    Ability to spell common words and street names correctly from oral communications

    Knowledge of typewriter keyboard and ability to type information into forms with
        minimum errors

    Ability to fill out forms appropriately and with minimum errors

dimensions, and an attempt was made to use test item content that reflected the tasks for which a given KSAO was originally generated. An oral directions/typing test was designed to measure the applicant's memory ability and technical/clerical skills. This test had four components: (a) spelling, (b) telephone call recording, (c) monitoring, and (d) typing. The first three components of this test were administered using a tape recorder (information coming to the job incumbents was mostly aural, from incoming emergency calls). The applicants listened to the information and questions presented on tape and responded in writing on answer forms that resembled the computerized form used on the job. In the spelling test, the applicants had to spell a series of street and place names not idiosyncratic to the local area. In the telephone portion of the test, the applicants listened to recordings of emergency calls and then recorded key information onto a standardized form similar to that used by the incumbents when typing critical information into the computer system. In the monitoring part of the test, the examinees listened to a series of conversations that gave information about the nature and the location of police units and their activity and were then asked questions about this information. Finally, applicants were required to type the basic information about a call (name, address, nature of incident, and so on) onto a standardized form.

The second component of the test was a situational interview in which candidates were asked to indicate how they would react to a series of incidents. Answers to these questions were scored by trained raters using a behaviorally anchored rating scale, the anchors of which reflected good and bad answers to the questions. The interview questions were based on critical incidents of good and bad job performance. In generating the critical incidents, the researchers asked job incumbents to describe incidents in which they, or someone else, did something that was particularly effective or ineffective. In describing these incidents, the focus was on identifying the behavior involved, the situation, and the outcomes of the behavior. Because applicants were unlikely to have the job experience necessary to deal with the critical incidents mentioned by the job incumbents, the questions generated from the incidents were adjusted to involve situations with which job candidates would have had some knowledge or experience. Examples of interview questions and the critical incidents from which they were generated are presented in Table 1.7. The interview was used to assess four KSAO categories: communication skills, emotional control, judgment, and cooperativeness.

The final portion of the exam consisted of a phone call simulation that was designed to assess examinees' communication skills, emotional control, and judgment by focusing on the important operator tasks of obtaining and recording critical information accurately. Each

Table 1.7   Examples of Situational Interview Questions and Corresponding Critical Incidents Used for Selection of Emergency Telephone Operators

Interview Question	*Critical Incident*
1. Imagine that you tried to help a stranger, for example, with traffic directions or to get up after a fall, and that person blamed you for his or her misfortune or yelled at you. How would you respond?	1. Telephone operator tries to verify address information for an ambulance call. The caller yells at the operator for being stupid and slow. The operator quietly assures the caller an ambulance is on the way and that she is merely reaffirming the address.
2. Suppose a friend calls you and is extremely upset. Apparently, her child has been injured. She begins to tell you, in a hysterical manner, all about her difficulty in getting baby-sitters, what the child is wearing, what words the child can speak, and so on. What would you do?	2. A caller is hysterical because her infant is dead. She yells incoherently about the incident. The operator talks in a clear, calm voice and manages to secure the woman's address, dispatches the call, and then tries to secure more information about the child's status.
3. How would you react if you were a salesclerk, waitress, or gas station attendant and one of your customers talked back to you, indicated you should have known something you did not, or told you that you were not waiting on him or her fast enough?	3. A clearly angry caller calls for the third time in an hour, complaining about the 911 service because no one has arrived to investigate a broken water pipe. The operator tells the caller to go to _____ and hangs up.

applicant talked with an experienced technician who was trained to play one of six different roles. The examinee's objective was to interview this "caller," obtain information about the emergency, and record that information into one of the forms used earlier in the test. The scores the applicants received on this test were based on the accuracy and completeness of the information they recorded and on ratings of their communication skills, emotional control, and judgment by raters who listened to tape recordings of these conversations. Finally, a total of the various test scores was computed and used to rank order candidates for the purpose of making hiring decisions.

In an effort to evaluate the degree to which these various test tasks represented the actual job tasks, the researchers asked eight experienced incumbents to make judgments about each exam component. Specifically, the incumbents were asked to indicate the degree to which each exam component provided information that was (a) essential; (b) necessary, but not as essential as other components; (c) useful, but not essential; or (d) not necessary or useful in judging applicants' skills in performing various aspects of the job. The agreement across judges was computed using Lawshe's (1975) content validity ratio, and the results of these judgments are presented in Table 1.5. A 1.00 in this table indicates unanimous agreement on the part of the judges that a component provided necessary or essential information about the candidates' ability to perform the job task, whereas a –1.00 indicates that the test task provided no information about the candidates' ability to perform a job task. The table indicates an adequate level of content validity as assessed by this group of judges, with the exception of one task dimension. No test tasks were judged to be representative of the category of tasks designated "dispatcher—coordinate requests across jurisdictions." However, all components of the test were perceived to be relevant to one or more task dimensions.

The research in this study is based on the notion that behavior observed in one situation (i.e., the test) should be consistent with behavior observed in another situation (i.e., the job) provided the same set of requirements exists. There was no independent verification of the fact that such consistency actually existed, but the whole test development process was undertaken with this notion in mind. The final test review summarized in Table 1.5 provides support for the content validity of this examination procedure. The reliability of tests and ratings was assessed as well. One major challenge in developing tests that are supposed to be relatively direct representations of a job is that the tests must be such that an inexperienced job candidate will be able to perform the tasks. In this case, modifications were made to the interview questions and role-players were used both to standardize the testing situation and to keep applicants from potentially harming any callers. In making such modifications to actual job tasks, developers of selection procedures must take care that the procedures possess psychological fidelity (i.e., require the same KSAO as is required on the job) and that major job components are represented in the total set of selection procedures. The whole test design process in content validation studies requires a great deal of creativity because of the demand for fidelity and representativeness on the one hand, and the need to be concerned about requiring reasonable types of tasks and levels of performance of job applicants without doing them physical harm on the other. A more complete description of this study is provided in Schmitt and Ostroff (1986).

Example 4: Executive Selection

In this last example, we describe the process whereby a company interested in replacing a vice president for human resources consulted with a psychologist to obtain recommendations concerning the person who should fill this position. In the area of personnel selection, this practice is usually called *individual assessment*. Because this selection practice is rarely, if ever, described in research reports, we have constructed an ideal example of individual assessment based on the selection model presented at the beginning of this chapter and on the results of a survey of individual assessment practices reported by Ryan and Sackett (1987). Obviously, selection of one person will not allow criterion-related validation, and given that there is little research available regarding the validity of this type of selection, we cannot rely on that research to justify our approach to this problem. However, we can rely on the general selection research model in describing the approach to executive selection, and we can rely on studies of managerial talent (e.g., Bray, Campbell, & Grant, 1974; Gaugler, Rosenthal, Thornton, & Bentson, 1987; Miner, 1978) to suggest what individual differences, if any, might relate to executive performance in a given job.

Before one can assess the abilities of a candidate for an executive position, it is important to know what he or she will be expected to do in the organization, just as was true in each of our previous examples. Ryan and Sackett's (1987) survey of individual assessment practices indicates that most people who engage in this work obtain organizational and job analysis information by reading job descriptions and by talking informally with organizational decision makers. In this case, we will assume that this information revealed that our vice president would be responsible for setting policy and managing organizational activities in employee compensation, recruiting and selection, training, and organizational development. Heads of these four areas would report directly to the vice president, and he or she in turn would report to the president of the company. The organization is expanding rapidly into new markets, and the new vice president would be expected to make certain that all human resource programs contribute in a complementary manner to provide the talent that will allow for these expansions to take place. The position would also carry with it a significant administrative and public relations burden.

From this basic description, the psychologist charged with evaluating applicants for this position inferred that the successful candidate should have at least general knowledge of the company's major product lines and the expertise required of employees in the company, and that he or she should understand the legal and union constraints governing hiring and compensation policy. Further, the successful candidate should have knowledge of various employee development practices. The psychologist also considered experience in several different human resource areas to be an important, but not necessary, qualification. On a personal level, the individual must be highly organized and capable of supervising and managing a large number of people. He or she must relate well to top members of the organization and the board of directors as well as individuals at lower levels of the organization. In addition, the candidate must be able to perform a public relations role in the local community and among individuals and organizations with whom the corporation interacts. Finally, this individual must be willing and able to handle multiple competing demands simultaneously.

In their survey of those doing individual assessments, Ryan and Sackett (1987) found that most (94%) used a personal interview and that about 80% relied on a personal history form, ability tests, and personality inventories. A much smaller proportion (38%) used a simulation exercise. In our example, a personal history form could be used to examine the degree to which candidates might possess the background experiences from which one might infer that they understand the job and have the knowledge required. It would also be of help in structuring an interview to pursue whether or not the applicants possess the specific knowledge and personal characteristics described above. The personal history form and interview could be used in combination to obtain similar information from all candidates upon which to make comparative judgments of their strengths and weaknesses. The interview could also be used to assess individuals' oral communication skills. General intellectual ability is almost always associated with performance in complex, demanding jobs (Hunter & Hunter, 1984), hence, a relatively difficult test of general intellectual ability might be used (the Watson-Glaser Critical Thinking Appraisal was popular among Ryan & Sackett's respondents). Personality instruments could be used to assess the candidates' extraversion, conscientiousness, agreeableness, and openness, which appear to be aspects of the Big Five (Digman, 1990) that would be relevant to successful performance on this job. A simulation in which each individual has to set priorities on work projects, organize and plan activities, delegate to staff, and handle frequent interruptions might provide information that could be very useful in the assessment of candidates. The point is that the person conducting this assessment can potentially make use of a variety of techniques to examine the extent to which each candidate possesses the characteristics required of the person who might hold this high-level position. If linked to required KSAOs and used in a consistent manner across candidates, these techniques should provide pertinent information that can be used in the assessment of the candidates' job-related abilities.

After evaluating the various candidates, the assessor makes recommendations to corporate personnel regarding the various candidates and their strengths and weaknesses. He or she also usually provides feedback to the candidates, in written and/or oral form.

Although individual assessment can and should involve (a) a job analysis that delineates the job responsibilities and the abilities required to meet these responsibilities and (b) standardized evaluation of the same set of abilities for all candidates, there is little research available on the validity of individual assessment. Most persons engaging in individual assessment do report following up the candidates they recommend to ascertain how successful they have been (see Ryan & Sackett, 1987, Table 13). As should be obvious, this process can involve a great deal of time and money. Development of individualized assessment tasks or simulations, or even interviews that focus on job-related issues or knowledge, can be very expensive; perhaps this is one reason organizations often employ particular individuals to assess candidates for multiple positions. As an assessor gains experience with a given company, he or she comes to an understanding of the work and culture characteristics of the organization and can much more quickly understand the job requirements, and thus may be able to use some of the same assessment devices and questions to make recommendations about who might fill different positions.

Research on the use of individual assessment will need to confront several difficulties. First, the problem of small samples will likely mean that any effort to conduct criterion-related validation studies will involve the use of data across organizations or positions. The comparability of performance data in these different contexts will be questionable. Simply obtaining an appropriate measure of an executive's performance in a single organization will be a formidable problem if the researcher is interested in correlating ability measures with actual performance data. In individual assessment, the assessor is using data from a variety of instruments and interviews to make decisions. The assessor in this instance becomes the final decision tool, so research must separate an assessment of the validity of the tools used by the assessor, for which there is a substantial database, from the validity of the assessor's use of that information in formulating recommendations. Finally, we have little evidence as to how these recommendations are actually used or implemented in the organizations that receive them.

Summary: Similarities Across Research Designs and Organizational Contexts

In this chapter, we have presented the general research model that has guided most of a century of research on personnel selection. We have identified various sources of evidence regarding the validity of selection procedures and presented the outline of this book on theory and research in personnel selection. We have also offered four examples that span the domain of personnel selection. Although all very different, these examples have a number of commonalities, and it is these common concerns that are most important. In each instance, the basic personnel selection research model guided the effort to develop and validate the selection procedures. The organizations in all of these instances were motivated by similar concerns when they launched these projects. All were concerned with the potential productivity and quality (though these characteristics usually are defined with respect to organizational goals) of the individuals they hired. With the exception of the organization in the fourth example, all were also motivated by concerns related to the diversity of the workforce (this was especially important for the first organization, because its employees work with people of different cultural and language backgrounds) and the degree to which their hiring procedures met legal standards. Although none made explicit mention of it, all four organizations were interested in people who would "fit" the organization, not only in terms of qualifications, but in terms of interests and values. Whereas the examples we have provided are very different, the motivations these organizations had for engaging in the research and development exercises described are similar.

There are technical commonalities among these cases as well, which are also very important. First, the research in this area always begins with a delineation of the work that will be performed by the persons to be selected. This examination of the job allows the researcher to form theories of work performance.

Second, the researcher forms hypotheses about the nature of the individual differences (KSAOs) required to perform the job. These hypotheses are based on the researcher's understanding of the job and her or his knowledge of the literature on ability-performance relationships.

Third, the researcher uses a variety of evidence to support the selection procedures that are developed. Our first example presented a case in which there was a great deal of attention placed on the manner in which some of the selection procedures represented a sample of the job performance domain, but criterion-related evidence was also collected. In Example 2, direct criterion-related evidence was used to evaluate ability measures for some jobs, but researcher and job expert judgments about the nature of the work and the required ability constructs underlay the use of tests for evaluation of applicants for other jobs. In Example 3, the procedures used were meant to sample the job performance domain in a relatively direct manner. In Example 4, there was heavy reliance on the judgment of the individual assessment specialist as to the ability domains required and assessed in making recommendations. In subsequent chapters in this book, we will identify the case in Example 1 as a criterion-related validation effort. Example 2 involves criterion-related validation and the transportability of the validity obtained when a researcher studies one job to support the use of tests in other jobs. The procedures used in Examples 3 and 4 are supported by content and construct validation as defined in Chapter 5.

Fourth, in all four instances, there were concerns with the implementation of the procedures similar to those discussed in connection with the first example. These concerns were legal, organizational, and financial. Finally, we should mention that organizational characteristics, the jobs studied, and the people involved make all applications different and challenging, even though the basic research paradigm used is similar and the patterns of KSAO-job performance relationships may be very similar across jobs. The uniqueness of organizational situations means that human resource professionals must be continuous learners. Learning about people and how they meet their work demands is certainly a major determinant of the excitement involved in this application of psychological and human resource research.

Personnel selection researchers have developed research methods to evaluate and assess the importance of each of these concerns. In dealing with these concerns, researchers have been informed by theory and research in basic psychology, particularly the area of individual differences. Personnel selection researchers have also contributed to both research methods and theory. In the remainder of this book, we will focus on both theory and methods, because we believe that they are by nature interconnected.

2 Developing Theories of KSAO-Performance Relationships

The Role of Job Analysis

Theory in selection research is essentially a theory of work performance. This theory is based on an analysis of the job and the organizational context in which the work takes place. The theory development aspects of job analyses are not often mentioned, but our position is that some form of theory development must occur at this stage of a selection research project. It may not be a very formal or systematic process, but it occurs. One result of the job analysis is the specification of important work behaviors. Using these work behaviors, the researcher generates a set of required knowledges, skills, abilities, and other characteristics. Measures of these KSAOs are subsequently developed, and scores on these measures constitute selection criteria. Specification of the tasks or behaviors that workers must accomplish also serves as the basis for the development of the criteria against which the researcher evaluates hypotheses about the nature of the KSAOs required to perform the job.

The detailed examination of a job, the specification of the required worker activities and corresponding required KSAOs, and, in a criterion-related validation study, the careful development of criteria corresponding to the major dimensions of work that will be described in this chapter are all time-consuming and expensive. Aspects of these analyses may be unnecessary if the researcher can abstract from many previous such analyses the basic structure of work and its attendant KSAO requirements. This abstraction is one of the basic objectives of science—that is, parsimony. The degree to which work structures and/or work behaviors are similar across jobs and the implications of this similarity for job analysis activities are detailed in the second major part of this chapter. Practically speaking, the ability to abstract allows for the streamlining of the activities described in this chapter. On a theoretical level, it means that the nature of work dimensions identified in a job analysis in one context is generalizable to other work contexts. By implication, jobs that are similar on these basic dimensions will also be similar in terms of the human characteristics required for successful performance.

A detailed approach to job analysis, with careful thinking about the ability-performance linkages that are likely present in some jobs, certainly adds to our ultimate understanding of those linkages. In practical terms, it may add significantly to the validity of the measures developed (see Adler, 1996, for a similar argument in the area of personality determinants of job performance). The detail provided regarding the necessary work activities, the required KSAOs, their linkages, and their relative importance may be of significant use in meeting other human resource needs, such as the development of training curricula, career development, compensation, and recruiting. For a very different position, see Schmidt, Hunter, and Pearlman (1981), who argue that no more than a very holistic (e.g., clerical, mechanical, managerial) description of jobs is necessary to determine the KSAOs required of workers. This is likely the case in many situations confronted by relatively experienced human resource personnel, but legal constraints often necessitate the collection of much more detail than is necessary to identify the requisite KSAOs (see also Guion, 1998). Detailed job analyses are most necessary when the validation of selection procedures relies solely on expert analysis of the domain of job tasks and the replication of these tasks in the selection procedures, as was the case in the telephone operator and executive selection examples presented in Chapter 1.

We begin this chapter with a description of the information a researcher might gather about an organization in preparation for job analysis interviews or the administration of job analysis surveys. This is followed by a discussion of the generation of work tasks and KSAOs. We then describe job analysis surveys in which tasks, KSAOs, and their linkages are evaluated by subject matter experts. Following that, we address the generation of a test plan and discuss the importance of various ability-performance linkages, concerns about the format of the test and assessments of relevant or irrelevant constructs, and the attendant practical concerns that arise in the measurement of some KSAOs. We also discuss the use of critical behaviors as a means of specifying the job performance in which the researcher is interested and as a source for measurement of both criteria and predictors. In the second part of the chapter, we describe efforts to generate a general taxonomy or theory of work. These theories are represented by the work of Fine at the U.S. Department of Labor and in subsequent work in many organizations (Fine & Getkate, 1995) and by attempts to develop general task inventories that are the basis of comparing jobs on a common set of dimensions.

Initial Preparation for Job Analysis

Prior to talking with job experts to find out what job tasks they are required to perform, it is always useful for the researcher to become as familiar with the job and the organization as possible. The researcher can do this by reading existing job descriptions and training and procedure or policy manuals, by talking with supervisors and workers, by touring the facility, and by observing the work being done. The review of background material as well as observations and conversations in the workplace usually allow the researcher to make a list of major job activities for use in the actual job analysis interviews.

In gathering this preliminary information, the job analyst will also want to assess the organization in which the work is being done. Organizational features such as leadership practices, the reward system, and structure have direct effects on employee behavior. These features may constrain or enhance the degree to which individuals are able to use their abilities, or may change the nature of the tasks performed and the KSAOs required. In addition, there may be characteristics of the external environment—such as the customers or clients of the organization, the competition for labor and materials, the sociopolitical environment, the suppliers upon whom the organization depends, and the technological sophistication of those with whom organizational members must interact—that affect the nature of the work and the required KSAOs. In any event, knowing about these issues allows the job analyst to ask more intelligent questions of subject matter experts and will certainly add to his or her credibility.

At this point, too, it is very important that the job analyst seek an understanding of the organization's goals—in a broad sense and specifically, as they relate to the selection of new employees. The analyst should explore questions regarding the motivation for an examination of the organization's selection procedures. What outcomes are the organization's leaders most interested in enhancing, or correcting, if they perceive problems? Are they concerned about the safety of employees, their promotability, turnover, quality, productivity, and so on? Are their concerns localized in a particular occupation, geographic location, organizational level, or unit? Is the organization's suggested solution (i.e., identification of talented employees) likely to solve the problem, or should the firm be exploring other human resource interventions, such as training or changes in the compensation system? Increasingly, the determination of organizational goals involves an exploration of what a company expects to do in the future, as opposed to the activities in which it is currently engaged. A consultant cannot determine organizational goals, but he or she can help organizational decision makers generate their best collective answer to problems.

When there are serious differences in the perceptions of organizational goals among important decision makers, or these decision makers anticipate significant changes in the direction of the organization, then specification of the required worker KSAOs using job incumbents in job analyses as described below can be misleading. Before the job analyst embarks on an effort to develop a selection-based solution to problems, it is very important that he or she determine the organizational goals and how they might influence the types of required KSAOs and the values and interests most critical to the organization and to the individuals who will have to work and adapt to life in the organization. For instance, in the example involving investigative agents described in Chapter 1, it was important to know that the organization was very concerned about the public image projected by its employees. Very often, employees took this for granted as they did their work, and they may not have recognized it as important, but the employees of this organization were frequently involved in incidents that received a great deal of news coverage. Insensitivity to public perceptions could have significant political ramifications that in turn would impede the work of these agents in other situations.

Generating Task Dimensions

The next step for the job analyst is to convene groups of individuals (usually three to six is optimal) who are very knowledgeable about the work required in a specific job. These subject matter experts (SMEs) will usually be job incumbents who have been in the job long enough to have experienced all of the various tasks required. Supervisors are sometimes asked to serve as experts in this phase of the job analysis, but only if they still actively participate in the work, as opposed to performing supervisory or administrative roles and tasks only. There has been some research as to individual differences (verbal ability, demographic differences, experience, and motivation) in abilities to provide ratings of task and KSAO information (see below), but little or no research has shown whether substantially different tasks or KSAOs are generated by different groups of people. Usually, the analyst will find it helpful to conduct group as opposed to individual interviews, as participants very frequently help each other in generating tasks or completing information about tasks. Because it is vital that any intervention in an organization be acceptable to the people affected, it is always important that different groups be represented in such expert panels and that the criteria for participation be clearly articulated.

After explaining the purpose of the interview and answering questions and addressing concerns about the project, the analyst presents the major task categories he or she has compiled based on a preview of the job. The analyst then asks the SMEs to modify this general

Table 2.1   Major Task Categories Relevant to Secretary's Job

1. Maintaining and developing databases and spreadsheets, including collecting and entering information
2. Preparing printed documents and reports
3. Creating and completing various company forms and ensuring that they are filed and distributed to the appropriate personnel
4. General clerical activities, including filing, answering the phone, handling mail, and duplicating
5. Note taking, typing, and letter preparation, including editing and revising
6. Coordinating office and building functions and maintaining equipment and supplies

framework as appropriate. An example list of the task dimensions for the job of secretary in one company is shown in Table 2.1.

Developing Task Statements

Once the group members reach consensus as to a framework, the analyst then asks them to specify the work tasks undertaken in each of the major task dimensions. The analyst should require that each task statement include four major components, as illustrated in Table 2.2. It is assumed that each task is performed by the job incumbent, so the subject of all task statements is left unspecified. The first word should be an action verb that specifies what worker activity is required to perform the task (such as *writes, types, sweeps, sews*). General terms such as *provides, responds,* and *evaluates* are not very good descriptors of worker activity. The next part of the task statement should specify to whom or what the activity is directed. This is followed by a specification of the purpose and the manner in which the activity is undertaken. If all of these components are included in each task statement, it becomes much easier to specify the KSAO required, the level of the KSAO required, and the need for special technical capabilities (e.g., use of word processing software). Table 2.3 presents some task statements from various jobs.

The job analyst then edits the first set of task statements generated and revises the statements to remove redundancies and improve their format. This process is repeated until the analyst gains little new information by interviewing more people. The analyst then uses the final set of task statements and their categorization as the basis for a

Table 2.2 Appropriate Form of a Task Statement

The statement should describe what the worker does, how the worker does it, and to whom/what, and why. The following example comes from the job of a secretary.

What?	To Whom/What?
Sorts	correspondence forms and reports

Why?	How?
to facilitate filing them	alphabetically.

The next example comes from the job of a supervisor:

What?	To Whom/What?
Informs	the next shift supervisor

Why?	How?
of the status of departmental work projects	through written or verbal reports.

Table 2.3 Task Statements Generated in Analyses of Different Jobs

1. Removes debris after fire is extinguished under the direction of a fire officer using shovel, mop, and bucket, broom, and squeegee to prevent accidents.
2. Answers phone from internal customers to give information on status of purchase orders, information on buyers, or other relevant information from a database (often while on the phone).
3. Plans operational and arrest activities, specifying time, location, personnel, activities, and unexpected events, to ensure safety and efficiency in arresting subjects or seizing property.
4. Assesses personality characteristics and views of others (e.g., suspects, informants, witnesses) using information from files, observations, personal contacts, etc., to determine the best approach to use in dealing with them.

second set of interviews with job experts in which the goal is to identify the knowledges, skills, and abilities required to perform the tasks.

Developing KSAO Statements

The job analyst meets with a second group of job experts and asks them to read the task statements and indicate what KSAOs are required to perform each task or group of tasks. The analyst defines KSAOs for the job experts and discusses some examples of KSAO statements. *Knowledge* refers to the foundation upon which abilities and skills are built; it involves an organized body of information—

usually facts, rules, and procedures—that, if used, makes good job performance possible. *Skills* refers to the capability to perform tasks with ease and precision. Most often, they involve psychomotor-type activities that people perform using body movements, arms and hands, vision, and so on. *Abilities* usually refers to the cognitive capabilities necessary to perform a job function; these often require the application of some knowledge base. In addition, the analyst asks the job experts to generate lists of other characteristics—such as willingness to work under relevant adverse conditions—and personality traits that may be helpful for the performance of certain tasks (e.g., persistence, tolerance of others' viewpoints). The distinctions among knowledge, skills, abilities, and other characteristics are not important; what is important is the notion that each type of human characteristic should be considered in the generation of a comprehensive list of capabilities. The KSAO statements must be specific enough that they can be useful to the analyst in building assessment exercises or writing test items that accurately reflect what is required on the job. What the KSAO is, in what contexts the worker is expected to use the KSAO, with what level of accuracy or quality a worker is expected to display the KSAO, and with what result may all be relevant aspects of a desirable KSAO statement. The inclusion of this information in KSAO statements allows for appropriate test development.

As with the generation of task statements, the analyst reviews and edits the results of the initial interview and repeats the process with a new group of experts until little new information is acquired with additional interviews. In the case of both task and KSAO generation, there is usually no need to conduct more than three or four interviews. Table 2.4 presents a list of some KSAO statements generated for various jobs.

Evaluating Tasks and KSAOs by Surveys

When sufficient numbers of job incumbents are available and the analyst wants to collect job information on a wider and more representative group of people (occasionally, a researcher may do this simply to develop wider support for a human resource program, rather than because he or she needs information beyond that provided by the interviews), he or she may construct surveys to assess the

Table 2.4   Examples of KSAO Statements for Different Jobs

Knowledge of the information contained in a database and how it is accessed

Ability to question a customer to determine precisely the customer's needs

Ability to translate technical knowledge in a way that will be understood by a client or customer

Ability to calm a caller with an emergency so as to acquire information that will help resolve
the caller's problem

Knowledge of digital operating systems

Ability to develop, use, and organize a filing system

Knowledge of supervisor's personal traveling preferences

Ability to follow instructions in completing forms

importance of various tasks and KSAOs in the accomplishment of various job activities or responsibilities. The analyst then has job incumbents rate each of the tasks and KSAOs on a variety of response scales. Three of the most frequently used response scales on which tasks are rated are the time spent, difficulty, and criticality scales reproduced in Table 2.5. Levine (1983) has combined ratings on these three scales to produce a task importance value using the following formula:

$$\text{Task Importance} = \text{Difficulty} \times \text{Criticality} + \text{Time Spent}.$$

The importance value is used as the basis upon which to develop various human resource interventions, such as selection or training programs. The logic of this importance formula is apparent if one considers the arithmetic computations involved. The task will receive the highest importance value if it is both difficult and critical. If it takes up a large amount of time on the job, it will be considered even more important. Because criticality and difficulty are multiplied in this formula, they will influence the importance value greatly. Other methods of using these ratings and other possible rating schemes are available, but their primary purpose, at least in personnel selection, is to identify the tasks that are most important. Usually, these ratings are used to shorten the task list; that is, some importance value is used as the cutoff below which tasks are no longer considered as a source of test content or as the basis on which to develop KSAOs.

Many different possible rating scales have been used, and we review some of the research into how these ratings are combined below.

Table 2.5   Scales Commonly Used to Evaluate Task Statements

Time spent: a measure of time spent per week (or day, month, or year, depending on the complexity and usual repetition of job tasks) doing a task relative to all other tasks within a given job

1 = rarely do

2 = very much below average

3 = below average

4 = average (approximately half of tasks take more time, half take less)

5 = somewhat more than average

6 = considerably more than average

7 = a great deal more than average

Task difficulty: difficulty in doing a task correctly relative to all other tasks within a single job

1 = one of the easiest of all tasks

2 = considerably easier than most tasks

3 = easier than most tasks performed

4 = approximately half of tasks are more difficult, half less difficult

5 = harder than most tasks performed

6 = considerably harder than most tasks performed

7 = one of the most difficult of all tasks

Criticality/consequences of error: the degree to which an incorrect performance would result in negative consequences

1 = consequences of error are not at all important

2 = consequences of error are of little importance

3 = consequences of error are of some importance

4 = consequences of error are moderately important

5 = consequences of error are important

6 = consequences of error are very important

7 = consequences of error are extremely important

However, we should mention here one potential problem with these scales. If one is interested in comparing job analysis data across jobs, the rater's frame of reference is critical. If the rater is rating the task relative to other tasks on her or his job, one cannot legitimately expect to use these data in making cross-job comparisons. Only when the rating task is framed as a comparison across jobs and the rater is knowledgeable about other jobs are such cross-job comparisons possible.

The KSAO statements can also be rated by the job incumbents. Commonly used scales in the evaluation of KSAOs are presented in Table 2.6. We want to know how important the KSAOs are and whether possession of a particular KSAO would allow us to identify a superior

Table 2.6 Scales Commonly Used to Evaluate KSAOs

How *important* is this KSAO to effective performance of the _____ job?
  1 = not important
  2 = minor importance
  3 = important
  4 = major importance
  5 = critically important

To what extent does possession of this KSAO *distinguish a superior worker from an average worker*?
  1 = very little or none
  2 = to some extent
  3 = to a great extent
  4 = to a very great extent
  5 = to an extremely great extent

Is it important to have this KSAO at the *time of appointment*?
  1 = definitely no, or probably no
  2 = definitely yes, or probably yes

This last scale would be used to evaluate only the knowledge statements:
What *level of recall* of this knowledge is needed at the time of appointment?
  1 = general familiarity (A person must be aware of general principles and be able to locate pertinent details efficiently in source documents and/or seek help from others.)
  2 = working knowledge (A person must be able to apply general principles and specific details from memory in typically encountered occurrences, but can refer to source documents or seek guidance from others for applying specifics in unusual circumstances.)
  3 = full recall (A person must be able to apply both general principles and specific details in a wide variety of occurrences from memory without referring to source documents or seeking guidance from others.)

versus an average or marginal employee. We also want to know whether the worker must have the KSAO when he or she is first hired, in which case we should measure the degree to which applicants possess the KSAO (as opposed to developing a training component around the KSAO). In the case of knowledge, we also want to know the degree to which job incumbents must have the knowledge in memory or whether they can simply be generally familiar with a topic. Ratings on these scales are used to decide whether to develop or select measures of these KSAOs for measurement of job applicants' skills. A KSAO would be measured if it is something required of new applicants, if it is relatively important, if it will help to some degree to distinguish workers with varying levels of capability to perform the job, and, in the case of knowledge, if full knowledge and recall of the KSAO (usually knowledge) is required to perform some job task(s).

Note that the KSAOs are generated from a consideration of what is needed to perform the job tasks. In a content validity approach to test development (the test tasks are based on the experts' judgments that they represent a sample of actual job tasks), it is now appropriate to consider the tasks that generated a particular KSAO in the development of test tasks. For example, if a good sense of balance is required of a firefighter when he or she climbs ladders, it might be appropriate to design a test task in which the job applicant is required to climb a ladder. Or if a police officer has to have writing skills that allow her or him to complete a checklist with a brief description of a traffic violation, then a task that requires a similar writing task might be used to assess writing skills. In developing items with content validity in mind, test constructors often distinguish between psychological fidelity and physical fidelity. In the case of the description of the traffic violation and the assessment of writing skills, a checklist and brief written description of an athletic event might possess psychological fidelity, although it would not be physically the same task.

In the emergency telephone operator example presented in Chapter 1, the ability to take oral directions was considered important by the job experts. In developing a content valid measure of this dimension, it was important to know that the oral direction ability was often exercised in the context of a task that was extremely urgent and that the directions given by the caller were apt to be highly emotional. The type of test item or exercise developed in this instance should be very different from the type used to test oral directions ability in a bank teller's or secretary's job, for example. Knowledge of the task in which an ability is exercised allows for the development of exercises with psychological fidelity and, when possible and necessary, physical fidelity as well.

Linkage Judgments

After the tasks and abilities are generated and evaluated, many job analysts will require that another panel of job experts judge the extent to which each KSAO is required by the tasks that are generated. Note that KSAOs were originally generated from the task statements, so this final linkage process is a reaffirmation of the degree to which the KSAOs are indeed required by important job tasks. This linkage process also serves as the basis on which to develop and weight the measures of the individual KSAOs. That is, those KSAOs that are reflected in a large number of important tasks are the ones for which tests are developed, and they ought to receive the greatest weight in a test battery. These data are used to develop the *test specifications,* that is, the plan that specifies which KSAOs will be measured in the tests and how much each is weighted in the final composite measure of an applicant's measured ability to perform a job.

Development of Test Plans

At this point, the test constructor develops test specifications or plans by which the relevant KSAO dimensions can be assessed. He or she considers the nature of the KSAO dimensions, available selection procedures, the literature regarding these procedures (i.e., their validity in assessing certain constructs and their susceptibility to method effects, such as social desirability), and the practical feasibility of using various procedures. When content or face validity (KSAOs measured are apparent to test takers and users and seem appropriate for the purpose) of the procedures is a concern, the format and context of the test items should match as closely as possible the type of tasks required on the job. Test procedures should never introduce an *irrelevant* level of difficulty or "construct" such as reading comprehension. Table 1.1 in the previous chapter represents one such test plan. To illustrate how these various considerations affected the construction of that table, consider the KSAO dimension labeled "ability to write effectively." Given the type of individual KSAOs included in this dimension, and using knowledge of critical incidents regarding writing tasks, several sets of video and written test materials were constructed. Examinees were instructed to use these materials to write an essay describing the series of events described in the test stimuli. The essays were scored for the degree to which relevant details were recorded, for how well organized they were, and for how well they reflected basic knowledge of spelling, grammar, and sentence construction rules. The job incumbents were frequently asked to write similar reports of their activities, and the quality of their essays often made a significant difference in legal cases. Important practical considerations included the time needed to score these essays and the degree to which raters of the essays could agree on scoring them. Both of these concerns were addressed in a series of pilot studies before a final decision to use this testing format was made. There is little or no scientific literature on the validity of written essays, but the literature on job samples (this test represents very closely the type of writing required of job incumbents) used as selection procedures is very encouraging (Hunter & Hunter, 1984; Schmitt, Gooding, Noe, & Kirsch, 1984). In the case of other selection procedures used (i.e., cognitive ability tests), the considerations were very different. In this case, we have many encouraging validity data, especially for jobs involving the relatively complex KSAOs required in this job, and practically, cognitive ability tests are easy to administer and score, but there were concerns about face validity and the degree to which these tests exhibit large differences between different ethnic groups.

We stated above that test constructors in a content validity study often try to construct assessment devices that mirror important job tasks, as was true in the writing simulation and the telephone operators' need to take oral directions described above. In many instances, however, the test tasks cannot very closely replicate the job tasks as in the examples cited above, for a variety of practical reasons, such as the expense of developing replicated situations, risk of injury to test takers, and inability to simulate a very great portion of the job tasks in a limited period of time. In these instances, it is useful to perform a linkage analysis after the test tasks are developed. In the linkage analysis, the analyst asks job experts (usually supervisors or experienced job incumbents) to make judgments of the degree to which each KSAO required to perform the job tasks is important in the performance of each test task. If there are a large number of important KSAOs and test tasks, this linkage and the other linkage described above can be a very tedious task. Sometimes this task is divided among groups of job experts, or the KSAOs are grouped such that the total number of judgments required is minimized. This latter linkage analysis affirms that the test developer did produce test tasks that are measures of the KSAOs deemed important in the performance of a job. In brief, these two sets of linkage judgments confirm that the targeted KSAOs are indeed required to perform important aspects of the job and that these KSAOs are reflected appropriately in the components of the selection battery. These two sets of linkages in combination also represent the set of hypotheses about ability-performance relationships held by the subject matter experts.

The choice of job experts is critical in all phases of the type of job analysis we have just described, but in the linkage phase, this choice is particularly important. The job experts must know the test items well and must know the KSAO as it is reflected in the target job tasks. For this reason, the KSAOs measured by the test should be clearly defined for the job experts and the experts should be required to take the test whenever logistically possible and to be informed as to the scoring of the test. Of course, the job experts should also be thoroughly familiar with the requirements of the job itself.

Role of Critical Performance Incidents

During the job analysis interviews, many job analysts will also collect critical performance incidents that describe effective, average, and ineffective performance observed by the job experts. These incidents complement the information obtained from tasks and KSAOs by providing examples of how individuals perform effectively and ineffectively. Beyond helping the researcher/test constructor gain a better understanding of the job's performance requirements, these performance incidents are also extremely useful in the development of the content of various predictor and criterion measures in personnel selection research. Performance incidents serve as the basis for questions asked in situational or experience-based interviews (see Latham, Saari, Purcell, & Campion, 1980; Pulakos & Schmitt, 1995), situational judgment tests (Motowidlo, Dunnette, & Carter, 1990), and various simulations (Pulakos & Schmitt, 1996; Schmitt & Ostroff, 1986).

The analyst must provide some training or explanation to the job experts when he or she asks them to generate performance incidents. This training should describe the features of a good incident:

1. It concerns the actions of an individual job incumbent. It should be clear that the individual worker was responsible for the incident.

2. It tells what the worker did (or failed to do) that indicated he or she was effective or ineffective.
3. It describes clearly the background of the incident.
4. It provides the consequences of the incident.
5. It should be short; it should not specify unimportant details of the background, the activity itself, or the consequences of what the agent did.

In this training of the job experts, the analyst may also include a description of the types of errors made in writing incidents, using examples of good and bad incidents. The analyst may then have the experts practice writing incidents, which he or she will then critique and, if necessary, have the experts rewrite. The analyst then usually asks each job expert to write one or more performance incidents at each level (effective, average, ineffective) for each major task category.

After these incidents are generated, the analyst or test constructor must sort them into major task categories as a means of organizing them and linking them back to the tasks that describe the work done by the job incumbents. Examples of incidents generated for a variety of positions are listed in Table 2.7.

At this point, the researcher has a comprehensive list of the tasks performed by the job incumbent, the KSAOs required to perform those tasks, and a large number of behaviors that reflect the kind of job activity deemed important and effective/ineffective by job experts. Given this information base, the researcher should be well equipped to construct a test that accurately reflects the job requirements.

Research Issues in Generating Job Information

Most of the research on job analysis has focused on (a) the quality of the task and KSAO ratings produced in surveys of job incumbents and (b) the nature of the underlying dimensions of work and human ability. We will summarize the latter area of research in a later section of this chapter. The three major sources of job analysis information are the job incumbents, supervisors of those incumbents, and trained job analysts. Use of each of these groups as a primary source of job information has some advantages and disadvantages. Incumbents certainly ought to be the best-informed individuals about the work they do, but they occasionally do not possess the conceptual or verbal

Table 2.7   Examples of Critical Performance Incidents From Various Jobs

When a worker was asked to lecture a group of students on the nature of work in her organization, the worker prepared a presentation, used various visual aids, and was able to answer questions adequately. The students and their faculty sponsor were delighted with the presentation and asked the presenter if she would consider giving the presentation again to a different group.

This officer received a phone call regarding an alleged assassination plot against a federal judge. The officer failed to research the validity of the complaint and notified the investigative unit in his department. As a result, a great deal of time and effort was wasted investigating a complaint that proved to be a hoax.

When this officer was charged with the accounting responsibilities of an undercover operation in her department, she tediously reviewed all vouchers, receipts, invoices, and rental agreements from the start of the operation. The officer discovered that a rental car company had been double-billing the organization for many thousands of dollars. The money was refunded.

A caller was abusive when talking to a customer service technician. The technician became angry and verbally abused the customer, using derogatory language. The caller reported the incident to a local newspaper, which published a report of the incident, producing a great deal of embarrassment to the organization.

A secretary does not keep a record of the directories and files in which he stores documents. When the secretary is absent and someone needs to make changes in a document prepared by the secretary, a great deal of time is wasted searching all files and directories to find the appropriate file.

skills to provide good descriptions of their job tasks, and especially the required KSAOs. If they suspect that the collection of job analysis information will have implications for their compensation, they may also tend to exaggerate the nature of their duties. Supervisors sometimes are not familiar with all job tasks, especially in jobs that require the use of complex and changing technologies. They may, however, not have the conflicting motivations or verbal deficits that are sometimes characteristic of incumbents. Trained job analysts may be able to produce the most reliable and consistent cross-job ratings, but they must also spend a great deal of time familiarizing themselves with the job prior to rating it, and without adequate preparation they are likely to produce ratings that are a function of any stereotypes they hold regarding the job (Harvey & Lozada-Larsen, 1988).

Smith and Hakel (1979) found that the ratings provided by supervisors and incumbents were higher than those of trained job analysts, though the shapes of the profiles of ratings across elements of a task inventory called the Position Analysis Questionnaire (McCormick, Jeanneret, & Mecham, 1972) were similar. Meyer (1959) and Hazel, Madden, and Christal (1964) found that supervisors and subordinates agreed on the tasks performed in a job on between 58% and 63% of a set of tasks rated. Harvey (1990) found that subordinates failed to rate as applicable 30% of the tasks that supervisors said were part of the job. Among trained job analysts, interrater reliabilities of task ratings tend to be in the .70-.90 range (Cragun & McCormick, 1967; Geyer, Hice, Hawk, Boese, & Brannon, 1989; Schmitt & Fine, 1983; Wilson, Harvey, & Macy, 1990), though for some physical demands and temperament dimensions, the reliabilities are less than .50. Given disparities in the reliability and agreement across raters, it is difficult to ascertain who is providing an incorrect/correct view of a job. We should also note that an equally interesting and perhaps more important question is the degree to which different raters or rater groups generate a common set of tasks or KSAOs. Interrater or cross-rater group studies have been conducted to determine raters' evaluations of a fixed set of tasks or KSAOs, either indicating whether a task was performed or the task or KSAO's level, importance, or frequency.

In the discussion of task ratings above, we presented a formula for task importance that combines three other ratings of tasks (criticality, frequency, and difficulty). Occasionally, raters are asked to judge importance directly. Some research has been conducted to determine how raters form these judgments of the importance of a task. Of ratings on six different dimensions, Sanchez and Levine (1989), using policy capturing methods, found that incumbents in most jobs used a linear combination of task criticality and difficulty of learning a task when they made judgments about the overall importance of a task. Harvey (1991), who reviewed research by Friedman and Wilson, argues that there is a great deal of variability in these judgment policies when they are considered at the individual level as opposed to aggregated over raters of a given job. Because of these large individual differences in rater use of different scales, Harvey believes that any significant reduction in the number of scales used cannot be achieved. This small body of research is clearly not very satisfying. It seems reasonable to think that, at least within a job, a group of raters would rely on similar task characteristics in judging importance. The method of data collection (i.e., large numbers of tasks rated by a relatively large number of scales), the use of regression analysis of highly correlated rating dimensions to determine the importance of different rating dimensions, and the relatively small number of studies on this issue regarding a limited range of jobs contribute to the conclusion that more data on this question would be useful.

It is possible, however, that individuals see a job differently, or that different persons with the same job title are performing significantly different tasks. Early studies of individual differences in raters led industrial/organizational psychologists to accept the conclusion that rater sex and job effectiveness (and perhaps other individual differences as well) do not influence job analysis survey ratings (Arvey, Davis, McGowen, & Dipboye, 1982; Arvey, Passino, & Lounsbury, 1977; Wexley & Silverman, 1978). More recent literature indicates that sex, race, experience, and effectiveness of raters have some impact on the way in which tasks are rated (Ferris, Fedor, Rowland, & Porac, 1985; Sanchez, 1990; Schmitt & Cohen, 1989). However, these studies usually report only small effect sizes and a small number of significantly different ratings across rater subgroups, and there remains little attempt to provide any theoretical explanation of these results. Perhaps the most interesting of these studies are those reporting that raters' levels of job performance effectiveness were related to the type of critical incidents they reported (Mullins & Kimbrough, 1988; Ronan, Talbert, & Mullett, 1977). As indicated above, differences in ratings have been most frequently studied; of perhaps more importance are differences in the material that gets generated and is presumably rated in subsequent phases of the job analysis. It may also be interesting to study within-job variability in ratings as a variable in its own right. Variability may be indicative of lack of clear understanding of the responsibilities of a job or some meaningful and effective role differentiation (Ilgen & Hollenbeck, 1991) among job incumbents.

The validity of job analysis data is very difficult to assess. Some attempts have been made to assess the degree to which relative time spent ratings correspond to actual time spent on various job tasks. Carpenter, Giorgia, and McFarland (1975) found that the average actual time spent was approximately equal to the average difference between ratings of time spent and actual time spent (i.e., the error in ratings of time spent). Efforts to assess accuracy using phony task statements (Green & Stutzman, 1986) and by repeating task statements (Wilson et al., 1990) have found evidence for significant inconsistencies that have usually been attributed to rater carelessness. A common approach to bolster confidence in the comprehensiveness of a task list is to ask incumbents what percentage of their job is represented by a task list (e.g., see Fine & Getkate, 1995). Wilson (1990) provided job incumbents with two lists of task statements, one of which showed only 30% as many tasks as the other. Incumbents estimated that the tasks on the short list constituted 77% of their job. The two task lists themselves may have been redundant. If so, Wilson's demonstration would not be as discouraging as it seems at first. However, this overall judgment does seem like a difficult one to make, especially if the job is complex and some tasks occur at widely differing intervals in time.

Usefulness of Detailed Job Analysis and Need for a General Theory of Work

Perhaps the one issue that is most controversial is whether or not the detailed job analysis described above is required. Some researchers suggest that to determine the appropriate KSAOs on which to make selection decisions, all one needs to know is the general job family to which a job belongs (e.g., managerial, clerical, mechanical). This controversy and the conflicting points of view are well summarized by Harvey (1991). Comparisons between the selection procedures and the *outcomes* (e.g., test plans, test items and tests, test validity and utility) produced by these procedures when different types of job analyses are conducted have rarely been attempted (see Levine, Ash, Hall, & Sistrunk, 1983, for an example), are difficult to design, and have been inconclusive.

There are several reasons the type of job analysis described above should and does play an important role in selection research. First, continued careful examination of job behavior is important as jobs change. Accepting the notion that the same basic KSAOs are required to perform job tasks with no reexamination of this hypothesis seems shortsighted, especially in light of the speed of technological innovation and the increasingly rapid changes in the types of jobs people are required to perform (Bridges, 1994). Second, careful examination of jobs and efforts to develop content valid tests (tests that represent samples of job behavior) may be at least partially responsible for significant advances in the development of selection procedures (e.g., situational judgment tests) and greater understanding of existing procedures (e.g., the interview). Third, if the job analysis procedures described in this chapter are used as the basis upon which to develop test content, the likelihood that the tests will appear valid to test takers and corporate users is greater. Such perceptions of face validity are related to test fairness perceptions and perhaps a variety of other reactions to an organization (Gilliland, 1993; Smither, Reilly, Millsap, Pearlman, & Stoffey, 1993). Fourth, in cases that have involved litigation, the courts almost always have examined the care with which job analyses have been conducted and the degree to which the results of those analyses have been linked to selection procedures. An organization that faces the threat of litigation regarding the manner in which employees are selected would be well advised to follow the procedures outlined above and in a very similar chapter by Goldstein, Zedeck, and Schneider (1993). It is also almost certainly true that legal pressures have produced a needless and unthinking compulsiveness about the way in which job analyses are conducted (Landy, 1986). In summary, there are good theoretical and practical reasons to conduct the type of careful job analysis described above.

Having made these arguments, we should also note that there are also good reasons researchers and practitioners do not want or need to engage in this time-consuming, expensive process. The progress of a scientific discipline is often measured by the parsimony of its explanations for complex events. If personnel selection is to progress as a scientific discipline, we cannot maintain that there is no generality to work tasks and their human ability requirements. The hypotheses regarding work-ability linkages derived from a job analysis of the type described above should be similar to hypotheses derived in similar situations in other contexts. Hence, we have developed general theories of the structure of work and theories about human performance on these jobs, and have at least worried about the need for general taxonomies that link dimensions of work and human ability dimensions. We describe our efforts to develop a general theory of work in the remainder of this chapter.

Theories of the Structure of Work

In 1977, the fourth edition of the *Dictionary of Occupational Titles* (*DOT*) was published by the U.S. Employment Service. The *DOT* provides information on approximately 20,000 jobs that is potentially useful for determining job requirements or for confirming the information one might have gathered about a similar job. *DOT* job codes are also required in most federal government reports regarding employees. The *DOT* is also important because it describes a job classification that amounts to a theory of work and a well-defined method for gathering information about a job. This theory of work is the result of Sidney Fine's efforts to standardize the way in which job analysis information is collected and jobs are compared (Fine & Getkate, 1995; Fine & Wiley, 1974). The way in which Fine suggests that job tasks be written has been generally adapted by most professionals and is represented by the examples in Table 2.2. A trained job analyst gathers information about the job, interviews job incumbents, writes the task statements, and then rates the job on 10 dimensions that reflect Fine's theory of work and its complexity.

Functional job analysis (or FJA, Fine's name for his approach) is a conceptual system used to define the level and orientation of worker activity. Fine asserts that all work activity involves the way in which workers physically relate to things, mentally relate to data, and interpersonally relate to people. The difficulty and orientation (percentage of time spent relating to data, people, and things) constitute six of the dimensions along which work tasks are compared. In addition, a Worker Instructions scale defines the level of the worker's discretion in determining how she or he goes about doing a task. Reasoning, Math, and Language scales define the general educational levels required to do the work. The levels of data, people, and things hypothesized by Fine and Getkate (1995) and used to rate tasks are displayed in Figure 2.1 and are applied, along with ratings on the other dimensions, to two tasks in Figure 2.2.

Using these basic dimensions in a standardized manner allows for the comparability of tasks and, by aggregation, jobs. With the Worker Instructions and educational development scale ratings, one also has some information about the KSAOs required to perform these tasks. When these comparative data are available on all jobs, solutions to many different applied problems are possible. If a worker loses her or

Task Code:

Worker Function Level & Orientation						Worker Instructions	General Educational Development		
Data	%	People	%	Things	%		Reasoning	Math	Language
2	80	6	10	7	10	4	5	1	5

Task 25: Writes test specifications which represent the important knowledge, skills and abilities or tasks identified in the job analysis, drawing upon information gathered from those familiar with the job in order to develop a strategy for designing a content valid test.

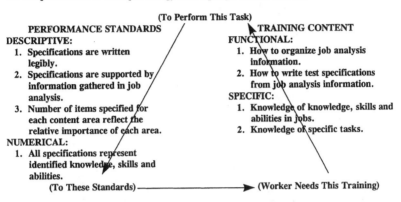

Task 26: Reviews/examines/evaluates various job analysis techniques (i.e., FJA, PAQ, checklist, critical incidents, observations, etc.) with regard to information required, time commitment, and cost to the organization, drawing upon knowledge and experience with job analysis in order to select most appropriate technique.

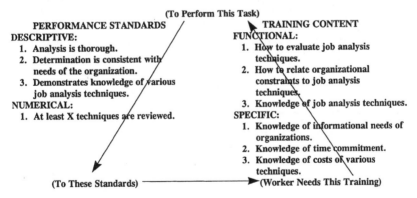

Figure 2.1. Functional Job Analysis Task Statement and Ratings

his job, we can tell what other jobs might require similarly rated tasks and, hopefully, a similar set and level of KSAOs. The worker's interest in doing the tasks on another job can also be inferred from the

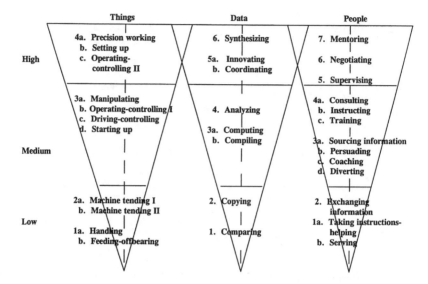

1. Each hierarchy is independent of the other. It would be incorrect to read the functions across the three hierarchies as related because they appear to be on the same level. The definitive relationship among functions is within each hierarchy, not across hierarchies. Some broad exceptions are made in the next note.
2. Data is central since a worker can be assigned even higher data functions although Things and People functions remain at the lowest level of their respective scales. This is not so for Things and People functions. When a Things function is at the third level, e.g., Precision working, the Data function is likely to be at least Compiling or Computing. When a People function is at the fourth level, e.g., Consulting, the Data function is likely to be at least Analyzing and possibly Innovating or Coordinating. Similarly for Supervising and Negotiating. Mentoring in some instances can call for Synthesizing.
3. Each function in its hierarchy is defined to include the lower numbered functions. This is more or less the way it was found to occur in reality. It was most clear-cut for Things and Data and only a rough approximation in the case of People.
4. The lettered functions are separate functions on the same level, separately defined. The empirical evidence did not support a hierarchial distinction.
5. The hyphenated functions, Taking instructions-helping, Operating-controlling, etc. are single functions.
6. The Things hierarchy consists of two intertwined scales: Handling, Manipulating, Precision working is a scale for tasks involving hands and hand tools; the remainder of the functions apply to tasks involving machines, equipment, vehicles.

Figure 2.2. FJA Functional-Level Rating Scales

SOURCE: From *Benchmark Tasks for Job Analysis* (Figure 1.1), by S. A. Fine and M. Getkate, 1995, Mahwah, NJ: Lawrence Erlbaum Associates. Copyright 1995 by Lawrence Erlbaum Associates, Inc. Adapted with permission.

similarity of the orientations to data, people, and things. Training requirements can also be inferred from the similarity of the level ratings on data, people, things dimensions across jobs as well as from the ratings of general educational development. Of most relevance to this book, we should also be able to tell what previous job experiences are relevant when we evaluate applicants for a job. Whether these vocational, career, training, and selection applications are possible depends on the adequacy of Fine's theory of work. To our knowledge, research on the adequacy of functional job analysis ratings in these contexts has not been validated empirically. One could envision a comparison of the training required or the level of specific skills required as one switches jobs across varying levels of data, people, and things dimensions.

Other theories of the structure of work are implicit in various general task inventories. Whereas Fine generated different tasks across different jobs and gained comparability across jobs by comparing these jobs using the FJA dimensions and rating scales, the objective in constructing general task inventories was to provide a set of tasks that could be used to represent all jobs. The first attempt to provide an instrument that would reflect all work activity on various jobs (and hence be useful in analyzing any job without generation of new task statements) is represented by the Position Analysis Questionnaire (PAQ; McCormick et al., 1972). McCormick and his colleagues (1972) used an information-processing model (input, processing, and output tasks as well as tasks related to the context of work) to organize the generation of worker-oriented items. Worker-oriented items were intended to be free of the specific technologies or products associated with work and refer only to worker activity. McCormick et al. reasoned that this approach was the only way in which an instrument that would be of general use could be constructed. Their 194-item instrument has been used in various consulting and research projects for 25 years and has produced a great deal of useful data about the structure of work.

To discover (or confirm) the underlying structure of work across many jobs, McCormick and his colleagues used a technique called factor analysis to isolate the underlying dimensions of job behavior and to confirm the appropriateness of their information-processing model of work activity. The original factor analysis of responses to the PAQ yielded five major factors: (a) decision making/communication/social responsibilities, (b) performance of skilled activities, (c) physical activity relative to environmental conditions, (d) operation of vehicles or equipment, and (e) processing of information. Subsequent factor analysis of the PAQ and other structured job analysis instruments produced more factors of different types. Harvey

(1991) has provided a useful integration of the factor analyses of these different instruments organized around the FJA data, people, and things dimensions and a work context dimension (see Table 2.8). That we find this degree of convergence across various methods and data collection instruments suggests that, overall, the field may have produced a reasonable taxonomy of worker activity.

McCormick and his colleagues have analyzed a large number of jobs using the PAQ over the past 25 years and have maintained and updated a database on these jobs that adds to the utility of the instrument. When new jobs are analyzed, their characteristics are examined in light of what is known about other similar jobs. For example, if a previously analyzed job requires the same level of activity on the PAQ dimensions as does the new target job, then it is likely that similar worker characteristics (KSAOs) will be required to perform the job. This goal—that is, an empirically verified theory of the structure of work—has tremendous practical implications for various human resource activities, including selection. The *DOT,* mentioned above, is being revised, and one of the goals of this revision effort is to produce an interactive computer module that can access information about jobs and link that information to individuals' education, training, experience, and interests as well as job opportunities to provide vocational counseling to individuals. The same information could be used by employers to determine the types of skills they should search for when filling job vacancies. These applications all depend on standardized and comparable information on the various available jobs.

As Harvey (1991) concludes, additional research is needed to improve upon the degree to which standardized task inventories can and do index a comprehensive set of work constructs. At this point, it is probably true that no one instrument indexes the entire domain of work, and that some of the means by which data are collected (that is, the rating scales) do not allow appropriate cross-job comparisons because of the use of scales or directions that give raters a within-job frame of reference. When raters do not have experience with a range of jobs, it is important that anchors on rating scales be specific and behavioral, so that ratings across different jobs can be compared meaningfully. Research and theory that provide a taxonomy of work and the means to use that taxonomy to measure jobs may be the most important practical and theoretical need in selection research.

Table 2.8 Taxonomy of General-Purpose and Managerial Dimensions

Interpersonal (FJA's "people")
   Internal contacts
      Communication/instruction/consulting/coordinating
      Supervision/direction of employees
         Lower level
         Mid/upper level
   External contacts
      Public/customers
      Professional/industrial
      Legal/regulatory
   Personally demanding situations
   Personal services for others

Information processing (FJA's "data")
   Resources/assets/financial
   Planning/scheduling/budgeting
   Production/operations/systems analysis/management
   Physical environment sensing/judging
   Decision making/conflict resolution
   Policies/procedures
   Multiple language use
   Contract management
   Taking/exchanging information
   Clerical activities

Mechanical/technical/physical activities (FJA's "things")
   Adjust/tend/repair equipment
   Operate equipment
      Office
      Production/manufacturing
      Light vehicles
      Heavy vehicles
      Tools
   Gross body activities
      Strength/endurance
      Coordination/balance
   Graphic/quantitative/measurement activities

Work context
Apparel	Task/skill variety, repetitive activities
Work schedule	Task significance
Reward system	Feedback
Unpleasant physical environment	Task identity
Risks and hazards	Licensing/certification
Autonomy	Training/education experience

Theories of Work Adjustment

To this point, we have focused on the requirements that organizations and jobs impose on workers or that are necessary if the worker is to be able to do the job. This ability to do the job must be accompanied by a willingness or motivation to do the job. Such issues are often included as the "other" characteristics in a list of required KSAOs, but they have also been studied explicitly by some researchers, particularly a group at the University of Minnesota (Dawis, 1991; Lofquist & Dawis, 1978). These researchers have focused on the importance of interests, values, and preferences of potential employees, defined as the stable dispositions people develop as a result of affective evaluations of their previous life experiences. Measures of these interests, values, and preferences are predictive of occupational membership, tenure, and change and of job and career satisfaction. They are also related, to a much lesser degree, to employees' success at their jobs. The implication of these relationships is that job analysts should consider the reward aspects of jobs (Schneider & Schmitt, 1986) as well as job demands.

Holland (1976, 1985) has made this notion explicit in developing a measure of organizational environments that matches the basic dimensions that he believes are representative of all human interests. Holland has generated considerable evidence, using responses to the various editions of the Strong measure of vocational interests, that these dimensions include realistic interests (building, repairing, working outdoors), investigative interests (researching, analyzing, inquiring), artistic interests (creating or enjoying art, drama, music, writing), social interests (helping, instructing, caregiving), enterprising interests (selling, managing, persuading), and conventional interests (accounting, organizing, processing data). Holland (1985) maintains that these interests are matched by organizational environments of the same basic types, and that individuals will be most happy and committed to jobs and organizations that provide a match to their interests. The implication for job analysis activity is that the organizational environment and the nature of the work required should be measured and matched to the individuals' interests.

Work with the Minnesota Importance Questionnaire, which is described as a measure of work values, indicates that the factors measured in this instrument are different from Holland's interest dimensions. The following factors emerged from several large-scale studies of the structure of work values (Seaburg, Rounds, Dawis, & Lofquist, 1976): achievement (environments that encourage accomplishment), comfort (environments that are comfortable and not stressful), status (environments that provide recognition and prestige), altruism (environments that encourage harmony and service to others), safety (environments that are predictable and stable), and autonomy (environments that stimulate initiative). Underlying the theory of work adjustment is the notion that workers whose values fit the environment in which they find themselves are apt to be more satisfied and motivated. Rounds, Dawis, and Lofquist (1987) found that measures of the correspondence between individuals and their occupations were relatively highly correlated (i.e., .30 to .50) with their job satisfaction.

We mentioned at the beginning of this chapter that job analysis should begin with a discussion of organizational goals. If one of the organization's goals is to recruit a satisfied, committed, and highly motivated workforce, then it would seem useful for the job analyst to determine the types of environments provided by the work and units within the organization and attempt to assess the degree to which workers match their environments. Perhaps beyond organizational goals, human resource professionals should be concerned about the reward attributes of jobs and the welfare and satisfaction of the people involved. The work adjustment approach to job analysis is rarely employed explicitly, although, as mentioned above, it is often implicit in the KSAOs generated during traditional job analyses.

Use of Different Approaches to Job Analysis

Clearly, there are multiple approaches to job analysis, many of which will lead to similar delineations of desired worker KSAOs. The approach to job analysis an individual uses is a function of many different considerations. Sometimes, it is a matter of the personal preference of the analyst or the analyst's previous experiences with a job. Other times, it is a function of legal considerations or the size of the incumbent worker group. If we consider the job analyses conducted in the examples in Chapter 1, we see a variety of approaches. In the case of the investigative officers (Example 1), a detailed listing of tasks and KSAOs was generated in focus interviews and a survey was conducted of a representative group of incumbents working at different assignments and locations. This choice of job analysis procedure was partly a function of the legal considerations being confronted by the organization, but it was also a function of the fact that there were many job incumbents working in various places and at different assignments, and we wanted to ascertain the nature of these differences. In the second project, it would have been impossible to conduct interviews with incumbents in each of the many jobs involved to develop comprehensive task and KSAO lists. Because we were concerned primarily with differences and similarities in KSAOs across jobs, we used the Fleishman taxonomy of human abilities as a starting point and derived profiles of required human abilities across jobs as a means of determining what tests might be appropriate to select applicants for the many jobs. In the project involving telephone operators (Example 3), we conducted a very detailed job analysis because the small sample precluded any criterion-related validation effort. Also, the organization was very concerned that the tests be accepted by higher-level administrators and applicants. These considerations meant that we needed to rely on the test development process itself to justify the use of the tests and that the tests themselves needed to match the job tasks insofar as was possible. In the example of individual assessment targeted at the selection of an executive, there was no large group of incumbents or supervisors to interview or survey. The job analysis consisted of interviews with high-level organizational personnel who defined the executive officer's job and indirectly determined the kinds of KSAOs evaluated and the selection tasks developed.

Summary and Research Issues

In this chapter we have provided a description of various job analysis activities as the basis upon which hypotheses may be formed about ability-performance relationships in the workplace. We have provided detail regarding the development of job information, both the work accomplished and the KSAOs required to do that work. We have also provided a very brief introduction to efforts designed to shortcut and standardize the work of job analysts by using theories of work and the measurement procedures designed to operationalize given theories. The development of these theories or taxonomies of work is critically important for all human resource functions, including selection. We have also advocated explicit consideration of work adjustment factors in job analysis. Whereas we have addressed the nature of work in this chapter, we will consider the nature of work performance and models of work performance in the next.

We mentioned earlier in this chapter several research issues concerning the generation of job analysis information; we would now like to highlight some of these issues as well as others. First, we think that more work should be done on what determines differences in job incumbents' perceptions of the importance and criticality or even frequency of various job tasks. If these within-job, across-incumbent differences are real, how do they develop—as a function of the situation, the colleagues with whom people work, or the perceivers' own abilities and motivations? Second, it would be useful to have more information on the capability of various people or groups of people to ascertain the KSAO requirements of jobs. Are incumbents or supervisors appropriate judges, or should human resource professionals with a background in the psychology of individual differences make these judgments after carefully studying the nature of the work? Third, perhaps the most intriguing issue that remains to be addressed is the value of incorporating ideas from the work adjustment research and the results of traditional job analysis. Would assessment of jobs and organizations lead us to the assessment of human characteristics that would better predict worker satisfaction, commitment, and withdrawal behavior as well as performance? The existing literature suggests that values and interests are good predictors of individual reactions to jobs, but do not predict performance well (Dawis, 1991). Performance, however, is usually quite well predicted with measures derived from more traditional job analyses. Fourth, there continues to be a need to taxonomize worker tasks and abilities. This effort has occupied psychologists for at least half of the 20th century and remains an important practical and theoretical limitation in selection research.

 **3** The Nature of Work

Performance and
Its Measurement

I n Chapter 2, we considered the nature of the work that is performed
on various jobs. In this chapter, we consider the nature of work
performance and its measurement. Work performance is a variable of
considerable societal concern and central to selection research. We
measure human ability and characteristics in an effort to predict the
subsequent work performance of the individuals who are asked to
become members of our organizations. As we indicated in the preceding chapter, measures of work performance should be derived from
the information collected in the job analysis and the theories of work
derived from that analysis. That is, the job analyst develops measures
of how well workers perform the various activities that represent their
jobs. Before we proceed to measurement issues, however, we believe it
will be useful to discuss what we mean by *performance* and how
previous researchers have treated this construct. Our conceptualization of the performance construct is important because it determines

what KSAOs we consider in selecting employees and because this conceptualization determines the measures we use to evaluate the selection process itself.

Performance has often received little attention from those doing selection research. It has been defined simply as that which is to be predicted, the dependent variable, or "the effectiveness and value of work behavior and its outcomes" (Society for Industrial and Organizational Psychology, 1987, p. 39). Recently, Campbell and his colleagues have proposed a "theory of job performance" that hypothesizes that this construct comprises eight major dimensions, each of which consists of several more-specific features as well (Campbell, Gasser, & Oswald, 1996; Campbell, McCloy, Oppler, & Sager, 1993). In general, Campbell et al. (1993) define performance as "goal relevant actions that are under the control of the individual, regardless of whether they are cognitive, motor, psychomotor, or interpersonal" (pp. 40-41).

The eight general factors listed below are meant to describe the universe of things people do (not the results of their actions) across all jobs, though one or more of the factors may be missing or irrelevant in any given job. *Job-specific task proficiency* behaviors are those technical or core tasks that are central to the job. These define the substantive content of what gets done by computer programmers, college professors, carpenters, and so on. *Task proficiency of a non-job-specific nature* includes those things that people across jobs are often required to perform in organizations. For example, in many workplaces, all individuals are required to help keep the workplace clean and to be watchful for unsafe conditions. Many jobs require that individuals be proficient in various *written and oral communication tasks*. People in most jobs are required to *demonstrate effort*, in that they must commit themselves to the performance of work tasks, exert a high degree of effort, and persist in that effort. They must also exercise a degree of *personal discipline*, in that they are required to arrive at work on time, avoid substance abuse problems, and abide by company rules and policies. In many jobs, an important element of performance is the degree to which workers *facilitate peer and team performance*. This factor is very similar to the concept of organizational citizen behavior (Organ, 1988), which includes behavior related to helping colleagues with work-related and personal problems, serving as a role model, and promoting participation of colleagues in the organization's work.

Table 3.1   Comparison of the Position Analysis Questionnaire (PAQ) and Campbell et al.'s (1993) Theory of Performance

Campbell et al.	PAQ[a]
1. Job-specific task proficiency	—[b]
2. Non-job-specific task proficiency	—[b]
3. Written and oral communication	Communications: Oral & Written
4. Demonstrating Effort	Job Demands
	Job Structure
5. Maintaining Personal Discipline	Responsibility, Work Schedule, Job Demands, Apparel Worn, Supervision Received
6. Facilitating Peer and Team Performance	Personal and Social Aspects
	Job-required personal contact
Other organizational activity	
7. Supervision/Leadership	Supervision and Coordination
	Personal and Social Aspects
8. Management/Administrative	Mental Processes: Decision-Making, Planning, Information-Processing

a. Listed in this column are section titles in the PAQ.
b. The PAQ developers sought to exclude items that were job specific (McCormick et al., 1972). Much of the Input section and a large amount of the Work Output tasks in the PAQ relate to task proficiency, both job specific and non-job specific as defined by Campbell et al. (1993).

Supervisory/leadership behavior is directed at influencing the behavior of subordinates. *Management and administration tasks* include those tasks that help to manage, report, or define what an organization does without direct interaction with subordinates, as would be the case for supervisory tasks.

In Chapter 2, we described the Position Analysis Questionnaire (PAQ) developed by McCormick and his colleagues as a theory of the structure of work. Table 3.1 represents an attempt to map the sections of the PAQ approach against Campbell et al.'s (1993) dimensions. As can be seen in the table, there is some similarity in the way in which Campbell et al. have defined the nature of job performance and the manner in which the structure of work is defined in the PAQ. Both Campbell et al. and McCormick, Jeanneret, and Mecham (1972) recognize that some aspects of their models will not apply to all jobs. Provision for nonapplicability in the PAQ is made by allowing an NA (not applicable) response to tasks that do not occur on a given job. In making these comparisons, it is important to remember that the PAQ was constructed to assess what work is being done; Campbell et al. are concerned with how well that work gets done.

There are also some dissimilarities between these two approaches. McCormick and his colleagues (1972) have deliberately avoided the use of job-specific tasks, because they were interested in producing an instrument that would be generally useful across all jobs. Much of what is defined by Campbell and his colleagues (1993, 1996) as job-specific and non-job-specific task proficiency appears in the Input and Work Output sections of the PAQ. The Campbell et al. dimensions and the PAQ sections and items also differ in that Campbell et al.'s Demonstrating Effort and Maintaining Personal Discipline are not directly measured in the PAQ. The sections listed as parallel sections of the PAQ involve items that require an inference that effort and discipline are required. It should also be noted that an examination of the levels of involvement with data, people, and things dimensions used in functional job analysis (see Figure 2.2) would reveal considerable overlap with Campbell et al.'s performance dimensions, but as with the PAQ, there is no differentiation between job and non-job-specific tasks, and the Effort and Discipline dimensions are not explicitly mentioned.

These comparisons across very different approaches to the nature of work and its performance are reassuring in that there is conceptual overlap. However, in testing whether the conceptualization of job performance provided by Campbell et al. (1993), or any other construct definition, is appropriate, we must have adequate measures of all the relevant dimensions. Consequently, we turn next to a discussion of the ways in which job performance has been, or can be, measured, and how these measurement methods can provide information regarding the performance construct as defined above. We then describe efforts to test general theories of work performance. Some of these efforts have examined the nature of performance constructs themselves. Other research, described in Chapter 4, has been directed to a study of the determinants of these constructs. In the last section of this chapter, we examine the idea that performance constructs change as a function of job tenure.

Performance Measurement

In most research on job performance, ratings by supervisors, peers, and subordinates, as well as self-ratings, have been used to measure performance. This has been partly a matter of convenience, given that other measures of work performance are unavailable, but ratings may also be the best, and most flexible, approach to job performance measurement. In this chapter, we will also describe performance as measured by the outcomes of work (e.g., products, sales), job samples, withdrawal behavior (tardiness, absence, turnover, "bad" attitudes), and customer outcomes. Each of these latter measures may appear to be superior to ratings, but each also has significant problems. Outcome measures are preferred by many researchers and organizational personnel, but these measures are often not fully under the control of the individual worker (see Campbell et al.'s definition of performance above). Such lack of control is often termed *opportunity bias*, meaning that workers differ in terms of their opportunities (e.g., different sales territories, different equipment, different coworkers) to produce valued organizational outcomes.

Some or all of these outcome measures can be assessed using rating measures as well. For example, supervisors could be asked to assess aspects of customer service or withdrawal behavior. Presumably, a supervisor could "correct" for some of the errors in the actual output variables such as opportunity bias. However, use of supervisory ratings as the source of all performance data may introduce other problems. It is important in any discussion of various output measures to distinguish between problems that are inherent in the nature of the construct being measured (e.g., the fact that turnover is relatively rare and dichotomous) and those that are a function of the way in which the variable is being measured (e.g., ratings or archival measures). Perhaps the best approach is to assess performance using a variety of measures, recognizing the strengths and weakness of each.

The use of job samples—specially constructed job tasks that allow for the measurement of work process and outcome (Green & Wigdor, 1991)—usually does not allow for the performance of the full array of job tasks, necessitating a sampling from the domain of job tasks. Perhaps most important, a job sample can rarely be taken in a situation that replicates the motivational context of the job and organization.

In some organizations and for some jobs, only attendance behavior is relevant. Hulin (1991; Hulin, Roznowski, & Hachiya, 1985) has argued that tardiness, absence, and turnover are parts of a general process of withdrawal from an organization that may begin with individual predispositions and job attitudes. Withdrawal behaviors certainly match the Campbell et al. (1993) Effort and Personal Discipline dimensions and perhaps affect Peer and Team Performance Facilitation, but they also may not be completely under the control of the individual worker, and they present other significant definitional and measurement problems. Finally, customer satisfaction (Fierman, 1995; Schneider, Parkington, & Buxton, 1980) is increasingly used as a measure of employee performance, but it too is only partially under the control of the worker. We discuss below the research on each of these approaches to job performance measurement, with a view toward measuring the performance construct as defined by Campbell et al. (1993).

Ratings

Ratings are probably most frequently made on 5- or 7-point scales ranging from *poor* to *excellent* on several different dimensions considered important by management. These ratings have often been criticized, for a wide variety of reasons. There is some support for the notions that people tend to rate more highly others they perceive to be like themselves (the *similar-to-me effect*; Wexley, Alexander, Greenawalt, & Couch, 1980); that some raters are more *lenient* than others (independent of the job behavior of their ratees); that raters are sometimes unwilling to provide extreme ratings (the *central tendency error*); and that individuals tend to make their ratings primarily on the basis of one dimension that is particularly important to them (*halo error*). Considerable research has been invested in correcting these and other errors associated with ratings. This research has focused on the format of the rating scale, the training provided to raters, and, in an effort to discover how to explain rating errors, on the cognitive processes involved in the rating task (Landy & Farr, 1980). One problem with these studies is that there is often no "true" performance measure against which to evaluate the accuracy of ratings; hence, much effort has gone into developing measures of rating accuracy (Sulsky & Balzer, 1988). We will not review this research on the quality of ratings, but the references cited above should direct the interested reader to this body of literature. The following descriptions of rating scale development, rater training, and the process of making ratings are meant to reflect the findings of this research.

The development of rating scales should involve the following steps:

1. Using the results of the job analysis, the job analyst identifies the major job performance dimensions. These dimensions are defined as precisely and behaviorally as possible through the analyst's work with job experts. If the analyst is interested in testing the Campbell et al. (1993) theory of job performance (or any other theory), consideration as to how each of these dimensions fits the theoretical framework is appropriate; of particular importance would be the recognition that one or more of the major dimensions identified by Campbell et al. are absent. This may be consistent with the nature of the job, or it may represent a deficiency in the job analysis.

2. The analyst identifies the critical incidents that were generated during the job analysis for each of these major performance dimensions. If the job analysis did not include the generation of critical incidents, then the analyst collects these behaviors using the procedures outlined in Chapter 2.

3. The analyst has a panel of job experts reassign a scrambled list of these critical incident behaviors to the major dimensions. If 50%-80% of the experts cannot reassign a behavior to the same dimension (preferably the same dimension for which it was written), the incident is dropped. Dimensions for which a preponderance of the original incidents are not reassigned are also dropped, because they are not defined clearly enough to represent distinct behaviors or dimensions in the experts' minds.

4. The job analyst has the same group of experts or another similar group rate each statement as to the level of performance it represents on a particular dimension. Statements covering the full range of performance on a given dimension are used to anchor the scale points on the rating scale for that dimension. Ratings of these statements by the panel of experts should also have low standard deviations, indicating that the experts agree on the level of performance represented by the incident. Occasionally, several incidents are available to anchor a specific point on a rating scale, and a "behavioral summary" involving this group of incidents can be prepared as an anchor.

5. The analyst constructs the final instrument, which consists of at least one rating scale for each major performance dimension. Each scale is anchored by several statements indicating different levels of performance. An example of the resulting behaviorally anchored rating scale (BARS) is presented in Figure 1.2.

This method of scale construction was first proposed by Smith and Kendall (1963) as a means of eliminating or alleviating the problems of central tendency error, halo error, and leniency referred to above. Although subsequent research generally did not support the notion that these rating errors are any less evident in the use of BARSs than they are in other rating formats, behaviorally anchored scales do have other important advantages. In our own experience, we have found that the greater participation that workers and supervisors have in developing these scales leads to all employees' taking the rating process much more seriously, and this in turn produces positive motivation toward the whole rating process. This result may, of course, occur with any rating format when the employees are involved in development. A second positive result of the use of a BARS is not directly relevant to the use of ratings as criteria in selection, but is important when the ratings are used as performance feedback or as a means of developing employees. The definitions and anchors do make explicit to the rater what performance is being evaluated. Finally, BARS formats are more face valid and often more acceptable, not just to employees, but also to legal personnel who scrutinize the criteria used in our validation efforts. Securing the trust and confidence of the raters is often key to collecting good-quality rating criteria, and using instruments that clearly reflect the performance domain helps tremendously in this regard. Bernardin and Beatty (1984, chap. 6), who provide a comprehensive comparison of rating formats, conclude that the most difficult and most expensive approaches to rating performance (one of which is the BARS) are also the best, but that much depends on the context in which ratings are collected. We believe it is still important, even when a researcher cannot engage in the rather cumbersome rating scale development process described above, that rating dimensions and anchors be defined as behaviorally and specifically as possible.

Research has also shown that the quality of performance ratings (particularly those that are collected for research purposes only) can be improved with appropriate rater training (McIntyre, Smith, & Hassett, 1984; Pulakos, 1986, 1991). Such training usually has three elements. First, criteria for the selection of raters are carefully laid out to ensure that the raters have had time to observe the ratee's job performance. The second component of efforts to improve ratings involves an explanation of the importance of the ratings, provided on both organizational and personal levels. The third component is an effort to explain the nature of common rating errors and how they can be avoided. Raters are encouraged to acknowledge both the strengths and the weaknesses of the ratees, to consider only performance-related information, and to evaluate performance over time, not just single instances of outstanding or awful performance.

As indicated above, researchers have also investigated the extent to which cognitive process models account for performance ratings. These process models hold that person categories (i.e., implicit theories, person schemata, or prototypes) help to process information.

These person categories specify the relationships among traits, characteristics, or behaviors in a particular domain. In the case of performance ratings, these would include a notion of how people and organizations operate, and raters who hold these person categories would judge their ratees accordingly. There is support for the role that these person categories play in determining ratings (Feldman, 1981; Landy & Farr, 1980) and the fact that there are individual differences in the use of these category systems (e.g., Hauenstein & Alexander, 1991). Rater training, as described above, is really designed to encourage raters to adopt the organization's implicit theory of performance in a particular occupation.

Defining performance carefully, selecting appropriate raters, and training the raters all can help to improve the quality of ratings as measures of performance. One way of assessing the quality of ratings is to evaluate the degree to which two or more raters provide the same evaluations of a group of ratees. Rothstein (1990) aggregated studies of the reliability of ratings over a large number of studies and found that interrater reliability asymptotes at about .60. Consistent with the recommendation above that raters be selected who have an opportunity to observe ratees is Rothstein's observation that the experience of the rater was correlated about .70 with the reliability of the ratings.

When the raters are from different levels of the organization (i.e., subordinates, supervisors, and peers), interrater reliability is typically lower (Harris & Schaubroeck, 1988; Schmitt, Noe, Meritt, & Fitzgerald, 1984) than the asymptotic figure reported by Rothstein (1990). The fact that these reliabilities are not higher could be a function of different frames of reference being applied in judging job performance (as the cognitive process models suggest), different opportunities to observe on the part of raters, or the ratees' actually behaving differently in the presence of different raters. However, with appropriate estimates of reliability, we can correct our estimates of the relationship between ratings and other variables of interest (see the discussion of the correction of attenuation in Chapter 6), such as measures of relevant KSAOs. Campbell et al. (1993) also note that there are other important reasons to use ratings in gathering performance information. First, and perhaps most important, is the fact that the content of ratings can be constructed to conform to an underlying theory of performance—that of Campbell et al. or any other. As our discussion of performance measures other than ratings will show, it is often not likely that these alternate measures could completely encompass the performance domain. Moreover, when constructed and used competently (C. H. Campbell et al., 1990), performance ratings can be reliable and relevant measures of job performance. Finally, the reliability of ratings can also be improved, in those instances in which multiple raters are available, through the use of composites of several raters' judgments.

Performance Outcomes or Results

Researchers have often favored so-called hard or objective criteria of job performance as opposed to soft criteria or ratings. These objective criteria might include the number of objects produced in a given period of time, the number of products sold, or the amount of scrap produced in a given period of time. Although these measures may have utility in some instances, problems of contamination often preclude the use of production measures as job performance indices. Salespeople may, by chance, have territories in which it is easier or harder to sell. A particular typist may be assigned all the difficult letters and papers to type because he or she has a reputation for doing excellent work in a reasonable amount of time. Or the operator of a punch press may have an older machine at which safety considerations make it impossible for him or her to produce as much as a coworker with a newer machine. All of these are examples of cases in which performance is not under the control of the worker; recall the basic definition of performance cited above. Further, use of products as performance measures will allow for consideration of factors such as Effort, Personal Discipline, and Facilitation of Peer and Team Performance only indirectly, if at all.

Occasionally, those who use products as performance measures will also attempt to assess the quality of what is produced. Certainly, quality indices face the same potential for contamination as do simple counts of products. Secretaries with newer printers and more sophisticated software ought to be producing better-quality briefing papers and graphics. Further, the assessment of quality often involves some type of rating; if one is concerned about the quality of ratings, the use of quality indices may not preclude the various rating errors described above.

Job Samples

Green and Wigdor (1991) advocate the use of performance on specially constructed tasks that represent a sample of the entire domain of job tasks. For example, a mechanic may be asked to repair an electronic ignition, or a secretary may be asked to correct a manuscript. The outcome would then be scored as a measure of the person's job performance. In some instances, such tasks may require the production of some output, and both quantity and quality of this output can be measured. The process of accomplishing these tasks can also be observed and rated, which would allow for the measurement of the use of safe procedures and/or the conservation of the materials used. For those concerned with the products actually produced by a company, job samples have great appeal. However, it may not be practical to use job samples as job performance measures. For complex jobs, it may be very difficult and expensive to construct enough job samples to represent adequately the full range of tasks performed, or even a representative sample of those tasks. A second concern, voiced by Campbell et al. (1993), is that performance on job samples is probably mostly a function of the ability of the workers to do the job, not their motivation to do the job in a realistic organizational context. Hence, the use of job samples as performance measures may be deficient. It is true that job samples are very well predicted by KSAO measures (Schmitt, Gooding, Noe, & Kirsch, 1984), but this may be because the predictors in the studies reviewed were ability measures. With little or no variance in the criterion attributable to motivation, and none of the predictors being motivational in nature, the correlation of job samples with measures of ability should be higher than the correlation of other job performance measures, such as ratings, with the predictors.

Sackett, Zedeck, and Fogli (1988) examined the relationship between performance on a job sample, termed a maximum performance measure, and typical job performance. The researchers measured speed and accuracy of grocery store checkout personnel using a specially constructed grocery cart containing 25 items. Employees were told that they were part of a research study and that their speed and errors would be measured as they processed the job sample carts. Similar speed and accuracy measures were recorded routinely at each actual workstation. In addition, supervisory ratings of the performance of these checkout persons were made. Maximum and typical performance measures were nearly uncorrelated, as were speed and accuracy. Sackett et al. interpreted the lack of correlation between the job samples and the everyday performance measures as a function of the fact that the job sample performance was a result of checkout persons' ability, whereas typical performance was a product of both ability and motivation. This is consistent with the notion that job samples are deficient. The supervisory rating in this study, however, which should be a function of both motivation and ability, was most highly correlated with the maximum performance measure. The store managers explained this anomaly on the basis of the fact that their most frequent opportunities to observe the checkout personnel were during the busiest store times, when it was necessary that the workers work at their maximum. Clearly, more work on the nature and inter-relationships of job performance measures would be useful.

Withdrawal Behavior

In some jobs, the critical aspect of performance is the presence of the employee. In jobs in which the production process is controlled by an assembly line and the quality of what gets done is not under the control of the worker (provided the task is completed), the most important performance variable is whether the worker comes to work and remains at work. In such jobs, if one worker is absent, it is frequently the case that other workers may not be able to complete their tasks or will be forced to work more slowly. In these instances, tardiness, absenteeism, and turnover are often used as the performance measures. In these cases, using the Campbell et al. (1993) definition of performance, it would seem that only the Effort and Personal Discipline dimensions might be important, though even in these jobs, it is probable that some degree of Peer and Team Facilitation may occur. In any event, for these types of jobs, Maintenance of Discipline and Effort would seem to be the major relevant dimensions of performance. However, absence, tardiness, and turnover used as measures of these dimensions produce a variety of measurement problems, and performance on these variables themselves is often not completely under the control of the individual worker. For example, a person may change jobs because a spouse relocates, or may be absent from work because of a sick child or because transportation to work is unavailable.

Hulin (1991) asserts that job dissatisfaction leads to one or more of a set of adaptive behaviors. Voluntary absenteeism, tardiness, and turnover constitute one set of the potential adaptive behavior (called withdrawal behavior) in which a worker may engage when faced with an unpleasant work situation. When such behavior is blocked by organizational policy, external job availability, or personal contingencies, it is Hulin's hypothesis that the person will engage in other forms of adaptive behavior. For example, the person who wants a different job but finds it impossible because of the local job market or owing to her or his age and training may deal with dissatisfaction by missing meetings, coming to work late, stealing supplies, filing grievances (Gordon & Miller, 1984), or working a different shift. Alternatively, the satisfied worker may engage in activities of the type referred to as organizational citizenship behavior (Borman & Motowidlo, 1993; Organ, 1988); such a worker may organize parties, clean up the work area, or volunteer for special assignments.

This theory of adaptive behavior also suggests that researchers will achieve greater understanding of such behaviors by studying them in combination rather than as isolated measures of performance. The theory also suggests that because these withdrawal variables are a function of the same processes, they should be correlated and should have common antecedents. Some of these common antecedents may be individual in nature, and therefore may be KSAOs that are potentially useful in a selection context. Empirical research on the interrelationships among withdrawal variables has often been disappointing (Hackett & Guion, 1985). However, when various statistical artifacts are accounted for, these relationships are more impressive (Carsten & Spector, 1987). Moreover, Hulin (1991) points out that each of these withdrawal factors likely has specific determinants (see models of turnover and absenteeism by Mobley, 1977; Steers & Rhodes, 1984) as well as common determinants, so the true relationship between the variables is likely much less than 1.00.

The statistical artifacts referred to would make the estimate of relationships with these withdrawal behaviors appear low even when their true values may be quite substantial. All of these behaviors tend to be relatively rare, hence, product-moment correlations with these variables will be lower than the correlations with a theoretically continuous underlying construct, such as withdrawal or adaptation. This is referred to as the base-rate problem, long a concern of persons interested in research on absenteeism and turnover (Bass & Ager, 1991; Hunter & Schmidt, 1990a; Williams, 1990). Similar to the base-rate problem is the skewed nature of the distribution of variables like absenteeism and tardiness (i.e., most people are absent very little, but some are absent very often).

A second problem about which we have less information is how to determine the correct time span within which to study the relationships among these variables and their hypothesized determinants, and the correct time period over which to add up the number of instances of absenteeism or tardiness. We might want to aggregate over a long period of time to provide for a variable that is more continuously distributed and/or reliable, but in so doing we create a behavior composite that is not likely related to a specific work-related attitude. This concern is not as relevant in selection research, in which we are more likely to be interested in stable individual difference determinants of performance. The time period is important, however, if we hypothesize a long process of withdrawal leading to a set of behaviors such as those that might be related to turnover. An individual usually does not decide to quit a job on the spur of the moment, but how long does the process take? Clegg (1983) introduces the possibility that some measures of employee withdrawal also influence their determinants; that is, being absent from work may reduce attitudinal variables such as organizational commitment and job satisfaction, which are generally considered determinants of the withdrawal process. It is almost certain that the withdrawal process differs across individuals, which suggests that longitudinal data collection is essential and that techniques such as latent growth curve modeling (Duncan & Duncan, 1996; Willett & Sayer, 1994) should be employed to assess individual difference correlates of the process.

Other problems of measurement are also unique to these withdrawal behaviors. In the past decade or so, much has been written about the voluntary or involuntary nature of withdrawal behavior and how we can measure voluntariness (Mathieu & Baratta, 1989). Note that this concern is directly relevant to our definition of performance as acts under the control of the worker. In measuring turnover, there has also been concern about its functional or dysfunctional nature (Boudreau & Berger, 1985), functional turnover being turnover of workers who are not doing a very good job or turnover that allows the organization to recruit individuals with new ideas or greater capacities to perform well on the job. Again, if performance is defined as a set of goal-relevant actions, we should be interested in the functional nature of turnover. Much has also been written about the appropriate way of counting absences (Gaudet, 1963); that is, should each day an individual is not present be counted as an absence, or should each uninterrupted period of absence be counted as an absence? Clearly, a 1- or 2-day absence (or even absences at different times of the week) may have different implications for the organization and different individual and organizational determinants. These measurement issues, as well as the substantive meaning of withdrawal behavior itself, have led researchers to explore the utility of a variety of new ways of analyzing withdrawal data (Harrison & Hulin, 1989; Morita, Lee, & Mowday, 1989). All of these problems make it difficult to assert that withdrawal indices are relevant indicators of employee performance, but they also make this a very interesting area of research.

In summary, withdrawal behaviors (or job involvement and engagement) may provide an important and relevant measure of performance on some jobs. This measure may not be fully under the control of the worker, however, as models of absenteeism (Steers & Rhodes, 1984) and turnover (Mobley, 1977) make very obvious. Further, these behaviors are relatively rare events, which poses some significant problems for the use of the Pearson product-moment correlation in analyzing their relationship with other constructs. Viewing these behaviors as indicators of a more general worker effort to adapt to work may help to resolve some of the measurement problems while also providing a better psychological understanding of the nature of this group of variables. That, in turn, may help to determine what role worker attributes (i.e., KSAOs) play in determining workers' responses to their environment.

Customer Satisfaction

Customer satisfaction with the products produced is indirectly important to manufacturing organizations, but very directly tied to organizational goals in service organizations. Sales personnel, entertainers, counselors, bank tellers, postal employees, medical personnel, and others may, in fact, constitute the product that is sold, or, in many instances, may be the only source of variance in the product sold, as the products are of equal quality and price. The majority of American workers are engaged in service activity of one type or another. Given that service is so central to the organizations for which they work, it is surprising that until recently, customer satisfaction was rarely considered as an index of employee performance (Schneider, 1972; Schneider & Schmitt, 1986). Customer satisfaction is not directly mentioned in Campbell et al.'s (1993) description of the job performance dimensions, but it certainly could fit in the job-specific task category for many service occupations and in the Effort, Maintaining Discipline, and Facilitating Peer and Team Performance dimensions for other service organizations. In a very important sense, customer satisfaction is an output variable, like number of products produced or sold, so it is not entirely under the control of the worker. Some customers will always be irritable, perhaps because of factors that have nothing to do with service personnel, including, in some instances, the quality of what the organization makes.

Recently, there has been increased interest in customer satisfaction, both as a measure of individual employee performance and as an index of organizational performance (Beauchamp, 1994; Fierman, 1995). In the latter case, researchers have been able to tie various facets of employee satisfaction to levels of customer satisfaction and organizational profitability (see also Schneider, 1990). Our interest in this book is on individual performance and its antecedents, but much of the recent research has been directed toward the role that group or organizational climates for service may play in determining individual behavior (Schneider, 1990; Schneider & Bowen, 1985; Schneider et al., 1980). Schmit and Allscheid (1995) provide an initial test of an attitude-behavior model linking individual employee attitudes to customer satisfaction. Their model is similar to, and has the same basic social psychological origin as, the model of employee withdrawal behavior mentioned above (Hulin, 1991). When linking climate measures to customer satisfaction, it is important to remember that individuals make up these aggregate groups and organizations, and the interplay between climate as an organizational variable and job attitudes and behavior as individual variables produces challenging substantive and measurement issues, often referred to as levels of analysis issues (Klein & Kozlowski, in press; Rousseau, 1985). Measures of customer satisfaction may be relevant indices of job performance, but concerns about the relevant level of analysis must be addressed. In a strict sense, we are saying that the measure of customer satisfaction must be one over which the individual worker has some control.

Studies of the Construct of Performance

Having discussed various possible ways in which job performance can be measured, we turn now to research directed toward an understanding of the performance construct(s) underlying these measures. Certainly, the most extensive effort to date aimed at developing measures of performance and examining the nature of the underlying performance construct is represented by the U.S. Army's Selection and Classification Project A, which was conducted by the Army Research Institute and a group of research firms during the 1980s. C. H. Campbell et al. (1990) describe the effort to develop job performance measures that included armywide measures of performance on 11 BARSs and overall measures of performance and promotability, five measures of combat readiness, six personnel file measures (e.g., awards, disciplinary actions, training courses), and additional file information. They also developed a set of job-specific measures, including BARSs, training achievement tests, job knowledge tests, job sample test performance, ratings on the job samples, and self-reports of job experiences for each of nine different jobs. The general procedure used to develop these measures included a literature review, job analyses, conceptual development, scale construction, pilot testing, scale revision, field testing, and management review.

Given the thoroughness with which project staff developed measures of performance and the breadth of measures used, the Project A data provide an excellent opportunity to examine the underlying nature of performance. Campbell, McHenry, and Wise (1990) describe a series of exploratory and confirmatory factor analyses designed to assess the degree to which a similar set of dimensions underlay job performance across different jobs. These analyses led to the conclusion that a model that includes five major performance dimensions (see Table 3.2) is a reasonable representation of performance across nine different jobs. Each of these performance dimensions is represented by two or more of the different types of measures

Table 3.2 Performance Constructs and Indicators Based on Project A

Construct	Measures
Core Technical Proficiency	
This performance construct represents the proficiency with which the soldier performs the tasks that are "central" to the MOS. The tasks represent the core of the job and they are the primary definers of the MOS. For example, the first-tour Armor Crewman (MOS 19E) starts and stops the tank engines, prepares the loader's station, loads and unloads the main gun, etc. This performance construct does not include the individual's willingness to perform the task or the degree to which the individual can coordinate efforts with others. It refers to how well the individual can execute the core technical tasks the job requires, given a willingness to do so.	Work samples for specific jobs Job knowledge tests for specific jobs
General Soldiering Proficiency	
In addition to the core technical content specific to an MOS, individuals in every MOS also are responsible for being able to perform a variety of general soldiering tasks—for example, determines grid coordinates on military maps, and puts on, wears, and removes M17 series protective mask with hood. Performance on this construct represents overall proficiency on these general soldiering tasks. Again, it refers to how well the individual can execute general soldiering tasks, given a willingness to do so.	Work samples in common across jobs Job knowledge in common across jobs
Effort and Leadership	
This performance construct reflects the degree to which the individual exerts effort over the full range of job tasks, perseveres under adverse or dangerous conditions, and demonstrates leadership and support toward peers. That is, can the individual be counted on to carry out assigned tasks, even under adverse conditions, to exercise good judgment, and to be generally dependable and proficient? Although appropriate knowledge and skills are necessary to successful performance, this construct is meant to reflect the individual's willingness to do the job required and to be cooperative and supportive with other soldiers.	Peer and supervisory ratings Administrative awards and certificates

(continued)

Table 3.2. Continued

Construct	Measures
Personal Discipline	
This performance construct reflects the degree to which the individual adheres to U.S. Army regulations and traditions, exercises personal self-control, demonstrates integrity in day-to-day behavior, and shows a commitment to high standards of personal conduct.	Peer and supervisory ratings Administrative disciplinary problems Administrative measures of promotion rate
Physical Fitness and Military Bearing	
This performance construct represents the degree to which the individual maintains an appropriate military appearance and bearing and stays in good physical condition.	Peer and supervisory ratings Administrative awards and certificates

SOURCE: This table combines material from Borman and Brush (1993, Table 3) and J. P. Campbell et al. (1990, Figure 1).

described by C. H. Campbell et al. (1990). A comparison of these five dimensions with the general performance model that Campbell et al. (1993) propose reveals that Written and Oral Communication, Supervision and Leadership, and Management or Administration dimensions are missing. Given that these are mostly entry-level jobs within the military, it seems reasonable that these dimensions do not account for variance in job performance. The Physical Fitness and Military Bearing dimension is uniquely military, perhaps, but may also represent aspects of the Facilitating Peer and Team Performance measure in that soldiers who score high on Physical Fitness and Military Bearing may represent models for their peers. The intercorrelations of those factors that J. P. Campbell et al. (1990) did find ranged from .032 to .590; the median intercorrelation was .27. These interrelationships indicate that the five factors are relatively different facets of performance. As these researchers point out, it is not certain that all of these factors (and certainly not their indicators) will be replicated in a nonmilitary sample. Further, they describe a considerable amount of exploratory analysis of all their data prior to their confirmatory tests of the common five-factor structure. Further studies of the nature of performance in other organizations on other jobs should be undertaken.

One rationale for specifying the dimensionality of performance is that different KSAOs might be useful in predicting different dimensions. If so, these differences themselves constitute further evidence of the meaningfulness of the performance constructs and the practical utility of treating performance as a multidimensional construct. Results of such examinations of the degree to which different predictor domains are correlated with the performance dimensions in Project A are reported by McHenry, Hough, Toquam, Hanson, and Ashworth (1990). Measures of achievement, dependability, and adjustment were clearly the best predictors of Effort and Leadership, Maintaining Personal Discipline, and Physical Fitness and Military Bearing whereas measures of verbal, quantitative, technical, spatial, and psychomotor ability were the best predictors of Core Technical Proficiency and General Soldiering Proficiency (see McHenry et al., 1990, Table 2A). These results are consistent with the notion that there are at least two major dimensions of work performance, rather than five, that are related to substantially different sets of worker attributes.

Several studies concerning jet engine mechanics, conducted for the U.S. Air Force, involved an exploration of the dimensionality of job performance (Lance, Teachout, & Donnelly, 1992; Vance, Coovert, MacCallum, & Hedge, 1989; Vance, MacCallum, Coovert, & Hedge, 1988). These studies compared performance on different tasks in a single job measure with supervisor, peer, and self-ratings of the performance of the same tasks on the job. These studies affirmed the existence of several technical proficiency factors. The Lance et al. (1992) study also included measures that all loaded on an interpersonal factor (e.g., ratings of initiative and effort, abiding by organization rules and policies, integrity, leadership, military appearance, self-development, and self-control). In addition, each of these studies also reported that methods factors (factors identified by the method of measurement or source of ratings) accounted for substantial portions of the variance in the performance measures. These methods factors may be errors associated with a particular way of collecting data, which has been the traditional psychometric view of source or method factors, but they could also be a result of the fact that each measurement perspective provides a valid look at different parts of the performance construct. Without a substantive theory about performance *and* the nature of the methods variable(s), it is really impossible to determine how these methods factors should be treated (Schmitt, 1994; Schmitt, Pulakos, Nason, & Whitney, 1996). The fact that these studies also reported the existence of several proficiency factors (though they are highly correlated) raises the possibility that some of the major dimensions hypothesized by Campbell et al. (1993) may themselves be constituted of meaningful subfactors of performance in some groups of jobs. This introduces the prospect of job or occupational moderators of performance dimensionality. Perhaps the relatively fine-grained analysis of job task requirements provided by measures like the PAQ could form the basis of jobs homogeneous with respect to job performance. McCormick et al. (1972) originally proposed a similar approach to grouping jobs to facilitate the identification of KSAO measures that would predict performance across different groups of jobs.

The presence of methods factors or other contaminants of performance measurement has been a primary concern in many of the studies on performance measurement. Recently, investigators have turned from simple descriptions of these contaminants to studies of how they occur. For example, Lance, LaPointe, and Stewart (1994) provide three potential explanations of halo error (high intercorrelations among conceptually distinct performance measures) in a laboratory study: a general impression model, in which the rater simply decides that a ratee's overall performance is good or bad and then rates her or him accordingly on all dimensions; a salient dimension model, in which one performance dimension (e.g., tardiness) is extremely important and noticeable to a rater and therefore influences ratings on other performance dimensions; and an inadequate discrimination model, in which the rater is influenced by behaviors that have been incorrectly assigned to a particular aspect of performance. Lance et al. tried to provide a frame of reference consistent with one of these three halo explanations for raters, who then proceeded to rate videotapes of teachers. The general impression model of halo was the best explanation of error regardless of the context provided to the raters. In a field study, Oppler, Campbell, Pulakos, and Borman (1992) described and examined the presence of three different explanations for race effects on ratings of three performance dimensions. They found minimal effects for all race effects, but there was some support for the notion that performance was interpreted differently by Black soldiers when rating their Black colleagues than when rating their White peers.

Empirical studies of the dimensionality and nature of performance as well as theories of performance are very much needed. Analysis techniques such as confirmatory factor analysis, which was employed in several of the studies described briefly above, provide a helpful means of testing alternate models of performance. All the models described above using confirmatory factor models point to a multidimensional model of job performance, but Viswesvaran's (1996) recent meta-analysis of the relationships among different measures of job performance supports the existence of a sizable general factor in job performance not unlike the general factor that seems to be present in measures of cognitive ability.

Whether performance is best represented by a single factor or by multiple factors, the existing research base included in any meta-analysis is one in which researchers seldom looked for or seriously considered dimensionality of performance. In fact, the practicalities of selection research and decisions usually meant that single-criterion models were preferable (see Schmidt & Kaplan, 1971, for a review of these considerations). The primary focus was usually on the predictors, and the criterion was needed only as a basis upon which to evaluate the predictors.

In the first selection research example described in Chapter 1, supervisory ratings on 10 behaviorally anchored rating scales (see Figure 1.1 for an example) plus an overall effectiveness dimension were collected as standards against which to evaluate the validity of the selection procedures. Table 3.3 contains the means, standard deviations, and intercorrelations of these 11 rating scales. These data are fairly representative of ratings collected on multiple dimensions and can be used to illustrate some of the concerns mentioned above. First, 4 is the midpoint of the 7-point scales and was defined as "fulfills expectations." The average on all 11 scales is between 4 and 5. In this case, the means do not indicate that the raters were being excessively lenient. The standard deviations of all of the scales also indicate that the raters were making discriminations among the ratees. However, for the most part, the raters did not assign ratees to the lowest 2 points on the scales. Across the 11 scales, the proportion of ratees assigned to these rating levels ranged from 1% to 8%.

If these rating dimensions are really different, then the correlations between scales should be relatively low. In this case, most of the correlations are in the .40s and .50s. These relatively high intercorrelations represent what we have referred to above as evidence of halo error, though as we mentioned in that discussion, it is difficult to ascertain the "real" correlation between these performance dimensions. Use of factor analysis to define the major dimensions (see

Table 3.3   Means, Standard Deviations, and Intercorrelations of Performance
Ratings Collected in a Study of Investigative Officers ($N = 467$)

	Mean	SD	A	B	C	D	E	F	G	H	I	J
A. Recording and Writing	4.34	1.13	—									
B. Making Presentations	4.41	1.13	.57	—								
C. Gathering Information	4.62	1.17	.52	.58	—							
D. Analyzing Information	4.58	1.17	.61	.59	.72	—						
E. Planning and Organizing	4.36	1.21	.59	.58	.64	.61	—					
F. Monitor Work/Detail	4.37	1.18	.60	.53	.54	.61	.63	—				
G. Danger Situations	4.69	1.18	.21	.38	.39	.32	.38	.38	—			
H. Develops Relationships	4.78	1.33	.31	.42	.38	.37	.43	.40	.37	—		
I. Effort and Initiative	4.94	1.33	.41	.44	.57	.53	.51	.54	.44	.43	—	
J. Professional Image	4.97	1.14	.35	.47	.41	.39	.53	.45	.47	.57	.48	—
K. Overall Effectiveness	4.61	1.06	.59	.61	.65	.64	.57	.58	.40	.43	.59	.44

Chapter 4 for a brief description of this data-analytic technique)
indicates that two major factors account for most of the variance in
these ratings (in fact, the first of these two factors accounts for 54%
of the variance in ratings, and the second accounts for 11%). The first
six dimensions define the first dimension, and the last four define the
second dimension. Although these ratings were not developed with
the Campbell et al. (1993) model in mind, these two factors do correspond conceptually to the Core Technical Proficiency and Effort
dimensions in the model.

The Changing Nature of Performance

Thus far, we have been speaking of performance as though it were
a stable characteristic of persons. The presence of change is important
for two reasons. The first is that when current employees are employed
as participants in criterion-related validation research, they may include individuals with varying levels of job experience. If performance
changes over time, then the existence of any ability-performance
relationships will be hidden or confounded. Second, if the nature (i.e.,
dimensionality) of performance changes over time, it is likely that any
characteristic associated with performance at one time would likely
not relate to performance at a different point in time.

Change in performance has been examined in three ways. First, studies of the existence of mean performance changes over time are in general agreement that performance on most jobs improves rapidly at first and then becomes nearly asymptotic for most of the individual's work life, and that the period of time before performance levels off varies with the complexity of the job (Avolio, Waldman, & McDaniel, 1990; Jacobs, Hofmann, & Kriska, 1990; Schmidt, Hunter, Outerbridge, & Goff, 1988). For complex jobs, this initial time period is often assumed to be no longer than 5 years (Jacobs et al., 1990; Schmitt & Schneider, 1983), but there is little direct empirical evidence concerning the time at which job performance asymptotes.

The second way in which change has been studied is through the examination of the test-retest correlation of performance over time— that is, the degree to which people are rank ordered similarly in terms of their performance over time. It is assumed that any change in rank order is evidence of a change in the underlying dimensionality of performance. When the job is constant and motivational effects can be controlled, some data indicate considerable consistency across time (Hanges, Schneider, & Niles, 1990; Rambo, Chomiak, & Price, 1983; Rothe, 1978; Vinchur, Schippmann, Smalley, & Rothe, 1991). Correlations across years, however, seem to decline in a regular pattern, and this finding has generated a tremendous amount of debate as to whether this implies a change in the skills and abilities required to perform a job as individuals gain job experience (for the most recent expression of the issues involved in this debate, see Ackerman, 1989; Henry & Hulin, 1987, 1989).

The third approach to change in performance addresses the issue of concern about the size of test-retest correlations of performance measures more directly. The concern is really about the stability of the dimensions of performance across time. Perhaps the first study to address this issue directly was conducted by Fleishman and Hempel (1955), who showed that the factors underlying performance on a discriminant reaction time task changed as a function of practice. Fuchs (1962) found the same phenomenon when he examined the factors important at different stages of learning a complex tracking task, such as that involved in flying an airplane. More recently, Kanfer and Ackerman (1989) have provided evidence of changes in the ability and motivational requirements necessary for performance on a complex air traffic control simulation. Their explanation of performance changes over time is that the demand on the individuals' cognitive resources at the beginning of the task was so great that any self-monitoring associated with a goal-setting or motivational manipulation was distracting. After participants had an opportunity to gain some skill at the task, motivational influences on performance became more important.

All three of the research efforts just cited were laboratory studies done in the context of training "workers" in relatively new tasks; it is unclear to what extent these changes in the factor structure of performance take place on real jobs, or what the time period over which these changes occur might be. The discussion of changes in the factor structure of performance is similar to the discussion of alpha, beta, and gamma change in the organizational development literature. Golembiewski, Billingsley, and Yeager (1976) hypothesize that changes often occur in the dimensionality and scaling of variables in intervention studies so that comparisons of average changes across time are no longer meaningful. If our performance constructs change across time, our measurement of those constructs must change, and it would almost certainly be the case that different KSAOs would be involved in performance at different stages of an individual's learning a job. The Schmidt et al. (1988) study cited above provides some preliminary evidence that such changes are unlikely, but actual data on performance change across time are almost completely unavailable, even for the simpler types of change discussed in the preceding paragraphs.

Among the reasons we do not have much evidence on change in performance over time are the impracticalities of data collection and the long-term persistence demanded of the researchers, organizations, and research participants involved. Another reason is found in the complexities of the data analysis required to identify these different types of changes. Methods used to assess alpha, beta, and gamma change may be helpful in this regard (Millsap & Hartog, 1988). Similar techniques are used to assess change in individual growth curves (Hofmann, Jacobs, & Gerras, 1992; Willett & Sayer, 1994). These techniques allow assessment of mean change and factorial change in the constructs underlying the measures. These latter methods also provide the capability of assessing individual difference correlates of these different types of change. Clearly, the whole area of performance change has not received appropriate attention; it would seem to provide ample opportunity for meaningful contributions by behavioral science researchers interested in both the theory and practice of personnel selection.

Summary and Conclusions

Our intent in this chapter has been to describe efforts to understand the performance construct, which is the ultimate variable of interest in selection research. In efforts to assess the validity of measures of KSAOs as predictors of this performance construct, investigators make a number of inferences that are often unstated or even unrealized. The evidence regarding these inferential linkages constitutes the basis for our discussion in this chapter and the next four chapters. Binning and Barrett (1989) have provided useful distinctions among and discussion of these inferences, which are depicted in Figure 3.1; we discuss these inferences fully in Chapter 6. In selection research, we are concerned with relationships between KSAO and performance constructs, labeled Linkage 3 in Figure 3.1. To investigate this relationship, we usually relate measures of the ability construct(s) to measures of the performance construct(s). The extent to which our empirical estimate of this relationship between ability and performance is an accurate estimate of the relationship between the constructs of ability and performance depends on two other linkages. The measures of our performance construct must be appropriate, which is Linkage 4 in the diagram. This linkage has been the focus of this chapter. We began with a definition of performance and a discussion of its major dimensions. We then discussed various measures that have been used to index performance and how they conform to the Campbell et al. (1993) definition that we have adopted. We then examined several tests of the dimensionality of performance and the possibility that this dimensionality might change with experience or training on the job.

In Chapter 4, we discuss the nature of the KSAO domain, and in Chapter 5, we address actual measures of ability constructs—both aspects of Linkage 2. In the latter part of Chapter 4, we discuss the degree to which the current literature allows us to develop taxonomies of ability-performance linkages, represented by Linkage 3. In Chapter 5, we also provide a review of the existing data regarding some ability-performance relationships. In Chapter 6, we discuss the technicalities associated with empirical efforts to evaluate these various linkages.

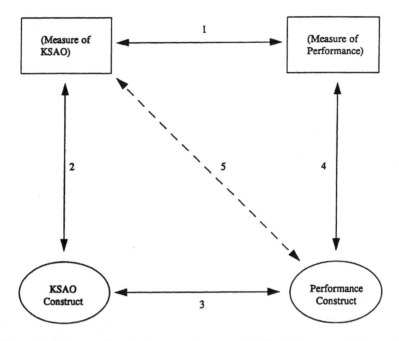

Figure 3.1. Inferences Involved in Investigations of Ability-Performance Linkages in Selection Research

SOURCE: Adapted from Binning and Barrett (1989).

Before we proceed to Chapter 4, we believe it would be useful to review the major research issues raised in this chapter. First, the most important concern should be the development and evaluation of theories of performance. We have presented and used Campbell et al.'s (1993) notions about performance, but this theory should be evaluated in other than military contexts. Such examination may lead to refinement or change of these ideas about the nature of performance. Second, we have discussed only briefly a very large literature on the process and determinants of performance ratings. If ratings continue to be used as the primary measure of performance (and the research cited in this chapter supports this use), then more should be done in this area. In particular, it would be useful to explore why supervisor, subordinate, peer, and self-ratings are often so dissimilar. Given that interrater reliabilities within these different groups are usually much higher than those across groups, it seems reasonable to suppose that raters are reporting something consistently. Whether each of these groups is reporting a relevant part of the job performance construct or what might be considered some form of contamination should receive attention. Third, there should be more work on the inter-relationships among various measures and performance constructs, particularly research that addresses questions related to the functional relationships among these variables—that is, the degree to which performance on one dimension causes performance on other dimensions. Fourth, when researchers investigate methods factors, they should better delineate the nature of the methods factors proposed, and, whenever possible, should include measures that will allow for the assessment of these alternate explanations of the research. Fifth, research on customer satisfaction is just beginning, so any information on its nature and antecedents would be helpful. In particular, the degree to which customer satisfaction is under the control of the worker or determined externally is a particularly important issue if measures of customer satisfaction are to be used as performance indices. Sixth, longitudinal studies of performance are almost nonexistent; in this context, it would be very useful if research could identify what if any changes occur in the dimensionality of performance over time and then what individual difference variables might relate to those changes. Seventh, efforts should be undertaken to confirm or negate Hulin's (1991) hypotheses about the nature of withdrawal processes in organizations. In this case, job attitudes are an intermediate variable between the organizational context and the person's attributes on the one hand and these withdrawal behaviors on the other. This suggests that researchers should begin to investigate the KSAOs that lead to particular job attitudes and how they might interact with organizational situations (Schneider, 1987), and how KSAOs might affect the withdrawal process. Finally, the material we have presented in this chapter underscores the need for researchers to educate themselves about, and perhaps begin to conduct studies on, several new analysis issues. We introduced concerns about levels of analysis issues when we mentioned organizational climates for service, but these might be relevant for other performance measures as well. Novel methods of analysis may be appropriate for the investigation of some aspects of withdrawal behavior. Confirmatory factor analysis and latent growth curve techniques (Willett & Sayer, 1994) may be very useful for researchers working on hypotheses about both mean changes and relationship changes in performance.

4 General Theories of Human Characteristics and KSAO-Performance Relationships

The successful measurement of human ability originated with the development of individual tests of academic ability by Binet and Simon (1905). Binet and Simon's effort was commissioned by the French government and was directed toward the identification of children with learning problems as opposed to emotional problems. Binet's measure was translated and adapted by Terman and his colleagues at Stanford (Terman, 1916). The Stanford-Binet has been revised several times since then, most recently in 1985, and remains, along with the Wechsler tests, one of the major individual tests of intelligence. Terman further developed the concept and coined the term *intelligence quotient* (or IQ), and soon his measure was perceived by some at least as a general measure of academic ability, although Binet's original notion was that his test was useful only in discriminating between normal children and those with emotional impairments. These early tests, beginning with the Binet-Simon measure, included a variety of academic tasks (memory, vocabulary, comprehension) and everyday tasks and knowledge (e.g., knowledge of body parts and names for very young children). Scores on these tests were related to success in academic environments (they were keyed to reflect teacher ratings of students), but the tests were not useful on a wide scale because they were individually administered.

During World War I, Yerkes (1921) and his colleagues developed tests that could be administered simultaneously to large groups of people. The U.S. government was faced with selecting, training, and placing a very large number of military recruits in appropriate job assignments very quickly to aid in the stalled Allied war effort in Europe. Individual tests of ability were impractical. Yerkes's group tests were used successfully to classify soldiers entering military service, and similar tests were developed and used by industry after the war.

As the interest in test use grew, so did interest in understanding the underlying dimensionality of ability. The development of tests of different or more specific abilities was also undertaken. Both of these objectives were furthered by the development of factor-analytic techniques. Factor analysis helped to determine a parsimonious list of factors that appeared to be the source of the intercorrelations among many different types of test items, which in turn led to the development of the Primary Mental Abilities Test (Thurstone, 1938). The primary mental abilities tested included measures of verbal comprehension, word fluency, number (arithmetic computation), spatial relations and visualization, associative memory, perceptual speed, and induction or general reasoning. This multiple aptitude test battery is very similar to many batteries developed since that time, including the General Aptitude Test Battery (GATB), the Armed Services Vocational Aptitude Battery (ASVAB), and the Differential Aptitude Tests (DAT).

Development of tests of different aptitudes led to a spirited debate about the meaningfulness and practical utility of considering these different aptitudes versus a single general aptitude (Spearman, 1927). Hence, concern about the structure of intelligence (or a theory of intelligence) arose and became one of the most persistently researched issues in the area of individual differences and personnel selection. Consideration of different abilities also led to consideration of individual differences in other domains of human activity. Personality, interests, physical abilities, and other characteristics were studied as well. In this chapter, we attempt to provide a review of the individual difference constructs and theories that seem relevant to the world of work, beginning with the structure of cognitive ability. At the end of the chapter, we consider those efforts that have been most centrally directed to the consideration and testing of theories of ability-performance relationships. By describing the variety of attempts to develop generalizable KSAO taxonomies and KSAO-performance taxonomies, we hope to provide the conceptual basis for the next chapter, in which we discuss the measurement of ability and other individual difference constructs.

Most of the existing ability taxonomies have resulted from the collection of data on a large number of tests or measures and the ascertainment of what these measures have in common. To derive these common dimensions or factors underlying a large number of measures, researchers have used a technique called factor analysis. Before we proceed with the major objectives of this chapter, we will describe briefly the objectives, interpretations, and terminology associated with factor analysis.

Factor Analysis

The central notion in any factor analysis is that a large number of observed behaviors are direct results of a smaller number of unobserved, or latent, variables. This basic principle is used in empirical studies to isolate a set of underlying common factors that represent the major sources of differences among individuals and groups. A factor analysis starts with correlations among tests. The product of a factor analysis should be an understanding of what underlying latent variables, or factors, produced those correlations. The results of a factor analysis, as far as interpretation of any one test is concerned, are a function of the companion tests, the group of people whose responses to the tests are being analyzed, and the technique of factor analysis employed, as well as sampling error.

Consider the set of correlations in Table 4.1. If one examines the correlations in this table and the labels of the six tests that are intercorrelated, it is likely that one would reach the conclusion that there

Table 4.1 Correlations Among Six Ability Measures

	1	2	3	4	5	6
Verbal analogies	1.00					
Reading comprehension	.66	1.00				
Word knowledge	.59	.70	1.00			
Arithmetic reasoning	.43	.45	.34	1.00		
Data comprehension	.46	.46	.37	.62	1.00	
Math knowledge	.45	.35	.36	.59	.61	1.00

are two group factors. The first might be characterized as a verbal factor, whereas the second could be labeled a quantitative factor. The first three variables are relatively highly correlated, as are the last three variables. Intercorrelations across these two sets of tests are lower. We use this correlation matrix to demonstrate the main features and ideas of factor analysis.

The results of the first factor analysis we will discuss are based on the notion that the two underlying factors are uncorrelated. As we shall see, some of the equations discussed below change when the factors are correlated. Every respondent is thought to have a true score on each of the factors resulting from a factor analysis. The factor loading describes the correlation of the observed variable with this underlying latent factor. As with other correlations, there are sampling errors associated with these correlations, which means the loadings will change from sample to sample, especially when the sample sizes are small.

The unrotated and rotated (see the discussion of rotation of factors below) factor loadings resulting from a principal axis factoring are presented in Table 4.2. The first underlying factor represents the weighted combination of variables that accounts for the maximum amount of the covariation among the observed variables. Subsequent factors account for maximum portions of the remaining covariation. Each of the measured variables that is factored is composed of variance it shares with these common factors, termed common variance, and unique variance not associated with any of the common factors. In a matrix in which all correlations are substantial, like that in Table 4.1, the first factor accounts for a great deal of variance and all the variables load highly and positively on that factor. Subsequent factors account for smaller portions of variance and are by definition uncorrelated with previous factors.

When to stop factoring is one decision that a researcher using factor analysis must make. Sometimes this is done a priori based on substantive knowledge of the measures; for example, in this case, a verbal and quantitative factor might be hypothesized based on previous experience with cognitive measures. When the analysis is purely *exploratory,* researchers often decide to interpret factors whose *eigenvalue* (sum of the squared factor loadings) exceeds 1.00. Some will also examine the eigenvalues for a series of factors and decide to cease extracting factors when change in the eigenvalues from one factor to the next becomes relatively small. The latter decision rule is called the *scree criterion* (Cattell, 1966). In this example, all these considerations, plus our examination of the correlation matrix, lead to the conclusion that there may be two factors.

The *factor loadings,* which are correlations of the observed variables with the factors, are used to interpret the factors, but the unrotated factor loadings are not usually of much help in this regard. If we view factors as axes in space, the position of the factor axes can be changed so that each variable is defined primarily by a single factor (for good examples, see Cronbach, 1990; Nunnally & Bernstein, 1994). Mathematically, varimax rotation is done so that the sum of the squared factor loadings for each factor (i.e., the eigenvalues) is a maximum. This means each variable will load high on one factor and not very high on others. This rotation provides for the more interpretable factor loadings identified in Table 4.2 as the *rotated solution.* As you can see, verbal analogies, reading comprehension, and word knowledge are correlated highly with the first factor and not very highly with the second factor. The reverse is true for the arithmetic reasoning, data comprehension, and math knowledge tests. So the first underlying factor might be identified as a verbal factor, whereas the second might be called a quantitative factor.

The percentage of variance accounted for by the factors is equal to the eigenvalue divided by the number of tests or test items factored and is another gauge of the importance of a particular factor in explaining the covariation among the observed variables. As can be seen in Table 4.2, the eigenvalues and percentage variance are less in the rotated solution than in the original (unrotated) solution. This results from the principal axis factoring of less than the total number of factors (i.e., six) that would be required to account for all the covariation in this matrix.

Table 4.2   Results of an Exploratory Factor Analysis of the Data Presented in Table 4.1

| | Unrotated Solution | | Rotated Solution | | |
	Factor 1	Factor 2	Factor 1	Factor 2	Communality
Verbal analogies	.74	−.20	.66	.37	.58
Reading comprehension	.79	−.39	.84	.27	.78
Word knowledge	.70	−.38	.76	.22	.63
Arithmetic reasoning	.70	.33	.27	.72	.59
Data comprehension	.73	.33	.29	.75	.64
Math knowledge	.68	.37	.23	.73	.59
Eigenvalue	3.48	1.05	3.12	.69	
Percentage variance	58.1	17.5	52.10	11.50	

The *communality* tells what proportion of the variance in a given test (or observed variable) is a function of the underlying factors. One calculates the communality by summing the squared factor loadings of the test on each of the common factors. For example, the communality of the verbal analogies test (.58) is the sum of the square of its factor loading on the first factor (.44) and the second factor (.14). If the factors are rotated so that they are oblique or correlated, as might be appropriate in this instance, these computations would be more complicated because of the necessity to account for the intercorrelation among factors. Suppose we also know that the reliability of the verbal analogies test is .75, so that 25% of the variance in the test is due to error variance. The variance in this test could then be divided into three parts: 58% is due to the two common factors, 25% is due to error variance, and 17% is due to variance specific to the verbal analogies test or to some other common factor we chose not to extract. Recall that we could have chosen to interpret and rotate more than two common factors.

Exploratory factor analysis similar to that described briefly above is the basis for many of the explanations of the nature of individual differences described in this chapter. As should be obvious from our description, the researcher must make many judgments in the process of doing a factor analysis. Although not mentioned above, decisions must also be made about the type of factor analysis method to use and the method of rotation, as well as others. In addition, as we stated at the outset, the results of a factor analysis are a function of the set of tests whose intercorrelations are considered and the group of people whose responses to the tests are analyzed. Given these multiple determinants of the results of a factor analysis, it is perhaps surprising that the empirical results of many different studies have converged on sets of major individual difference constructs in areas such as cognitive ability, physical ability, interests, and personality.

In the past two decades, *confirmatory factor analysis* has become increasingly popular. Instead of relying on the data analysis to reveal the factors (probably never completely true in exploratory factor analysis), the researcher begins by indicating the number of factors, the variables that load on the factors, and any expected inter-relationships among the factors. If this set of hypotheses about the structure of the data is true, then this particular pattern of factors and factor loadings should account for the intercorrelations, or covariances, among the variables. Even when sampling error can account for any departures of the data from the hypothesized structure (i.e., by statistical criteria, the model is confirmed), we are not confident that the researcher's structure is the best or only explanation of the data, but we do know that the data do not contradict the hypothesized structure. In point of fact, many other structures may also fit the data (MacCallum, Wegener, Uchino, & Fabrigar, 1993).

A hypothesized structure for the data in Table 4.1 might look like Figure 4.1. In this figure, the ovals represent the two hypothetical factors, or *latent variables,* and the rectangles represent the observed variables, or *indicators* of the latent variables. Each of the tests (indicators) is determined partly by a specific factor (labeled U in Figure 4.1), variance not shared with the common underlying factors. The lines with arrows at the ends represent the hypothesized explanations for the intercorrelations among these six tests. Each test is considered to be a function of one of the underlying factors and some unique variance component. Unlike the exploratory analysis described above, the curved arrow between the two factors indicates that they are thought to be related. It is also possible to rotate factors to an *oblique,* or correlated, solution in exploratory factor analysis.

The results of the confirmatory factor analysis are displayed in Table 4.3a and in Figure 4.1. The factor loadings for the two sets of analyses (i.e., the confirmatory factor analysis and the exploratory factor analysis) are very similar, except for the fact that in the confirmatory factor analysis there are no loadings of the verbal tests on the Quantitative factor and no loadings of the quantitative tests on the Verbal factor (compare Table 4.3a and Table 4.2). This is consistent with the

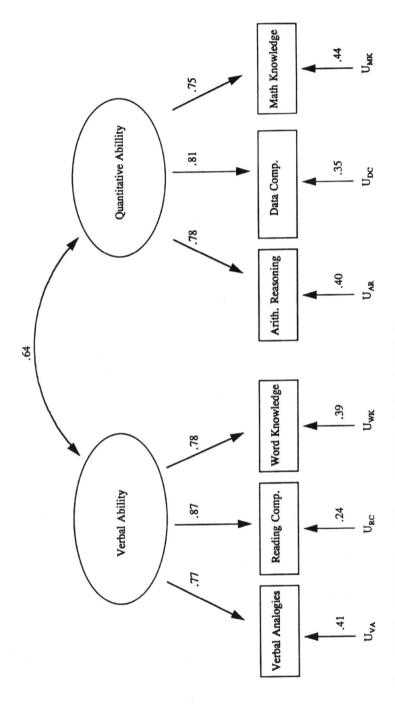

Figure 4.1. Hypothesized Factor Structure Underlying the Data in Table 4.1

Table 4.3   Results of Confirmatory Factor Analysis of Data Presented in Table 4.1

| | a. Summary of Confirmatory Factor Analysis | | | |
	Verbal	Quantitative	Communality	Unique/Error
Verbal analogies	.77		.59	.41
Reading comprehension	.87		.76	.24
Word knowledge	.78		.61	.39
Arithmetic reasoning		.78	.60	.40
Data comprehension		.81	.65	.35
Math knowledge		.75	.56	.44

Correlation between Verbal and Quantitative factors = .64

| | b. Reproduced and Original Correlation Matrix[a] | | | | | |
	Verbal Analogies	Reading Comprehension	Word Knowledge	Arithmetic Reasoning	Data Comprehension	Math Knowledge
Verbal analogies	1.00	.67	.60	.38	.40	.37
Reading comprehension	.66	1.00	.68	.43	.45	.42
Word knowledge	.59	.70	1.00	.39	.41	.38
Arithmetic reasoning	.43	.45	.34	1.00	.63	.58
Data comprehension	.46	.46	.37	.62	1.00	.61
Math knowledge	.45	.35	.36	.59	.61	1.00

a. Values below the diagonal are the observed correlations also presented in Table 4.1. Values above the diagonal are the correlations reproduced using the estimates of factor loadings presented in the first part of this table.

hypotheses regarding the nature of these measures. Another difference in the confirmatory analysis was that the two factors were allowed to correlate, and the estimate of their correlation was relatively high (.64).

As we indicated above, the central idea underlying confirmatory factor analysis is that we examine the degree to which our model of these interrelationships is likely given the actual data. This examination begins with the computation of a reproduced correlation matrix. For ease of comparison, we present both the observed and *reproduced* correlation matrix in Table 4.3b. The differences between corresponding elements in these two matrices are referred to as *residuals*. To obtain the reproduced correlations, it is easiest to examine the diagram in Figure 4.1, which includes the factor loadings in Table 4.3a. One can obtain the reproduced correlation by computing the product of the factor loadings, or pathways, that connect any two variables. For example, the reproduced correlation between verbal analogies and reading comprehension is .67 (.77 × .87). The observed correlation is .66; hence, the residual, or the degree to which the model is inaccurate as an estimate of the observed correlation, is –.01 (.66 – .67). Reproduction of the correlations between variables loading on different factors is more complicated because we must take into account the level of intercorrelation between factors. For example, the reproduced correlation between verbal analogies and arithmetic reasoning is .38 (.77 × .64 × .78). The observed correlation between these two tests is .43 and the residual is .05 (.43 – .38). Reproduced correlations can be computed from an exploratory analysis as well, and were the basis of the evaluation of various models of cognitive ability by such early psychologists as Spearman and Thurstone (see the discussion below).

Formally testing overall models of the interrelationship of variables and evaluating the fit of competing models has become commonplace only in the past couple of decades (Jöreskog & Sörbom, 1979). The fit of the overall model to the observed relationships among a group of variables can be evaluated in many ways (Bollen & Long, 1993). The first index of fit developed and used widely was a chi-square, which is a measure of the discrepancy between the sample or observed correlations (or covariances) and the fitted (i.e., reproduced) correlation or covariance matrix. This chi-square is a *badness-of-fit* measure in that a small chi-square corresponds to good fit and a large chi-square indicates a bad fit. In the model presented in Figure 4.1, the chi-square fit index was 15.74 ($df = 8$, $p > .01$). The chi-square has 8 degrees of freedom because we have 21 independent elements in the correlation matrix and have estimated 13 parameters ($df = 21 - 13$). This chi-square indicates that the overall difference between the reproduced and observed correlation matrix does not exceed what might be expected on the basis of sampling error ($p > .01$).

Perhaps of equal or greater importance is the use of the chi-square statistic to compare different models that are nested within one another. *Nested* means that starting with some model, we propose or test another model with fewer parameters estimated than was true of the original model (see Bollen, 1989, for a more thorough discussion of nesting). The second, more parsimonious model is said to be nested within the first model. The model discussed above can be compared with one that restricts the correlation between the two latent factors to .00. This model, which is nested within the original model, had a chi-square equal to 83.82. The difference between the two chi-squares is also distributed as a chi-square with degrees of freedom equal to the difference in degrees of freedom associated with the two models. In this case, the difference chi-square is 68.08 (83.82 – 15.74). With one degree of freedom (i.e., 13 – 12), this chi-square is very large and statistically significant, indicating that a model that posits that these two factors are independent is clearly an inappropriate representation of these data.

Chi-square is heavily dependent on the sample size associated with the estimates of the correlations between variables, so that with large sample sizes, models will produce statistically significant chi-square values, resulting in the rejection of these models even if they are theoretically reasonable. Hence, investigators have developed many alternate indices of fit. Tucker and Lewis (1973) presented a fit index that measures how much better the model fits the data than does an *independence model,* which specifies that all relationships between variables are zero. This logic spawned the normed and nonnormed fit indices of Bentler and Bonett (1980). Another more intuitively simple index is the *root mean square residual,* which is simply the average amount by which elements of the reproduced and observed correlation or covariance matrix differ. In the case of the data presented in Table 4.3, the value of the root mean square residual is .033. Values of the normed and nonnormed indices are both .97 (values of these indices should range from .00 to 1.00). Steiger (1990) has proposed the root mean square error of approximation (RMSEA), which is a measure of discrepancy per degree of freedom. A value of the RMSEA less than .05 is considered good fit, values over .10 are considered bad fit, and those of intermediate value are considered indicative of moderate fit. The RMSEA for the model presented in Figure 4.1 is .07. These indices are relatively popular, but the literature comparing the utility and appropriateness of these fit indices is still developing. Good summaries are provided by Jöreskog and Sörbom (1993), and critical examinations of various indices are contained in Bollen and Long's (1993) edited volume. In substantive research, it has become increasingly common to rely on multiple indices when evaluating a model in order to obtain convergent evidence in the assessment of model fit.

In addition to overall evaluation of the model, a test is provided for the significance of each parameter (factor loading in this instance) as well as modification indices for parameters that are not included in the model. Modification indices are the value by which the chi-square would be reduced (indicating better fit) if a parameter were estimated and included in the model. The modification indices and the test statistics and the residuals can be used to modify or "trim" the original model when it does not fit the data well. Such modifications are no longer confirmatory, however. They represent a variation on the same approach that has been taken in the use of exploratory factor analysis. That is, a series of factor analyses of the same and different data are conducted to determine the best representation of the factors underlying human performance in a given area. A very brief, but readable and informative examination of the relative strengths and weaknesses of these two approaches is provided by McArdle (1996). Theory and previous research in some broad individual difference domains are ready for confirmatory analyses; others are still primarily at the exploratory stage. We hope that this brief explanation of the purposes and mechanics of exploratory and confirmatory factor analyses will lead our readers to a greater appreciation of the subsequent discussion of the structure of human characteristics and the means by which these structures have been developed.

Structure of Intellect

Just as there have been attempts to develop a general theory or structure of work performance (as discussed in Chapter 3), there have been attempts to develop theories of the structures of individual differences in various KSAO domains. As in the case of work, the search is for a parsimonious set of job-related dimensions along which individuals vary. In this section, we present an overview of the key issues in conceptualizing the structure of the domain of cognitive ability.

At the most general level, we can define cognitive abilities as latent or hypothetical individual difference attributes that are manifest when individuals are performing tasks that involve the active manipulation of information. These abilities may be broad (i.e., applicable across a wide variety of task domains) or narrow (i.e., applicable to specific task domains), and they may also be interrelated (Murphy, 1996). Theories of cognitive structure differ in terms of the generality/specificity of ability constructs postulated and the nature of the interrelationships among these constructs.

The issue of whether the structure of cognitive ability should be characterized as a single general ability factor or multiple distinct ability factors has its scientific origins in the debate between Spearman and Thurstone. In Spearman's (1927) theory, all conceivable measures of cognitive ability are related to a common general cognitive function. Not all measures, however, are equally good indicators of the common general cognitive function. Spearman assumed that all cognitive measures could be partitioned into two components: a general (i.e., g) component and a specific (i.e., s) component. The g component of a measure is determined by what the measure has in common with all other cognitive measures. The s component is specific to each measure. This assumption implies that the correlation between two cognitive measures will be determined by the ratio of g to s in each of the measures. As the ratio increases, the correlation increases. Several empirical implications follow from Spearman's theory. One is that intercorrelations between cognitive measures should all be positive. Another implication is that the best indicator of cognitive ability is defined in terms of an aggregate index based on diverse measures of the common cognitive function. Also, measures with higher loadings on the common cognitive function are deemed better indicators of cognitive ability, or g. Spearman developed methods for analyzing correlation matrices that provided the foundation for factor analysis. He was probably the first to analyze a correlation matrix of psychological measures and to assert that the understanding of a measure can be obtained through the analysis of the relationships between the measure and other measures. Spearman's analyses are precursors of the construct validation procedures psychologists use today that assess the validity of a measure by examining the nomological network of relationships surrounding the measure.

Thurstone (1938, 1941) thought that the idea of construing cognitive ability as g was an oversimplification. Intrigued by Spearman's factor-analytic methods for analyzing correlation matrices, Thurstone "turned the question around and asked *how many and what kinds* of factors are needed to account for the observed correlations among tests of ability" (Nunnally, 1978). Thurstone found that correlations between measures belonging to two separate classes (e.g., spatial visualization tests versus verbal tests) are likely to be lower than the correlations among measures belonging to the same class. Hence, Thurstone concluded that correlations between cognitive measures would be determined not only by a shared general ability factor but also by similarity in specific ability factors that are shared by a subset of measures. Thurstone originally assumed that the structure of intellect is composed of several independent specific ability factors (e.g., verbal comprehension, memory) but later concluded, in the light of subsequent factor-analytic studies, that the specific ability factors are correlated.

The correlated factor solutions left Thurstone without a convincing refutation of Spearman's theory, because Spearman's g may account for the correlations among specific factors. Cattell (1971) reconciled Spearman's theory and Thurstone's theory by postulating a hierarchical structure of cognitive ability. The single general factor g is represented at the apex of the hierarchy and is at a higher level of abstraction than the specific ability factors that collectively define it. Thus, each specific factor is defined by a subset of the diverse cognitive measures, whereas the general factor is defined by the entire set of measures. This hierarchical structure of intellect provides the conceptual basis for contemporary constructions and interpretations of cognitive ability measures.

In addition to the work of Spearman and Thurstone, there were other major efforts to identify the structure of intellect. One well-known example is Guilford's (1967) *structure-of-intellect* model. Guilford based his theory on a three-dimensional taxonomy of cognitive tasks. He maintained that cognitive tasks differ with respect to the dimensions of operations, contents, and products. *Operations* refers to what the individual must do to perform the task appropriately. *Contents* refers to the nature of the information the individual is required to operate on. *Products* refers to the outcomes of the operation of the ability on any kind of contents. Guilford presented five operations (cognition, memory, convergent thinking, divergent thinking, evaluation), five contents (auditory, visual, symbolic, semantic, behavioral), and six products (units, classes, relations, systems, transformations, implications), resulting in 150 distinctly different abilities. Guilford asserted that it is possible to develop measures that assess each of these distinct abilities.

Guilford's (1967) theory has been criticized on conceptual, methodological, and empirical grounds. Critics have objected to the over-extraction of the factors, the subjectivity of the factor-analytic rotational methods, and the forced independence of the factors (Carroll,

1968; Horn & Knapp, 1973, 1974; Undheim & Horn, 1977). Empirically, Guilford's (1964) findings of near-zero intercorrelations among cognitive tests have been criticized for the use of unreliable measures and samples that were restricted in range of cognitive ability (e.g., Brody & Brody, 1976). Guilford's findings were also contrary to the consistent findings of positive intercorrelations among cognitive measures. In a confirmatory factor-analytic study, Bachelor (1989) reanalyzed Guilford's data using confirmatory factor analyses of the type described above and found that Guilford's a priori models of 25 abilities involving cognition, convergent thinking, and divergent thinking did not provide significant incremental model fit over random multifactor or single general factor models.

Another major effort to conceptualize the structure of cognitive ability was Sternberg's (1977) componential analysis method for studying individual differences in intelligence. The cognitive components method is a theory-driven and process-oriented approach. A componential analysis begins with a theory of the task of interest, which is typically one of the items actually found on standard psychometric tests, such as analogies, series completion, and syllogisms. The theory postulates the components essential for successful task performance and specifies the combinatory rules for the components. For example, Sternberg and Gardner (1983) analyzed task performance on an analogy problem into three components (encoding, inference, and application) and specified that, in solving the problem, subjects perform these components serially and that the solution time for an item is the sum of the time required for executing each of the component processes.

In componential analysis, subjects are typically tested via computer, and the primary dependent variable is usually reaction time, with error rates and response choice patterns as secondary dependent variables. The values of the dependent variables as a function of each of the three components are estimated. Scores on the components are correlated with each other and with scores on standard psychometric tests. The interest is not in whether there is any correlation between cognitive task performance and psychometric test scores, because the tasks analyzed are typically taken directly from psychometric tests. Rather, the interest is in identifying the relative importance of the components in determining successful task performance.

Sternberg (1988) also proposed that the traditional measures of intelligence and the multiple aptitude test batteries were deficient in that they did not assess the degree to which people develop practical intelligence, or the ability to resolve daily life problems and to adapt their behavior as circumstances demand. Sternberg asserted that this capability does not come about from any formal training and that it is relatively unrelated to academic learning. In the job arena, Sternberg's concept of practical intelligence is most directly represented by measures of situational judgment, such as those used in the first example in Chapter 1, involving the selection of investigative officers.

Theory may specify certain components to have intertask generality, so that, in principle, a taxonomy of cognitive components can be developed to explain performance on different cognitive tasks. Estimates of component importance should generalize to new tasks, so that an individual's performance on a new task can be predicted from his or her component scores derived from the tasks analyzed. The cognitive components approach is best represented by Sternberg's work (Sternberg, 1977; Sternberg & Gardner, 1983). Similar componential analyses have been conducted by Alderton, Goldman, and Pellegrino (1985) and Carpenter, Just, and Schell (1990).

The theory-driven, process-oriented, and construct-oriented nature of the cognitive components approach should represent substantive progress beyond psychometric approaches in our understanding of the structure of cognitive ability. Understanding of cognitive performance is obtained through the development and testing of explicit models of task performance. However, a critical problem in the componential analysis approach is that, to date, there is little evidence that task components identified are generalizable beyond the specific tasks analyzed. Like Guilford's theory, the componential analysis approach has failed to account adequately for the existence of the positive correlations among cognitive ability measures.

Hierarchical models of cognitive ability (e.g., Carroll, 1993; Harnqvist, Gustafsson, Muthen, & Nelson, 1994; Horn, 1988) postulate a single general factor g collectively defined by different specific ability factors. These models reconcile the idea of intellect as a general ability factor and the idea of intellect as specific ability factors. They also account for positive correlations among all cognitive measures. As mentioned earlier, hierarchical models of cognitive ability provide the conceptual basis for contemporary constructions and interpretations of cognitive ability measures. Unlike the single general factor model, which postulates an undifferentiated intellectual capacity, hierarchical models provide an adequate basis for sampling cognitive abilities, and the models facilitate identification and investigation of different intellectual domains.

An example of a contemporary hierarchical model is Carroll's (1993) three-stratum model of cognitive ability. On the basis of a large number of factor-analytic studies, Carroll proposes a structure of intellect consisting of three levels of specificity: general, broad, and narrow. The highest stratum or the most general level is simply a single g factor. The next level (broad stratum) consists of seven broad abilities: fluid intelligence, crystallized intelligence, general memory ability, broad visual perception, broad auditory perception, broad retrieval ability, and broad cognitive speediness. Each of these broad abilities can be characterized in terms of a number of more specific abilities (narrow stratum). For example, induction and spatial relations are narrow specific abilities corresponding to the broad abilities of fluid intelligence and visual perception, respectively.

Murphy (1996) argues that hierarchical models suggest that general versus specific ability constructs should be used for different purposes. The single general factor g may be all that is needed if the purpose is parsimonious prediction of performance. A series of studies by Ree and colleagues has demonstrated that abilities that are unrelated to g do not make any incremental contribution to predicting important job-relevant criteria (Ree & Earles, 1991, 1992, 1993; Ree, Earles, & Teachout, 1994). On the other hand, if the purpose is to understand and explain performance, then specific abilities at lower levels of the hierarchy are more useful. Linking relevant specific abilities to performance helps describe the nature and content of the tasks performed by the individual.

Predictive efficiency is insufficient for the understanding of a construct. High positive intercorrelations between different cognitive abilities per se do not constitute direct evidence for an underlying general intelligence factor. Many proponents of g (e.g., Ree and colleagues) have often interpreted the observation of high positive intercorrelations between performance in different cognitive domains (i.e., positive manifold) and the extraction of a single factor accounting for a substantial amount of common variance based on a traditional exploratory factor analysis as evidence for the psychological reality of a unitary construct of general intelligence underlying behavior. This interpretation is flawed. Positive manifold per se does not imply any particular causal structure or theoretical relationship between the cognitive variables. Traditional exploratory factor analysis, which is based solely on intercorrelations, can never reveal the underlying causal structure because different incompatible interpretations (causal schemes) can be consistent with a given pattern of intercorrelations. A high positive correlation between two variables V_1 and V_2 does not necessarily imply an underlying common causal factor. As we noted above in discussing confirmatory factor analysis, the positive correlation is consistent with several different theories about the relationships between these two variables. V_1 may cause V_2; V_2 may cause V_1; both V_1 and V_2 may be the result of some underlying factor (a third variable) or both variables may affect each other. Although one or more of these models can be rejected (falsified) because it does not fit the data, none can be confirmed merely on the basis of good fit, because alternative models may provide equally good, if not better, fit. The model specifying a single general factor producing a correlation between V_1 and V_2 (the third possibility listed above) is just one of many possible models for the observed intercorrelations between cognitive variables, and to date, there has been no clear evidence of the superiority of this model over others (e.g., hierarchical models) in terms of goodness of fit, parsimony, and consistency with a substantive theory of intellect.

A good question at this point is whether these theories of cognitive ability have any influence on organizational selection practices. Many times, cognitive ability is treated as a single dimension, as the advocates of *g* would suggest is appropriate. For example, a very popular cognitive ability test used in organizations is the Wonderlic Personnel Test (Wonderlic, 1984). This test includes a variety of items, including vocabulary, verbal analogies, arithmetic problems, number series, and spatial problems. Probably more often, separate dimensions of cognitive aptitude are considered. As we have indicated, in the situation described in Example 1 in the first chapter, three tests of verbal aptitude and three tests of numerical aptitude were used. This probably conforms most closely to Carroll's (1993) perspective on cognitive ability in the sense that verbal and numerical dimensions underlie more specific abilities in each area. The second example in Chapter 1 includes an even greater variety of cognitive aptitudes and reflects very directly the influence of those who followed Thurstone's lead in developing multiple aptitude test batteries. Also fairly representative of the use and empirical research on multiple aptitude batteries is Hunter and Hunter's (1984) meta-analysis of research on the General Aptitude Test Battery, used by the U.S. Employment Service for several decades to evaluate the aptitude of job seekers. Hunter and Hunter show that it was meaningful to posit that the GATB scores were best represented by three major dimensions: a general ability factor consisting of both numerical and verbal aptitude, a spatial dimension, and an index of motor ability (i.e., manual and finger dexterity and coordination). Most researchers would not consider the motor ability factor a component of cognitive aptitude, but measures of these aptitudes are often parts of a multiple aptitude battery. Hunter and Hunter show that the complexity of the job was related to the validity (relationship between test performance and supervisory ratings of job performance) of the test. Scores on the general ability factor were most highly related to performance in highly complex jobs, and the tests of motor ability appeared to be most valid for jobs of low complexity. The validity of spatial perception measures did not vary as a function of job complexity. So, theories of cognitive ability are rarely mentioned in selection studies, but they are implicit in the measures used and the manner in which tests are scored and used by human resource professionals.

In summary, correlations among cognitive ability measures are uniformly positive. In predicting external criteria, a first general factor seems to be all that is needed to account for substantial variance. However, analyses of multiple aptitude batteries almost always show evidence for verbal and quantitative factors and a spatial aptitude dimension. If the concept of ability is expanded to include measures of psychomotor ability, these measures usually constitute a separate factor (e.g., see Hunter & Hunter, 1984). In a very real sense, how many factors one decides to accept is a function of how generally or how specifically one wants to describe human ability. The component approach to ability represents an effort to understand at a deeper level various ability measures. In Chapter 9, we discuss the potential contribution of cognitive methods to furthering this understanding.

Personality and Motivational Constructs

Implicit in most problems and procedures in personnel selection are theories or assumptions about human nature. Because personality and motivational theories are about human nature, they should provide the conceptual bases for generating predictor constructs and hypotheses concerning predictor-criterion relationships. These theories should also be sources of principles that underlie the measurement of personality or motivational predictor constructs. However, researchers' interests in personality and motivational theories have varied over time in the history of personnel selection. Further, these theories have originated with concerns about "mental health" rather than work behavior, hence, the applicability of measures from these theories or taxonomies has sometimes been marginal or nonexistent. In this section we provide a brief overview of these changing interests. We discuss the empirical research on and measurement issues in the assessment of personality/motivational predictor constructs in more detail in Chapter 5.

In addition to Guion and Gottier's (1965) assertion that personality theory and measures seem to be unrelated to work behavior, there have been significant attacks on the very concept of personality. In 1968, Mischel published a highly influential book in which he argued against the trait conception of personality and asserted that behavior is explained more by differences across situations than by differences across individuals. Mischel's work sparked a heated situation-trait debate that lasted about two decades. By the late 1980s, the consensus among personality psychologists was that both situational and individual differences are important because they interact to affect behavior (Kenrick & Funder, 1988; Snyder & Ickes, 1985).

One of the most important lessons that personnel selection researchers learned from the situation-trait debate was that the personality predictor construct under examination needs to be relevant to the criterion construct. At the workplace, this means that traditional personality measures, such as the MMPI, which are designed for clinical use, are likely to be irrelevant to the kinds of work-related criteria personnel psychologists are interested in predicting (Weiss & Adler, 1984). Within this trait-in-context environment, personnel selection researchers gathered evidence for the validity of personality variables. Both primary studies and meta-analytic studies of the criterion-related validities of personality measures have demonstrated the usefulness of these measures in personnel selection (e.g., Barrick & Mount, 1991; Gellatly, Paunomen, Meyer, Jackson, & Goffin, 1991; Ones, Viswesvaran, & Schmidt, 1993; Pulakos, Borman, & Hough, 1988; Schmitt, Gooding, Noe, & Kirsch, 1984; Tett, Jackson, & Rothstein, 1991).

Researchers have also begun to focus on taxonomic issues—that is, questions regarding the structure of personality. Personality taxonomies are important because they provide conceptual organizing principles that enable researchers to link personality constructs to job-relevant criteria. Personality tests and test batteries include measures whose labels indicate that hundreds of different constructs are being measured. Although there are several personality taxonomies relevant to the workplace (e.g., Hogan's six-factor taxonomy, 1991; Hough's nine-factor taxonomy, 1992), the most recognized taxonomy among personnel selection researchers is probably the five-factor model (e.g., Costa & McCrae, 1995; Digman, 1990; Goldberg, 1990, 1993; Goldberg & Saucier, 1995; John, 1990; McCrae & John, 1992). The personality constructs described in the five-factor model (known as the Big Five) are Conscientiousness, Agreeableness, Neuroticism, Openness to Experience, and Extraversion. Hough and Schneider (1996) have reviewed the history of the five-factor model and evaluated the usefulness of the taxonomy. They conclude that there is evidence that the model is replicable across time, samples, methods of data collection, and, to some extent, cultures. However, Hough (1992) maintains that greater understanding and predictive utility can be obtained using a structure of personality that includes a greater number of specific work-related constructs, such as *need for achievement.* More research may be needed to determine the best trade-off between parsimony (use of measures of one or more of the Big Five dimensions) and comprehensiveness or specificity (use of measures of a wider set of specific job-related dimensions such as those suggested by Hough, 1992) in capturing the domain of work-relevant personality constructs.

Meta-analytic studies have demonstrated the usefulness of the Big Five factors, especially Conscientiousness, in personnel selection. In a meta-analysis of 117 criterion-related validity studies in which personality measures were used as predictors, Barrick and Mount (1991) coded the personality variables in terms of the Big Five structure. They found that Conscientiousness predicted significantly all job performance criteria for all occupational groups represented in the data analyzed. The remaining four factors also predicted some dimensions of work behavior for some occupations. In another meta-analysis, Tett et al. (1991) also found the Big Five factors to have predictive validity for a variety of job-relevant criteria, but identified Agreeableness as the factor with the highest predictive efficiency.

To summarize, substantial progress has been made regarding the development of taxonomies for describing the structure of personality and for providing conceptual organizing principles to establish personality-criteria construct linkages. Specific and conceptually adequate linkages between personality and criterion constructs provide the key to greater understanding of the role of personality variables in determining work behavior.

Interests

In this section, we discuss the structure of individuals' interest in work or career. Personality and interest are similar constructs in some ways (e.g., both are concerned with typical behavior patterns), but interest measures and constructs are usually oriented toward the determination of what work tasks and environments are of interest to individuals, whereas personality measures usually address the manner in which people behave in some predictable fashion across a variety of environments, including the work environment. The primary reason for considering and measuring interests lies in the notion that a person will be happiest and most productive when working in an occupation in which he or she is interested. Interest measures have been used more frequently in vocational guidance situations than in personnel selection, but the goal of selection, most broadly, is to find persons whose personalities, abilities, motivations, and interests best fit those of the organization. Dawis (1991) summarizes research indicating that personality and interest measures have relatively low correlations. As we mentioned in Chapter 2, measures of interest are related to worker satisfaction, but are not very highly related to worker performance. Personality variables are related to worker performance.

Certainly, the most widely accepted taxonomy of interests is that developed by Holland (1985), who suggests that both people and organizations have "personalities" and that fit is determined by the similarity between an individual's interests and the degree to which an environment provides for engagement in activities of interest to the individual. According to Holland, individuals and environments can be characterized along six major dimensions. Realistic persons (and environments) are usually interested in dealing with concrete things and relatively structured tasks. High scorers on the realistic dimension are police officers, engineers, farmers, and carpenters. High scorers on the investigative dimension are scientists, who are usually interested in discovering explanations for the phenomena they observe. Artistic individuals include actors, musicians, architects, and others engaged in creative activities. Those interested in working and helping others, including teachers, social workers, flight attendants, and mental health workers, score high on Holland's social dimension. Enterprising individuals include managerial personnel and sales-people. These individuals like the challenge of making opportunities for themselves. Finally, those with high conventional interests include accountants, bankers, and Internal Revenue Service agents. Holland does not propose that individuals high in one interest area have no interests in other areas, but rather that the interest patterns people have are organized in a fashion that may be depicted as a hexagon (see Figure 4.2). People are likely to have some interest in areas that fall next to their primary interests, but are likely to have less interest in areas that lie opposite to their primary interest areas on the hexagon.

This structure has been used to organize responses to the Strong Vocational Interest Blank in its recent revisions and has received a great deal of corroborative support from a variety of researchers in addition to Holland (Hansen & Campbell, 1985; Harmon, Hansen, Borgen, & Hammer, 1994; Tracey & Rounds, 1993, 1996). These same researchers report that the long-term stability (i.e., test-retest corre-lations) of these interest scales is in the .60s and .70s for periods extending up to 20 years. In addition to the six basic dimensions, the Strong Vocational Interest Blank, which is the measurement instru-ment used to assess interests, includes scores on 25 basic interest scales (e.g., agriculture, public speaking, religious activities, mathematics, science) and 211 specific occupational scales. Efforts have also been made to link interest patterns with self-reported skills (Campbell, Hyne, & Nilsen, 1992), in recognition of the fact that a person's interest in an occupation must be accompanied by an appropriate level of skill.

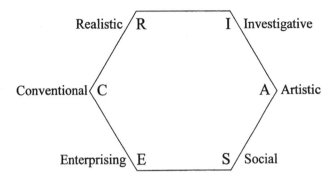

Figure 4.2. Holland's Model of the Structure of Interests

The search for the nature, number, and organization of basic interests parallels those conducted in the area of primary mental abilities and personality. In all three instances, the dimensions "discovered" are a function of the specific questions asked, the people who respond, and the manner in which the data are analyzed. Holland's framework for the structure and understanding of interest dominates the field of counseling and vocational guidance.

Physical Ability

For the most part, psychologists ignored the measurement of physical abilities until issues related to the fair employment of women in jobs that require a certain level of physical ability became important considerations for employers in the 1960s and 1970s. Fortunately, a great deal of basic research on the measurement and dimensionality of physical ability had been done by Fleishman (1964) prior to that time. Physical abilities measurement also requires interdisciplinary contributions from a variety of fields in addition to individual differences psychology, including physiology, industrial engineering, and biomechanics, which probably continues to show advances in the measurement and use of physical abilities in personnel selection.

Personnel selection research on physical abilities has relied heavily on the dimensions and job analysis procedures developed by Fleishman

Table 4.4   Fleishman's Physical Ability Dimensions

Static Strength: The ability to use continuous muscle force to lift, push, pull, or carry objects. This is the maximum force that one can exert for a brief period of time using the hand, arm, back, shoulder, or leg.

Explosive Strength: The ability to use short bursts of muscle force to propel oneself or an object. This requires gathering energy for bursts of muscle effort over a very short period of time, rather than continuous use of muscle force.

Dynamic Strength: The ability of the muscles to exert force repeatedly or continuously over a long time period; the ability to support, hold up, or move the body's own weight or objects repeatedly over time. This involves muscular endurance and resistance of muscles to fatigue; it does not include cardiovascular fitness.

Trunk Strength: The ability of the stomach and lower back muscles to support part of the body repeatedly or continuously over time. This ability involves the degree to which the muscles in the trunk area do not fatigue when they are put under such repeated and continuous strain.

Extent Flexibility: The ability to bend, stretch, twist, or reach out with the body, arms, or legs. This involves the degree of bending rather than the speed of bending.

Dynamic Flexibility: The ability to bend, stretch, twist, or reach out with the body, arms, or legs, both quickly and repeatedly. This involves both speed and repeated bending or stretching as well as the degree to which muscles "bounce back" during these repeated activities.

Gross Body Coordination: The ability to coordinate the movement of the arms, legs, and torso in activities in which the whole body is in motion. This is not involved in coordinating arms and legs while the body is at rest.

Gross Body Equilibrium: The ability to keep or regain one's balance or to stay upright when in an unstable position. This ability includes maintaining one's balance when changing direction, either while moving or while standing motionless. It does not include balancing objects.

Stamina: The ability of the lungs and circulatory system of the body to perform efficiently over long periods of time; the ability to exert oneself physically for a long time without getting out of breath.

and his colleagues. These procedures involve the assessment of the nine major physical ability dimensions first identified by Fleishman in basic research conducted for the U.S. Navy. These dimensions are listed and defined in Table 4.4. Subsequent applied research in a variety of contexts has reaffirmed these basic dimensions (for summaries of this research, see Fleishman, 1988; Hogan, 1991). Measures of these dimensions are relatively uncorrelated (compared with cognitive ability dimensions and personality dimensions), and they are differentially valid across performance in different jobs. Fleishman and Reilly (1992a) have developed scales for the analysis of job requirements for each of these dimensions that are anchored in everyday physical tasks, which should facilitate the generalizability of the measurement, analysis, and use of these dimensions and the Fleishman taxonomy. An adaptation of one of these scales is shown in Figure 4.3.

Hogan (1991) provides a summary of the validation research using physical ability measures, most of which are measures of the Fleishman dimensions. This research indicates a relatively high degree of relationship with job performance measures in many different contexts. However, in some contexts the validity of the physical ability measures is high for the group as a whole, but relatively low or zero within male and female groups. This finding is consistent with the very large gender differences observed for measures of physical ability, especially for measures of upper-body strength. It is also consistent with the notion that individual differences within gender groups may not be related to job performance because those difference are not large. Across gender groups, however, there are large and important job-related differences.

The Question of Fit

Kristof (1996) has redirected the attention of personnel selection researchers to the importance of a fit between the individual differences reflected in people and the environments in which individuals find themselves. In doing so, she has drawn attention to different types of fit. Kristof maintains that person-organization (P-O) fit is more useful to an understanding of work behavior than are the more general person-environment models such as Holland's, described above. Her model of P-O fit is presented in Figure 4.4. This model recognizes the importance of two different types of fit. *Supplementary fit* is represented as the relationship between the fundamental characteristics of the organization, such as culture, climate, values, goals, and norms, and the characteristics of the individual, such as values, goals, personality, and attitudes. *Complementary fit* includes the degree to which

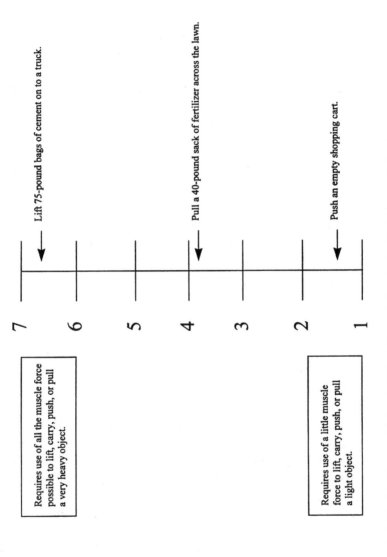

Figure 4.3. Scale Used to Measure the Level of Static Strength Required to Perform Job Tasks
SOURCE: Adapted from Fleishman and Reilly (1992a).

124

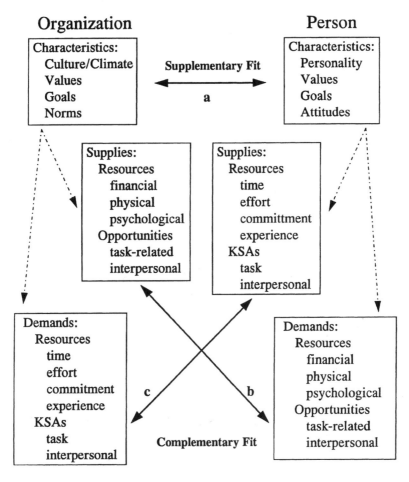

Figure 4.4. Supplementary and Complementary Fit: Aspects of Person-Organization Fit
SOURCE: Kristof (1996, p. 4). Reprinted by permission of Personnel Psychology, Inc.

the organization and the individual have needs that are supplied by
the other party. For example, the organization may demand time,
effort, and ability, and the degree to which the employee supplies these
resources contributes to complementary fit. Supplementary fit, as
defined in this model, is similar to the approach espoused by Holland,
who maintains that individual interests must match the nature of the
work environment. Complementary fit is similar to ideas that underlay much of personnel selection research—namely, that a person's

abilities and other characteristics must match the needs of the organization and vice versa. A good example of the degree to which P-O fit influences work-related outcomes (job performance and turnover) is provided by Chan (1996a), who found that worker performance was highest when the problem-solving demands of an organizational environment matched the cognitive style of problem solving of the organizational members. Given the degree to which notions of fit underlay the science and practice of personnel selection, it is surprising that more research directly assessing fit hypotheses has not been conducted. More research should be conducted on models such as that presented by Kristof (1996). Certainly, the distinction between complementary and supplementary fit ought to stimulate work on the relative utility of these two conceptualizations of fit. Evaluation of fit models often requires the use of complex data-analytic methods. Recent advances in the analysis of such data (e.g., Edwards & Harrison, 1993) should contribute to the development of this research area as well.

We have just summarized ideas from four major individual difference domains: cognitive, personality, interests, and physical ability. Do selection personnel evaluate job applicants along all four dimensions, and does each dimension provide useful, nonredundant information? In the first example in Chapter 1, the researchers used both cognitive ability and personality measures. Physical ability was assessed in another part of the selection process and by means of a medical examination. Interests were not explicitly evaluated, though some of the interview questions probably indirectly assessed the nature of the applicants' interests in the job. In Example 2, the main focus was on cognitive ability. In Example 3, personality and aspects of cognitive ability were likely measured, but when job samples or simulations are used in selection, it is very difficult to assert that a single KSAO dimension is being measured. Performance on these simulations, like performance on a job, is likely to be multidimensional. The fourth example also represented a situation in which personality and cognitive ability were measured. Interest may have been assessed in the interview. Physical ability was not considered in either Example 3 or Example 4, and probably was not relevant to performance in these jobs. A clearer specification of what is being measured from these relatively nonredundant individual difference areas may allow a more precise evaluation of the relative role each plays in work performance.

Taxonomies of Human Characteristics

To this point, we have discussed findings relevant to taxonomies of individual differences in general domains of human behavior (i.e., cognitive ability, personality, physical ability, and interests). Attempts have also been made to taxonomize all human characteristics. For example, Fleishman's ability requirements approach has been used to specify 52 human abilities in the four broad domains of cognitive abilities, physical abilities, sensory/perceptual abilities, and psychomotor abilities (Fleishman & Quaintance, 1984; Fleishman & Reilly, 1992b). Fleishman and Reilly (1992b) provide definitions of each of these abilities, the jobs and tasks in which these abilities might play a role, and existing measures of each of these abilities. Recently, the same methods have been employed to extend this taxonomic effort to include interpersonal abilities (Abod, Gilbert, & Fleishman, 1996). The research cited above on physical abilities indicates that these dimensions are relatively consistently replicated in various studies, but the research base for the distinctiveness and importance of dimensions in some of the other domains Fleishman and his colleagues have addressed is not as extensive. This is particularly true of the interpersonal domain. Nevertheless, these efforts represent a useful and important advance in the study of individual differences in the ability to perform various tasks.

The revision of the *Dictionary of Occupational Titles* that is now being undertaken is organized around what is thought to be a comprehensive content model (recall our discussion of the *DOT* and functional job analysis in Chapter 2). This model provides a schema for identifying, defining, and organizing relevant types of information about people, jobs, and work environments. The content model proposed by Peterson, Mumford, Borman, Jeanneret, and Fleishman (1995) is organized in four sections: (a) worker attributes, (b) work context, (c) work content and outcomes, and (d) labor market context. The model is intended to provide the basis for a comprehensive occupational infrastructure that would be reflected in the *DOT*. For purposes of this discussion, however, the most interesting part of the *DOT* content model (now called O*Net) is the worker attributes section. Definitions of the major worker attribute categories are as follows: (a) aptitudes and abilities, which are particular classes or categories of mental and physical functions, including cognitive, spatial/

perceptual, psychomotor, sensory, and physical abilities; (b) fundamental developed abilities, which are required to some degree in all jobs, such as reading, writing, and arithmetic; (c) cross-functional skills, such as information gathering, oral communication, problem analysis, negotiating, organizing, and planning; (d) occupation-specific skills, such as ability to read blueprints, to repair electrical appliances, or to operate a forklift; (e) occupation-specific knowledge, such as financial planning and analysis skills, foreign-language skills, or computer software knowledge; and (f) personal qualities, including work style and personality characteristics. The content model organizes worker attributes into a hierarchy or continuum that varies in level of description and analysis from the very general (aptitudes, personal qualities, and workplace basic skills) to those specific to the performance of a small range of jobs. The cross-functional skills are defined at a moderate level of generality and are expected to be applicable to relatively wide ranges of jobs. The Fleishman taxonomy and the O*Net model include very similar worker attributes, as does the Project A effort described below.

There have been frequent calls for more attention to the development of a taxonomy of human characteristics (e.g., Dunnette, 1976; Fleishman & Quaintance, 1984; Peterson & Bownas, 1982) and there have been successes in some relatively broad domains, as outlined above. There have also been calls for an integration of the taxonomic efforts in the worker attributes realm with the taxonomies in the job tasks area, as we have noted in Chapter 1 (see Burke & Pearlman, 1988). The latter efforts have been less frequent and less successful. Burke and Pearlman (1988) mention three important problems or issues that must be addressed in attempts to integrate worker attributes and job characteristics. The first concerns what worker attributes should be included in the taxonomy. How comprehensive or representative must the set of characteristics be to explain adequately the nature of human performance in a given context? This, of course, demands that performance be clearly defined, which is the focus of our discussion in Chapters 2 and 3. Second, we must decide how generally or specifically we should define the worker attributes. What we want is a situation in which an attribute is maximally related to performance of a given work task, but relatively unrelated to performance of other work tasks. This is the issue being addressed in the research by Ree and his colleagues described earlier in this chapter. The third issue involves the way in which the importance of worker attribute-job performance linkages is derived. This can be done through the collection of the judgments of subject matter experts or, as is usually preferred by industrial/organizational psychologists, through actual empirical assessment of the relationships between worker attributes and performance on worker tasks.

Psychologists have probably spent much more time quantifying the relationships between worker attributes (i.e., KSAOs) and performance through validity studies than they have in addressing the comprehensiveness or representativeness of either the worker attribute domain or the performance domain, or in determining just how general or specific they must be in specifying these domains. There are at least two strategies that can be used to address these questions. One involves the use of meta-analytic methods (Hunter & Schmidt, 1990b) to summarize the available data on worker attribute-job performance relationships using tests of moderator hypotheses to determine how specific or general the categories in the attribute and performance domains must be. However, the existing database is insufficient in many cases because researchers have not collected the right data (e.g., on various performance dimensions) or they have not reported appropriate data. A second approach to these questions would be to employ what Peterson and Bownas (1982) have described as a grand design. This grand design requires a massive, large-sample, predictive validation study involving measures in all the attribute taxonomies, a wide range of jobs, and the collection of a broad range of performance criteria.

Perhaps the closest the discipline has ever come to having the opportunity to conduct a study of such grand design is the U.S. Army's Project A. In 1990, a special issue of *Personnel Psychology* was devoted to the overall design of the project and a description of the results of efforts to meet its major objectives ("Project A," 1990). In addition, many other research articles have described Project A work in addressing specific problems in selection research (e.g., McCloy, Campbell, & Cudeck, 1994; Oppler, Campbell, Pulakos, & Borman, 1992; Pulakos, White, Oppler, & Borman, 1989). The Project A researchers began with an overall specification of the predictor space, which they obtained by asking a group of experts to estimate the validity of 53 predictor variables for 72 different criterion elements. Using these judgments, the researchers clustered the predictor space as shown in Table 4.5 (Peterson et al., 1990).

Similar care was taken to specify the entire criterion space across jobs. The latter effort (C. H. Campbell et al., 1990) yielded a large number of measures for the assessment of performance across all the 19 army jobs studied. These included paper-and-pencil measures of training achievement; five indices from administrative records (number of awards and letters of commendation, physical fitness qualification, number of disciplinary infractions, rifle marksmanship scores, and promotion rate); 11 behaviorally anchored rating scales designed to measure factors not specific to a given job, such as giving peer leadership and support, maintaining equipment, and self-discipline; single overall ratings of job performance and leadership potential; and 40-item summated rating scales for the assessment of expected combat performance. In addition to these general measures of performance, the researchers collected measures specific to each job (job samples, ratings, and knowledge measures). Efforts to model this overall performance domain (Campbell, McHenry, & Wise, 1990) led to the development of five overall dimensions of performance: Core Technical Proficiency, the proficiency with which the soldier performs the tasks central to her or his job; General Soldiering Proficiency; Effort and Leadership; Personal Discipline; and Physical Fitness and Military Bearing.

The degree to which this massive effort was successful is apparent if one examines the validity of the predictor measures for the five major performance domains. These indices are presented in Table 4.6. Several observations are relevant to the questions posed above about taxonomic efforts. All validities (both observed and corrected) represent practically significant and high correlations relative to the existing literature; careful specification and measurement of the various attribute and performance domains likely added to the overall validity of these groups of predictors. It is also apparent that validities vary across cells in this table in theoretically sensible ways. For example, ability measures are most highly related to the Core Technical Proficiency and General Soldiering factors, whereas the personality, interest, and motivational measures are more highly related to performance in the areas of Effort and Leadership, Personal Discipline, and Physical Fitness and Military Bearing. These differences are relevant

Table 4.5   Hierarchical Map of Predictor Space

Constructs	Clusters	Factors
1. Verbal comprehension		
5. Reading comprehension		
16. Ideational fluency	A. Verbal ability/general intelligence	
18. Analogical reasoning		
21. Omnibus intelligence/ aptitude		
22. Word fluency		
4. Word problems		
8. Inductive reasoning: concept formation	B. Reasoning	
10. Deductive logic		
2. Numerical computation	C. Number ability	COGNITIVE ABILITIES
3. Use of formula/ number problems		
12. Perceptual speed and accuracy	N. Perceptual speed and accuracy	
49. Investigative interests	U. Investigative interests	
14. Rote memory	J. Memory	
17. Follow directions		
19. Figural reasoning	F. Closure	
23. Verbal and figural		
6. Two-dimensional mental rotation		
7. Three-dimensional mental rotation		
9. Spatial visualization	E. Visualization/spatial	VISUALIZATION/ SPATIAL
11. Field dependence (negative)		
15. Place memory (visual memory)		
20. Spatial scanning		
24. Processing efficiency		
25. Selective attention	G. Mental information processing	INFORMATION PROCESSING
26. Time sharing		
13. Mechanical comprehension	L. Mechanical comprehension	MECHANICAL
48. Realistic interests	M. Realistic versus artistic interests	
51. Artistic interests (negative)		

(continued)

Table 4.5   Continued

Constructs	Clusters	Factors
28. Control precision		
29. Rate control	I. Steadiness/precision	
32. Arm-hand steadiness		
34. Aiming		
27. Multilimb coordination	D. Coordination	PSYCHOMOTOR
35. Speed of arm movement		
30. Manual dexterity		
31. Finger dexterity	K. Dexterity	
33. Wrist-finger speed		
39. Sociability	Q. Sociability	
52. Social interests		SOCIAL SKILLS
50. Enterprising interests	R. Enterprising interests	
36. Involvement in athletics and physical conditioning	T. Athletic abilities/energy	
37. Energy level		VIGOR
41. Dominance	S. Dominance/self-esteem	
42. Self-esteem		
40. Traditional values		
43. Conscientiousness	H. Traditional values/ conventionality/nondelinquency	
46. Nondelinquency		
53. Conventional interests		
44. Locus of control	O. Work orientation/locus of control	MOTIVATION/ STABILITY
47. Work orientation		
38. Cooperativeness	P. Cooperation/emotional stability	
45. Emotional stability		

SOURCE: Peterson et al. (1990, pp. 252-253). Reprinted by permission of Personnel Psychology, Inc.

to the questions above concerning the appropriate degree of specificity of any attribute-performance taxonomy. The Project A data could have been reported at other levels of specificity and generality, but the researchers in this study made decisions based on their sense of what were practically and theoretically meaningful ways in which to report the data. Their decisions appear to have been appropriate, given data like those reported in Table 4.6.

Opportunities to collect data employing this type of grand design are very rare. We do, however, have other examples of smaller

Table 4.6   Mean Within-Job Corrected and Uncorrected Validities for the Composite Scores Within Each Predictor Domain

Job Performance Factor	Predictor Domain					
	General Cognitive Ability (K = 4)	Spatial Ability (K = 1)	Perceptual- Psychomotor Ability (K = 6)	Temperament/ Personality (K = 4)	Vocational Interest (K = 6)	Job Reward Preference (K = 3)
Core Technical Proficiency	.63 (.43)	.56 (.38)	.53 (.32)	.26 (.15)	.35 (.24)	.29 (.13)
General Soldiering Proficiency	.65 (.47)	.63 (.47)	.57 (.37)	.25 (.15)	.34 (.25)	.30 (.14)
Effort and Leadership	.31 (.22)	.25 (.14)	.26 (.15)	.33 (.30)	.24 (.20)	.19 (.12)
Personal Discipline	.16 (.11)	.12 (.08)	.12 (.07)	.32 (.31)	.13 (.11)	.11 (.09)
Physical Fitness and Military Bearing	.20 (.16)	.10 (.08)	.11 (.08)	.37 (.36)	.12 (.13)	.11 (.10)

SOURCE: McHenry, Hough, Toquam, Hanson, and Ashworth (1990). Reprinted by permission of Personnel Psychology, Inc.
NOTE: Validity coefficients were corrected for range restriction and adjusted for shrinkage. Uncorrected Rs are in parentheses. K is the number of predictor scores.

scale studies that represent tests of theoretical models of ability-performance relationships. Such smaller-scale studies can be useful for testing portions of a grand design or taxonomy. In addition, the focus of some of these studies is to test the process by which individual difference variables influence work performance; a simple taxonomy of ability-performance relationships does not address such mediating effects. In the final section of this chapter, we discuss several of these studies.

Modeling KSAO-Performance Relationships

To represent these tests of the manner in which ability and other worker attributes affect performance, we have chosen studies by Schmidt, Hunter, and Outerbridge (1986); Borman, White, Pulakos, and Oppler (1991); Schmit, Motowidlo, DeGroot, Cross, and Kiker (1996); and Pulakos, Schmitt, and Chan (1996). Schmidt et al.'s (1986) theory of ability-performance relationship is an extension of Hunter's

(1983) path-analytic model of job performance. Hunter conducted a path analysis using data from 4 civilian and 10 military studies to examine relationships among cognitive ability, job knowledge (as measured by paper-and-pencil tests), task proficiency (as measured by work sample tests), and supervisory ratings of job performance. Hunter found that the job knowledge-performance ratings path coefficient was three times larger than the task proficiency-performance ratings path coefficient. Cognitive ability had a substantial indirect effect on performance ratings, primarily through its influence on job knowledge. Schmidt et al. extended Hunter's model by including job experience as an additional exogenous variable. Schmidt et al.'s results essentially replicated those obtained in Hunter's original model. In addition, job experience had direct paths to both job knowledge and task proficiency, but the effect was much greater for job knowledge than for task proficiency. Job experience was found to have a moderate effect on performance ratings, primarily through its influence on job knowledge.

Borman et al. (1991) built on the work of Hunter (1983) and Schmidt et al. (1986) and added several variables to help explain the variance in supervisory ratings of performance. Using the Project A database, Borman et al. developed their theory of ability-performance relationship by expanding the ability domain to include two personality variables (achievement orientation and dependability) and two personnel record indices (awards and disciplinary actions). The expanded model accounted for more than twice the variance in performance ratings as was explained by the Hunter model variables alone, suggesting that the addition of noncognitive variables such as the personality/motivational-type variables in the Project A database could account for substantial incremental variance in performance ratings over the variance accounted for by cognitive variables alone. Borman et al.'s results for cognitive ability were essentially the same as those found by Hunter and Schmidt et al. However, task proficiency had the largest direct effect on performance ratings; job knowledge had no direct effect on performance ratings. Job knowledge mediated the cognitive ability-task proficiency relationship.

Schmit et al. (1996) provide another example of a theory of ability-performance relationship that expands the attribute domain to include personality variables. These authors suggest that the mechanism through which personality affects performance is similar to the mechanism through which cognitive ability affects performance. Just as the cognitive ability-performance relationship is mediated by task job knowledge, Schmit et al. propose that *contextual job knowledge* mediates the personality-performance relationship. They define contextual job knowledge as knowledge of workplace expectations (i.e., workplace norms, values, or goals) and what the appropriate behavior is for dealing with social situations that arise in the work context, given these expectations. Schmit et al. make the distinction between task job knowledge and contextual job knowledge to correspond to the task and contextual components of job performance (see Chapter 3) proposed by Borman and Motowidlo (1993). Schmit et al.'s model hypothesizes that the Big Five personality traits have both direct and indirect effects (through contextual job knowledge) on contextual performance. Using a sample of 160 sales associates, Schmit et al. tested the relationships among three of the Big Five personality traits (Conscientiousness, Agreeableness, Extraversion), contextual job knowledge, and contextual performance. They assessed contextual job knowledge through a situational interview and used supervisory ratings of customer service to assess contextual performance. They found that extraversion had direct effects on both contextual job knowledge and contextual performance. In addition, extraversion had an indirect effect on contextual performance through contextual job knowledge.

A similar performance model using the data from Example 1 in Chapter 1 was evaluated by Pulakos, Schmitt, and Chan (1996). This model, depicted in Figure 4.5, is similar to the model developed by Borman et al. (1991). Cognitive ability and a situational judgment measure of practical intelligence are seen as determinants of performance on two job samples, which in turn are thought to be reflected in performance ratings. Cognitive ability is also thought to influence job knowledge, which in turn should be reflected in performance ratings. Finally, a measure of motivation was thought to be directly related to performance ratings. Pulakos, Schmitt, and Chan found that this model was generally consistent with the data, and the same model seemed to fit data for different gender and race groups. Of special interest in this study was the evaluation of the impact of each of the paths between cognitive ability, practical intelligence, and motivation and the performance ratings. These direct and indirect effects are summarized in Table 4.7. For example, as the table shows, the results suggest that there is no direct effect of cognitive ability on perfor-

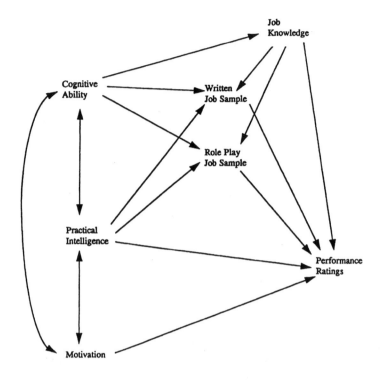

Figure 4.5. Model of Job Performance Ratings of Investigative Officers

mance, but that cognitive ability influences job knowledge and performance on the job samples, and these in turn influence performance
as indicated by the supervisors' ratings. By contrast, the measure of
practical intelligence is directly related to performance ratings, with
little or no impact on the job sample measures. This is perhaps
consistent with the notion that practical intelligence is dependent on
the context in which performance is required. As we cautioned at the
beginning of this chapter, one must remember that other models with
different interpretations of the observed correlations may fit the data
as well.

The four studies discussed above represent a progression in which
increasingly complex models are evaluated. Interestingly, these studies
added complexity by expanding the number and nature of the ability
constructs considered. Adequate theories of ability-performance
relationships and, more generally, KSAO-performance relationships

Table 4.7   Direct and Indirect Effects of Determinants of Job Performance as Modeled in Figure 4.5

Cognitive ability on performance	
Direct	.000
Indirect	
By job knowledge	.051
By job knowledge, written	.002
By job knowledge, role-play	.014
By written	.029
By role-play	.028
Total	.124
Practical intelligence on performance	
Direct	.128
Indirect	
By written	.008
By role-play	.016
Total	.152
Motivation on job performance	
Direct	.087
Indirect	.000
Total	.087
Job knowledge on job performance	
Direct	.110
Indirect	
By written	.005
By role-play	.031
Total	.146
Written on job performance	
Direct	.078
Indirect	.000
Total	.078
Role play on job performance	
Direct	.191
Indirect	.000
Total	.191

SOURCE: Adapted from Pulakos, Schmitt, and Chan (1996).

should also recognize the multidimensionality of job performance, as we have emphasized in Chapter 3 and as represented in the Project A effort. Even on variables such as work experience, there is a need to consider the type, amount, and relevance of work experience as it relates to the performance of work tasks (Quiñones, Ford, & Teachout, 1995).

The ability-performance or KSAO-performance relationships described by Hunter (1983), Schmidt et al. (1986), Borman et al. (1991), Schmit et al. (1996), and Pulakos, Schmitt, and Chan (1996) are all conceptualized in terms of *static forms* of covariance structure models and tested using cross-sectional data. One of the problems of conceptualizing and testing KSAO-performance relationships as such is that these models are at best a "snapshot" of a dynamic *process* linking KSAO and performance occurring over *time*. A potentially useful approach toward increasing our understanding of KSAO-performance relationships would be to incorporate KSAO and performance variables into models that are more process oriented and temporally sensitive.

Campbell, McCloy, Oppler, and Sager's (1993) theory of performance provides a promising example of a process-oriented model that emphasizes the multidimensionality of both the KSAO and performance domains. As described in Chapter 3, Campbell et al. propose that there are eight core performance components (e.g., job-specific task proficiency, demonstration of effort), and that each component is a function of three categories of performance determinants: declarative knowledge, procedural knowledge and skills, and motivation. These performance determinants constitute the mediating *processes* between individual difference and situational variables on the one hand and performance components on the other. Campbell et al.'s theory has significant implications for the way researchers should conceptualize and test models of KSAO-performance relationships. For example, the substantive nature of the major performance component should be specified in the KSAO-performance relationship. Different performance components may have different relationships with the same KSAO constructs. In addition, models of KSAO-performance relationships should go beyond simple correlations between KSAO predictors and performance criteria to explicate the substantive content of the domains of knowledge, skill, and choice behavior (i.e., Campbell et al.'s performance determinants) that mediate the KSAO-performance relationships. McCloy et al. (1994) describe a test of a model that includes such mediating variables.

Finally, the person-organization fit model described above (Kristof, 1996) underscores the importance of matching KSAO dimensions to requirements of jobs and work performance. Thus, it makes little sense for the personnel selection researcher to ask what KSAO construct has the highest predictive validity without specifying the substantive content of both the KSAO predictor construct and the performance criterion construct and the substantive nature of the specific KSAO-performance relationship.

Summary and Conclusions

In his review of the literature on personality and work behavior, Adler (1996) argues that studies that increase our understanding of personality at work come about only when researchers think through carefully the potential mediating linkages between personality constructs (not personality measures) and target criterion constructs. Adler's thesis should be generalized to other KSAO domains as well. These considerations constitute the basic objectives of studies such as those described in the section above on modeling KSAO-performance relationships and are basic to the Campbell et al. (1993) performance model. A central theme throughout this chapter has been the critical importance of specifying the substantive nature of the KSAO-performance relationship under examination. A productive study of the relationship of KSAO dimensions to work performance behavior requires careful consideration of the substantive content of both the KSAO predictor domain and the performance criterion domain and the substantive nature of the critical linkages between the two domains in the theoretical model.

Personnel selection researchers are beginning to pay more attention to construct and predictor-criterion linkage issues in their research. The recent debate on appropriate levels of specificity or broadness of personality traits is one example of an increased focus on construct issues in the examination of KSAO-performance relationships (Hogan & Roberts, 1996; Ones & Viswesvaran, 1996; Schneider, Hough, & Dunnette, 1996). Another example is research that emphasizes the multidimensionality and multilevel nature of the construct of work experience (Ford, Quiñones, Sego, & Sorra, 1992; Ford, Sego, Quiñones, & Sorra, 1991; Quiñones et al., 1995). Additional research in these areas, together with continued emphasis on the substantive nature of job performance variability (Campbell et al., 1993) and increased interest in P-O fit studies (Kristof, 1996), will help to provide a foundation for a better understanding of KSAO-performance relationships.

Finally, continued attention should be paid to taxonomic issues with regard to both KSAOs and performance areas. The relative utility of measures from various predictor domains in the prediction of performance should be investigated. Consistent use of a given taxonomy would facilitate aggregation and meta-analyses of empirical studies. With the cumulation of research data, the relative strength of various KSAO-performance relationships can be specified more confidently.

5 The Measurement
of Job-Related
Characteristics

In Chapter 4, we discussed the nature and dimensionality of individual differences. In this chapter, we focus on the success with which human resource professionals have measured these individual differences. To begin, we discuss the basic ways in which these methods of measuring individual differences are evaluated—namely, reliability and validity. After defining these basic concepts, we address various methods of measurement, such as paper-and-pencil techniques, interviews, biographical data, and simulations, in light of these criteria. In the preceding chapter, we focused on the nature of individual difference constructs; in this chapter, we focus on the practicality of measuring these constructs. Of course, we believe that the field of personnel selection will be advanced most significantly if researchers attend to the nature of the constructs measured as well as the substantial practical outcomes that accrue from personnel selection.

Reliability

Most simply stated, reliability is the consistency of measurement across time. This *test-retest* reliability is most often evaluated through the computation of a correlation of scores on a test given at two different points in time. Because the purpose of using selection procedures is to predict across time, adequate test-retest reliability is usually considered a necessary quality of tests. A test cannot predict job performance if it cannot predict scores on the instrument itself.

More broadly, the computation of reliability is based on a theory of test scores that posits that any observed test score is a combination of a true score and an error. The error and true components of the observed score are uncorrelated, and errors across administrations of a test are also assumed to be uncorrelated. Given these assumptions, it is also true that the variance in a set of observed scores is equal to two independent sources—true and error—and that the reliability of a measure is that proportion of the observed variance that is a function of true variability among individuals on the trait of interest (see Nunnally & Bernstein, 1994, for a presentation of various classical reliability formulas). What is defined as the true and error component of a test depends on the test user's purpose, or the types of decisions to which he or she hopes to generalize (Cronbach, Gleser, & Rajaratnam, 1972). In the case of test-retest reliability, the true score component is the component of the test score that is stable across time, and error is the portion of test variance that changes across time. Other sources of error that might be important in some applications include test content and differences in observers or raters.

Many times, an assessment of test-retest reliability is not practical, because examinees cannot be tested twice, or because memory or practice effects would influence the second test scores. In such instances, two forms of a test may be developed, and the correlations of examinees' scores on these two alternate forms used to assess reliability. Depending on the time elapsed between the administrations of these two forms of the test, there are two potential sources of error involved in this *parallel forms* reliability. The first source of error is the difference in the actual items contained in the two alternate forms. If the alternate forms are administered with a substantial intervening time period, there may also be other changes in test scores that are a function of the examinees' intervening experiences.

If a parallel form is not available, reliability may be assessed using the *split halves* method. Test items are split randomly into two halves, and examinees are scored on each half of the test; the scores on the two halves are then correlated. This correlation represents an estimate of the reliability of either half of the test. The reliability of the full-length test is obtained by using the Spearman-Brown correction formula. The general form of this formula is as follows:

$$\text{corrected reliability} = n(r_{xx})/[1 + (n-1)r_{xx}], \qquad [5.1]$$

where r_{xx} is the correlation between the two half tests and n is the number of times the test length is multiplied to obtain the corrected reliability. In the case of split-half reliability, n is equal to 2, because the length of the full test is double the length of either half. This formula expresses the relationship between the length of a test and its reliability and can be applied to other instances when a test is either shortened or lengthened to estimate the reliability of a test of differing length. The main assumption underlying the use of the formula is that the items added to, or subtracted from, the test are equal statistically to the items upon which the original estimate of reliability was obtained. In the use of the split-half estimate of reliability, the main source of error is the content of the items in the two different halves, because all of the test is administered at the same point in time.

There are many possible ways in which to split a test. If one were to split a test in all possible ways and compute the estimates of split-half reliability as described above, the average of these various split-half reliabilities would be *coefficient alpha,* which is a frequently used *internal consistency* estimate of reliability. Fortunately, the computation of alpha does not require the computation of all these split halves; it can be estimated using the following formula:

$$\text{coefficient alpha} = \frac{n^2(\text{average covariance among all items})}{\text{variance of the test}}, \qquad [5.2]$$

where n is the number of items in the test. Because all items on the test would be administered at the same point in time, the major source of error affecting this estimate of reliability is the content of the items. The use of coefficient alpha *assumes* that the items are measures of a unidimensional construct; the degree to which this index is less than one is a function of the degree to which the test measures more than one construct and the degree to which random error affects the test item responses.

Many of the measures used by personnel selection researchers involve the use of raters. When raters are used as the source of information about an important KSAO, the reliability of ratings is important, and differences among raters are an important source of error. The reliability of a single rater can be estimated through the correlation of the ratings of two raters of a group of people. If both raters' ratings are used to index some trait or work performance, then the Spearman-Brown correction formula can be used to estimate the reliability of the composite of these two ratings. In this case, n would be 2, because a two-rater composite is twice as long as the rating of a single individual. If three or more raters' ratings are combined to assess examinees' ability, as is the case in some panel interviews or assessment centers (discussed below), the composite reliability can be obtained through the computation of the covariances among the multiple raters' ratings and computation of coefficient alpha as described above—that is, treating raters as items. This interrater reliability would be influenced by any differences among raters; if the researcher is also interested in the influence of time as a potential error source, he or she should collect ratings from different raters at different time periods. This would be an appropriate way to estimate the reliability of an employment interview, for example, because in such a case the researcher is interested in estimating the error associated with different raters, but is also interested in the cross-time predictability of the KSAOs measured in the interview.

It should be obvious that different reliabilities can be calculated for the same test, depending on what sources of error are of interest. These differences in the various reliability estimates, as well as the experimental requirements of each form of reliability, are summarized in Table 5.1. Aside from the fact that reliability is a necessary characteristic of any measuring instrument, it can also be used to estimate the relationships among the true sources of variance in different measures, ruling out the effects of the different sources of measurement error cited above in our discussion and presented in Table 5.1. This estimate of the "true" relationship is very important when one is interested in scientific questions related to the actual interrelationships among constructs. The true relationship is provided by

Table 5.1 Methods of Estimating Reliability and Sources of Error

Method	Number of Test Forms Required	Number of Test Sessions Needed	Sources of Error Variance
Test-retest	1	2	Time
Alternate forms (same time)	2	1	Item content
Alternate forms (different times)	2	2	Item content; time
Split-half	1	1	Item content; type of split
Cronbach's coefficient alpha	1	1	Dimensionality of test; item content
Interrater	1 or more	1	Scorer differences

the correction for attenuation formula, which involves dividing the observed correlation between two measures by the product of the square root of their reliabilities. In estimating the true validity of predictor-criterion relationships, standard practice involves a correction for unreliability in the criterion but does not include a correction for unreliability in the predictor. This is because the same test is usually used as the estimate of a KSAO in other situations, hence there will be no change in the construct measured. Validities are also corrected for restriction of range (see Chapter 6), reflecting the fact that the range of the KSAO dimension (e.g., cognitive ability) in the sample on which a test is validated will often be less than that of the applicant pool in which the test will ultimately be used. With lower variability in scores, the estimate of validity will be lower. In our discussion of various tests in this chapter, we often mention corrected validities. These validities are estimates of the "true" validity, after correction of observed validities both for unreliability in the criterion using the correction for attenuation mentioned above and for range restriction using the formula presented in the next chapter. Corrected validities are very important in theoretical discussions because they represent the true underlying relationships between constructs; in the personnel selection context, these constructs are usually ability and performance constructs.

We have stated that reliability is a necessary psychometric characteristic of a measuring device, but it is not sufficient. Tests used in a selection context must be valid as well, and we turn next to a consideration of test validity.

Validity

Validity is the degree to which the inferences drawn from test scores are accurate. When scores on the Law School Admissions Test are used in the process of selecting among applicants for law school, the inference is that a particular score indicates that an applicant will (or will not) be successful in law school and perhaps successful as a lawyer as well. When an integrity test is used to reject an applicant for a job, the inference is that the individual's score on the test indicates that he or she would engage in some counterproductive activity if employed. When a test of spatial ability is used to select auto mechanics, the inference is that the test scores show which applicants will do well (or poorly) as auto mechanics. The validity of all such inferences can be evaluated in a variety of ways; in fact, several different inferences are often being made when a test is used in an employment situation. We discuss the nature of validity and the variety of experimental designs and evidence used to establish validity in the next chapter. In the employment situation, the most frequently used estimate of validity is a correlation between a predictor (e.g., a test, interview, or job sample) and a measure of job performance. In our discussion of the validity of various selection procedures below, we will be speaking of this approach to validity unless we specify otherwise. The literature on personnel selection refers to this estimate of inferential accuracy as *criterion-related validity*. Ordinarily, one might think that a reliable test that produces scores that are highly correlated with a job performance measure would be useful to an organization. However, there are a number of aspects of the organization itself and the situation in which tests are used that may modify the appropriateness of this expectation. In the next section, we discuss the situational aspects that affect the utility of a test.

Utility

Utility refers to the practical usefulness of a test. Certainly, validity affects the utility of a test; if there is no correlation between a test and any important performance outcomes, then the test will not be useful to the selection process. The inferences one would make from such a test would be no better than those one would make on the basis of chance. In the selection situation, other factors also influence the practical usefulness of tests. In 1939, Taylor and Russell described and tabulated the effects of the selection ratio (the proportion of applicants hired), the base rate (the proportion of present employees or the proportion in the applicant pool who are considered successful), as well as the validity of a test on test utility. Table 5.2 presents a part of the tables Taylor and Russell constructed for the situation in which the base rate is .50 (half of the current employees are considered successful). The values in the table are the percentages successful when the test is used. Examination of Table 5.2 reveals that (a) with .00 validity, the proportion of successful employees will always be equal to the base rate; (b) increases in validity will produce increases in the proportion of applicants selected who are subsequently successful; and (c) low selection ratios will produce the greatest increases in proportion of selected applicants who are successful. In addition, if we were to present Taylor-Russell tables for a broader range of base rates, it would be possible to see that the greatest increases in percentage of successful selected applicants would have occurred when the base rate is equal to .50, as opposed to either high or low levels of base rate. Taylor and Russell's tables were extremely helpful in determining when a test might be useful, but this formulation did have some liabilities. Use of the base rate and proportion successful required that the outcome variable be dichotomized, when, in most situations, performance outcomes are continuous; that is, there is no definite point at which a person is considered a success or a failure. Also, this approach did not take into account the cost of testing.

Brogden (1946, 1949) provided solutions to both of these problems. First, he showed that validity is directly and linearly related to utility expressed as a standardized criterion value. This notion is embodied in Table 5.3, which was first produced by Brown and Ghiselli (1953). Examination of the values in this table reveals that the expected mean criterion score increases linearly as a function of validity, and that low selection ratios produce the largest expected increases. The base rate is no longer relevant, as the outcome variable is expressed in increases in a standardized performance measure in a continuous fashion. Brogden (1949) also demonstrated the effect of testing costs on these expected utility values. With high testing costs and over a limited time frame, an organization could expect to lose money with either high or low selection ratios. With low selection ratios, many people would

Table 5.2 The Effect of Validity, Base Rate, and Selection Ratio on Proportion of Applicants Considered Successful for Base Rates .20 to .50

Employees Considered Satisfactory	r	Selection Ratio										
		.05	.10	.20	.30	.40	.50	.60	.70	.80	.90	.95
20%	.00	.20	.20	.20	.20	.20	.20	.20	.20	.20	.20	.20
	.10	.26	.25	.24	.23	.23	.22	.22	.21	.21	.21	.20
	.20	.33	.31	.28	.27	.26	.25	.24	.23	.22	.21	.21
	.30	.41	.37	.33	.30	.28	.27	.25	.24	.23	.21	.21
	.40	.49	.44	.38	.34	.31	.29	.27	.25.	23	.22	.21
	.50	.59	.52	.44	.38	.35	.31	.29	.26	.24	.22	.21
	.60	.68	.60	.50	.43	.38	.34	.30.	.27	.24	.22	.21
	.70	.79	.69	.56	.48	.41	.36	.31	.28	.25	.22	.21
	.80	.89	.79	.64	.53	.45	.38	.33	.28	.25	.22	.21
	.90	.98	.91	.75	.60	.48	.40	.33	.29	.25	.22	.21
30%	.00	.30	.30	.30	.30	.30	.30	.30	.30	.30	.30	.30
	.10	.38	.36	.35	.34	.33	.33	.32	.32	.31	.31	.30
	.20	.46	.43	.40	.38	.37	.36	.34	.33	.32	.31	.31
	.30	.54	.50	.46	.43	.40	.38	.37	.35	.33	.32	.31
	.40	.63	.58	.51.	47	.44	.41	.39	.37	.34	.32	.31
	.50	.72	.65	.58	.52	.48	.44	.41	.38	.35	.33	.31
	.60	.81.	74	.64	.58	.52	.47	.43	.40	.36	.33	.31
	.70	.89	.82	.72	.63	.57	.51	.46	.41	.37	.33	.32
	.80	.96	.90	.80	.70	.62	.54	.48	.42	.37	.33	.32
	.90	1.00	.98	.90	.79	.68	.58	.49	.43	.37	.33	.32
40%	.00	.40	.40	.40	.40	.40	.40	.40	.40	.40	.40	.40
	.10	.48	.47	.46	.45	.44	.43	.42	.42	.41	.41	.40
	.20	.57	.54	.51	.49	.48	.46	.45.	44.	43	.41	.41
	.30	.65	.61	.57	.54	.51	.49	.47	.46	.44	.42	.41
	.40	.73	.69	.63	.59	.56	.53	.50	.48	.45	.43	.41
	.50	.81.	.76	.69	.64	.60	.56	.53	.49	.46	.43	.42
	.60	.89	.83	.75	.69	.64	.60	.55	.51	.48	.44	.42
	.70	.95	.90	.82	.76	.69	.64	.58	.53	.49	.44	.42
	.80	.99	.96	.89	.82	.75	.68	.61	.55	.49	.44	.42
	.90	1.00	1.00	.97	.91	.82	.74	.65	.57	.50	.44	.42
50%	.00	.50	.50	.50	.50	.50	.50	.50	.50	.50	.50	.50
	.10	.58	.57	.56	.55	.54	.53	.53	.52	.51	.51	.50
	.20	.67	.64	.61	.59	.58	.56	.55	.54	.53	.52	.51
	.30	.74	.71	.67	.64	.62	.60	.58	.56	.54	.52	.51
	.40	.82	.78	.73	.69	.66	.63	.61	.58	.56	.53	.52
	.50	.88	.84	.78	.74	.70	.67	.63	.60	.57	.54	.52
	.60	.94	.90	.84	.79	.75	.70	.66	.62	.59	.54	.52
	.70	.98	.95	.90	.85	.80	.75	.70	.65.	.60	.55	.53
	.80	1.00	.99	.95	.90	.85	.80	.73	.67	.61	.55	.53
	.90	1.00	1.00	.99	.97	.92	.86	.78	.70	.62	.56	.53
	r	.05	.10	.20	.30	.40	.50	.60	.70	.80	.90	.95

SOURCE: Taylor and Russell (1939).

have to be tested for a very few to be hired; hence, those selected would have to be very productive to offset the costs of the large number tested. With high selection ratios, nearly everyone is hired, but all are tested so as to reject a few whose predicted criterion scores are low. To recognize a positive result in this instance, it must be very important to the organization to reject these few persons. The latter result implies a consideration of the costs associated with selecting a person who does badly (or the benefits accrued from the rejection of low-performing persons), whereas to this point, the emphasis was on the positive outcomes associated with the persons who are hired. It is also possible that we can consider the negative outcomes associated with not hiring highly qualified persons. The costs of testing and the consideration of all possible outcomes associated with selection decisions were comprehensively outlined by Cronbach and Gleser (1965).

The widespread application of the ideas of Brogden (1946, 1949) and Cronbach and Gleser (1965) did not take place until Schmidt, Hunter, McKenzie, and Muldrow (1979) presented a method to estimate the size of the standard deviation of employees' economic contribution to the organization. This estimate was important because Brogden estimates of the utility of a test were expressed in standard deviation units (i.e., standardized criterion scores). Schmidt et al.'s solution to this problem was to ask job experts to estimate the economic contribution of employees who performed at the 50th percentile (average employees) as well as the economic contribution of employees who performed one standard deviation below (approximately the 15th percentile) and one standard deviation above average (approximately the 85th percentile). The differences between the judges' estimates of the 50th and 15th percentiles and the 50th and 85th percentiles produced two estimates of the standard deviation of employees' contributions to the organization. These estimates could then be averaged to produce a single estimate for each judge. This proposed estimate produced a large number of attempts to estimate the utility of a variety of human resource functions, including selection (see Cascio, 1987b), as well as a great deal of research designed to assess the appropriateness of this estimate of the standard deviation (see Boudreau, 1991, for a comprehensive review). A review of a number of attempts to assess the size of this standard deviation has revealed that it is normally between 40% and 70% of the average salary for the position an employee holds (Schmidt, Hunter, & Pearlman, 1982).

Table 5.3 Mean Standard Criterion Score of Accepted Cases in Relation to Test Validity and Selection Ratio Based on Brogden Formulation

Selection Ratio	Validity Coefficient																				
	.00	.05	.10	.15	.20	.25	.30	.35	.40	.45	.50	.55	.60	.65	.70	.75	.80	.85	.90	.95	1.00
.05	.00	.10	.21	.31	.42	.52	.62	.73	.83	.94	1.04	1.14	1.25	1.35	1.46	1.56	1.66	1.77	1.87	1.98	2.08
.10	.00	.09	.18	.26	.35	.44	.53	.62	.70	.79	.88	.97	1.05	1.14	1.23	1.32	1.41	1.49	1.58	1.67	1.76
.15	.00	.08	.15	.23	.31	.39	.46	.54	.62	.70	.77	.85	.93	1.01	1.08	1.16	1.24	1.32	1.39	1.47	1.55
.20	.00	.07	.14	.21	.28	.35	.42	.49	.56	.63	.70	.77	.84	.91	.98	1.05	1.12	1.19	1.26	1.33	1.40
.25	.00	.06	.13	.19	.25	.32	.38	.44	.51	.57	.63	.70	.76	.82	.89	.95	1.01	1.08	1.14	1.20	1.27
.30	.00	.06	.12	.17	.23	.29	.35	.40	.46	.52	.58	.64	.69	.75	.81	.87	.92	.98	1.04	1.10	1.16
.35	.00	.05	.11	.16	.21	.26	.32	.37	.42	.48	.53	.58	.63	.69	.74	.79	.84	.90	.95	1.00	1.06
.40	.00	.05	.10	.15	.19	.24	.29	.34	.39	.44	.48	.53	.58	.63	.68	.73	.77	.82	.87	.92	.97
.45	.00	.04	.09	.13	.18	.22	.26	.31	.35	.40	.44	.48	.53	.57	.62	.66	.70	.75	.79	.84	.88
.50	.00	.04	.08	.12	.16	.20	.24	.28	.32	.36	.40	.44	.48	.52	.56	.60	.64	.68	.72	.76	.80
.55	.00	.04	.07	.11	.14	.18	.22	.25	.29	.32	.36	.40	.43	.47	.50	.54	.58	.61	.65	.68	.72
.60	.00	.03	.06	.10	.13	.16	.19	.23	.26	.29	.32	.35	.39	.42	.45	.48	.52	.55	.58	.61	.64
.65	.00	.03	.06	.09	.11	.14	.17	.20	.23	.26	.28	.31	.34	.37	.40	.43	.46	.48	.51	.54	.57
.70	.00	.02	.05	.07	.10	.12	.15	.17	.20	.22	.25	.27	.30	.32	.35	.37	.40	.42	.45	.47	.50
.75	.00	.02	.04	.06	.08	.11	.13	.15	.17	.19	.21	.23	.25	.27	.30	.32	.33	.36	.38	.40	.42
.80	.00	.02	.04	.05	.07	.09	.11	.12	.14	.16	.18	.19	.21	.22	.25	.26	.28	.30	.32	.33	.35
.85	.00	.01	.03	.04	.05	.07	.08	.10	.11	.12	.14	.15	.16	.18	.19	.20	.22	.23	.25	.26	.27
.90	.00	.01	.02	.03	.04	.05	.06	.07	.08	.09	.10	.11	.12	.13	.14	.15	.16	.17	.18	.19	.20
.95	.00	.01	.01	.02	.02	.03	.03	.04	.04	.05	.05	.06	.07	.07	.08	.08	.09	.09	.10	.10	.11

SOURCE: Brown and Ghiselli (1953).

With an estimate of the standard deviation of employee worth, researchers and practitioners could use the Brogden table to make estimates of the economic benefits resulting from the introduction of a human resource intervention such as selection. For example, if we have a selection ratio of .20 and a test with a validity of .30, Table 5.3 suggests that we should expect that the average standardized outcome value for the employees selected in this situation would be .42. Assuming no previous valid selection method were available, the average expected performance would be the mean, or .00. If the estimate of the standard deviation of employee worth is $10,000, then each employee hired using this procedure would produce $4,200 (.42 times $10,000) more than would have been the case previously with no valid selection procedure in place. If 100 employees are selected, the benefit would be $420,000. From this value, we would have to subtract the cost of testing 500 people (100 divided by .20, which is the selection ratio) to estimate the annual benefit.

Once this estimate of the standard deviation of performance in economic terms was available, researchers began to make refinements or adjustments to the overall utility estimates. The average tenure of the employees selected could change the overall return significantly, as the estimates of the standard deviation were always made on annual bases. However, adjustments then need to be made for inflation (dollars earned in the years to come will be worth less than they are today), the fact that the organization may have to pay a higher rate of taxes if it is more profitable, and the possibility that the organization may have to sell its products for less if greater productivity results in surplus. In addition, other researchers have considered the implications of recruiting costs designed to lower selection ratios and the fact that the most desirable recruits may not accept offers of employment (Murphy, 1986). Boudreau (1984) has also analyzed the degree to which various parameters in the utility model (e.g., validity, selection ratio, standard deviation of worth) can be varied downward to the point at which the costs of testing equal the projected returns. Others have varied these same parameters through a range of possible values to determine the degree to which overall utility is sensitive to variability in specific parameters (e.g., Boudreau & Berger, 1985). All of these refinements have made the basic utility formulations extremely complex, and some have questioned the logical basis and necessity of the various financial accounting methods (e.g., Hunter, Schmidt, & Coggin, 1988). These complexities may outstrip the understanding and the credibility of both human resource professionals and their managerial clients (Rauschenberger & Schmidt, 1987). In fact, there is some evidence that managers react negatively to utility arguments (Latham & Whyte, 1994).

Researchers should keep these three characteristics of a selection procedure in mind when deciding on the use of a technique. It should be pointed out that all three are partly a function of the test and partly a function of the situation in which the test is being used, including the characteristics of the people being evaluated. Because reliability, validity, and utility are partly determined by situational variables, it is not possible to make unqualified statements as to the qualities of particular selection procedures. For instance, aptitude test batteries are normally quite reliable, but if the range of ability represented by the sample being tested is small, then reliability will be lower. Validity for aptitude test batteries may be relatively high when assessed against a sample of employees' job performance, but not very high against a criterion that assesses their willingness and capability to work as members of a team. The nature of the inference being made is important. Utility, of course, is a function of validity, but it is also a function of the ability of the organization to recruit a sizable number of applicants so as to realize a reasonably low selection ratio. The cost of testing is usually an inherent characteristic of a selection procedure, but even the cost of testing may vary as a function of the cost of hiring the raters or interviewers who are necessary components of some selection procedures.

In addition to the implications of test use for predicted performance levels, legal and social constraints (as well as a sense of social responsibility) have led many organizations to consider the implications of test use for the demographic diversity of their workforces. When test scores differ across particular groups (usually by race or gender), the proportion of the lower-scoring group hired is usually smaller. How much smaller is determined by a complex interaction of the validity and reliability of the tests, the size of the subgroup difference on the tests and the criterion, and the manner in which tests are used, as well as other factors. The interplay of some of these factors and their implications for both minority hiring and organizational performance have been examined in various studies (e.g., Cronbach, Yalow, & Schaeffer, 1980; Murphy, 1986; Sackett & Roth, 1996; Schmitt & Noe, 1986; Schmitt, Rogers, Chan, Sheppard, & Jennings, 1997). For the most part, the courts have used the four-fifths rule to determine whether there is prima facie evidence that a particular selection procedure produces *adverse impact* on a particular group. To apply the four-fifths rule to a particular procedure, one must have the percentage of individuals hired from a minority group and the percentage of individuals hired from the majority group. If division of the minority percentage by the majority percentage produces a value less than four-fifths, or .80, then the test is considered discriminatory unless the organization can produce evidence that test scores are related to performance.

Another legislative development, the Americans with Disabilities Act of 1990 (ADA), has had great practical impact on the tests and questions that can be used in a selection context and the types of accommodations that must be made so that persons with disabilities can be evaluated fairly in testing contexts. The ADA prohibits medical screening of applicants before a job offer is made, based on the reasoning that such screening would permit employers to discover the presence of disabilities and discriminate on that basis. Some psychological tests have been viewed as medical screens—for example, when the test is administered or interpreted by a health care professional in a medical setting, when the test is designed to reveal psychological health, and when the employer's purpose is to determine applicants' psychological health. Many personality tests, including the integrity tests mentioned below, probably fit this description. Hence, these tests are often administered only after a job offer is made, and the employer then must justify withdrawing an offer if test results indicate that the potential employee has significant problems that would preclude his or her performing the job in an acceptable manner. The other problem that the ADA has presented for test users is the fact that the effects of adaptations of test administration (e.g., using readers for the visually disabled or dropping time limits for learning disabled individuals) are not known, and it is difficult to accumulate samples large enough to study the effects of these accommodations on test scores and their reliability and validity. This latter problem applies to all test use, not just personality measures. We discuss both the ADA and diversity concerns in more detail in Chapter 7, where we address "external pressures" on selection.

In the discussion of various selection techniques that follows, we make what we consider to be justifiable statements about the reliability and validity of various procedures for different uses, but generally do not make statements about their utility, recognizing that utility, in particular, is highly determined by the selection context. In the cases of reliability, validity, and even subgroup differences, a great deal of information is available about various selection procedures; we attempt to summarize that literature in the next several sections.

Paper-and-Pencil
Measures of Cognitive Ability

Beginning with the development of the first group-administered test of intelligence (Yerkes, 1921), tests of general cognitive ability have been used in the employment context. The use of these tests has been shown to be valid in many industrial studies (Ghiselli, 1966, 1973; Schmidt, Hunter, Pearlman, & Shane, 1979). Schmidt et al. (1981) have claimed that these tests have at least nonzero validity for virtually all jobs. Representative of the general cognitive ability test is the Wonderlic Personnel Test (Wonderlic, 1984), which is probably also one of the oldest and most frequently used of these tests. As described in the previous chapter, this 12-minute test contains 50 items that are quite varied in content, covering vocabulary, arithmetic reasoning, spatial visualization, number series, and other areas. There are about a dozen different forms of the Wonderlic, and the publishers have collected a very large amount of normative data for various groups and members of different occupations as well as validity data for a wide range of jobs. Although reliable and valid, the Wonderlic usually displays large differences in test scores between members of minority groups and Whites, and the use of this test is often viewed negatively by legal authorities and courts in spite of a great deal of positive evidence regarding its validity. Items similar to the type that often appear in general tests of cognitive ability are presented in Table 5.4.

Reflecting the notion, discussed in Chapter 4, that ability is really multidimensional (Thurstone, 1941), most ability testing involves the use of multiple aptitude test batteries and reflects to some extent the primary mental abilities Thurstone believed were represented in these tests. Three such batteries include the Differential Aptitude Tests (DAT; Psychological Corporation, 1992), the Basic Skills Tests (Ruch, Weiner, McKillip, & Dye, 1985), and the General Aptitude Test Battery

Table 5.4   Test Items Similar to Those on the Wonderlic and Other "General
             Intelligence" Tests

---

1. Forward is the opposite of:

    a. obverse   b. adverse   c. converse   d. reverse

2. In the following set of words, which is different?

    a. pig   b. chicken   c. cow   d. corn

3. Pencils sell for $.30 apiece or $3.00 for a dozen. How much is saved by purchasing pencils
   by the dozen?

    a. nothing   b. $.10   c. $.60   d. $1.20

4. Look at the series of numbers below. What number should come next?

    1   2   4   12   36

    a. 60   b. 72   c. 108   d. 144

5. How many of the pairs of numbers below are different?

17692	17692
13987654	13987554
63297512	63297512
18765322	18865322
77891542	78891542

    a. 1   b. 2   c. 3   d. 4   e. 5

(GATB), used in U.S. Employment Services offices as a basis for referral of individuals to corporate employers. The Basic Skills Test is perhaps most directly targeted at specific job-related skills, as is evident in the titles of some of its subtests (e.g., Forms Checking, Coding, Filing Names, Typing, Following Oral Directions), whereas the DAT is more general and is targeted most often toward use in vocational counseling, in which abilities of a general nature are most useful. The GATB provides scores on what are generally thought to be three major dimensions: cognitive ability (general intelligence, verbal ability, and numerical ability), perceptual ability (spatial ability, form perception, clerical perception), and psychomotor ability (motor coordination, finger dexterity, and manual dexterity).

More validation data are available on the GATB than on perhaps any other multiaptitude test battery because of the long-term support of the U.S. Department of Labor. Hunter and Hunter (1984) found an average observed validity of .25 for the three major components of the GATB across all jobs for 515 validity studies. As mentioned in the preceding chapter, these validities were moderated, however, by the complexity of the jobs in which the research participants were engaged, such that cognitive ability was most valid for jobs high in complexity and least valid for jobs low in complexity, and psychomotor ability was most valid for jobs low in complexity and least valid for jobs high in complexity. No differences in validity across levels of complexity were observed for the perceptual tests. Hartigan and Wigdor (1989) report that 264 more recent studies of the validity of the GATB found lower validities (average of .15) than were found in Hunter and Hunter's work. Paper-and-pencil cognitive ability tests display validity across a wide range of jobs, though there is certainly variability in the magnitude of these validities, most likely representing differences in the extent to which the job makes cognitive demands on the incumbents. In addition, when the validity of these tests is corrected appropriately for attenuation due to unreliability in the criterion measure and restriction of range problems in the predictor, the validity is always considerably higher.

Of practical as well as theoretical importance (see Chapter 4) is the issue of the need for more than one ability construct for the prediction of performance. The research of Ree and his colleagues (e.g., Ree, Earles, & Teachout, 1994) has been supportive of the notion that only a general factor contributes to the prediction of performance. The usual moderate to high intercorrelations among the various measures in multiple aptitude test batteries also suggest that these measures are redundant and that when combined to predict some performance outcome are unlikely to contribute uniquely to prediction.

As for general aptitude tests like the Wonderlic, the most significant liability of multiple aptitude test batteries (at least the cognitive components of these batteries) is the degree to which there are subgroup differences on test scores. In many instances, these differences are as large as one standard deviation, though a recent summary of the available published data on general cognitive ability measures indicates an average difference of .83 standard deviations (Schmitt, Clause, & Pulakos, 1996). Although there is little evidence that these subgroup differences provide underprediction of minority members' performance (e.g., Hartigan & Wigdor, 1989), the magnitude of these differences is such that if the test is used as a basis on which to hire people, it is almost always the case that the four-fifths rule (described above) will be violated.

Personality Tests

Structured Personality Tests

Measures of personality were first developed for clinical purposes, and, not surprisingly, they provided scores on scales that relate to various hypothesized psychological problems (Hathaway & McKinley, 1943). This health care-related orientation is reflected in many subsequent personality test batteries, such as the California Psychological Inventory (CPI; Gough, 1987) and the Sixteen Personality Factor Questionnaire (16PF; Cattell, Eber, & Tatsuoka, 1970), though more recent personality test batteries such as the Hogan Personality Inventory (HPI; Hogan & Hogan, 1986) and the Personality Research Form (PRF; Jackson, 1967) were constructed so as to have wider applicability than the earlier, more clinically oriented, measures. All of these test batteries are "structured" in the sense that examinees are required to answer questions by choosing among available responses (e.g., a 5-point scale ranging from *strongly disagree* to *strongly agree,* or possible answers of *yes, no,* or *maybe*). The research on the structure of personality by Costa and McCrae (1992a) has spawned the development of the NEO Personality Inventory (NEO-PI; Costa & McCrae, 1992b), which is a relatively "nonclinical" measure of the Big Five constructs (as noted in Chapter 4, these constructs are Openness to Experience, Neuroticism, Extraversion, Agreeableness, and Conscientiousness). Items representative of the Big Five constructs are presented in Table 5.5.

In any consideration of the reliability of personality measures, it is important that the measures be consistent over time, because one is usually interested in predicting future performance. Most of the personality measures described produce relatively stable across-time scores. For example, Costa and McCrae (1992b) report reliabilities of .53 to .81 for up to a period of 7 years. The stability of personality varies, of course, with the time period and the instrument; a user should always seek this information from a test manual or the relevant literature. Internal consistency reliabilities are important as a means of determining the relationships between true scores on various constructs, but they are also important in the measurement of multiple personality dimensions. In these cases, these dimensions should be relatively unrelated, so as to provide information about nonredundant

Table 5.5   Items Representative of the Constructs Measured by the NEO-PI

Openness: I like to travel to countries I've never been before.

Extraversion: I love to go to parties and have fun.

Agreeableness: I avoid an argument if I can.

Neuroticism: I am always concerned that I will not do the right thing.

Conscientiousness: My workplace is always clean and orderly.

NOTE: The items shown here are not included in the NEO-PI, but they match the constructs that test measures.

aspects of a measure. If the internal consistency reliabilities of two measures are no larger than their intercorrelation, then their true scores are correlated 1.00 (see the discussion of the correction for attenuation above). The internal consistency reliabilities, the intercorrelations of the scales within a battery, and the standard error of the differences among scales (Nunnally & Bernstein, 1994) are all important information if a profile of scores is to be considered as the basis for any personnel decisions.

The validity of personality measures in the prediction of a variety of job performance measures has generally been thought to be quite low (Guion & Gottier, 1965; Hunter & Hunter, 1984; Schmitt, Gooding, Noe, & Kirsch, 1984), though there was a relatively more favorable early review (Ghiselli, 1973). Ghiselli (1973) considered the theoretical relevance of a particular personality construct for a particular performance construct in organizing the results of validation studies. A similar approach by Hough, Eaton, Dunnette, Kamp, and McCloy (1990) produced encouraging estimates of validity. Barrick and Mount's (1991) meta-analysis is generally credited with the rebirth of personality measurement as a valid predictor of performance. Their study found that the construct of conscientiousness was generally valid across most occupations, though the average observed validity (.13) and corrected validity (.22) were not much different from those in earlier reports (e.g., Guion & Gottier, 1965) that had discouraged use of personality tests in the work context. Finally, the work of Tett, Jackson, and Rothstein (1991) indicates that some loss in estimated validity is a function of retaining the sign of validity coefficients in summarizing across studies. These researchers point out that often a negative validity is consistent with theory and should be considered positive rather than negative evidence.

Integrity Tests

One aspect of personality, integrity, has received a great deal of attention in the personnel selection arena in the past two decades. Sackett and colleagues have provided a series of four reviews of the use of measures of integrity, honesty, dependability, or trustworthiness, the most recent of which is by Sackett and Wanek (1996). Ones, Viswesvaran, and Schmidt (1993) have reported on a meta-analysis of the validity of these measures. Integrity tests are usually divided into two major categories: Overt integrity tests measure attitudes and beliefs about theft and admissions of theft and other wrongdoing, including drug and alcohol abuse; personality-based measures are not usually aimed at wrongdoing, but include items that address dependability, conscientiousness, thrill seeking, conformity, and hostility. Murphy and Lee (1994) have linked the latter types of tests to the Big Five construct of Conscientiousness.

In their review, Ones et al. (1993) report that the average corrected validity of integrity tests as a whole is .34 against supervisory ratings of performance and .47 against counterproductive behavior. Although this meta-analysis included a very large database, many of the studies included features that served to inflate these estimates of validity. Sackett and Wanek (1996) examined those studies using a predictive validity strategy, an applicant sample, and external or non-self-report criteria. For the seven studies of theft criteria that were characterized in this fashion, the average observed validity was .09 (corrected .13) for overt tests. For nontheft criteria, the corresponding validities were .27 and .39 averaged across 10 studies. For personality tests of integrity and nontheft criteria, the observed validity was .20 and the corrected validity was .29 averaged over 62 studies. These data indicate more modest, and probably realistic, estimates of validity; they also indicate that there are relatively few high-quality assessments of the validity of integrity tests as predictors of theft. Because of the difficulty in collecting good criterion data and because of the fortunate low occurrence of these behaviors (for a discussion of this base-rate problem, see Martin & Terris, 1991; Murphy, 1987), these studies are particularly difficult to conduct. Integrity tests are very widely used, though controversial.

In addition to the usual technical issues of reliability and validity summarized briefly here, examinees often react negatively to these measures, though the review of this literature by Sackett and Wanek (1996) suggests that this problem may be overstated. A potential user of integrity tests would be well-advised to read Sackett and Wanek's (1996) and Ones et al.'s (1993) reviews, as well as the critical reviews of various individual integrity tests provided in the 1997 volume of *Security Journal.*

Response Sets

One significant problem associated with structured personality instruments is what researchers have called response sets. Some response sets may be deliberate, in which case they constitute faking; others are the unintentional side effects of respondents' desire to look good. Paulhus (1984) calls these two types of social desirability responding *impression management* and *self-deception.* When engaging in impression management, the examinee is aware that his or her responses are inaccurate or untrue; in contrast, the respondent who engages in self-deception gives socially desirable or positively biased responses that may be inaccurate or untrue, but that the respondent actually believes otherwise. Paulhus presents measures of these two response sets; examples of items from his measures are displayed in Table 5.6. Other items are designed to identify the careless respondent (Hough et al., 1990). For example, consider your response to "All cattle are (a) cars, (b) trees, (c) animals, (d) round."

Perhaps the earliest example of recognition of this problem is represented by the three validity scales of the Minnesota Multiphasic Personality Inventory (MMPI; Hathaway & McKinley, 1943). The Lie scale is a set of items that make the respondent look very good, but are unlikely to be answered in the favorable direction if the person is truthful (e.g., I never tell a lie). The K scale is more subtle; a scored response to a large number of items on this scale is thought to indicate defensiveness or an attempt to fake good. Scores on the K scale are sometimes used to correct scores on some of the clinical scales, the thought being that the latter scores are lower than they otherwise would be if the person were not faking. The F scale comprises a set of items that are rarely answered in the scored direction; a respondent with a high score is either careless or deliberately distorting her or his answers to the questions. The F and L scales are usually used to

Table 5.6   Self-Deception and Impression Management Items

Self-deception items

    My first impressions of people usually turn out to be right.

    I always know why I like things.

    I am fully in control of my fate.

Impression management items

    I never cover up my mistakes.

    When I hear people talking privately, I avoid listening.

    I don't gossip about other people's business.

SOURCE: These items are taken from 20-item measures of these two social desirability scales presented in Paulhus (1984).

determine the overall validity of a person's responses to the instrument.

Evidence regarding the validity of these validity scales is not conclusive, at least in the personnel selection area. Personality tests can be faked (e.g., Hough, Barge, Houston, McGue, & Kamp, 1985; Krahe, 1989; Orpen, 1971), but evidence regarding the extent of faking and its effects on selection decisions and the validity of selection tests is less clear. Using a large U.S. Army sample, Hough et al. (1990) found similar scores between actual applicants and a group of examinees who had no motivation to distort responses. These authors also found that validities of the personality measures examined remained stable regardless of possible distortion by examinees in either unusually positive or negative directions. Hough et al. (1990) used a random response scale (like the MMPI F scale) and scale called Unlikely Virtues (like the MMPI K scale) to assess fakability and its effects on validity. In another paper, Hough (1995) has suggested that scores on the Unlikely Virtues scale may actually be valid indicators of job performance on some jobs, because the individuals who know what is correct behavior in some situations are those who are more likely to behave correctly in socially demanding situations, such as those found in some jobs.

An opposing view has been presented by Douglas, McDaniel, and Snell (1996). Using college student subjects and a test of integrity, they found that their research participants could fake and that this had an effect on the test's validity. In addition, they showed that with a relatively high test score cutoff, most of the persons who had been selected would have achieved their high scores at least partially as a function of their faking good on the test. Clearly, more research is needed to sort out the effects of faking and how faking should be dealt with in a selection context.

Projective Tests

A second major approach to the measurement of personality is the use of projective tests. In a projective test, an examinee is provided with an ambiguous stimulus and is asked to give an interpretation or a description of the stimulus. The first such test was the Rorschach inkblot test (Rorschach, 1921), in which the examinee was asked to look at a series of inkblots and describe what he or she saw in each picture. The examinee's responses were interpreted in light of a clinical interview, though standardized scoring systems have also been developed (Erdberg & Exner, 1984). A less ambiguous set of stimuli is represented by the Thematic Apperception Test (TAT; Murray, 1938). The TAT uses a series of black-and-white pictures about which respondents are asked to write stories. The stories told by examinees are scored for a variety of psychological needs, at least one of which (i.e., need for achievement) has received a great deal of attention as a potential predictor of success in a variety of leadership and job performance situations (Andrew, 1967; Atkinson, 1958, 1981). The most successful projective test has been the Miner Sentence Completion Blank (Miner, 1978). This test, which has been used for managerial selection, consists of a series of incomplete sentences (e.g., "My supervisor . . . ") that the examinee must complete. These responses are then scored on six "managerial role" scales. Reviews of the literature on the validity of the Miner Sentence Completion Blank by Cornelius (1983) and Miner (1978) have revealed surprisingly high validities against sales success and promotion criteria. In the case of all projective tests, standardized scoring methods and interscorer reliability are critical. As described by Cornelius (1983), for the TAT, interscorer reliability is frequently quite low (i.e., .30 or less). In summary, there are many different personality test batteries and methods of measuring personality, as well as many dozens of hypothesized personality constructs. Perhaps in no other area of individual difference measurement are the choices of measuring devices so diverse. In choosing among the methods available, personnel selection researchers must carefully evaluate the reliability, validity, and appropriateness of the construct measured given the performance construct of interest.

Summary and Evaluation

There is little evidence that personality measures (either structured or projective) produce any sizable subgroup differences (Hough, 1994; Schmitt, Clause, & Pulakos, 1996), hence, these measures rarely produce adverse impact as defined above. Further, the correlation between personality and ability measures such as those discussed above is usually quite low, so that incremental validity produced by the use of personality in combination with cognitive ability usually produces more valid prediction than either would alone. There remain, however, some significant questions about personality. We referred to the issue of the structure of personality in Chapter 4; this has obvious relevance for measurement as well. In addition, concerns about examinee reactions to these measures (see Rynes & Connerly, 1993; Stone, Stone-Romero, & Hyatt, 1994) and about how some measures might be viewed from the perspective of the ADA make their use problematic in some contexts. Finally, even though recent research findings and professional opinion are generally positive with respect to the validity of personality in predicting a broad range of performance criteria, these validities are still modest (Barrick & Mount, 1991). Further, much of the literature base is still highly atheoretical (and frequently not of very high quality, at least by today's standards), which makes it difficult to make general statements about validity. Comments about the need to examine the performance construct carefully and then match the predictor to that construct (Schneider & Schmitt, 1986) are particularly appropriate in the personality measurement domain.

Biodata

The scoring of biographical data, or biodata, was originally developed as a method for making systematic use of the information filled in by applicants on job application forms. An attempt was made to

Table 5.7   Examples of Biographical Data Items

If you are working with a group of people, what role do you usually take?

    a. Wait for someone else to make task assignments so as not to appear "bossy."

    b. Avoid task assignments, because the work usually gets done anyway.

    c. Take the lead in organizing the project and making work assignments.

    d. Try to make all people enjoy working together.

If you were at a party at which you didn't know many people, what actions would you take?

    a. Greet the few people you do know, then leave.

    b. Spend the time talking with those you do know.

    c. Introduce yourself to as many people as possible.

    d. Ask the people you do know to introduce you to others.

How many times did you change your college major?

    a. Never

    b. Once

    c. Two or three times

    d. Many times

In college, which type of class did you like the most?

    a. English

    b. History

    c. Science

    d. Math

---

relate individuals' specific past experiences, education, and interests to job performance outcomes. When such a relationship was found, it became the basis for a scoring key applied to subsequent application forms (England, 1971). As the technique proved useful, the types and number of items used were expanded, and today a biodata form looks very similar to a multiple-choice test (see Table 5.7 for examples). Based on the rather simple idea that an individual's past behavior is the best predictor of her or his future behavior, early studies of the validity of biodata indicated that they were good predictors of a variety of performance criteria (Ghiselli, 1966; Henry, 1966). In the several decades since then, the validity of this approach to personnel selection has been reaffirmed (see Hunter & Hunter, 1984; Mumford & Stokes, 1992; Schmitt, Gooding, et al., 1984). Over the course of several decades of research, three major issues have occupied the bulk of researchers' and practitioners' time: the cross-validity or specificity of the biodata scoring key, empirical versus rational approaches to scoring key development, and the nature of the constructs measured by biodata.

Because of the empirical and atheoretical approach to the development of biodata, the scoring keys must be cross-validated. Even after successful cross-validation (applying a scoring key and checking its validity in a separate sample of research participants from the same population), the validity of scoring keys was often found to be very specific to time and organizational context. For example, Brown (1981) found that the same biodata inventory provided meaningfully different validities across different companies within the same industry. Rothstein, Schmidt, Erwin, Owens, and Sparks (1990), however, have shown that such specificity might be the result of the manner in which item keys are developed. These researchers initially selected items for their study because they thought the items addressed some aspects of the individuals' backgrounds that might be relevant to job performance. In addition, they developed scoring keys based on large samples from multiple organizations and retained items only if they showed validity across multiple organizations. The average observed validity in the prediction of first-line supervisory job performance was .30 (corrected .36), and most of the variability in validity across organizations (i.e., 58%) was accounted for by various artifacts. Moreover, there was little evidence of any large differences in validity as a function of race, sex, education, tenure, or supervisory experience. Rothstein et al.'s results suggest that if one proceeds to develop a biodata inventory with generalization to different contexts in mind, then the end result need not be a key that is situationally specific. However, it is also important to note that this particular set of biodata items and key may or may not generalize to other jobs; that is, biodata are not like cognitive ability tests, which seem to predict well for various occupations.

The most significant attempt undertaken to date to understand the meaning of biodata is found in the research of Owens and his colleagues (Owens, 1968; Owens & Schoenfeldt, 1979; Mumford & Stokes, 1992). Owens and Schoenfeldt (1979) state that the differences in people are the result of differences in developmental patterns, resulting from major life-history experiences. The *developmental integrative* model classifies people according to what has been done to them and what they have done in the past. Biographical information is predictive of future behavior because it signifies prior development of the knowledge, skills, abilities, and other characteristics required of an individual in a new situation. Using the developmental model as the basis for hypotheses, one looks for prior experience in the performance domain in question and those items that may be related to experience in that domain. Individuals learn from prior experiences, are thought to be conditioned to select new situations similar to those previously experienced, and do best in such similar situations. The *ecology model* of biographical information focuses on the motivational influences that result in a pattern of selected situations in which to engage. It is thought that people select situations for the reinforcement value associated with the outcome of such a selection and the potential satisfaction of their needs and values. An individual's pattern of behavior results from his or her seeking situations that are rewarding and rejecting situations where goal attainment fails to satisfy needs and values. Not everyone seeks the same types of experiences, due to differences among subgroups (Mumford & Stokes, 1992). These are two alternative explanations for the results of longitudinal research (Mumford, Stokes, & Owens, 1990; Owens & Schoenfeldt, 1979; Stokes, Mumford, & Owens, 1989) that indicate that subgroups of people tend to behave the same way in similar situations and that subgroups are relatively stable over time.

When interested in performance on a specific job, some researchers have employed a rational or deductive approach to item development, both to select or construct items and to score them. This approach has been used both to provide greater understanding of what was being measured and to overcome some of the instability in scoring keys referred to above. When using this approach, the researcher writes the items to reflect the KSAOs identified in a job analysis as being important to performance of particular job tasks. Mitchell and Klimoski (1982) compared this approach to biodata development with the empirical approach described at the beginning of this section and found that the empirical approach unexpectedly yielded better cross-validity. Based on their review of the literature, Mumford and Stokes (1992) report, however, that rational scaling does provide better scales that produce less shrinkage in criterion-related cross-validation than do empirical approaches. With the empirical approach and a large set of items, the final instrument should reflect the factorial nature of the criterion; if an important KSAO is ignored or dropped in the rational development of a biodata instrument, validity may be lower. This may explain some of the contradictions in this area of research. Another vehicle often used to try to understand the nature of biodata is factor analysis. Because of the number of items in biodata inventories and the noncontinuous nature of the scoring of many items, this method often yields results that are difficult to interpret.

The nature of biodata items has evolved over the past several decades. Originally, biodata items assessed relatively factual and verifiable aspects of the individual's background (e.g., How many siblings do you have? How many sports did you play in high school?). Today, biodata items are often indistinguishable from personality test items (e.g., Of the following statements, which one describes you best? or The kind of supervision I like best . . .). This change to more "personality-like" items has meant that some of the same problems (i.e., faking) that occur with personality tests are also likely to be of concern with the use of biodata. On a more positive note, the relationship between biodata and traditional personality items may yield useful information about the nature of the constructs measured (Mumford & Stokes, 1992).

Biodata have certainly proven to be a valid and reliable selection tool. Data on subgroup differences most often indicate that there are minimal differences in validity and means (Reilly & Chao, 1982). However, the blind empirical approach to scoring key development may sometimes inadvertently lead to items that are related to race or gender (Pace & Schoenfeldt, 1977). In addition, some researchers have reported that different keys must be developed to achieve equivalent validities across subgroups (Life Insurance Marketing Research Association, 1979), and in at least two studies, gender differences were observed on factor scores derived from a biodata inventory (Eberhardt & Muchinsky, 1982; Owens & Schoenfeldt, 1979). As noted above, however, Rothstein et al.'s (1990) work indicates that biodata scales are equally valid for race and gender subgroups. The issue of gender and race differences in both validity and scale means deserves additional attention. Finally, further work should be conducted on the meaning of biodata scales; we strongly prefer a rational and theoretical approach to item and scoring key development, with the usual empirical verification of hypotheses.

Interviews

Anyone who has ever applied for a job has likely encountered the employment interview. Most organizations use the interview in some part of the recruitment and employment process, and many hundreds of studies have assessed the reliability and validity of the employment interview. Early reviews of the interview literature reported relatively negative findings with respect to the psychometric quality of the interview (e.g., Schmitt, 1976; Ulrich & Trumbo, 1965; Wagner, 1949). Beginning with Arvey and Campion's (1982) review, however, there appeared to be evidence that, with certain improvements in the ways in which interviews were conducted, both reliability and validity could be improved. In a recent meta-analytic review of the validity of interviews, McDaniel, Whetzel, Schmidt, and Maurer (1994) found that the average validity of the interview across 160 studies was .20. More important, these authors identify several moderators of interview validity that are related to recent improvements in the conduct of the interview.

Among the improvements that seem to have increased the validity and reliability of the employment interview are the following. The interview content is important; that is, the interview questions are based on the findings of a job analysis and are demonstrably job related. The interview is structured, in that the same questions (and probes, if they are used) are asked of all applicants, and the interviewers use rating scales that specify the nature of good and bad answers to each question (see an example of an interview rating scale in Figure 5.1). Interviewer training that specifies how the interview is to be conducted, provides practice and feedback with respect to the conduct of the interview, and details the types of interviewer errors (e.g., first impression or recency effects, contrast and context effects, similar-to-me effects, and "talking too much" effects) that might serve to diminish the quality of the interview is helpful. This training often includes suggestions as to how to avoid such errors; for example, interviewers are instructed to take notes during the interview and to make their ratings after the interview and after they have reconsidered the responses to all of the interview questions. If possible, the use of multiple independent interviewers whose judgments are combined will usually increase the reliability and validity of the interview. Examples of the use of these "improvements" indicate that the inter-

E. Train, Develop, and Evaluate Associates

Ability to train associates and give feedback, individually or as a group, adapting teaching methods to meet associates' needs and evaluating/testing associates' progress in learning and performing a task.

Low	Moderate	High
• Applicant failed to demonstrate the ability to train or effectively evaluate others.	• Applicant demonstrated a competent level of training ability.	• Applicant demonstrated an exceptional ability to train others.
• May lack a systematic, methodical approach to training or may give training that is disorganized and incoherent.	• Can develop a coherent, systematic training regiment and can effectively impart the information to others.	• Develops highly organized training programs or utilizes novel and ingenious teaching techniques.
• May fail to recognize or acknowledge different learning styles, or may refuse or lack the ability to modify training to the needs of the trainee.	• Develops training programs that are understood by a majority of trainees.	• Is highly proficient at modifying his/her teaching style to the needs of the trainees.
• May be unrealistically critical or overly tolerant of others performance or progress.	• Is generally patient in training situations and demonstrates the ability to evaluate the performance of others.	• Demonstrates the ability to effectively evaluate the progress of others and give feedback that is constructive and targeted at improving performance.
① ②	③ ④ ⑤	⑥ ⑦

Figure 5.1. Example of a Rating Scale Used to Appraise the Answer to Interview Questions Regarding the Ability to Train Subordinates

view can be used very effectively as a selection tool (Campion, Pursell, & Brown, 1988; Pulakos & Schmitt, 1995, 1996). Strong support for the notion that interview validity is increased when the interview is structured and job related is found in the moderator analyses conducted by McDaniel et al. (1994) as well.

Much of the interview research conducted since the work of Webster (1964) has focused on the way in which the interview decision is made and has viewed the interview as a social and information-processing event (e.g., see Dipboye & Gaugler, 1993). This literature has presented evidence for the influence of a variety of biases in causal attributions (i.e., the explanation for the interviewee's behavior is incorrect), rating effects (e.g., halo, leniency, contrast effects), and the influence of irrelevant characteristics of the applicant (e.g., similarity to the interviewer, sex, race). Causal attributions may affect the way in which interview data are encoded and interpreted, but the research in social cognition also suggests that many of the problems with interviewer memory arise from the cognitive representations that interviewers form regarding applicants. Interestingly, this whole body of research seems to be oriented toward the discovery of what *irrelevant* constructs are measured in the interview. One way of viewing the success achieved in recent studies of the interview is that researchers have found ways to control or minimize these irrelevancies or biases. Some of the complexity associated with interview decision making is depicted in Figure 5.2. As this figure shows, the interview decision comes out of the complex interplay among the situation and the characteristics and behavior of both interviewer and interviewee.

We believe that much more attention should be directed toward ascertaining what constructs are measured in an interview. Ulrich and Trumbo (1965) suggest that interpersonal skills and motivation are most validly assessed in interviews. Campion et al. (1988) found high correlations (.27 to .54) between cognitive ability tests and the structured interview. This led them to suggest that the structured interview in their case might represent an orally administered cognitive ability test. This might be true if the questions were similar to those asked on cognitive ability tests, but we doubt it would be the case when the questions asked represent different content or constructs. Most researchers have written about the validity of the interview (and some other methods of measurement as well) as though it makes no difference what might be asked in the interview. The distinction between

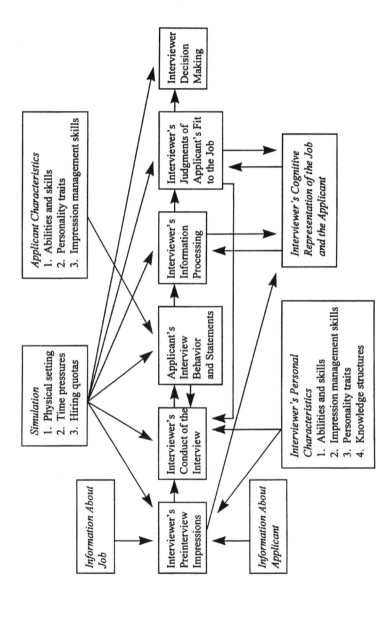

Figure 5.2 Representation of Various Influences on Interview Decisions

Table 5.8   Examples of Experience-Based and Situational Interview Questions

Experience-based questions
  a. Think about a time when you had to motivate an employee to perform a job task that
     he or she disliked but that you needed the individual to do. How did you handle that
     situation?
  b. Think about a time when you were confronted with a serious problem that needed to
     be solved quickly. Tell us about this problem, the steps you took to solve it, and the
     outcome.
Situational questions
  a. Suppose you were working with an employee who you knew greatly disliked
     performing a particular job task. You were in a situation where you needed this task
     completed, and this employee was the only one available to assist you. What would
     you do to motivate the employee to perform this task?
  b. Suppose you were working on the production of a new machine assembly when you
     noticed a quality problem. How would you proceed to identify the cause of the
     problem and correct it?

SOURCE: Pulakos and Schmitt (1995).

test method and test content (Chan & Schmitt, 1997; Schmitt, Clause, &
Pulakos, 1996) is crucial to other areas in personnel selection research
as well, including subgroup differences in test performance and test
reactions. We will return to this important distinction when we discuss
subgroup differences in test performance and reactions in Chapters 7
and 9.

Many of the questions posed in well-developed interviews require
applicants to relate past experiences in particular situations or
how they would react to given situations in the future. Pulakos and
Schmitt (1995) compared the validity of these two types of questions (see
Table 5.8 for examples) and found that experience-based questions
yielded higher validities than did future-oriented situational questions. This finding is consistent with a review by Campion, Campion,
and Hudson (1994), who also found large differences in validity
favoring the experience-based interview ($r = .51$) over the situational
or future-oriented interview ($r = .37$). There is no consensus regarding
the superiority of one format over another (for an opposing view, see
Latham & Sue-Chan, in press), however, and no one has provided an
explanation for the difference in validity. In the case of both types of
questions, interview validity is usually much superior to that reported
in the past for unstructured interviews (e.g., see Schmitt, 1976).

As indicated above, recent studies of interview validity have
reported relatively positive findings. Moreover, the interview is usually

unrelated to other valid parts of a selection battery; hence, its incremental validity is usually quite good (e.g., Pulakos & Schmitt, 1996). Part of this improvement is very likely due to the improved interrater reliability of the interview (Campion et al., 1988; Pulakos & Schmitt, 1995). The most important reliability in the case of the interview is provided by the correlation between ratings supplied by independent interviewers of the same applicants. Large differences in the interrater reliability of the interview have led some investigators to examine the question of interviewer differences in validity. Dipboye, Gaugler, and Hayes (1990), Dougherty, Ebert, and Callender (1986), and Kinicki, Lockwood, Hom, and Griffeth (1990) have all reported very large differences in the validity of different interviewers' judgments. It is usually suggested that these differences arise from differences in how information is gathered and processed. Pulakos, Schmitt, Whitney, and Smith (1996), using a large number of different interviewers ($N = 62$), showed that differences in validity across interviewers could be a function of sampling error.

Race (Parsons & Liden, 1984), gender (Hitt & Barr, 1989), physical attractiveness (Pingitore, Dugoni, Tindale, & Spring, 1994), and age (Avolio & Barrett, 1987) have been related to interviewer judgments, but results have been mixed and are often a function of a complex interaction of several factors (e.g., Heilman, Martell, & Simon, 1988). Most of the studies in this area have been laboratory studies; studies conducted in the field usually indicate relatively small differences between subgroups (Pulakos & Schmitt, 1995, 1996; Schmitt, Clause, & Pulakos, 1996).

Work Samples

In a job or work sample test, an applicant performs a selected set of actual tasks that are psychologically and, sometimes, physically similar to those performed on the job. Perhaps the most common job sample test is the typing test typically given to candidates for a secretarial position. Work samples provide applicants with an opportunity to show that they can perform relatively small and manageable segments of the job tasks or duties. Used as tests, these measures have produced excellent validities (Hunter & Hunter, 1984; Robertson & Kandola,

1982) and lower levels of subgroup differences than traditional cognitive ability or achievement measures (Schmidt, Greenthal, Hunter, Berner, & Seaton, 1977; Schmitt, Clause, & Pulakos, 1996). Often, work samples provide products that can be counted or judged as to quality, and, frequently, the process of work performance can also be judged (Hattrup & Schmitt, 1990). The interrater reliability of product indices is usually quite high, but consistency of performance across tasks in some job samples is quite low, suggesting that different capabilities are being measured. Test-retest reliability is usually adequate, but is probably lower as a function of the number of tasks performed and the degree to which task performance is or is not dependent on equipment differences. Shavelson (1991) reports on a study in which time and tasks accounted for a relatively large portion of the variance in examinees' scores. In addition to the generally positive psychometric characteristics of work samples, most examinees react positively to the use of these tests, presumably because they are credible representations of the jobs for which they are applying (Dreher & Sackett, 1983). These favorable examinee reactions may produce a number of positive side effects (Gilliland, 1993; Smither, Reilly, Millsap, Pearlman, & Stoffey, 1993), such as increased rates of job acceptance, more positive views of the organization and its products, and better subsequent work attitudes, though these causal effects remain to be documented in empirical research.

Work samples also have a number of practical and scientific liabilities. First, most work samples involve only a relatively small number of the total job tasks. The sampling issue was a major stumbling block in the development of work samples in the military (Wigdor & Green, 1991). Second, for jobs in which there are significant physical demands, work sample tests may pose a danger to the examinees. Third, the use of a work sample is appropriate only when the applicants are expected to know and be able to perform the job tasks without training. This particular problem has been addressed to some degree by miniaturized training tests (Siegel, 1983), which require that the examinee actually learn some of the skills necessary to perform the test during the testing session. This idea has been used to develop tests for emergency telephone operators (Schmitt & Ostroff, 1986) and for clerical tasks requiring the use of computers (Schmitt, Gilliland, Landis, & Devine, 1993). A fourth problem is that most work samples are costly to develop, maintain, and administer. They often require expensive equipment, and the testing situation often involves one examiner for each applicant. Fifth, and more theoretically, the work sample is not very informative if one is interested in determining the underlying constructs being measured; most work samples will be multidimensional, and the scoring process rarely allows the isolation of these multiple dimensions. This liability can also be practical in those instances in which the examiner wants to provide feedback to applicants and cannot really isolate the reason for a less-than-adequate test score (Schmitt, Gilliland, et al., 1993). Finally, work samples are likely to be measures of *maximum performance* rather than *typical performance*; the motivational components associated with everyday work performance probably play a minimal role in work sample performance (Sackett, Zedeck, & Fogli, 1988). This difficulty regarding assessment of maximum performance capability versus typical performance levels may not be unique to job sample tests. A similar situation may exist for cognitive ability tests, for example; they measure what a worker *can* do, but not necessarily what he or she *will* do. An analogous situation exists for personality, situational judgment, or motivational measures in the form of social desirability response sets. In one sense, responses to these measures reflect what the applicants say they will do, not necessarily what they actually will do.

Assessment Centers

Assessment centers have been used primarily in managerial selection and promotion. Here, *assessment center* refers to an evaluation method or process rather than a physical location, although typically those being assessed are evaluated in one central physical location. The evaluation process usually includes a day or more of exercises, some of which are meant to replicate, at least psychologically, the major components of the managerial job. The exercises may include paper-and-pencil tests, interviews, in-basket tests (in which participants are given papers, memos, and messages upon which they are required to take action), and group discussions in which the participants are required to interact (cooperate or compete) to resolve some problem or achieve some goal. These exercises and discussions are observed by various trained assessors. At the end of the exercises, the assessors or raters report their observations to each other and are then asked to rate the candidates on various job-related dimensions. Problem analysis, decision making, interpersonal sensitivity, leadership, oral and written communication skills, and organizing or planning ability are some commonly rated dimensions. These ratings are then used as one basis on which selection and promotion decisions are made. Lists of the exercises and dimensions rated in three very different assessment centers are provided in Table 5.9.

Beginning with the early research on assessment centers at AT&T (Bray & Grant, 1966), researchers have reported that the interrater reliability of assessor ratings is high; a meta-analysis of 50 studies of assessor ratings produced an average observed validity of .29 (corrected .37) (Gaugler, Rosenthal, Thornton, & Bentson, 1987). Moreover, examinee reactions to the "face validity" of this technique are usually positive. Positive developmental effects for the assessors have also been reported (Lorenzo, 1984). A large-scale study of more than 13,000 candidates yielded virtually equal estimates of male and female capability (Moses & Boehm, 1975). Schmitt (1993) found a mean difference of approximately .40 standard deviations between minority and majority candidates for school principal jobs.

Assessment centers are obviously time-consuming and expensive to administer. There have also been some questions as to the nature of what gets measured in assessment centers. Klimoski and Brickner (1987) present the hypothesis that individuals who are rated highly in assessment centers are those who can maneuver their way up the promotional ladder in the organization rather than those who are most effective. According to this explanation, assessor ratings correlate with subsequent promotion because assessors, instead of looking for behavioral evidence of the intended dimensions or constructs, in fact make observations and evaluations on the basis of their knowledge of those factors needed to advance in the organization (i.e., to get promoted). Hence, assessors are "capturing the policy" when making assessments in the center, in the sense of attempting to mimic what future decision makers might do in making promotion decisions (Klimoski & Brickner, 1987, p. 247). These policy factors may or may not be based on job performance. Klimoski and Brickner based their hypothesis partly on the fact that most of the reported criterion-related validity studies available at the time of their research had involved the use of number or rate of promotions as criteria. In Gaugler et al.'s (1987) meta-analysis, there was evidence that studies

Table 5.9   Brief Descriptions of Three Different Assessment Centers

| | *Position for Which Candidates Are Evaluated* | | |
	School Administrator	*First-Line Supervisor*	*Middle Manager*
Length of time for candidate evaluation	1 day	1 day	3 days
Length of time for assessor integration meetings	1 day	1 day	2 days
Assessor/candidate ratio	1:2	1:3	1:4
Exercises	In-basket Personal interview Leaderless group discussion of case Role-play exercise with student Role-play exercise with teacher	In-basket Interview Group exercise involving human relations problem Problem-solving group exercise Biographical questionnaire Mechanical test Situational questionnaire	Intelligence test Projective test In-basket Group discussion of case study Assigned role exercise Self-report Personality tests Oral report
Sample of rated dimensions	Communication skills Persuading/motivating Interpersonal sensitivity Visionary leadership Administrative skills Community awareness/involvement	Organizing and planning Analyzing Decision making Controlling Influencing Oral communications Interpersonal relations Flexibility	Judgment Initiative Adaptability Planning and organizing Originality Abstract reasoning Interpersonal sensitivity Impact Technical expertise Oral and written communication

SOURCE: Adapted from Schneider and Schmitt (1986).

using promotion criteria yielded higher validities than those using performance criteria (.40 versus .25 average observed validities), but both validities would normally be practically useful. In a sample of police officers, Chan (1996b) found that assessment center ratings predicted subsequent promotion (within 2 years after assessment) after controlling for the predictability afforded by current supervisory ratings of job performance. This incremental validity has applied value, because many organizations will use assessment center ratings *in addition to* supervisory ratings of performance to make promotional decisions. Chan's finding is consistent with Klimoski and Brickner's (1987) hypothesis. This finding also indicates that assessment center ratings may contain information regarding the potential for success in the target job that is not related to the dimensions or constructs embodied in the supervisory ratings of performance on the current job.

Another major criticism of assessment center ratings relates to their construct validity. Some assessment centers require ratings to be made on the same dimensions in different exercises. Sackett and Dreher (1982) found that within-exercise ratings of different dimensions correlated more highly than cross-exercise ratings of the same dimension. Factor analyses of multiple ratings of the same trait collected as a function of participation in different exercises produce factors defined by the exercises rather than by the dimensions that are thought to be measured (e.g., Bycio, Alvares, & Hahn, 1987). This result has proven to be highly replicable and robust with respect to attempts to minimize the role of these exercise or methods factors (e.g., Schneider & Schmitt, 1992). Center ratings may be related to various performance criteria, but the constructs or traits that account for this relationship remain something of a mystery.

New Technology in Selection

For the past two decades, various paper-and-pencil tests have been administered and scored by computer. When computer hardware and software are available, this is a very cost-effective and rapid way to collect test data. In addition, the past two decades have seen the development and implementation of computer-adaptive tests. In computer-adaptive testing, items are selected from a large bank of items that have been calibrated using item response theory (Hambleton, Swaminathan, & Rogers, 1991). In computer-adaptive testing, each item is matched to the computer's best previous estimate of the person's ability (at the beginning of the test, the test mean is the best estimate), so that the margin of error associated with the computer's estimate of ability is minimized with each new item administered. Computer-adaptive tests have a number of advantages. Accurate measurement of a person's standing on a measure can be obtained with very few items (relative to standard tests), and test security issues are minimal. A different set of items is given to each examinee depending on his or her ability level, so with a sufficiently large bank of calibrated items, there is little likelihood that efforts to "steal" the items will succeed. Computer-adaptive testing has been used primarily with ability tests, but personality test applications are beginning to appear.

In a review of the data on the parallelism of paper-and-pencil tests, computer versions of these tests (sometimes labeled computer-based tests), and computer-adaptive tests, Mead and Drasgow (1993) found that computer-based measures were equivalent to their paper-and-pencil counterparts when the tests were not timed for speed. If speed was a factor in the test, then correlations between paper-and-pencil tests and their computer versions were only moderate (.72). Beyond the speed component, computer-adaptive tests were equivalent to paper-and-pencil tests except that the former were shorter. For example, McBride and Martin (1983) found that their 15-item adaptive tests of verbal ability had better psychometric properties than did conventional computerized tests of 30 items. At this point, computer-adaptive tests can be constructed only when the item pool is unidimensional, though one can always develop computer-adaptive tests of each important construct. In addition to computerized versions of paper-and-pencil tests, computers have also been used to measure perceptual/psychomotor abilities that have proven difficult to assess using paper-and-pencil tests (McHenry, Hough, Toquam, Hanson, & Ashworth, 1990).

Psychologists have also experimented with the video presentation of test stimuli. This mode of testing is particularly useful in presenting work situations in which interactions among people are of interest, or when it may be desirable to minimize the reading requirements of a test and perhaps also minority-majority subgroup differences in test performance. In our own work, for example, we have found that paper-and-pencil situational judgment tests exhibited much larger subgroup differences in test performance (favoring White over Black examinees) than did their video counterparts, and that these differences were attributable to reading requirements in the paper-and-pencil version of the test (Chan & Schmitt, 1997).

In the past decade, rapid advancements in computer, video, and CD-ROM technology have greatly expanded assessment possibilities. Ashworth and McHenry (1993) describe an interactive computer simulation used to select insurance claim adjusters, and Dyer, Desmarais, and Midkiff (1993) report on a similar effort to assess IBM employees. Perhaps the most ambitious of such efforts is described by Drasgow, Olson, Keenan, Moberg, and Mead (1993), who designed a CD-ROM test of managerial skills in which examinees interact with computer people in a simulation. Given the nature of examinees' responses to particular situations, they are directed to different situations or test tasks. This necessitates the development of equivalent scoring keys across different response paths. Such technology provides many opportunities to develop very realistic work samples, but these simulations are very expensive to develop and administer, and are probably not feasible in very many companies or situations. Although the preliminary data regarding the validity of these methods of assessing ability are encouraging (McHenry & Schmitt, 1994; Mead & Drasgow, 1993), we are only beginning to explore the potential of these tests and the nature of the constructs measured in these ways.

Summary and Conclusions

In this chapter we have discussed many different ways of assessing ability, personality, and motivation, but we have not specifically addressed some others, such as interest tests (Hogan & Blake, 1996), situational judgment tests (Motowidlo, Dunnette, & Carter, 1990), peer judgments (Kane & Lawler, 1978), self-assessments (Mabe & West, 1982), and tests of physical abilities (Campion, 1983; Hogan, 1991). For interested readers, the references just cited provide good descriptions of these different measures.

How should personnel selection researchers choose which methods of assessment to employ? First, we believe that the choice process should begin with a consideration of the major KSAOs identified as important to success in performing job tasks. That is why it is important to know what constructs are measured by a test and why data on the "validity" of a particular method of assessment are not as useful as they might be if good information were also available about the constructs measured. It is also why we have included in this chapter a discussion of the correction for attenuation (to provide an assessment of the relationship between the underlying performance construct and the predictor), and why we described exploratory and confirmatory factor analysis in Chapter 4. Second, the researcher should seek out information about the reliability and validity of the method for assessing skills; we have provided such information or sources for that information for all of the methods described above. Third, the researcher should also be interested in how applicants are likely to react to the measures used, based on the belief that this may affect the quality of the information collected, as well as long-term reactions to the organization. Fourth, socially and legally, selection researchers must be aware of the impacts of the measures they choose on various subgroups. Finally, issues of cost and administrative time and effort must be considered, along with the situational context (i.e., the selection ratio, the capability to recruit talented applicants, the expense of training new recruits as opposed to selection) in which selection decisions will be made.

These statements regarding the choice of a selection instrument suggest some of the research issues that need to be addressed. Our knowledge of the constructs measured in the cognitive ability domain, and perhaps the personality area, is relatively good, but much more needs to be done with other selection instruments. First, researchers must avoid talking about the validity of interviews, biodata, personality, and so on. Rather, the questions they address must concern the validity of specific methods (e.g., interviews) for the assessment of different constructs. If research begins with a clearly articulated statement of the nature of the performance construct, and the selection or development of predictor instruments is tied to the KSAOs judged to be involved in the performance of this construct, the analyst will be better able to understand and interpret the relationships between predictor and construct. The inclusion of measures that are well understood in a test battery and the correlations of new or experimental measures with these better-known measures can provide the basis for the interpretation of new measures. Use of factor analysis, both confirmatory and exploratory, can also be helpful in the interpretation of the underlying constructs measured.

Construct issues are particularly difficult for some methods of data collection, such as the assessment center, situational judgment tests, and work samples. These methods of data collection do not allow for the disaggregation of the applicant's responses in item-level units, and the scores derived from these instruments are often by their nature multidimensional. Work on the construct validity of assessment centers suggests that the test performance situation in which worker

KSAOs are measured may be very important; more work needs to be done on the nature of these situations and the interactions between individual differences and these situations.

The use of new technology described above provides selection researchers with new challenges and opportunities to measure new constructs. For example, it may be possible to teach a candidate new concepts and directly measure his or her capacity to learn new material. Such learning ability is likely to be more important in the future if changes in jobs and technology continue to escalate. At the same time, selection researchers should be interested in measuring individuals' willingness to adapt and learn. Computers also expand opportunities to collect data. For example, some researchers have experimented with the use of reaction time measures and the possibility that these may indicate efforts to deceive in personality. Reaction time measures may also represent alternate ways to measure ability on tests of cognitive ability or aptitudes.

Even though most efforts to find job-irrelevant demographic correlates of measures of KSAOs have been unsuccessful, these efforts should continue. In trying to find race, age, and gender correlates of test performance, it is necessary that researchers have firm theoretical reasons to suspect differences before they proceed. Without such hypotheses, it is almost certain that any post hoc explanations of differences will be confusing and tentative, as has been true in the past. Whitney and Schmitt (1997) provided choices on a biodata instrument that reflected hypothesized differences between Black and White respondent subgroups. When responses across individuals from different cultures correspond to the values implicit in those cultures, the researcher can have more confidence in his or her interpretation of these differences, and can expect that the findings will replicate. Demographic differences research that does not begin with such a priori hypotheses will not likely contribute to the understanding of any observed differences.

Thus far, we have discussed the importance of a theory of performance and how that theory gets translated into measures of performance. We have also discussed taxonomies or theories of human characteristics and, in this chapter, how those characteristics are measured and the quality of some of these measurements. In Chapter 6, we discuss how research is designed and data are analyzed to evaluate our hypotheses about KSAO-performance relationships.

6 Estimating
KSAO-Performance
Relationships

In the preceding chapters, we have described the ways in which personnel selection researchers study jobs and form hypotheses or theories about KSAO-performance relationships. In this chapter, we describe the research designs and the methods of collecting and analyzing data used to evaluate these hypotheses and theories. This process of designing research and testing theories of KSAO-performance relationships is usually referred to as *test validation.* In Chapter 5, in describing very briefly the concept of validity, we indicated that validity is the degree to which the inferences we draw from test scores are accurate. When a retail salesclerk is required to take an honesty test as a condition for employment, the inference made by the employer is that the individual's score will tell him or her something about the probability that the employee will engage in theft or reveal confidential information. Or when a prospective CEO is evaluated using the procedures described in Example 4 in Chapter 1, the inference is that the judgments about the applicant made by board members or others with access to selection procedure data will tell them something about the applicant's capability to direct the company productively.

Validation of tests can proceed in several different ways, and usually researchers will attempt to collect a variety of evidence to support these inferences. In the 1998 version of the *Standards for Educational and Psychological Testing* (AERA, APA, & NCME, 1998), the types of inferences made are summarized using the model depicted in our Figure 3.1 in Chapter 3, which is adapted from Binning and Barrett (1989). In this figure, the numbers 1 through 5 represent five different inferences. Inferences 2 and 4 involve the notion that the actual measures or operationalizations of a particular KSAO or performance construct are appropriate. These inferences are supported by the thoroughness with which a job and its KSAO requirements are analyzed and by the manner in which the performance domain is conceptualized or defined. Much of our discussion in Chapters 2 through 5 is relevant to these inferences. Inference 1 refers to the degree that scores on a test (predictors) relate to workers' status on some performance measure. A great deal of the research in personnel selection has concentrated on the correlation between predictors and criterion, and for some predictor-criterion relationships, huge bodies of literature exist that have been summarized using the meta-analytic techniques described later in this chapter. Inference 3 involves the relationships between KSAO constructs and performance constructs, or the "true" validity of a KSAO. To the degree that the measures of predictor and criterion are adequate representations of the underlying ability and performance constructs, the empirical relationship between predictor and criterion (Inference 1) is an appropriate estimate of the strength of the relationship between the constructs (Inference 3).

Inference 5 is the relationship of most interest in personnel selection research; that is, we want to know to what degree our fallible measures of applicant KSAOs are associated with the underlying performance construct. As scientists, we are likely most interested in Inference 3, but as scientist-practitioners who must use a predictor that is a less-than-perfect representation of the underlying KSAO construct, we are most concerned with the inferences we make using this imperfect predictor about the performance construct. As we have addressed various aspects of predictor and criterion development in earlier chapters (i.e., Inferences 2 and 4), we devote most of this chapter to a discussion of the ways in which researchers develop evidence regarding the linkage between predictor and criterion (Inference 1) and use that evidence to support their conclusions about Inferences 3 and 5. It should be noted that these methods were used to generate the data on test validity summarized in Chapter 5. In dealing with data analyses issues, we will describe those procedures that are peculiar to validation research in some detail. We will not address more general data analysis procedures, such as regression analysis, as there are many comprehensive textbooks available on correlation and regression.

Research Design in Criterion-Related Validation Research

The basic research paradigm in criterion-related validation of tests is to collect test or predictor score data and job performance data and to compute the correlation between these two sets of data as an estimate of the validity of the test. There are two basic research designs. In *predictive criterion-related* studies, information on the required KSAOs is collected prior to the making of any hiring decisions. Hiring decisions are made without using these data, ideally on a random basis. After employees have had an opportunity to learn the job and performance has become relatively stable, measures of job performance are collected. The predictor measures (administered prior to hiring) are then correlated with the job performance or criterion measures. Obviously, implementation of this predictive design requires a significant period of time. In those instances in which the numbers of employees hired during a given period are low and the job requirements are complex, it may be several years before a large enough number of new employees has been hired to allow for an adequate estimate of the validity of the test.

In most criterion-related research, a *concurrent, criterion-related* design is employed. In this case, predictor and criterion data are collected simultaneously from a group of job incumbents. Concurrent validity studies differ from predictive studies in two ways: in the time required to conduct the study and in the research participants. These differences produce some threats to the quality of the evidence regarding predictor-criterion relationships. The research participants may be less motivated to do well on the tests than would job applicants, and to the extent that experience on the job influences performance on the test (which might be a significant problem when the tests are developed to be samples of the actual job tasks), the estimate of the validity of the tests may be distorted. Sussmann and Robertson (1986) point out that the distinction between concurrent and predictive designs is too simplistic. These researchers identified 11 different validation designs that vary in terms of the timing of the measurement of predictor and criterion, the degree to which the new and experimental tests are used, and the type of participant in the research (incumbent versus applicant). They then compared the research designs on the various facets of validity described by Cook and Campbell (1976): statistical conclusion validity, internal and external validity, and construct validity. Their analysis of the strengths and weaknesses of various criterion-validation designs is particularly informative and should be consulted routinely by any researcher planning a project of this type. Although it seems that these design differences should have some impact on estimates of criterion-related validity, there seems to be little empirical difference in the validities reported in concurrent versus predictive research (Schmitt, Gooding, Noe, & Kirsch, 1984).

A concurrent criterion-related validation design was used to support the use of the selection procedures developed in Example 1, described in Chapter 1. In that case, current investigative agents were asked to respond to all selection procedures at the same time that supervisors evaluated the agents' job performance. The agency for which the project was conducted clearly provided significant support and emphasized its desire that all participants respond to the best of their ability. Participants were also given assurances that no test data would be released to agency personnel or supervisors. Likewise, supervisors from whom performance ratings were collected were assured that the ratings they made were for research purposes only, and that no agency personnel would have access to them. Even with these necessary and helpful assurances, it seemed strange to many participants to be interviewed and evaluated for a job they already held.

As we have noted in earlier chapters, support for the selection procedures used in Examples 3 and 4 described in Chapter 1 came solely from the test construction process itself. In these studies, the researchers were concerned with Inferences 1 and 3 in Figure 3.1, typically labeled content validity or construct validity. Personnel selection researchers want to know that a test includes all relevant aspects of the construct with which they are concerned. In these examples, the following steps were critical: (a) job analysis that carefully specifies what workers do; (b) job analysis that details what KSAOs are required to perform the job tasks; (c) construction or selection of measures of the KSAOs that reflect as nearly as possible the format and difficulty level of the job tasks from which they were derived; (d) analysis of the measurement properties, including reliability, of the measures produced; and (e) review of the examination procedures to establish that there are appropriate linkages between job tasks and KSAOs and between KSAOs and test items or procedures. The role of subject matter experts' judgments is critical. These steps are detailed by Goldstein, Zedeck, and Schneider (1993).

Importance of Criteria

In the assessment of validity using criterion-related research designs, the criterion is central. If the criterion measure is inappropriate, then estimates of the validity of the test to which it is correlated will be distorted, most likely in unknown ways. Traditional analyses of the criterion begin with the notion that there is an ideal or ultimate criterion. This ultimate criterion may be the overall lifetime contribution of an individual to an organization. Overlap between the ultimate criterion and the actual measures of job performance represents the degree to which the actual criterion measure is *relevant*. If aspects of the ultimate criterion are not part of the actual measure (e.g., a salesperson's courtesy with customers is an aspect of the ultimate criterion and the actual measure used is sales volume), the criterion measure is said to be *deficient*. A predictor measure designed to rate a person's ability to relate in a courteous manner to customers may not correlate with sales volume because the latter is a deficient criterion measure and not because the predictor is unrelated to the ultimate criterion. Of equal concern are those instances in which the criterion measure is partly a function of behavior or worker characteristics that have nothing to do with the ultimate criterion. These aspects of the criterion measure represent what has been called *contamination*. Of special concern are those contaminants related to the demographic characteristics of the workers, but there are also instances in which some workers have special opportunities that others do not have, such as a secretary with new word-processing equipment and software. If this person's performance is compared with that of others who are still working with typewriters or outdated hardware and software, he or she will have an unfair advantage.

A particularly difficult situation occurs when a predictor is correlated with the contamination or bias in a criterion measure. In instances of such *predictor-related criterion bias,* the research will indicate that a predictor is important when in fact it predicts the bias or contamination in an outcome measure. An example would be a case in which supervisors provide the performance ratings that are used as a criterion, and some supervisors mistakenly believe that all members of a particular group perform poorly and so do not really make an effort to evaluate the performance of members of that group. If a predictor is related to group membership, as is true in some cases (see Chapter 5), then that predictor's validity may be overestimated as a function of its relationship with what amounts to bias. Studies of predictor-related criterion bias are very rare because of the difficulties of defining and measuring the constructs of interest as well as the bias.

Schmitt, Pulakos, Nason, and Whitney (1996) provide an example of the difficulty of identifying such bias; in their study, there was no evidence that bias affected the estimate of predictor validity. These researchers used the data collected as a pilot for the work described in Example 1 in Chapter 1. They hypothesized that perceived interpersonal similarity and likability of raters to ratees in the interview and role-play simulations, as well as raters and ratees on the performance end of the KSAO-performance relationship, might constitute a form of predictor-related criterion bias. Using measures of perceived similarity on social and political bases and leisure activities and social (as opposed to work-related) likability, they found that sociability and likability were related to interview- and role-play-generated ratings of KSAOs as well as supervisory ratings of job performance, but none of these "biases" affected predictor and criterion in the same way. Hence, there was no effect on the estimates of predictor-criterion relationships.

As mentioned above, subgroup differences in performance have been of particular concern in selection research. When those differences occur on the criterion, there is always concern as to whether these differences represent bias or are evidence of real subgroup performance differences. This is especially true when the performance measure is a rating that may be subject to various rater errors or biases. In a review of the literature in which both African American and White raters have evaluated members of the opposite race subgroup, Kraiger and Ford (1985) found that African American and White raters assigned slightly higher ratings to ratees of their own race than to ratees of the other race. Ratee race effects were found to be largest in field studies in which the African American group represented a small percentage of the workforce. In a follow-up study, Ford, Kraiger, and Schechtman (1986) found similar differences between these two subgroups for objective performance criteria and subjective criteria (i.e., ratings) when both sets of criteria were collected on the same research participants. In a military study that included nearly 40,000 participants, Pulakos, White, Oppler, and Borman (1989) found significant differences across gender and race of ratee, as well as interactions between rater and ratee demographic standings. However, these main effects and interactions accounted for only tiny amounts of the variance in ratings. This study is particularly convincing, because in a large number of cases both African American and White raters were available to rate members of the same and different racial subgroups.

The studies mentioned above (i.e., Ford et al., 1986; Kraiger & Ford, 1985; Pulakos et al., 1989) may be reassuring with respect to the presence of bias related to race and gender, but there may remain subtle forms of bias. The work of Heilman and her colleagues has explored the notion that minimal overall effects for gender do not rule out the presence of stereotypic decision making on the part of raters. Heilman and Saruwatari (1979) found that women who were attractive seemed to be disadvantaged by their appearance when they applied for managerial jobs. This attractiveness disadvantage was even more pronounced for managerial women in the evaluation of their work and in their likelihood of being recommended for organizational rewards (Heilman & Stopeck, 1985a). Heilman and Stopeck (1985b) found that the success of high-level corporate personnel was more likely to be attributed to ability, as opposed to luck, in the case of attractive men than in the case of attractive women. Heilman and Martell (1986) found that gender discrimination could be overcome, provided there had been previous exposure to multiple women in the occupation for which personnel evaluations were being made. Heilman, Martell, and Simon (1988) also found that very competent women were overvalued relative to male applicants for extremely male sex-typed jobs, but that otherwise women were undervalued. The work of Heilman and her colleagues is relevant because it underscores the subtleties of bias and the importance of the context in which evaluation takes place. Because of the obvious social implications of decisions that affect members of demographic subgroups, it is important that personnel selection researchers and practitioners continue to examine the criteria used to assess worker performance.

In conducting this research, it is important that researchers have clear notions of the nature of the predictor and performance constructs as well as theories about the manner in which contaminating factors influence the measurement of these factors. Finding that race and sex differences influence these measurements is not very helpful unless one also knows the psychological mechanisms responsible for these differences. When these mechanisms are understood, it is more likely that appropriate remedial action can be taken. The work of Heilman and her colleagues and that of Schmitt, Pulakos, et al. (1996) represent examples of research in which specific hypotheses about the nature of potential contaminants have been tested.

In this section, we have talked of the ultimate criterion as though the performance of individuals in a work situation could be reduced to a single number. It should be obvious that this is unrealistic if the theories of performance discussed in Chapter 3 are realistic and when the criterion is multidimensional. In these instances, each dimension of the performance construct may have different problems related to contamination or deficiency as well as different KSAO determinants. The measurement and use of a specific criterion measure against which to validate predictors is further complicated if and when the criterion changes over time, as was also suggested by research reviewed in Chapter 3. If the performance construct changes with time, then the time frame or tenure of study participants becomes an important consideration in the conduct of a validity study. Some KSAOs may be very relevant if performance is assessed early in workers' careers and relatively irrelevant later in their careers.

Estimating the
Predictor-Criterion Relationship

As indicated above, the estimate of the criterion-related validity of a predictor is provided by the correlation between the predictor and the criterion. This correlation assumes that the distribution of predictor and criterion measures is normal and that the relationship between the predictor and the criterion is linear. The nature of the underlying distribution of variables in psychological research is unverifiable; we can develop tests to select items so that the distribution of test scores is normal, or we can transform raw test scores so that the end result is a normal distribution. In either case, however, the assumption of normality cannot be proved or disproved.

The linearity assumption can be evaluated, and it has been in numerous studies. The overwhelming evidence is that the relationship between predictor and criterion is linear, at least given common operationalizations of these variables and within the range of scores normally investigated in criterion-related validation research. Perhaps the most thorough confirmation of the linearity of the predictor-criterion relationship has been carried out by Coward and Sackett (1990). Using 174 studies (average sample size of 210) of the relationship between nine scales of the GATB and job performance, these researchers found evidence for nonlinear relationships at less than chance levels.

Very often, more than one selection procedure is used, and in such an instance, the researcher computes a multiple correlation between the predictors and the criterion. This multiple correlation is a function of the validities of the individual predictors and their intercorrelations. The correlation matrix among the predictors and their standard deviations is used to produce a weighting of each predictor that optimizes prediction in the sense that squared errors of prediction of the criterion are minimized (for explanations and computational formulas for multiple correlation and regression, see, e.g., Cohen & Cohen, 1983). Predictors will receive large weights in these prediction equations if they are correlated well with the criterion and not correlated with other predictors in the system. Their lack of correlation with the other predictors means that they are explaining variance in the outcome measure that is nonredundant with that explained by other predictors.

Even when the design of a criterion-related study is relatively optimal and the assumptions underlying the computation of a correlation coefficient are met, the observed correlation between predictor(s) and criterion may be an inaccurate estimate of the criterion-related validity. In the following subsections we describe several of these problems and how, with some reasonable assumptions, a researcher can estimate the magnitude of their effects on the estimation of criterion-related validity.

Restriction of Range

One problem associated with the conduct of criterion-related research in organizations is called restriction of range. Organizations are understandably reluctant to hire individuals on a random basis or to wait until a test is validated before using it to make decisions, as is required for research design reasons. Frequently, tests are used to make decisions while validation data are being collected, or alternate measures correlated with the experimental measures are used to make decisions. If the organization rejects low-scoring individuals on these tests, no criterion data can be collected for these persons and they cannot be included in the validation study. In the case of concurrent validation studies, it is also probable that some of the low-scoring people have failed and been fired or left the organization and that some of the high-scoring people have been promoted out of the position. Another instance in which restriction of range can occur takes place when an organization employs a sequential strategy of making hiring decisions. For example, an organization may use a short screening test to eliminate some people, then a longer battery to assess skills in more depth, and an interview or assessment center to evaluate the remaining candidates. If the procedures used at different steps in this strategy are correlated, the scores on the tests used in the latter stages will be restricted. In the extreme, the problem of restriction of range is analogous to the conduct of an experimental study with a single level of the independent variable—that is, no relationship can be found because there is no variation to begin with.

Fortunately, the observed validity coefficient for range restriction can be corrected *if* the scores of all hired and rejected applicants have been retained and the standard deviations of the applicants' scores on the selection instruments can be computed. The corrected validity coefficient can then be computed using the following formula:

$$r_{xyc} = \frac{r_{xy}\left(\frac{SD_u}{SD_r}\right)}{\left(1 - r_{xy}^2 + r_{xy}^2\left(\frac{SD_u^2}{SD_r^2}\right)\right)^{1/2}}, \qquad [6.1]$$

where r_{xyc} and r_{xy} are, respectively, the corrected and uncorrected validities and SD_u and SD_r are, respectively, the unrestricted and restricted standard deviations. Consider a reasonably realistic situation in which the observed validity coefficient is .30 and half the applicants are accepted. With half of the applicants selected, the standard deviation of the selected group, assuming a normal distribution of test scores, is about 6.0 if the total applicant group's standard deviation was 10. Using these data and Formula 6.1, the corrected validity coefficient would be as follows:

$$r_{xyc} = \frac{.30\left(\frac{10}{6}\right)}{\left(1 - .09 + .09\left(\frac{100}{36}\right)\right)^{1/2}} = .46.$$

The corrected validity of .46 clearly indicates that the test has a higher functional validity than the empirically observed coefficient of .30. Similar corrections for the case of indirect restriction of range should be made when appropriate. Indirect restriction occurs when a test correlated with the experimental test is being used to make hiring decisions or when a sequential strategy is used and the tests used in earlier stages of the hiring processes are correlated with those used at later stages (see Thorndike, 1949). The latter correction for indirect restriction of range will not produce corrections as large as corrections for direct restriction in range.

These corrections are made to bivariate correlations—one at a time. Occasionally, selection researchers will use several predictors simultaneously and have data on the full range of scores on a subset of the total measures. Lawley (1943) has presented a general multivariate correction for range restriction in these situations. Rather than each validity coefficient being corrected separately, all of the correlations are corrected in one procedure considering the complete variance-covariance matrix. This multivariate correction, with formulas and a demonstration of its use, can be found in Ree, Carretta, Earles, and Albert (1994). A software program to make this correction is described by Johnson and Ree (1994), and differences between the bivariate corrections and the multivariate correction for one set of data are provided by Schmitt, Toney, and Ree (1997).

Corrections for Unreliability in the Criterion

In the discussion of the inferences involved in criterion-related research, we noted that the primary interest is in the inference from a predictor measure to the performance construct. In our earlier discussion on bias, we focused on systematic influences on the measurement of the criterion as a source of distortion of evidence on predictor-criterion relationships. Measures of the criterion can also be distorted because of measurement error or unreliability. This unreliability has the effect of diminishing the size of the correlations between predictor and criterion. Fortunately, these underestimates can be corrected if an appropriate estimate of the reliability of the criterion is available. This correction is referred to as the correction for attenuation due to unreliability. The general form of this formula is as follows:

$$r_{xyc} = \frac{r_{xy}}{r_{xx'}^{1/2} \, r_{yy'}^{1/2}} \qquad\qquad [6.2]$$

where r_{xyc}, r_{xy}, r_{xx}, and r_{yy} are the corrected and observed validity coefficients and the reliabilities of the predictor and criterion, respectively. In criterion-related research, the accepted approach is to correct for the unreliability of the criterion only because of the interest in Inference 5 in Figure 3.1. That is, we would remove $r_{xx'}^{1/2}$ from Formula

6.2 when performing the correction. If our interest were in estimating the true relationship between the predictor and criterion constructs ruling out the effects of measurement error, we would correct for unreliability in both measures as it is expressed in Formula 6.2. The effects of measurement error will serve to lower estimates of predictor-criterion relationships, but they will not have as serious an effect as will restriction of range. For example, even with a relatively low criterion reliability of .49, an empirical estimate of validity will be 70% (i.e., the square root of .49) as large as the "true" relationship.

The combination of restriction of range problems and criterion unreliability serves to produce empirical estimates of criterion-related validity that are inaccurately low. Schmidt, Hunter, and Urry (1976) display the impact of these two problems on estimates of criterion-related validity estimates for a range of situations. They also draw attention to the fact that when criterion-related research is conducted under these circumstances, the likelihood that a researcher will find a statistically significant relationship between the predictor and criterion is often quite low, particularly given the sample sizes usually available. This finding led Schmidt et al. to develop methods of aggregating research on validity coefficients estimating and correcting for the effects of various artifacts to estimate much more precisely the true level of the accuracy of inferences about performance. Their approach to meta-analysis is described in detail in *Methods of Meta-analysis* (Hunter & Schmidt, 1990b), and the basics of their approach are outlined below. In Chapter 5, we cited and summarized the results of many of these meta-analytic studies as related to predictor-criterion relationships in personnel selection.

The sample sizes available to researchers estimating predictor-criterion relationships seem to have improved in general (Schmitt, Gooding, et al., 1984), and there have been some studies in which the sample sizes have been such that there is very little sampling error. For example, the Project A studies include many thousands of individuals (see "Project A," 1990). Although these larger sample sizes reduce the likelihood that we will incorrectly conclude a test is not valid using statistical significance testing logic, the two problems (i.e., range restriction and criterion unreliability) still result in underestimates of the validity, and corrections for these artifacts should be made using appropriate estimates of reliability (Schmidt & Hunter, 1996) and

Table 6.1   Effects of Range Restriction and Criterion Unreliability on Validity Estimates

Predictors	Observed Correlations	Corrected for Range Restriction	Corrected for Unreliability
	Average Core Investigative Rating		
Cognitive ability	.21	.30	.41
Situational judgment	.20	.28	.38
Biodata	.22	.24	.33
Health fraud	.22	.28	.38
Structured interview	.34	.34	.47
	Average Effort and Professionalism Rating		
Situational judgment	.13	.17	.24
Biodata	.25	.25	.35
Structured interview	.35	.35	.49

NOTE: Corrections for unreliability were based on correlations between first-line and principal relief supervisor ratings. They were .53 for Core Investigative Proficiency and .50 for Effort and Professionalism.

estimates of range restriction based on the degree of range restriction that occurred in the sample(s) from which validity estimates were derived.

An example of the application of attenuation and restriction of range corrections is provided in Table 6.1. The data in the table were collected from job incumbents and applicants in the project described in Example 1 in Chapter 1. Data were collected on a group of 253 applicants to estimate unrestricted standard deviations for the paper-and-pencil tests used in the final selection battery. These estimates and similar restricted estimates of the standard deviations obtained from analysis of the incumbents' responses were used to make corrections to the obtained validity coefficients. Software provided by Ree (Johnson & Ree, 1994) was used to make these multivariate range restriction corrections. The observed validities are presented in the second column of Table 6.1, and the values corrected for range restriction are displayed in the third column. Additional corrections for unreliability in the criterion (estimated as shown in the note to Table 6.1) provide the estimates of validity contained in the last column of the table. Clearly, these corrections make a great deal of difference in our estimates of KSAO-performance relationships, and they should be applied when reasonable estimates of applicant and research participant standard deviations are available and criterion reliability can be estimated.

Estimates of Cross-Validated Multiple Correlation

As mentioned above, when selection researchers evaluate the multiple correlation of a battery of selection procedures, it is customary for them to weight these predictors using multiple regression. These weights are optimal weights in the sense that they maximize the relationship between predictors and criterion, but they are sample specific and will produce overestimates of the degree to which this set of predictors multiplied by the regression weights derived in a specific sample will predict a criterion in another sample. This second sample is referred to as the *cross-validation sample.* The overestimate of the cross-validated correlation is a function of the sample size, the number of predictors, and the degree of relationship between the predictors and the criterion.

One way of estimating the degree to which the weights derived in one sample will provide good prediction in another sample is to derive this estimate empirically. That is, weights are estimated in one sample from a population and these weights are then used to weight predictors in another sample from the same population, and the correlation between this weighted composite and the criterion measures in the second sample is taken as the estimate of cross-validated R. However, there are at least two reasons this is not an optimal solution to the estimation of R. First, it is a single estimate of the utility of these regression weights and is also subject to sampling error (Schmitt, Coyle, & Rauschenberger, 1977). Second, researchers often do not have available multiple samples, and total sample size is often not large enough to split into two groups—one to derive the weights and the other to estimate cross-validated R.

A second, more appropriate, approach is to estimate the cross-validated R by formula. The appropriate formula for use in estimating the population cross-validity is one presented by Cattin (1980). The population cross-validity is the value we would expect to get if we had an infinite number of samples available upon which to estimate cross-validity and we computed the average value of cross-validity across these samples. The formula used to compute the population cross-validity is as follows:

$$\rho_c^2 = \frac{\{[(N-k-3)\,\rho^4]+\rho^2\}}{\{[(N-2k-2)\,\rho^2]+k\}}, \tag{6.3}$$

where ρ_c is the population cross-validity, ρ is the population multiple correlation given by Wherry's formula (presented below), k is the number of predictors, and N is the sample size of the group upon which the weights were derived. Wherry's formula, which follows, provides an estimate of the degree of relationship between the predictors and the criterion in the population from which the sample is derived:

$$\rho^2 = 1 - \left[\frac{(N-1)}{(N-k-1)}\right](1-R^2), \tag{6.4}$$

where R is the multiple correlation between the predictors and the criterion in the sample from which the regression weights are derived and N and k are defined as above.

If N were 80, k were 12, and R were .40, the Wherry formula would produce the following calculation of the population multiple correlation:

$$\rho = \left\{1 - \left[\frac{(80-1)}{(80-12-1)}\right](1-.40^2)\right\}^{\frac{1}{2}} = .10.$$

The population cross-validity would be

$$\rho_c = \left(\frac{\{[(80-12-3)\,.1^4]+.1^2\}}{\{[(80-24-2)\,.1^2]+12\}}\right)^{\frac{1}{2}} = .04.$$

These formulas should always be used to estimate cross-validity, although there are two precautions. First, researchers often look at observed validities for a large number of predictors before deciding to do regression analysis on a subset of especially promising predictors.

In this case, the k in the formulas above should be the total number of predictors whose validities were estimated and examined. Second, when the ratio of N to k is less than approximately 3, the formula estimate of cross-validated R is likely to be inaccurate, because the sample R is likely to be inaccurate. In this latter instance, there is little alternative but to rely on an actual empirical estimate of cross-validity, although it would be wise to recognize that sampling error will play a significant role in determining the adequacy of this single estimate of cross-validity (Murphy, 1983).

To this point, we have discussed statistical problems that influence correlational estimates of the predictor-criterion relationship estimated in a single study. Two of these problems (range restriction and criterion unreliability) result in underestimates of the validity of a test and can be corrected by Formulas 6.1 and 6.2, presented above. The third statistical problem occurs when multiple predictors are weighted as a result of regression analysis. The multiple correlation resulting from this analysis is an overestimate of the cross-validated criterion-related validity of this battery. We have also provided a correction formula (6.3) to estimate the population cross-validity of regression-weighted composites. Single-study estimates of criterion-related validity, even when these three corrections are applied appropriately, are never as accurate as multiple studies of the same relationship; in the next section, we describe methods of analysis designed to provide an aggregated estimate of criterion-related validity of tests.

Aggregating Results From Validation Research to Assess Predictor-Criterion Relationships

Relationships between many KSAO constructs and performance constructs have been investigated numerous times. Researchers often have slightly different reasons for collecting these data, may employ different operationalizations of key constructs, and may use different research designs. Moreover, they often work within different organizational or situational constraints (e.g., labor markets, applicant demographics, sample sizes). The results of these different studies have often produced very different estimates of the validity of measures of the same construct or even the same test. For many years, selection researchers thought that the differences in research methods employed and differences in situations were responsible for the differences in observed validity of tests. Beginning in the late 1970s, Schmidt and Hunter (1977) developed procedures that have been used to demonstrate that much of the variability in observed validity coefficients is due to various study artifacts. The major artifacts investigated have been sampling error and differences across studies in the degree of range restriction and criterion unreliability. Schmidt and Hunter's meta-analysis methods have been employed to aggregate studies of many different KSAO measures and criteria, with the usual conclusions being that most procedures have nonzero validity for the prediction of important organizational outcomes and that those validities generalize quite well across study situations, with sampling error alone accounting for most of the variability in validity coefficients. In this section, we present a very basic form of meta-analysis using a correction for sampling error only. Schmitt and Klimoski (1991) offer a more complete description of meta-analytic reviews, and Hunter and Schmidt (1990b) provide a comprehensive treatment of meta-analytic methods and research.

Meta-analysis is the statistical analysis of the summary findings of many empirical studies. In such analysis, effect size data and data regarding study characteristics are coded from the original research reports. Before the data coding begins, the researcher should undertake a careful reading of the research literature, so that he or she clearly understands the domain of research studies available and the major dimensions along which studies in a given domain vary. This allows the researcher to formulate hypotheses regarding any potential moderators of the strength of predictor-criterion relationships. The researcher then trains the data coders and, as coding proceeds, monitors their accuracy and consistency in coding the primary research studies.

Summary estimates of effect size (predictor-criterion correlations, in this instance) are easily obtained. The average correlation across studies, $\bar{r}$, is usually weighted by the sample size in the study that produced the correlation as follows:

$$\bar{r} = \frac{\Sigma(N_i r_i)}{\Sigma N_i},$$
[6.5]

where r_i is the correlation recorded from Study i, Σ represents a summation over the total set of studies i, and N_i is the sample size in Study i. The variance of the observed relationships across studies is given as follows:

$$\sigma_{obs}^2 = \frac{[(1-\bar{r}^2)^2 k]}{\Sigma N_i}. \qquad [6.6]$$

If the researcher is interested in assessing the degree to which validity across studies is accounted for by sampling error, then the variance of sampling error can be calculated as follows:

$$\sigma_e^2 = \frac{[(1-\bar{r}^2)^2 k]}{\Sigma N_i}, \qquad [6.7]$$

where k is the number of studies. This formula uses the average r across studies as an estimate of the population correlation.

Table 6.2 displays a hypothetical set of data resulting from 10 studies of the relationship between interview ratings and performance ratings for two different forms of an interview. As can be seen, the average observed validity of the interview, $\bar{r}$, is .38. The variance of these validities, σ_r^2, is .0076, but .0033 or 43% of this variance is accounted for by variance in sampling error, σ_e^2, alone. Schmidt, Hunter, and their colleagues list a variety of other artifacts that may produce variability in estimated coefficients, such as unreliability in the measured variables, differences in the variability of one or more of the measured variables, differences in the factor structure of the measured variables, and differences in reporting errors. As indicated above, the portion of variance attributable to sampling error appears to account for most of the variability in the validity of tests (Schmidt & Hunter, 1981; Schmidt, Hunter, Pearlman, & Hirsh, 1985). However, the portion of variance due to sampling error will be dependent on sample size (McDaniel, Hirsh, Schmidt, Raju, & Hunter, 1986), and with larger sample sizes, other artifacts are likely to account for a larger portion of the variability in coefficients across studies. Unfortunately, actual data on these other artifacts are often unavailable. Given that their effects are likely minimal for the sample sizes usually available, it may be best to correct only for variability in sampling error. Correction

Table 6.2   An Application of Meta-Analytic Formulas to the Relationship Between Hypothetical Interview Ratings and Job Performance Ratings

Study	Type of Interview Question	N_i	r_i	N_ir_i	$r_i - \bar{r}$	$N_i(r_i - \bar{r})^2$
1	Experience based	57	.38	21.66	.00	.00
2	Situational	72	.19	13.68	−.19	2.60
3	Situational	98	.23	22.54	−.15	2.21
4	Experience based	212	.41	86.92	.03	.19
5	Situational	70	.23	16.10	−.15	1.58
6	Experience based	580	.39	226.20	.01	.06
7	Experience based	320	.50	160.00	.12	4.61
8	Situational	79	.26	20.54	−.12	1.14
9	Situational	412	.31	129.58	−.07	2.02
10	Experience based	291	.47	136.77	.09	2.36
		2191		833.99		16.77

$\bar{r}$ = (833.99)/2191 = .38

σ_r^2 = 16.77/2191 = .0076

σ_e^2 = 7.3/2191 = .0033

Summary of Moderator Analysis for the Interview-Performance Relationship

Situational Interview		Experience-Based Interviews	
$\bar{r}$ =	.28	$\bar{r}$ =	.43
σ_r^2 =	.0019	σ_r^2 =	.0022
σ_e^2 =	.0063	σ_e^2 =	.0028
σ_ρ^2* =	.0044	σ_ρ^2* =	.0008

*Indicates the population variability.

formulas for other errors do exist (see Callender & Osburn, 1980; Hunter & Schmidt, 1990b), and for those research areas in which artifact estimates are available, they should be used to correct the observed variability in coefficients.

The variance remaining after the correction for artifacts can be used to construct a credibility interval around the average effect size as a means of assessing expectations regarding any future studies of the relationship. For example, taking the square root of the variance remaining (i.e., $[.0076 - .0033]^{1/2}$) yields a standard deviation of .066. The 95% credibility interval then would be .38 ± 1.96 (.066), or .25 to .51. This means that we would expect to find that most validities would fall between .25 and .51.

Questions regarding the statistical significance of the meta-analytic estimate of validity require the computation of a confidence interval (Whitener, 1990).

For the data presented in Table 6.2, subtracting from the total variance the variance due to sampling error leaves a relatively large amount of remaining variance in the validity coefficients, and the credibility interval is relatively large. The remaining variance may be due to other artifacts in the studies reviewed, or it may be due to some moderator variable that causes differences in the correlation between interview ratings and job performance ratings. If the remaining variance were close to .00, then any apparent moderator effects would be totally explained on the basis of variability in sampling error.

We have constructed the hypothetical data in Table 6.2 so that there is a difference in the validities of the two different types of structured interviews. Meta-analysis can be used to assess the presence of moderator variables, but Sackett, Harris, and Orr (1986) have shown that unless there is a fairly large number of studies in each of the groups defined by a moderator variable, the likelihood of concluding that a moderator exists is very small, even when the estimate of effects in different groups of studies is large. If interview type is a moderator of the interview rating-job performance relationship, then the differences in effect size estimates in the two groups of studies should be large and the percentage of variance accounted for by artifacts in each group should be fairly large. That is, after artifacts are accounted for, the remaining variance should be close to zero when no moderator variable affects the relationship investigated.

As can be seen at the bottom of Table 6.2, the average correlation for the situational interviews is .28, whereas that for the experience-based interviews is .43. Moreover, the variance accounted for by sampling error alone exceeds the observed variability in validities. This frequently occurs when the number of studies included in the review is small, and is referred to as second-order sampling error. In any event, the hypothetical data in Table 6.2 support the hypothesis that the type of interview question moderates the validity of interviews.

Meta-analysis has produced a complete reversal among personnel selection researchers regarding the extent to which the criterion-related validity of tests generalizes across different organizational contexts. Twenty years ago, the standard belief was that there was little generalizability and that a new validation effort was required whenever a test was used in a new situation; today, there is general acceptance of the notion that when jobs require the same KSAOs, the same test should predict job performance. Meta-analysis has also provided the effect sizes used to test various models of job performance, which we will discuss below. Although the basic ideas of meta-analysis and validity generalization are relatively simple, refinements to the basic equations have become complex, and the estimation and inclusion of corrections for other artifacts have made the competent execution of a meta-analytic effort a challenging undertaking (see Hunter & Schmidt, 1990b).

Meta-analyses also require that the primary research studies report data on the size of the relationship between the study variables and data on various potential artifacts and moderators. Schmidt and Hunter and others have found these data missing in a large number of the studies they have used in their meta-analyses and have used assumed distributions of artifact data to perform various corrections. Raju, Pappas, and Williams (1989) have shown that the use of these assumed distributions can seriously distort the estimate of the variability of validities and consequently the conclusions about validity generalization. Finally, the body of literature on some predictor-criterion relationships is simply not large enough to warrant meaningful study of moderator effects. In those instances, it is still useful to provide an average estimate of the effect size while suspending judgment regarding the existence of moderators. Meta-analytic estimates of the validity of tests should be a good defense for inferences regarding test-criterion relationships, and this is recognized in the American Psychological Association's *Standards* (AERA, APA, & NCME, 1998), but there seems to be little dependence on validity generalization among practitioners. Perhaps more models in which validity generalization arguments are used should be provided. There would seem to be at least two requirements for a validity generalization defense. First, it should be demonstrated that the same KSAOs are required in a new performance situation as were required in the original studies of particular KSAOs. Second, it should be demonstrated that the test measures the same KSAOs as were present in the tests used in the actual studies. These demonstrations should be possible, but they are not available in the existing research literature. Moreover, they are usually more feasible than are new empirical studies of a test-criterion relationship.

Differential Prediction

One of the most researched and debated issues in the area of personnel selection over the past 30 years has been the degree to which test-criterion relationships are similar across different demographic groups. This issue is of great social and political importance. After the passage of legislation on employment discrimination in the 1960s, selection researchers became concerned with the fact that some tests produced significantly lower scores for minority individuals and women. In addition, most of these tests had been developed and normed using the responses of majority group members, so there was concern as to the meaning of the test scores for members of these groups. That is, did lower test scores mean that members of minority groups were indeed less competent on the constructs of interest, or did the tests measure different constructs when applied to members of these groups?

Before we proceed with an analysis of how measurement specialists have analyzed this problem, it is important that we define some terms. First, evidence of differences in scores across demographic groups is usually referred to as *impact*. When minority members score lower than majority group members on a test, the test is said to display *adverse impact*. In the presence of adverse impact, there may be an impression of a lack of *fairness* in the procedure. The fairness issue is primarily a perceptual or sociopolitical one, however, and it may or may not be coincident with statistical evidence that the test involved is biased. *Bias* is a statistical criterion and refers to the extent to which tests predict differently for different groups of people. In this section, we describe first how bias has been defined statistically. We then look at what is meant by *adverse impact* and what the implications are for minority hiring when there are test score differences between groups.

Evidence for differential prediction is usually analyzed through the regression of a performance variable on a predictor, then race, and then the product of race and the predictor (i.e., race × predictor) in hierarchical fashion—that is, one step at a time (Bartlett, Bobko, Mosier, & Hannon, 1978). Significance of the regression weight for the predictor is evidence of the validity of that predictor. If race predicts significantly after the effects of the predictor are partialed out, then a

$$\bar{X}_{verb} = 47.2, \text{SD}_{verb} = 12.3; \text{Males} = 1, \text{Females} = 2.$$

Equation: $\hat{y}$ = .030 (Verb) + .711 (Sex) - .016 (predsex) + 3.240

Males
     - 1SD Verb = .030(34.9) + .711(1) - .016(34.9) + 3.24 = 4.44

     +1SD Verb = .030(59.5) + .711(1) - .016(59.5) + 3.24 = 4.78

Females
     - 1SD Verb = .030(34.9) + .711(2) - .016(69.8) + 3.24 = 4.59

     +1SD Verb = .030(59.5) + .711(2) - .016(119) + 3.24 = 4.54

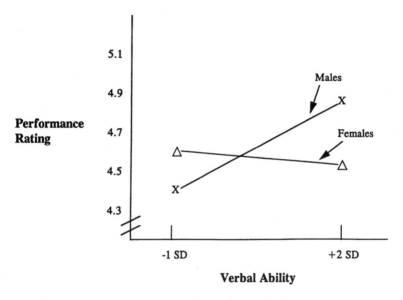

Figure 6.1. Regression Equation and Plot of the Relationship Between a Verbal Ability Test and Job Performance for Men and Women

form of bias called *intercept bias* is said to exist. In this case, there are race differences in performance after people are equated for ability as measured by the test. Those race differences would be taken as evidence of bias. If the race × predictor product term is statistically significant, then there is evidence of *slope bias,* in which case the test

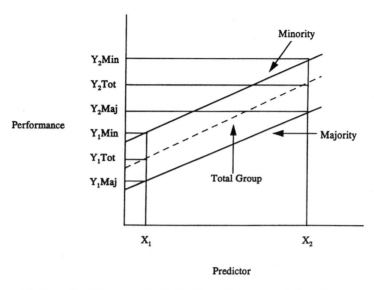

Figure 6.2. Example of Intercept Bias in Predictor-Criterion Relationship

is predicting better for one group than for the other. This Cleary model (1968) of test bias has been adopted by psychometricians (AERA, APA, & NCME, 1998; Society for Industrial and Organizational Psychology, 1987). To understand the implications of bias for one group or the other, plots of the regression lines for subgroups are usually constructed. One example of such a plot is contained in Figure 6.1. In this figure, we present the basic descriptive statistics for a verbal ability test used to predict the job performance of men and women in Example 1, described in Chapter 1. We also present the regression equation for the prediction of performance (in the second line from the top of the figure). In this equation, the ability measure is significant, as is the interaction, indicating some form of slope bias. Values for predicted performance are then calculated for men and women at 1 standard deviation below the mean and 1 standard deviation above the mean. These predicted performance values are then used to plot the graph. In this instance, the graph indicates that the test does predict the performance of men (i.e., the male slope is substantial), but does not predict women's performance (i.e., the female slope is almost flat). This differential prediction was a significant factor in the decision not to include this test in the final selection battery in the study described in Example 1.

Another case of differential prediction is depicted in Figure 6.2. In this case, the regression lines indicate intercept bias across minority and majority groups. There is a relatively constant difference between the predicted values of minority and majority performance across all levels of ability. If we were to ignore these differences and use a single regression equation (called the Total Group equation in Figure 6.2) to predict the performance of minority and majority group members' performance, the performance of minority group members would be underpredicted at all levels of ability, whereas the performance of majority group members would be overpredicted. This is illustrated by the values associated with Y along the Performance axis in the graph.

Most of the literature on test bias indicates that there are few instances of either intercept or slope bias (Bartlett et al., 1978; Jensen, 1980; Schmidt, Pearlman, & Hunter, 1980). This literature does not show evidence of underprediction of African American or Hispanic performance. Slope differences occur no more frequently than would be predicted by chance, and when intercept differences do occur, they usually indicate overprediction of minority group performance. Nor does there seem to be evidence that physical tests are statistically biased against women, even though there are large male-female differences on many physical tests (Hogan, 1991).

Even though there is little evidence that tests are biased as defined above, there are large subgroup differences on some tests. For example, measures of cognitive ability usually produce mean differences between African American and White groups equal to 1 standard deviation, and male-female differences of 1.5 standard deviations on tests of muscular endurance and larger for some other measures of physical ability (see Hogan, 1991) are common. The implications of these large subgroup differences is indicated in Table 6.3. The figures in this table are the proportions of a lower-scoring group that would be selected given various selection ratios and different levels of subgroup mean difference ranging from 0 to 1.5 standard deviations. If a test is used in the presence of a 1 standard deviation mean difference, we can see that about 1% of the lower-scoring (minority) group would be selected when 10% of the higher-scoring (majority) group is selected, and that 61% of the lower-scoring group would be selected when 90% of the higher-scoring group is selected. The ratio of these hiring rates is often taken as an index of adverse impact. So, for

Table 6.3 Minority Group Selection Ratio When Cutoff for Majority Group Is Set at 10%, 50%, and 90%

Standardized Group Difference (d)	Majority Group Selection Ratio		
	10%	50%	90%
0	.100	.500	.900
0.1	.084	.460	.881
0.2	.070	.421	.860
0.3	.057	.382	.836
0.4	.046	.345	.811
0.5	.038	.309	.782
0.6	.030	.274	.752
0.7	.024	.242	.719
0.8	.019	.212	.684
0.9	.015	.184	.648
1.0	.013	.159	.610
1.1	.009	.136	.571
1.2	.007	.115	.532
1.3	.005	.097	.492
1.4	.004	.081	.452
1.5	.003	.070	.413

SOURCE: Adapted from Sackett and Wilk (1994).

example, the ratio of the hiring rates (minority:majority) for the case in which the majority selection rate is .50 and the subgroup mean difference is 1.0 is .318 (.159/.50). This ratio is 1.00 when the hiring rates are equal, and when the ratio is lower than .80, legal guidelines assume some form of discrimination has occurred. An organization is then obligated to provide convincing evidence of the job relatedness of its selection procedures (EEOC, CSC, DOL, & DOJ, 1978). It is obvious from the data presented in Table 6.3 that even relatively small subgroup differences can result in significant adverse impact, especially when the selection ratio is low. This may lead to a perception of unfairness on the part of lower-scoring individuals, but adverse impact and fairness issues are separate from psychometric bias.

Similar analyses have been conducted at the test item level. There is a large literature on investigations of item bias and differential item functioning (*dif* in the item bias literature) that parallels the literature on test bias (Schmitt, Hattrup, & Landis, 1993). In this literature, too, there has been a tendency to confuse subgroup differences in the proportion of subgroups that get an item right with item bias. An item

Table 6.4   Number of People in Focal and Reference Groups at Different Ability
             Levels Who Get an Item Right and Wrong

| | Ability 1 | | Ability 2 | | Ability 3 | | Ability 4 | |
	Focal	Reference	Focal	Reference	Focal	Reference	Focal	Reference
Right	10	5	20	10	50	70	20	15
Wrong	20	25	30	25	20	40	30	10

is biased only when *equally* able members of two different groups have *unequal* probabilities of getting the item right. There are many different methods of detecting item bias (Berk, 1983; Holland & Wainer, 1993), but all depend on the analysis of item passing rates for members of different groups whose total test scores or some transformation of the total test scores are equal. The two major approaches to the assessment of differential item functioning are the Mantel-Haenszel (MH) statistic and differences in item characteristic curves (Drasgow & Hulin, 1990).

In computing the MH statistic, the first step is to divide the total test distribution into discrete score continua, each of which represents about an equal proportion of the total group of test takers. Then the proportion of each group that gets the item right at each score interval is calculated. Given the expectation that the proportions of the groups getting the item right should be equal at all ability levels, a chi-square test and effect size measures are calculated as indices of the extent to which an item might be biased (Dorans & Holland, 1993). The data in Table 6.4 display a case of a biased item because the individuals in the focal group are more likely than comparable individuals in the reference group to get the item right at ability levels 1, 2, and 3, but they are less likely to get the item right at ability level 4.

An item characteristic curve (ICC) represents the probability that a person with any given level of ability will get an item correct. Two examples of item characteristic curves are presented in Figure 6.3. ICCs can be represented by three parameters. The difficulty parameter is the value of the underlying ability of the person who has a 50-50 chance of getting the item right. Items for which the ICC lies to the right in Figure 6.3 are the most difficult. The discrimination parameter is the steepness of the item characteristic curve at its difficulty value. For example, Item 6 in Figure 6.3a would have a low discrimi-

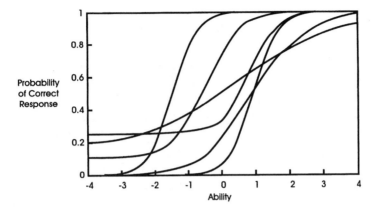

A. Three-Parameter Item Characteristic Curves for Six Typical Items

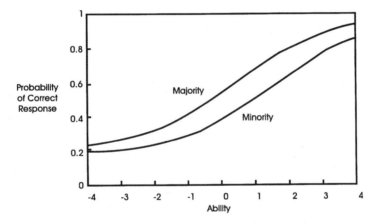

B. Item Characteristic Curves for Two Groups on an Item That Is Differentially
Difficult for White and Black Groups That Are Equally Able

Figure 6.3. Illustrations of Item Characteristic Curves

nation parameter relative to Items 1 and 4. Finally, the guessing parameter represents the probability that a person will get an item right if he or she has no ability on the underlying construct represented by the item. The guessing parameter is represented by the lower asymptote of the ICC. If ICCs for two different groups of people are significantly different, then there is evidence of dif. For example, in

Figure 6.3b, the item is differentially difficult for members of the two ethnic groups all along the ability continuum. In this case, equally able members of the two groups have differing probabilities of getting the item correct. Item response theory statistical tests for dif are provided in various sources (e.g., Thissen, Steinberg, & Wainer, 1993).

As in the case of test bias, there has been little evidence that the number of biased items in various studies exceeds chance levels. When biased items are identified and removed from a test, the result often is a highly unidimensional test that has reduced validity (Roznowski, 1987). We should point out that tests of both item bias and test bias depend on critical assumptions. In the case of test bias, the assumption is that the criterion against which one is evaluating predictive bias is unbiased. Analogously, in item bias studies the assumption is that the full-length test that is the representation of the KSAO is a unidimensional and unbiased estimate of the KSAO. The presence of dif is itself evidence that the test measures a second dimension related to subgroup status.

Personnel selection researchers and practitioners are left with a significant quandary. Some selection tests are valid in a predictive sense, but produce significant adverse impact such that if they are used, very few members of some subgroups will be hired. Recently, Schmitt (1997) summarized the results of efforts to reduce this adverse impact. One approach to the minimization of adverse impact is to employ tests of job-relevant KSAOs that typically do not display subgroup differences along with tests of cognitive ability that typically show a mean difference equal to 1 standard deviation. This approach was used by Pulakos and Schmitt (1996) to reduce subgroup differences from 1.03 (with a test of verbal ability only) to .63 when the verbal ability test was combined with three other predictors (a structured interview, a biodata form, and a situational judgment test). Although some reduction in subgroup differences was achieved, the .63 mean difference is still substantial and will produce adverse impact for most test use situations. Sackett and Roth (1996) and Schmitt, Rogers, Chan, Sheppard, and Jennings (1997) have confirmed that adverse impact is not reduced a great deal when one measure in a battery has high adverse impact and even when two or three other measures are unrelated to the demographic variable of concern.

A second approach to the reduction of adverse impact is to reduce the non–job-related reading or verbal ability requirements. For example, we recently compared African American and White examinees' performance on a video-based situational judgment test as well as a written version of the same test and found a significantly smaller subgroup difference when the test was given in the video format (Chan & Schmitt, 1997).

There is a small body of research that assesses the degree to which the test item format is responsible for subgroup differences. Research on this third approach produces some evidence that item format may have motivational impact on examinees, but there is little convincing evidence that one group or another performs better as a function of the format of test items used. The few comparisons of minority-majority differences on tests that are available usually completely confound the content or constructs measured in the tests with the format of the test items.

A fourth approach, the use of portfolio tests or accomplishment records (Hough, 1984), involves the careful documentation and scoring of past experiences that are relevant to the attainment of required KSAOs. These methods of assessment are usually difficult to score with any reliability, and there are concerns that all applicants have equal opportunity to achieve experiences relevant to the KSAOs measured. The major advantage of these methods appears to be their face validity, though Hough's (1984) study resulted in very much smaller subgroup differences as well.

Whereas the methods mentioned above seek to reduce adverse impact by changing the nature of the test, the use of test score bands achieves such reduction by changing the manner in which test scores are used to make hiring decisions. Instead of selecting first those individuals whose scores are the highest on a selection test, Cascio, Outtz, Zedeck, and Goldstein (1991) propose that organizations use test score bands as a basis of selection. This approach to the use of test scores started with the idea that individuals whose scores were not significantly different from that of the top scorer on the test should be treated as equally capable, and that selections from this group of individuals could be made on other bases, including education, racial/ethnic diversity, seniority, job performance, training, experience, and relocation preferences. To determine the size of this band, Cascio et al. propose calculating the standard error of the difference (which is equal to the standard error of measurement [the standard deviation of the test multiplied by the square root of 1 minus the reliability of the test] multiplied by the square root of 2). This value would then be multiplied by 1.65 (if one chooses the .05 level of significance) to determine the bandwidth. If the top score on a test were 100 and the bandwidth were 10, then all persons with scores between 90 and 100 would be considered equal, and some other means would be used to determine among this group of people who would be selected.

There are several different approaches to the use of bands, and the advisability and utility of banding has been hotly debated in the literature (e.g., Cascio, Goldstein, Outtz, & Zedeck, 1995; Schmidt, 1995). Aside from the considerable professional debate about the logic and merits of banding, we do not believe that this approach represents a workable or highly desirable long-term solution to the problem of subgroup differences in test scores. First, the efficacy of banding in producing increases in minority hiring is a complex function of at least the following variables: the size of subgroup differences on the test and any secondary predictors used, the reliability of the test (hence the size of the band relative to the distribution of scores as a whole), the confidence level chosen to set the band, and the intercorrelations among the tests and the other criteria used to make selections within a band. The fact that so many variables determine the outcome means that the manner in which bands are established will almost always be a post hoc consideration of several alternatives and their impact on minority hiring. When, and if, the post hoc manipulation and/or consideration of all these variables is explained to a court or jury, it may very likely be interpreted as deliberate "tampering" with test scores to achieve increases in minority hiring. Second, in many situations, the use of banding or sliding bands will not produce large increases in the proportions of minorities hired (Sackett & Roth, 1991).

In considering the research efforts and the literature on the reduction of adverse impact in selection, Schmitt (1997) has made the following suggestions. First, a very broad consideration of the organization's goals and the role it plays in the community at large should be considered in determining what performance criteria to predict. These considerations may mean that there are multiple, nonredundant, and relevant performance criteria (see also Chapter 3). This, in turn, will mean that a broad range of KSAOs will be required to achieve these criteria. Construction of measures to assess these KSAOs should not be guided by ease of administration, scoring, or interpretation, but rather by what is relevant to job performance. Face validity may also contribute to better perceptions of the fairness and appropriateness of selection procedures (see Chapter 7), which may lead to fewer legal problems and better-motivated test takers. Research on alternative testing methods and technologies should be continued as a means of gaining understanding of the subgroup differences and increasing the probability that appropriate remedial actions can be taken. Selection researchers should also be willing to admit that there are substantial differences between minority and majority groups that transcend particular tests used to measure ability, primarily in the cognitive domain. Rather than focusing on minimizing these differences or hiding "real" differences, researchers should concentrate on developing and supporting programs that will address the social, economic, and educational inequities that have produced these differences.

Use of Structural Equations to Evaluate Complex Ability-Performance Relationships

Most of the validity research described above has involved the correlation between a single predictor and a criterion or between a weighted composite of predictors and a criterion. In the past couple of decades, researchers have developed methods of analysis that test the plausibility of several prediction equations (or structural equations) simultaneously. In addition to the testing of several structural equations, hypotheses regarding the measurement model (Inferences 2 and 4 in Figure 3.1) can be included in these models. Methods to analyze data in this manner were popularized by Jöreskog and Sörbom (1982), and the actual analyses of these data were accomplished with a computer program called LISREL (Jöreskog & Sörbom, 1993). Since then, several other computer programs have been developed to analyze complex structural equation models, with probably the two most popular alternatives being AMOS (Arbuckle, 1995) and EQS (Bentler, 1985). Personnel selection researchers have begun to use these methods to analyze their data and to test theories about complex models of the KSAO-performance relationship. It is not our intent to provide instruction with respect to these methods of data analysis, but we will provide two examples of the use of these methods to illustrate their potential in explaining the roles of assorted variables in explaining job performance (Borman, White, Pulakos, & Oppler, 1991; Schmidt, Hunter, & Outerbridge, 1986). We mentioned these examples briefly in Chapter 4 as well. With the development of increasingly complex theoretical models of performance (see Chapter 3), it is appropriate that selection researchers understand and learn to use these methods of data analysis. Several excellent textbooks and software manuals that explain structural equations analysis are now available (e.g., Arbuckle, 1995; Bentler, 1985; Bollen, 1989; Bollen & Long, 1993; Hayduk, 1996; Jöreskog & Sörbom, 1993; Maruyama, 1998; Schumacker & Lomax, 1996).

Schmidt et al. (1986) were interested in a model of supervisory ratings of job performance that included general mental ability, job experience, job knowledge, and work sample performance. Their model represented the hypotheses that job experience and general mental ability exert impacts on supervisory ratings because they influence the degree to which employees acquire job knowledge and can perform job tasks. These authors used path analysis, which is actually a series of regression analyses, to estimate the parameters in the model displayed in Figure 6.4. The numbers in this figure are called path coefficients, and they represent, in standardized form, the strength of the effect of one variable on another (the directions of the hypothesized causal relationships are indicated by the arrows). The absence of paths in diagrams such as the one in Figure 6.4 also represents hypotheses. For example, the diagram indicates that the effect of general mental ability on supervisory ratings is not direct, but occurs through its influence on work sample performance and job knowledge. Note also that ability influences job knowledge, which is thought to influence work sample performance, which in turn influences supervisory ratings. So, there are three ways in which ability is thought to influence supervisory ratings, but there are no hypothesized direct effects. The size of the indirect effects can be computed through the multiplication of the path coefficients connecting two variables. The indirect effects implied by the model and estimates of path coefficients are computed at the bottom of the figure. All relationships among variables in a model are computed in the same fashion. The degree to which these estimates match the actual observed correlations between the variables represents the degree to which the model fits the data. In this case, the actual correlations between job experience and ratings and

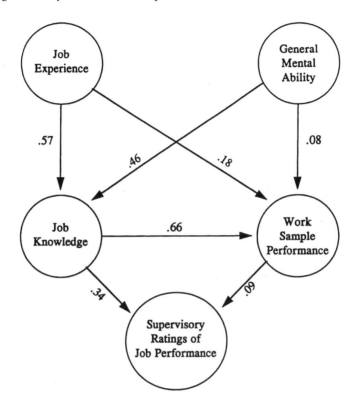

Figure 6.4. Model of Supervisory Ratings and Computation of Indirect Effects of General Mental Ability and Job Experience
SOURCE: Adapted from Schmidt et al. (1986).

ability and ratings were .16 and .33, respectively. These observed correlations compare quite well with the reproduced correlations of

.19 and .24 (see the bottom of Figure 6.4). Of course, it is important to recognize that many other models, some of which make theoretical sense and some of which do not, may fit the same data. The estimates of the paths in Figure 6.4 were also corrected for the influence of measurement error using the correction for attenuation as described above; the same is achieved by including aspects of the measurement model in a LISREL analysis or by correcting interrelationships before estimating the structural parameters.

A more complicated model, which is an expansion of the Schmidt et al. (1986) model, is represented by Borman et al.'s (1991) research. This expanded model includes the Schmidt et al. variables plus need for achievement, dependability, number of awards received, and the number of disciplinary actions taken against the individual. The model and the estimates (both observed and corrected for unreliability) are presented in Figure 6.5. The data were analyzed using the LISREL program, and overall indices of the fit of the model to the observed covariance matrix indicated that this model fit the data very well. Perhaps most important, this model explained nearly twice the variance in supervisory ratings (R^2 corrected for unreliability equaled .31) as did a simpler model based on the Schmidt et al. model. An examination of the model shows that a revised version of the Schmidt et al. model minus job experience is contained in the central part of this model. Job experience was relatively constant in these models and was not a hypothesized factor. The Borman et al. model also represents a different causal sequence than does the model tested by Schmidt et al. Ability is thought to influence the acquisition of job knowledge, which in turn influences the performance of job tasks, which finally influences how supervisors rate these military personnel. The Borman et al. model also makes conceptual sense and is a good example of what we mentioned above—that is, alternate models of the same data may provide reasonable explanations. The bottom and top portions of the Borman et al. model represent the role that personality, or temperament, plays in determining awards and disciplinary actions received. These intermediate criteria both influence supervisory ratings, and both personality variables also influence supervisory ratings directly. The curved arrows to the left of the model do not represent the evaluation of causal hypotheses; rather, they represent the intercorrelation between these independent or exogenous variables, which must be taken into account in the evaluation of the structural equations.

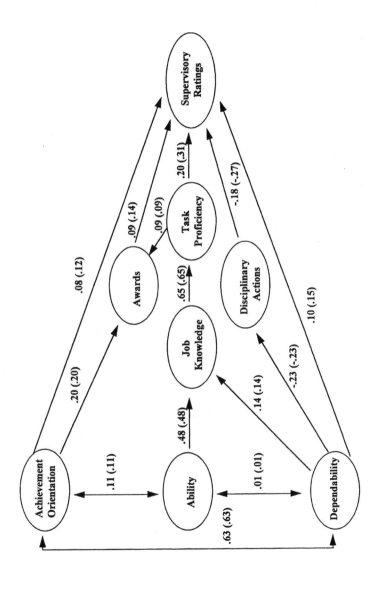

Figure 6.5. Revised Expanded Rating Model With Path Coefficients Based on Metacorrelations From Nine Jobs

SOURCE: From "Models of Supervisory Job Performance Ratings," by W. C. Borman, L. A. White, E. D. Pulakos, and S. H. Oppler, 1991, Journal of Applied Psychology, 76, p. 869. Copyright © 1991 by the American Psychological Association. Adapted with permission.
NOTE: Coefficients in parentheses were computed by correcting all variables for attenuation; the other coefficients were derived without correcting the ratings for attenuation.

The evaluation of both of these models was based on the use of meta-analytically derived estimates of the covariances between the variables in these models. In the case of Schmidt et al. (1986), the data were obtained from four military samples for which the relevant data were available. Borman et al. (1991) evaluated their model using data from nine different samples collected during the Project A work. Using data aggregated over several studies has obvious advantages. The role of sampling error is minimal as the number of research participants upon which the correlations are based increases. Idiosyncrasies of a particular sample or situation do not become the basis for support of a particular model, or such idiosyncrasies (moderator variables) can actually be identified and modeled. Meta-analyses and structural equation modeling, then, are two very powerful data-analytic tools that can be used to build and test the types of performance models we described in Chapter 3.

Aggregation of data from multiple studies, some of which were conducted decades ago, however, presumes that the data aggregated are of adequate quality and are reported in sufficient detail to allow for the estimation of effect sizes and various suspected artifacts. Estimates of reliability and restriction of range are rarely available, and hypothesized values of these artifacts have been routinely used (Hunter & Schmidt, 1990b). Restriction of range is dependent on the selection ratio and the variables used to make selections and is particularly difficult to estimate in the absence of actual data. Even descriptions of the sample or job in which research participants are engaged are frequently missing. Early studies were often not conducted with the same degree of experimental rigor as would be considered adequate today. For example, the use of overall and ambiguously defined performance rating scales was common, the extent of the use of cross-validation or shrinkage formulas to estimate cross-validated multiple correlations is not clear, and the possibility exists that disconfirming data were not reported. Also, the simple passage of time and possible changes in the ways jobs are viewed and tasks configured to constitute jobs may change the types of KSAOs required. For at least these reasons, we believe it is essential that criterion-related studies continue to be conducted and reported. The possibility of doing large-scale studies such as that represented by Project A is rare.

The opportunities such large projects afford are tremendous, but even smaller-scale studies are valuable when reported in sufficient detail and aggregated.

Summary and Conclusions

Research design and data analysis issues make substantial demands on personnel selection researchers. Most selection research is done in field situations in which the degree of control over extraneous variables is minimal, and sometimes the effects of these variables, or even their existence, are unknown. Advances in data-analytic strategies such as structural equations analysis, item response theory, and meta-analysis allow researchers to evaluate theoretical questions that could not be addressed even a couple of decades ago, but they also mean that researchers must be competent in executing these analyses. In this chapter we have highlighted those data-analytic techniques and problems that are likely to be of most importance to researchers in this area, but we believe that much more training is needed than can be provided in a single book, much less one short chapter.

On a substantive basis, we believe that additional criterion-related research would be helpful and informative with respect to the attributions that can be derived from test scores. Studies that continue to explore the nature of subgroup differences would also be valuable. Although most research indicates that inferences derived from tests are equally accurate for members of different subgroups, the role of item and test format—including the role of different options on multiple-choice tests (e.g., Whitney & Schmitt, 1997), the impact of the use of alternate technologies for test item presentation (e.g., Chan & Schmitt, 1997), and the effect of different types of tests on test-taking motivation and performance (e.g., Chan, 1997b; Chan, Schmitt, DeShon, Clause, & Delbridge, 1997)—should be addressed in future research studies. In addition, the evaluation of more complex models of job performance that include a variety of performance measures and hypothesized mechanisms through which KSAOs affect performance should be undertaken. Finally, the criteria used in validation research have been much neglected and are deserving of increased scrutiny. Organizational objectives and concerns beyond task-related performance measures, including those suggested by Campbell, McCloy, Oppler, and Sager's (1993) performance model, should be included in the criteria against which selection procedures are validated. Potential bias factors should be measured and investigated.

Data analysis is a very important part of selection research and can constitute a very exciting discovery process. Data analysis represents the culmination of a great deal of research planning and hypothesis generation. It is at this stage of research that we find out what theories or hypotheses are (or are not) supported and how confident we can be of our findings. The complex data analysis methods we have introduced in this chapter can be helpful in the development of appropriate interpretations of the data, but they should not substitute for careful planning, literature review, and theorizing at the beginning of the research. We also believe that data should always be explained or presented in the *simplest* terms *consistent with an appropriate interpretation.* This means that the use of graphs, tables, and simple bivariate correlations may sometimes be preferable to multiple correlation, factor analyses, and structural equations models. These simpler approaches often tell most of "the story," and they are much more easily communicated to the "consumers" of research.

7   Implementation
and Use of
Theory-Based Research

In Chapter 6, we described the major research designs, methods of analysis used, and the problems confronted in the evaluation of research hypotheses in personnel selection. In this chapter, we focus on implementation and use issues in personnel selection research. A central theme running through these issues is the "context sensitivity" of personnel selection. Personnel selection does not take place in a vacuum. Although meta-analysis and validity generalization results summarized elsewhere in this book (see especially Chapter 5) indicate there may be little variability in the relationship between ability and performance across organizations, there remains variability in the way procedures are implemented and the extent to which societal and legal constraints limit the implementation of valid selection procedures. The effective implementation and use of personnel selection systems has to take into account other organizational features and human resource practices, such as recruitment, training, and compensation, as well as various external pressures, such as legal constraints and societal values. Hence, unlike in previous chapters, our discussion in this chapter often moves beyond traditional individual-level research to the organizational level of analysis and to a systems perspective in which personnel selection is understood as one of several interacting human resource functions and as a means of satisfying certain legal demands and achieving goals related to social responsibility.

We begin with a discussion of efforts to assess the economic utility of selection research *at the organizational level of analysis.* Following that, we examine how the practical usefulness of selection can be influenced by recruitment, training, and compensation, and how selection can be used to accomplish particular organizational objectives or strategies. We will also discuss the influence of legal and societal pressures on selection. Finally, we will address the relatively recent interest in organizational justice and applicant reactions to selection procedures. Although all of the above issues represent practical problems, various theoretical assumptions and hypotheses are involved in each area. We will attempt to clarify the importance and relevance of these theoretical concerns and to show how theory can form the basis for consideration of implementation and use issues in personnel selection.

Assessments of the Economic
Utility of Selection Research
at the Organizational Level

From an economic perspective, the bottom line in personnel selection is the relative benefit an organization gains from the use of valid personnel selection procedures; this is the issue of utility. To put it simply, the more the benefits derived or to be derived from selection exceed the associated costs, the more the procedure is said to have utility (Cronbach & Gleser, 1965; Dunnette, 1966; Dunnette & Borman, 1979). In Chapter 5, we traced the history of utility analyses. As indicated in our review, results of utility research suggest that an organization can improve its effectiveness by using validated measures when (a) the measures yield a higher proportion of superior workers and (b) using the measures has more benefits than costs. But there is an important comparative utility question at the organizational level of analysis that is distinct from the focus on *an* organization's assessment of the merits of personnel selection based on an assessment of cumulated predictions about individual performance changes. This question concerns the relative effectiveness of one organization compared with another as a function of adopting particular selection procedures. With the increasing importance of intellectual capital as a competitive advantage, the organizational-level utility question is clearly of interest from an applied research perspective. Yet, traditionally, the selection researcher has emphasized individual performance as the criterion of interest and has neglected performance or effectiveness at the organizational level.

More than a decade ago, Schmitt and Schneider (1983), noting the lack of research on the contribution of personnel selection to organizational effectiveness criteria, outlined a research agenda. This agenda includes defining and assessing the organizational-level criteria of importance (e.g., increases in sales, turnover rate, market share) that might be related to various selection or other human resource interventions, surveying organizations and assessing their selection and human resource practices regarding various issues, and correlating the two sets of organizational assessments. Despite Schmitt and Schneider's call for research on the relationship between selection practices and organizational-level outcomes and the apparent recognition in the personnel and human resources management literature of the importance of selection utility at the organizational level, there remains a paucity of empirical research assessing selection utility at the organizational level. A few studies have examined human resource practices at the organizational level by identifying organizational characteristics (e.g., industry type, organizational size, competitive strategy use) as predictors or correlates of such practices as training, performance appraisal, and compensation (Cleveland, Murphy, & Williams, 1989; Jackson, Schuler, & Rivero, 1989; Saari, Johnson, McLaughlin, & Zimmerle, 1988). For example, Jackson et al. (1989) examined how four organizational characteristics—industry sector, the competitive strategy, the technology, and the organizational structure—are related to differences in the use of various personnel practices related to training, performance appraisal, and compensation. Survey results from 267 organizations supported these authors' general hypothesis that personnel practices vary as a function of organizational characteristics.

Researchers have noted that whereas the use and effectiveness of specific selection procedures might vary across organizations as a result of different human resource strategies, organizational characteristics, and external factors, the use of effective selection practices is likely to benefit most organizations regardless of their differing internal or external contingencies (Jackson et al., 1989; Schuler & Jackson, 1987; Terpstra & Rozell, 1993). However, although there is a massive empirical literature on the relationship between selection and individual performance (e.g., see Hunter & Hunter, 1984), Terpstra and Rozell (1993) have conducted probably the only systematic empirical study to examine directly the relationship between selection practices and organizational-level measures of performance. They surveyed 201 organizations and assessed the extent of use of five selection or staffing-related practices: (a) the use of follow-up studies of recruiting sources to determine which sources yield greater proportions of high-performing employees, (b) the use of validation studies for predictors used in selection, (c) the use of structured interviews in selection, (d) the use of cognitive ability tests in selection, and (e) the use of biographical information blanks (BIB) or weighted application blanks (WAB) in selection. Terpstra and Rozell also identified and assessed several organizational-level criteria of importance (annual profit, profit growth, and sales growth) and then examined the relationship between the two sets of organizational assessments. Their general finding was that organizations that employed relatively more of the practices examined in the study had higher levels of annual profit, profit growth, and overall performance, but the extent of use of the practices and sales growth were unrelated. Terpstra and Rozell suggest that, unlike profit and profit growth, which may be more directly influenced by good selection or staffing practices, sales growth is more dependent on external factors omitted in their study.

Terpstra and Rozell (1993) caution that the correlational nature of the data in their study does not allow the causal inference that the organizations' profit or profitability resulted from the use of the selection or staffing practices. It is possible that the more profitable organizations were simply more able to adopt these practices. Note that the three selection predictors that Terpstra and Rozell examined (cognitive ability tests, structured interviews, BIB/WAB) were among the most valid predictors of individual job performance (see Hunter & Hunter, 1984; Reilly & Chao, 1982; Schmitt, Gooding, Noe, & Kirsch,

1984). It would be interesting to include also organizations that use less valid (in predicting individual performance) selection predictors, such as personality tests and unstructured interviews. It would then be possible to determine whether the differential validities of predictors at the individual level are reflected in different degrees of organizational effectiveness.

Perhaps the influence of human resource management (HRM) practices has been most systematically studied by Huselid and his colleagues (Huselid, 1995; Huselid, Jackson, & Schuler, 1997), who have tried to document the impacts of HRM practices on firm profitability and productivity. In the Huselid et al. (1997) study, strategic and technical HRM effectiveness were distinguished as indicated in Table 7.1. *Strategic HRM effectiveness* involved the perceptions of senior HRM managers of the degree to which the HRM functions developed a firm's employees to meet its specific business needs. *Technical HRM effectiveness* refers to the perceptions of managers as to how well the HRM function performed the traditional personnel management functions, including recruitment, selection, training, performance appraisal, and the administration of compensation. Data on the performance of 293 firms were obtained from financial statements and other archival sources and included employee productivity and firm profitability indices. Both within and across time periods, strategic, but not technical, HRM practices were correlated with outcome variables after a variety of potential alternate explanations of the relationships were controlled for. Economic estimates of the impact of a standard deviation change in strategic HRM effectiveness yielded values between $8,800 and $9,700 per employee. These results suggest that HRM practices, among them selection, can contribute significantly to firm effectiveness, but these practices must fit the organization's strategy and objectives. Huselid et al. (1997) also recognize that there may be alternate interpretations to their data, including the possibility that their survey measures of HRM effectiveness may have been influenced by data on firm performance. Much more research should be done to isolate and measure the impacts of selection practices on a variety of organizational-level outcomes.

Much more conceptual and empirical work is clearly needed in the assessment of utility of selection research/practices at the organizational level. In particular, empirical studies that examine theory-driven linkages between organizational performance and organiza-

Table 7.1   Items Used to Assess Strategic and Technical Human Resource Effectiveness in the Huselid, Jackson, and Schuler (1997) Study

Strategic HRM Effectiveness	Technical HRM Effectiveness
Teamwork	Benefits and services
Employee participation and empowerment	Compensation
Workforce planning—flexibility and deployment	Recruiting and training
Workforce productivity and quality of output	Safety and health
Management and executive development	Employee education and training
Succession and development planning for managers	Retirement strategies
Advance issue identification/strategic	Employee/industrial relations
Employee and manager communications	Social responsibility programs
Work/family programs	EEO for females, minorities, etc.
	Management of labor costs
	Selection testing
	Performance appraisal
	Human resource information systems
	Assessing employee attitudes

tional implementation and use of selection are badly needed. Furthermore, the quality of the research base is dependent on the ability of the researcher and the constraints of the research situation to move beyond simple cross-sectional correlational designs to adopt longitudinal and quasi-experimental designs that would better address issues of causality. These more rigorous study designs are undoubtedly more demanding on research resources, but for a start, the practical implications of utility assessments at the organizational level should at least motivate selection researchers to begin conducting relatively simple empirical organizational-level studies. How aggregate individual ability and performance indices relate to various organizational measures of effectiveness remains largely unexamined. As we will see later (Chapter 9), the manner in which individual indices are aggregated must be linked to theoretical considerations.

Finally, it should be noted that selection utility assessment at the organizational level is more complex than a simple empirical estimation of the relationship between organizational performance and the use of selection practices or a direct application of some conventional utility model to arrive at expected utilities. Selection utility at the organizational level is context dependent and dynamic in nature. For example, Becker (1989) notes that the utility of a selection or other human resource system at the organizational level is in part a function of the labor market in which the organization operates. Becker argues that changes in labor market conditions and the responses of current and prospective employees as well as other employers to these labor market dynamics have been ignored in conventional utility models and concludes that conventional assessments are likely to result in overestimates of utility. Schmidt and Ones (1992), however, note that Becker's argument is theoretical, and that Becker provides no empirical evidence to support the argument. In addition, Schmidt and Ones assert that Becker seems to make unrealistic assumptions about levels of rationality and optimization among human resource managers. Notwithstanding the validity of Becker's conclusion on overestimation in conventional utility analysis, Becker raises the important point that selection utility assessment at the organizational level is a complex process that has to take into account not only organizational characteristics but also external environmental factors and responses from employee and employer to these factors. Similarly, Russell, Colella, and Bobko (1993) highlight the importance of incorporating in conventional utility models the strategic context faced by managerial decision makers. This context includes the changing strategic needs of the organization and the changing capacity of the selection system to meet those needs.

Similar, and additional, concerns are raised in an interesting and important paper by Johns (1993), who argues that industrial and organizational psychologists must view their practices, including selection, as organizational innovations that are subject to the mechanisms and processes described in the innovation diffusion literature, rather than as technical improvements that would be adopted by any rational manager who understands validity data. Johns presents a number of propositions, the central thesis being that variance in the adoption of psychology-based interventions is a function of the decision-making frame of managers, the nature of the industrial/organizational theory and research as presented to them, and critical events and players in the external environment of the adopting organization. Technically meritorious practices are sometimes not adopted because managers frame personnel practices as matters of administrative style rather than as technical innovations. A good example of this tendency occurred in one of the studies described in Example 1 in Chapter 1. In this case, a structured interview with excellent criterion-related validity was developed, validated, and introduced to the organization. After a short period of time, it was found that interviewers were asking the standardized questions, but were also adding some of their own "favorite" questions. Because of a concern that this nonstandardized change would affect the validity of the process, the organization introduced random recording and monitoring of the interviews.

Second, psychologists justify personnel practices from a technical perspective, not recognizing the relatively long causal chain and time from the introduction of a practice to an outcome and the ways social context can change or thwart any recommended technical change. Finally, crises, government regulation, and institutional factors all often overshadow technical merit. Anyone who has worked with organizations introducing selection systems can relate incidents in which procedures were developed but never used, or used very briefly, because of one or more of these concerns or issues. Psychologists must understand and do research on the innovation adoption and diffusion process as it relates to selection procedures if the impacts of selection innovations are to be optimized.

It appears that the "cutting edge" of extant research on utility is calling into question the simplifying assumptions made in traditional utility analyses and developing models that attempt to reflect organizational realities more accurately (Borman, Hanson, & Hedge, 1997). One of the organizational realities that has been neglected in traditional utility research concerns the interest managers and other decision makers have in the results of utility analyses and the perceived relevance of such analyses to organizational needs. Yet the primary purpose of utility analyses is presumably to communicate the value of selection procedures or other human resource practices to managers and decision makers. One recent research report included the troubling finding that a valid selection procedure actually received less support for implementation from managers when the procedure was presented with both validity and utility information than when it was presented with validity information only (Latham & Whyte, 1994). Research is clearly needed on how managers make judgments and decisions concerning the value and implementation of different selection procedures and the types of information that they find useful in meeting their needs. This reflects Johns's (1993) concern about how psychological interventions are presented. The call for research is not new. A decade ago, Rauschenberger and Schmidt (1987) emphasized the need for research on the ways of presenting utility information to organizational decision makers. Unfortunately, we could not find a single empirical study that has directly examined the utility *communication* question. For a start, utility researchers could begin systematically identifying and assessing the factors that affect the credibility and face validity of the utility message. The psychological research literature on persuasion and attitude or belief change as well as the literature on the adoption and diffusion of innovations should provide a relevant conceptual and empirical base for such investigations.

From the above discussion, it should be clear that utility assessment is a complex enterprise when we begin addressing the associated organizational realities and contexts. The complexity in selection utility assessment is not surprising when we appreciate that the implementation and use of selection is inextricably tied to other human resource functions, organizational strategy, and external pressures such as labor conditions, unions, legal constraints, and societal values. In the remaining sections of this chapter we will attempt to explicate some of these interactions.

Interaction of Selection
With Other Human Resource Functions

In this section, we examine the interaction of selection with other human resource functions, including recruitment, training, and compensation. It is beyond the scope of this chapter—and, indeed, it is not the purpose of this book—to review or evaluate the research on these other human resource functions. Excellent reviews are available elsewhere (e.g., on recruitment, see Rynes, 1991; on training, see Goldstein, 1991; on compensation, see Gerhart, 1992). In this section we focus on how the practical usefulness of selection can be influenced by recruitment, training, and compensation.

Recruitment

To put it simply, recruitment is concerned with how organizations attract competent individuals to fill job positions. With current and projected labor shortages in some fields (e.g., engineers, programmers), attracting and retaining competent applicants is becoming increasingly important for organizational success, because superior human resources provide organizations with a competitive advantage

(Jackson & Schuler, 1990; Offermann & Gowing, 1990; Rynes, 1991; Wright, Ferris, Hiller, & Kroll, 1995). Clearly, a valid selection procedure is of little if any value when competent individuals are not attracted to the job. Recruitment and selection are inextricably related. In this subsection, we focus on how recruitment can influence the practical usefulness of valid selection.

The literature on recruitment distinguishes between *internal* recruitment (filling positions with current employees) and *external* recruitment (filling positions with individuals outside the organization). Schneider and Schmitt (1986) note that the central issue in internal recruitment is employee retention; the focus is on understanding the job and organizational conditions that current employees find attractive enough that they want to be candidates for the job. Because the goal is to retain a pool of competent internal recruits, research on job satisfaction, organizational commitment, and turnover is directly relevant to internal recruitment. To *have* internal recruits, the organization needs to gain the commitment of satisfied employees. In addition, to have a pool of competent internal recruits, the organization must retain adequate information on employees, based on carefully developed staff appraisal and career management systems, so that wise internal choices can be made. In external recruitment, the central issues are the ways in which individuals (applicants or potential applicants) and organizations become attracted to, and seek out, each other (Breaugh, 1992).

Traditionally, research on external recruitment has concentrated on three topics: recruiters, recruitment sources, and realistic job previews. Rynes (1991) provides an excellent review of these three topics. Recent recruitment research has moved beyond these traditional topics to examine the role of organizational and individual difference variables in applicant perceptions of organizational attractiveness and applicant decision processes. From an organizational perspective, understanding organizational attractiveness and applicant decision processes is important because these processes can influence the utility of a valid selection procedure. Recruitment and selection practices likely interact or complement each other in determining attributes of an organization's workforce. When competent recruits decline offers of employment, less desirable recruits are often accepted in place of the more desirable recruits who received the initial offers. Murphy (1986) has shown that under realistic circumstances of applicant acceptance/rejection of job offers, utility formulas currently used could overestimate utility gains by 30% to 80%. Rejected offers have a negative effect on the utility of valid selection tests. In addition, negative impressions formed by applicants could also affect the practical utility of selection indirectly, through the negative impacts resulting from applicants' statements about the organization to other potential candidates. The larger the pool of qualified applicants to choose from, the greater the potential utility of the selection system.

Rynes (1991) suggests that a primary way in which recruitment activities influence applicant attraction to the organization (and eventually applicant decision) is by providing information about work conditions in the organization. That is, recruitment activities are thought to provide applicants with "signals" about the unknown job and organizational attributes (Breaugh, 1992; Rynes, 1991). This by no means implies that organizations should maximize the positive nature of these signals by presenting maximally favorable job and organizational attributes in recruitment activities in order to attract competent applicants to accept job offers. Presenting inaccurate information or insufficient information about work conditions (especially the negative attributes) is counterproductive for the organization in the long term, because unrealistically positive job information leads to unmet expectations, which in turn probably constitute the primary reason for turnover. Indeed, the premise for the effectiveness of realistic job previews is that accurate and realistic job information, both positive *and* negative, will reduce the probability of unmet expectations (Wanous, 1992).

With the changing demographic composition of the workforce (and the applicant pool), there is increased recognition of the need to implement recruitment and selection functions that attract competent minorities and women (Jackson & Schuler, 1990; Offermann & Gowing, 1990). In response to this need, recent recruitment research has begun to examine the effects of recruitment signals relating to the demographic composition of the organization and organizational policies concerning the valuing of demographic diversity on effective recruitment of minorities and women. Studies from this stream of research also provide good illustrations of the increasingly popular interactionist perspective, which emphasizes the importance of person-organization fit in the organizational attractiveness and applicant decision processes. Studies adopting this interactionist perspective examine whether and how individual difference characteristics moderate the effects of organizational characteristics on applicant attraction to the organization or the decision to accept a job offer (e.g., Bretz, Ash, & Dreher, 1989; Cable & Judge, 1994; Chatman, 1989; Judge & Bretz, 1992; Turban & Keon, 1993). Recruitment research on "demographic signals" to applicants is based on hypotheses regarding previous demographic diversity research involving current employees. For example, Ely (1994, 1995) provides some evidence that the presence of females at upper levels in an organization influences female employees' job satisfaction and perceptions about their likelihood of succeeding in the organization. On the basis of Ely's findings and those of other researchers who have studied perceptions of minority and women employees (e.g., Tsui, Egan, & O'Reilly, 1992), Marrs, Turban, Dougherty, and Roberts (1996) hypothesized that sex, race, diversity beliefs, and openness to experience would moderate individual attraction to racially diverse and gender-diverse organizations. Marrs et al.'s results support their hypotheses: Women, minorities, persons high in openness to experience, and persons with positive cultural diversity beliefs were more attracted to organizations with high racial and gender diversity than were men, nonminorities, persons low in openness to experience, and persons with less positive cultural diversity beliefs. Marrs et al.'s findings are consistent with the person-organization fit perspective, which specifies that individual difference characteristics moderate the effects of organizational characteristics on applicant attraction.

The results of the Marrs et al. (1996) study have practical implications for the effective recruitment of minorities and women. For example, Marrs et al. suggest that organizations have high-level minority and women managers meet with minority and women applicants. The differential impacts of organizational diversity-related attributes on minority versus majority and female versus male applicant attraction clearly indicates that the successful recruitment of a competent and demographically diversified workforce is not solely a function of the validity and adverse impact levels of the selection procedures. In fact, the success or failure of a recruitment program may determine the utility of a selection system and may also affect the level of adverse impact produced by the selection system.

Traditionally, recruitment has been viewed as the staffing function preceding selection. However, as the above discussion indicates, separating staffing practices and activities into recruitment and selection functions is artificial and potentially misleading. Recruitment and selection are both integral parts of a two-way decision process in which the organization and the individual make judgments and choices. Not only does the organization try to select the most competent from a pool of applicants, but applicants also form impressions of the organization during recruitment and decide whether to pursue and accept the job offer. Organizational attractiveness, which is affected by recruitment activities, influences the practical usefulness of valid selection. In addition to recruitment activities, the selection process itself could also influence applicant impressions. Later in the chapter, we will devote a substantial amount of discussion to the nature of applicant reactions to selection systems and their impact on the practical usefulness of selection.

Training

The utility of selection is also affected by its relationship to training with respect to the KSAOs required for successful job performance. If the critical job tasks can be learned quickly and cheaply by almost all applicants through training or brief on-the-job instruction, then it may not be worthwhile or even necessary to install a selection system. On the other hand, if it is costly or difficult (or perhaps practically impossible) to train individuals in the critical KSAOs for successful job performance, then it becomes important to have in place a valid system for selecting the right individuals, who can either perform the job or have a high probability of training success. Hence, the decision concerning the implementation and use of a valid selection procedure has to take into account both the trainability of the critical KSAOs and the cost of training. Note that even if the critical KSAOs are trainable and individual differences in asymptotic levels of training performance are minimal, valid selection may still be useful if training is highly expensive or impractical. Indeed, utility assessments of selection procedures should incorporate not only the cost-benefit considerations of recruitment and selection, but also those of training. The two organizations described in Examples 1 and 2 in Chapter 1 both attempted to recruit and select some highly trained and technically skilled people as well as individuals with the ability to write and converse in languages other than English.

Traditionally, selection research and training research have followed two different streams conceptually corresponding to the "two disciplines of scientific psychology" (differential psychology versus experimental psychology), first described as such by Cronbach (1957). Selection researchers have adopted the "differential" school and put the research emphasis on individual differences. In the selection context, KSAOs are viewed as stable individual difference characteristics or traits that predict job performance. Training researchers, on the other hand, have adopted the "experimental" school and put the research emphasis on the learning (development) process. In the training context, KSAOs are construed as important knowledge or skills to be learned and developed so that trainees can apply them on the job for effective performance.

On the surface, selection and training perspectives appear to be incompatible. We normally think of traits as stable individual differences, and hence very unlike the malleable skills to be learned in training. However, these perspectives need not be incompatible. The two can be integrated through the adoption of a person-situation interaction approach. The first step in this approach is that both selection and training views have to undergo a reconceptualization of residual variance—that is, variability in performance that does not appear to result from selection or training efforts. Residual variance is not entirely made up of error variance due to random measurement error. A substantial portion of the residual variance may be the effect of variables not considered by the researcher. These variables are likely to be provided by "the other view." Hence, the selection researcher should consider including relevant situational variables traditionally examined in training research (e.g., teaching metacognitive strategies to achieve better performance) to account for variance in job performance (or some other criterion) not accounted for by individual difference variables. For example, Hanisch and Hulin (1994) conducted a simulation study in which 91 college students completed ability tests and training relevant to an air intercept and traffic control operator task. These authors found that training performance provided practically and statistically significant incremental validity in the prediction of task performance after ability was included as a predictor. Conversely, the training researcher should consider including relevant individual difference variables traditionally examined in selection research (e.g., cognitive ability) to account for variance in job or training performance not accounted for by situational variables. Note that the discussion to this point reflects the notions that better training should lead to better job performance *and* that more competent persons ought to perform and learn more effectively. It is also possible that one or the other of these two sets of variables places constraints on, or optimizes, the effects of the other. For example, even very able employees may not be able to perform complex tasks without adequate training, and very good and extensive training may make it possible for workers with minimal skills to perform jobs effectively. Aptitude-treatment interaction studies, which examine whether treatments (training) have differential impacts on individuals of differing levels on some trait (Cronbach, 1957; Cronbach & Snow, 1977), in the training and educational literature are good examples.

Perhaps a very simple practical implication of this discussion is that an organization's training and selection functions must complement each other. If no money or time is spent on selection, then provisions must be made to train employees who lack the requisite skills. If the organization has extensive training and remedial education courses to which it is prepared to send all employees who lack the relevant KSAOs, then selection is unimportant.

Note that the purpose of including additional variables is not simply to increase the proportion of variance accounted for. Indeed, from an implementation or practical perspective, proportion of variance is often not a very meaningful or useful index unless it is tied to some practically significant effects. The basic purpose of the search for additional or alternate variables is to obtain a conceptually adequate and empirically supported model of performance determinants to increase our understanding of the construct of job performance. Clearly, theory is important and can form the basis for consideration of implementation and use issues in both selection and training. The person-situation approach to integrating selection and training gives primacy to the need for a theory of job performance. Chan (1997a) provides an example of how Campbell's (1990) theory of performance could provide a conceptual framework for organizing and relating potential individual difference constructs, learning constructs, and job performance components in a nomological framework.

Compensation

Selecting competent applicants and employing them has practical value to the organization to the extent that these competent individuals choose to use their skills and knowledge to perform the job well and help the organization reach productivity and quality goals. Hence, the organization must provide inducements to attract competent individuals to join the organization, to motivate them to exercise effort, to retain them, and to reward them for their contributions. Compensation is at the heart of this employment exchange relationship between the individual and the organization (Gerhart, 1992). Without an adequate compensation system that attracts, motivates, and retains competent individuals, a valid selection system is limited in its practical usefulness.

The administration of compensation can also affect the practical usefulness of selection. For example, a compensation system may be structured in such a way that selection mistakes cost the organization relatively little. An obvious example is a situation in which employees are paid piece rates; under this arrangement, the organization is "protected" from hiring low-productivity individuals because the wages vary directly with the individual's performance. If investment brokers, insurance salespersons, or even a door-to-door salespersons receive the bulk of their compensation based on commissions, it is not costly for the organization to hire individuals and let them fail. If enough are hired and a few succeed, the organization suffers relatively little from having low-productivity individuals because the wages of low-performing individuals will be proportionately low. In such situations, selection may not be necessary or cost-effective even if a valid system is available. This, of course, assumes that employees cannot actually harm the organization by treating customers inappropriately or by carelessly damaging or misusing organizational resources and equipment. It also assumes that the organization does not invest a great deal in training those who fail.

Researchers on compensation have used agency theory, reinforcement theory, expectancy theory, and equity theory to explain the potential influence of compensation programs on employee performance (for reviews, see Gerhart, 1992; Gerhart, Minkoff, & Olsen, 1995; Noe, Hollenbeck, Gerhart, & Wright, 1994). Although little empirical research has directly examined the relationship between compensation and selection at the organizational level of analysis, the theories used in compensation research provide a rich conceptual base for such theory-driven empirical research. For example, equity theory suggests that social comparisons affect how individuals evaluate their pay. When evaluating the pay or other benefits offered by an organization, applicants are likely to make external comparisons between what they would receive and what they believe is received by similar others in other organizations. Such comparisons should affect organizational attractiveness and applicant decisions, which, as discussed earlier, in turn have consequences for the practical usefulness of selection.

Selection as Strategy

Selection, like other human resource functions, occurs within the broader context of the organization's strategic business management. *Strategic management* refers to the process through which the organization addresses the competitive challenges it faces. The goals of strategic human resource management are to acquire, deploy, and allocate human resources in ways that provide the organization a competitive advantage. Many of the competitive challenges facing organizations today are related to changes in technology, communications, and the way work is organized and performed. We will discuss these specific changes and challenges for selection research in Chapter 8; in this section we focus more generally on how selection can be used to accomplish organizational objectives or strategies.

Before we address the idea of selection as strategy, it may be useful to distinguish between two distinct but interdependent components in the strategic management process: strategy formation and strategy implementation. During *strategy formation,* planners define the organization's mission, values, and goals; identify its external opportunities and threats; and determine its strengths and weaknesses. The planners then generate, compare, and select strategic alternatives. During *strategy implementation,* the selected strategy is carried out through the structuring of the organization, changes in the way work is performed, and the development and implementation of human resource programs. Selection as strategy implementation is a familiar topic in contemporary discussions on strategic human resource management. However, the idea of selection as strategy is applicable to both strategy formation and strategy implementation. Below, we first discuss strategy implementation, followed by strategy formation.

The focus in traditional selection research has been on the match between the person and the job. Although systematic efforts to maximize person-job fit may benefit staffing decisions in predictable organizational environments, the static person-job match approach becomes inadequate in many contemporary dynamic environments where jobs change because of technological advances and organizational innovations (Schneider & Konz, 1989; Snow & Snell, 1993). In the face of these changes and competitive challenges, selection must be linked to strategy management if it is to remain relevant. A commonly accepted linkage is to view selection as a component of strategy implementation (e.g., Miles & Snow, 1984; Noe et al., 1994; Snow & Snell, 1993). Selection can identify applicants with the necessary KSAOs that will help the organization achieve its strategic objectives. That is, the organization has to be staffed with individuals with the necessary KSAOs to perform their part effectively in implementing the strategy.

Selection, together with other human resource functions, including recruitment, training, and compensation, helps ensure that the right individuals are available to carry out the strategy. Organizations engaging in different strategies are likely to require individuals with different KSAOs. For example, borrowing from Miles and Snow's (1978) typology of strategic types, "defender" organizations (i.e., those that are efficiency oriented, with narrow and stable product or service market domains) are likely to require individuals who are different from those required by "prospector" organizations (i.e., organizations that are innovation oriented, with diverse and dynamic product or service domains). Individuals well suited to organizations engaging in a defender strategy may be those who are risk averse, prefer structure and stability, and are comfortable with repetitive functioning within a consensually agreed-upon problem-solving paradigm. On the other hand, individuals who are innovative, enjoy taking risks, and are comfortable with working outside the agreed paradigm or perceive the existing paradigm as part of the problem may be well suited to organizations engaging in a prospector strategy. To align with strategy, the selection system may have to consider selection KSAOs that match the strategic demands. For example, the adaptation-innovation cognitive style of problem solving at work (Kirton, 1976) appears to be a selection KSAO directly relevant to the defender-prospector strategy distinction. In Kirton's theory of cognitive style, *adaptors* are individuals who prefer to operate within consensually agreed-upon paradigms and are skilled in initiating changes that improve (adapt) current ways of doing things. *Innovators* are more likely to reconstruct the problem and tend to perceive the existing paradigm as part of the problem. They prefer to work outside the agreed-upon paradigm and are skilled in initiating changes based on different ways of doing things. There is some indirect evidence that the adaptation-innovation cognitive style is related to strategic demands. Specifically, individuals who operate in a relatively structured environment and whose work is focused on their own internal processes (i.e., groups predominant in adaptation demands) tend to be adaptors, as measured by Kirton's (1977) Adaption-Innovation Inventory. Examples of such adaptive groups include bankers, cost accountants, and those involved in maintenance or production, who largely operate in well-defined systems within which solutions to problems can be found (Gul, 1986; Hayward & Everett, 1983; Holland, 1987; Kirton, 1980; Kirton & Pender, 1982). Conversely, individuals who operate in relatively unstructured environments and whose work either embodies several systems or is focused on the interface between systems (i.e., groups predominant in innovation demands) tend to be more innovative in orientation. Examples of such innovative groups include those in consultancy, marketing, personnel, planning, research and development, and sales, who largely operate in fluid conditions under which existing paradigms may form part of the problem (Keller & Holland, 1978; Kirton, 1980; Kirton & Pender, 1982; Lowe & Taylor, 1986; Thomson, 1980).

In addition to effective job performance, selecting individuals who match the organization's strategic demands may also benefit the organization in the longer term through retention. In a heterogeneous sample of engineers performing either staff or research/development functions, Chan (1996a) found that the misfit between individual adaptation-innovation cognitive style and the style demands of the work context provided significant and substantial incremental validity in predicting turnover over the predictability provided by job performance. Finally, note that the linkage of selection to strategy implementation requires that strategy supplements the traditional job analysis as the basis for development of critical KSAOs. Strategy may also change the mix and weights of selection criteria (Butler, Ferris, & Napier, 1991).

Another example of the interaction between HRM practices and organizational practices is provided by the work of Youndt, Snell, Dean, and Lepak (1996). In a study of 97 plants in the metal-working industry, Youndt et al. analyzed the degree to which various "human-capital-enhancing practices," including selection, training, and compensation, were related to general manager self-report measures of several firm indices, such as product quality, employee morale, on-time deliveries, inventory management, employee productivity, equipment utilization, production lead time, and scrap minimization. The HRM practices were related to firm effectiveness, but Youndt et al. also found support for a contingency explanation of the HRM practices-firm effectiveness relationship. The impact of human-capital-enhancing practices was evident primarily when the manufacturing strategy emphasized product quality. Three of the interactions that Youndt et al. report are displayed in Figure 7.1. In each instance, the dotted line represents the main effect of HRM practices on a firm-level outcome. When firms are divided by manufacturing strategy, it is clear that HRM practices have their greatest impact when the firm emphasizes the manufacture of a high-quality product.

Selection assumes a subordinate role in its linkage with strategy implementation. This selection-strategy relationship is reversed in the linkage between selection and strategy formation. Selection can propel strategy formation (Dyer, 1983, 1984; Golden & Ramanujam, 1985). With the shortening of business cycles and acceleration of technological advances, many organizations find it increasingly difficult to develop and engage in a sustainable specific strategy (Ohmae, 1982). Strategy scholars suggest that in such dynamic and transitory competitive environments, people are likely to become the most sustainable source of competitive advantage (Pucik, 1988; Schuler & MacMillan, 1984). As noted by Snow and Snell (1993), because people can adapt to changes in the environment and learn new skills to meet new demands, they are a self-renewing resource, and the quality of human resources in an organization becomes the foundation of its competitive strategy. Selection then becomes a precursor to strategy in the strategic management process. The "best" individuals to be selected are not necessarily those who can effectively implement a specific

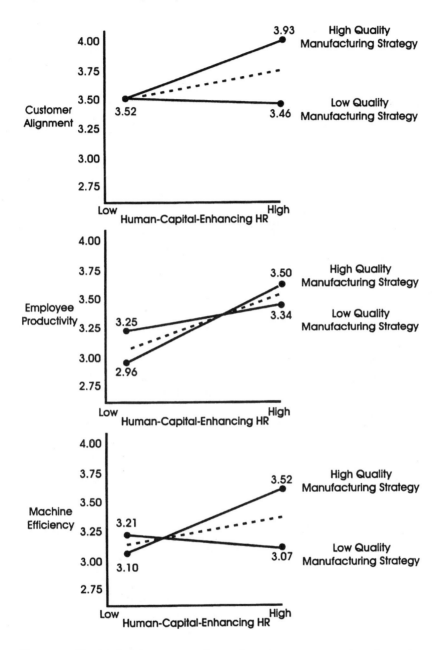

Figure 7.1. The Moderating Impact of Manufacturing Strategy on the Relationship Between Firm Performance and Human Resource Practices

SOURCE: Youndt et al. (1996). Reprinted by permission of the Academy of Management.

chosen strategy. Rather, they are those who possess the KSAOs that would make up a broad skill base that can be used to develop strategies rapidly for dealing with future competitive realities.

For selection to propel strategy formation effectively, selection research will have to move beyond the traditional individual difference predictors (e.g., cognitive ability, conscientiousness) and the static notion of person-job match. There is a need to examine more complex predictor constructs construed in terms of dynamic interactions between the individual's repertoire of behavior and the situation's changing demands. The recent literature on the construct of *adaptability* (Chan, 1997a; Kozlowski et al., 1994; Mumford, Baughman, Threlfall, Uhlman, & Costanza, 1993) provides a conceptual and empirical foundation for further examination of the selection-strategy formation linkage, which, at present, is more of a philosophy than a practice.

External Pressures

The capability of an organization or manager to use the results of a selection procedure in a rational manner—that is, selecting a small proportion of the total applicant pool whose predicted performance is the highest—is constrained by a variety of external pressures. Most obviously, the labor market may constrain the degree to which a manager can and cannot be selective. In addition, there are a variety of legal, social, and organizational constraints that sometimes make it difficult or impossible for managers to use tests optimally, as defined in psychometric terms (see Chapter 6 on test bias and differential item functioning).

Perhaps the most significant and controversial of these constraints have been legal. Some of the major legal developments of the past 35 years concerning personnel selection are summarized in Table 7.2. Beginning at least with the passage of Title VII of the Civil Rights Act of 1964, the courts have been involved in many hundreds of cases in which various parties have alleged that organizations' hiring practices are illegally discriminatory. Title VII made it illegal for an organization with more than 15 employees or a labor union or employment agency "to fail, refuse to hire, discharge any individual with respect to his compensation terms, conditions, or privileges of employment because

Table 7.2   U.S. Laws and U.S. Supreme Court Cases Affecting Employee Selection
Practices

Civil Rights Act of 1964: Title VII of this act made it illegal "to fail or refuse to hire or to
discharge any individual, or otherwise to discriminate against any individual with
respect to his compensation, terms, conditions, or privileges of employment because of such individual's race, color, religion, sex, or national origin." A federal
agency, the Equal Employment Opportunity Commission, was created to administer the law.

Executive Order 11246 (Office of Federal Contract Compliance, 1968): President Lyndon
Johnson issued an executive order in 1965 in which all organizations employing 15
or more persons having contracts with the federal government were prohibited
from discriminating on the basis of race, religion, color, sex, or national origin. This
order also required employers to take *affirmative action* to ensure that women and
minorities were hired. Employers were required to file timetables and goals in which
they reported areas of underutilization of protected groups and steps they would
take to remedy these deficiencies. The U.S. Department of Labor was given authority to investigate and monitor compliance with the order.

Age Discrimination in Employment Act of 1967: This act, passed in 1967 and amended in
1978, protects employees between the ages of 40 and 70 from discrimination on the
basis of age. Employers may use age as a qualification, but only if it is a legitimate
and necessary qualification.

Griggs v. Duke Power Co. (1971): The Duke Power Co. in North Carolina had a policy of
promoting employees out of the labor pool to higher-skill jobs only if they were
high school graduates and had passing scores on two aptitude tests. Black applicants
tended to score lower on the two tests and were less likely to have high school
diplomas. Consequently, they were more likely to be passed over for promotion.
The U.S. Supreme Court ruled that if selection procedures have an adverse impact
on the hiring of a protected group, the employer must show that the procedures are
valid even if the discrimination was unintentional. The Court also cited an early
version of the "Uniform Guidelines" (see EEOC, CSC, DOL, & DOJ, 1978) in
presenting the rationale for its decision.

Albemarle Paper Company v. Moody (1975): As in the *Duke Power* case, the Albemarle Paper
Company's use of tests led to discrimination against Black employees in hiring and
promotion. Unlike in *Duke Power,* the company in this case presented evidence for
the validity of its selection procedures. The U.S. Supreme Court ruled against the
employer largely on the basis of the poor technical quality of the validation research.
Again, the Court quoted and followed technical guidelines set forth in an early
version of the "Uniform Guidelines" of the EEOC in presenting the decision.

Regents of the University of California v. Bakke (1978): Allan Bakke, a White applicant for
admission to the Medical College of the University of California, alleged reverse
discrimination in two different years because minorities with substantially lower
scores than his were admitted under a special program for minorities who claimed
disadvantaged status. The U.S. Supreme Court ruled that Bakke's constitutional
rights had been violated and that Bakke should be admitted, but it also ruled that
under some circumstances (e.g., a past history of institutional discrimination)
racial diversity might be a legitimate consideration in admissions decisions.

(continued)

Table 7.2   Continued

Connecticut v. Teal (1982): In this case, the U.S. Supreme Court was asked to rule on the bottom-line concept that various steps in an employment process might produce unequal hiring rates if the overall process (or bottom line) produced relatively equal hiring rates. The Court ruled that the U.S. Constitution protects individual rights, hence, each step in an employment process must be examined and may be challenged. This ruling was very important to most organizations because some steps in many hiring processes are difficult to validate.

Watson v. Fort Worth Bank & Trust (1988): Asked to rule on the requirement that subjective supervisor recommendations be validated when they produce adverse impact, the U.S. Supreme Court indicated that subjective procedures do need to be validated. The Court, however, also stated that the plaintiff must identify the specific practice that is producing adverse impact along with evidence that this practice is causing a loss of equal opportunity. The Court also said that cost factors, both in developing alternative selection procedures and in conducting expensive validation studies, might be considered by the courts in their decision making.

Americans with Disabilities Act of 1990 (Bureau of National Affairs, 1990): This act makes it unlawful to discriminate against a qualified person with a disability in making employment decisions. *Disability* is defined broadly as including a physical or mental impairment that substantially limits one or more of the major life activities, a record of such an impairment, or being regarded as having such an impairment. A *qualified individual with a disability* is defined as an individual with a disability who, with or without reasonable accommodation, can perform the essential functions of the employment position. This act has yet to be interpreted in the courts.

Civil Rights Act of 1991: During the 1980s, the U.S. Supreme Court handed down several decisions that made it much harder for a person filing a suit (the plaintiff) to prove discrimination. The *Duke Power* case made it clear that if there is adverse impact against a protected group, the burden is on the employer to show that selection procedures are valid. In *Wards Cove Packing Co., Inc. v. Atonio et al.* (1989), however, the U.S. Supreme Court placed much more of a burden on the plaintiff. In the Civil Rights Act of 1991, Congress stated that "the decision of the Supreme Court in *Wards Cove Packing Co. v. Atonio,* 490 U.S. 642 (1989) has weakened the scope and effectiveness of Federal civil rights protections." Consequently, the act made into law the concepts set forth in *Duke Power* and also extended the Civil Rights Act of 1964 by allowing the plaintiff to have a jury trial and to claim punitive damages. However, this same act forbade the use of any adjustments to scores on selection procedures to ensure that greater proportions of any race or gender subgroup be hired.

Proposition 209, State of California (1996): Not a federal law or U.S. Supreme Court case, this proposition was passed into state law by California voters. It forbids the use of racial preferences in public employment, public education, and public contracting. Although obviously not binding on other states or the federal government, the passage of Proposition 209 has contributed to the consideration of similar laws in many other states.

of the individual's race, color, religion, sex, or national origin." Title VII, along with the development of case law in this area and the publication of the "Uniform Guidelines on Employee Selection Procedures" (EEOC, CSC, DOL, & DOJ, 1978), has very often placed organizations using some selection procedures in a difficult position. Especially in the case of cognitive ability tests, which are usually valid predictors of performance, the differences between majority and minority groups' scores are often high, producing adverse impact and the requirement that the organization present convincing information that its selection procedures are valid (see Chapter 5 for details on various procedures).

In addition to the Civil Rights Act of 1964, President Johnson's Executive Order 11246 required federal agencies and private organizations that do business with the federal government to have and to abide by equal employment policies, to analyze their workforces to determine whether women or minorities are underutilized, and to develop and use plans to remediate any underutilization. This order required organizations to develop affirmative action plans that were very often difficult, if not impossible, to accomplish. To meet these plans, some organizations were forced to hire women or members of minority groups whose qualifications, as defined by test scores, were lower than those of White males. This led in turn to cases in which White males alleged reverse discrimination. Affirmative action plans such as those originating in President Johnson's executive order have continued to be controversial, especially in the 1990s, and led President Clinton to set up a committee to study the advisability of the continuance of affirmative action plans. President Clinton accepted the committee's recommendation that affirmative action plans are still needed, but that aspects of their implementation should be changed.

Perhaps the best summary of research on the impact of affirmative action plans has been compiled by a committee of the Society for Industrial and Organizational Psychology (Kravitz et al., 1997). These researchers conclude that the target groups of affirmative action plans have gained in terms of employment rates, earned income, and promotion rates, but the gains have not been substantial, and there may be explanations other than formal affirmative action plans for these improvements. At the organizational level, scientists have argued that affirmative action would decrease organizational effectiveness because of the lowering of the qualifications of hired personnel; others have argued that organizations would be more effective because of the increased diversity of the workforce. There is no convincing evidence that organizational effectiveness has been influenced one way or the other by affirmative action, though charges of discrimination have often led to lowered stock values and public recognition of successful affirmative action plans has sometimes led to increased stock value. The latter finding, of course, could be a recognition of the legal costs associated with discrimination lawsuits. Attitudes toward affirmative action plans that rely heavily on demographic status are usually more negative than those toward plans that emphasize qualifications and equal opportunity. These attitudes are probably mediated by perceptions of fairness and self-interest. Clearly, however, the legal as well as the social impacts of affirmative action set constraints on how organizations employ and promote people. It is unfortunate that organizational scientists still understand very little about what makes for good affirmative action plans and how these plans and the public perception of these plans affect the organization's capability to recruit and employ an effective workforce as well as the organization's overall effectiveness.

As we mentioned in Chapter 6, the Americans with Disabilities Act of 1990 also complicates the use of many selection procedures. This act requires that organizations accommodate individuals with disabilities in testing situations so that their disabilities do not affect their performance on selection tests in ways that are not relevant to the assessment of the targeted KSAO. This can mean supplying a reader or a Braille version of a test for a blind examinee or the suspension of a test's time limits for an examinee with reading problems or learning disabilities. Given the normative interpretation of most tests and the fact that tests are usually normed under the conditions set out in the test manuals, scores of individuals for whom the testing conditions have been modified are of questionable interpretation. Because of the many different types of disabilities and accommodations, the number of individuals in each of these groups is very small, making it difficult to do research on the effects of any given accommodation.

The effects of hiring persons through affirmative action or based on provisions of the ADA on the motivation and performance of these people as well as the views of others in the organization have not been frequently studied. Most of this work has involved women who have been hired under affirmative action plans (Kravitz et al., 1997). These studies indicate that being hired in affirmative action circumstances can adversely affect the self-evaluation and self-efficacy of the hired persons, but there is little effect on the motivation level of these employees. Little work has been done on the performance of these people and the attitudes of others in the organization toward those who are hired as the result of affirmative action plans.

Legal and social developments have stimulated a variety of other scientific developments as well. During the 1970s, there was a great deal of research that investigated the degree to which tests are valid for different demographic subgroups; more basically, there was an examination of what constitutes test bias. The conclusions derived from this activity were that tests are usually valid for different subgroups (e.g., Schmidt, Berner, & Hunter, 1973) and that psychometric or test bias is most appropriately assessed using the Cleary (1968) approach (Linn, 1978), as described in Chapter 6.

The sometimes opposing objectives of affirmative action and merit hiring have been important concerns of organizations for the past 30 years. They have also created controversy over the degree to which psychologists reconcile these objectives in working for organizations and in recommending procedures for the selection of personnel. A highly controversial recent example involved the development of test procedures for the selection of entry-level police personnel in Nassau County, New York. A panel of psychologists was engaged by the Department of Justice and Nassau County (parties in continued litigation spanning about 15 years) to develop valid procedures that would minimize adverse impact. This panel recommended the use of a set of personality measures and a reading comprehension test as the basis for making selections. A number of psychologists expressed the view that this amounted to removing from consideration important cognitive skills (Gottfredson, 1996b) and that the result for Nassau County would be a serious decrement in the performance of its police personnel (Gottfredson, 1996a). The psychologists who developed the test battery replied that cognitive ability tests had not been highly valid predictors of performance in other police organizations (see Hirsh, Northrop, & Schmidt, 1986); that the organization was requiring a year of college as a basic qualification, thus potentially minimizing the need for cognitive ability assessment; and that the organization had a relatively academically rigorous training program. The criticisms of this test battery are marked by great emotionality and unnecessary and unjustified personal attacks, but they do indicate the complexity and seriousness of the stakes in this debate.

Another significant feature of the environment that may affect the way selection procedures are used is the unionization of the workforce. Union contracts frequently specify that those individuals who have served in an organization the longest be given preference in personnel decisions. Gordon and Johnson (1982) reviewed the literature on seniority and found that the evidence suggested there was little or no relationship between the length of time that a person was employed in an organization and measure of ability or performance. In fact, there may actually be a negative relationship between seniority and performance. Seniority can be used as a basis of reward for long-term committed service to an organization, but its use as a promotional mechanism may preclude the use of more valid procedures that would result in a workforce whose expected performance is greater.

Even when the position for which people are being recruited and selected is an entry-level position, it is likely that the union will be interested in the way in which employees are selected. In those instances, the organization and the psychologists developing and validating procedures will have to negotiate with union personnel in setting up those procedures. In one instance in which one of the authors was involved, a union flatly refused to allow a criterion-related validation effort because it would necessitate the collection of performance data.

Finally, there are always many issues in the local organizational culture or community that restrict or heavily influence an organization's decisions with respect to what procedures can be used. Introduction of a structured interview in an organization in which it has been traditional for managers to conduct and control the interview process will certainly be controversial and will require negotiation and continued monitoring if the intervention is to be successful. What competitors use to make selection decisions will often play a significant role in what an organization will use. These examples underscore Johns' (1993) argument that human resource procedures or policies are innovations that must be negotiated and fostered during the adoption, implementation, and diffusion phases.

Applicant Reactions

Traditionally, selection research has focused on the organizational perspective and, with the exception of the literature on realistic job previews (e.g., McEvoy & Cascio, 1985; Wanous, 1992), has paid little attention to the individual perspective of the applicant. But, as discussed earlier, selection is clearly a two-way street, with both the organization and the individual applicant having a series of decisions to make. Recent research has begun to recognize the importance of investigating the applicant's perspective when considering the implementation and use of selection. In this section, we focus on the recent surge of interest in applicant reactions research.

In recent years, a substantial number of studies have been conducted on applicant reactions to selection systems, as researchers have become more cognizant of the potential important practical implications of these reactions. Several researchers have noted the practical implications of applicant reactions for personnel marketing, applicant pursuit and acceptance of job offers, likelihood of litigation and successful legal defense of selection procedures, and test validity and utility (Arvey & Sackett, 1993; Chan, 1997b; Chan & Schmitt, 1997; Chan, Schmitt, DeShon, Clause, & Delbridge, 1997; Gilliland, 1994; Macan, Avedon, Paese, & Smith, 1994; Rynes & Connerly, 1993; Schmitt & Gilliland, 1992; Schuler & Fruhner, 1993; Smither, Reilly, Millsap, Pearlman, & Stoffey, 1993). Empirical evidence for some of these practical applications has been accumulating. For example, research has shown that job pursuit intentions and job choice decisions are influenced by college recruiting and interviewing practices (Harris & Fink, 1987; Powell, 1991; Rynes, Bretz, & Gerhart, 1991; Schmitt & Coyle, 1976). Smither et al. (1993) found that applicant reactions to a range of civil service examinations and their willingness to recommend the employer to others (assessed 1 month after the examination) were positively correlated. There is also some evidence to suggest that reactions to cognitive ability tests could influence test-taking motivation and performance on the test itself, and could account for a portion of the Black-White difference in test scores typically observed on standardized paper-and-pencil ability tests (Chan & Schmitt, 1997; Chan et al., 1997). For examples of the manner in which some of these reactions are measured, see the items presented in Table 7.3.

For both conceptual and practical reasons, it is important to identify what attributes of selection procedures contribute to favorable applicant reactions. Schmidt, Greenthal, Hunter, Berner, and Seaton (1977) found that perceptions of work sample tests were more favorable than

Table 7.3   Examples of Items Used to Measure Some Test Reaction Constructs

Face validity perceptions

I can see a clear connection between the test and what I think is required by the job.

The actual content of the test is related to job tasks.

I do not understand what the test had to do with the job.

Predictive validity perceptions

I am confident that the test can predict how well an applicant will perform the job.

The employer should be able to tell a lot about the applicant's ability to do the job based on the results of this test.

Failing to perform well on the test indicates that the applicant cannot perform well on the job.

Fairness perceptions

I feel that using this test to select applicants for the job is fair.

The use of the test would allow for the screening of all applicants fairly and giving them the same opportunity for the job.

Using the test would cut down on favoritism, which can sometimes be a problem when applicants are selected for jobs.

Using the test to select applicants for the job may introduce bias or discrimination.

Motivation

Doing well on this test was very important to me.

I tried my best on this test.

I was extremely motivated to do well on the test.

those of paper-and-pencil measures of cognitive ability. However, in Schmidt et al.'s study and in other studies demonstrating that selection procedures involving simulations (e.g., assessment centers, work samples) elicit more favorable examinee reactions than those using paper-and-pencil measures (e.g., Dodd, 1977; Macan et al., 1994; Smither et al., 1993), it is not clear which aspects of these tests are responsible for the positive reactions. These studies compared reactions across tests that differed in both the method of testing and the test content. For example, assessment centers and traditional cognitive ability tests differ in the method of testing (e.g., actual task performance versus paper-and-pencil) *and* presumably in the nature of the constructs measured (e.g., interpersonal-oriented dimensions versus general cognitive ability) due to different item content between the two tests. The distinction between method and content is crucial to increasing our understanding of test reactions and to the study of the reduction in adverse reactions to tests. The method-content distinction is particularly crucial to the study of subgroup differences (e.g., racial subgroup differences) in test reactions. To understand subgroup differences in reactions to different tests, one must isolate subgroup differences due to method and subgroup differences due to content.

An understanding of the determinants of subgroup differences may allow the reduction or even elimination of subgroup differences in test reactions through a change in the method of testing or the test content. For example, two different methods of testing may have the same test content measuring the same job-relevant construct, but one method may produce less subgroup difference in test reactions than the other. Subgroup difference in reactions that is a function of method of testing can then be eliminated through the use of the method with lower subgroup differences in reactions, assuming that subgroup differences in reactions are undesirable. In previous work, we have demonstrated how differences attributable to test method and those attributable to test content can be isolated to help clarify the aspects of tests responsible for test reactions (Chan, 1997b; Chan & Schmitt, 1997).

Early research on applicant or test reactions was descriptive rather than explanatory; that is, researchers focused only on the description of examinee reactions to different tests and comparisons of reactions across tests (e.g., Dodd, 1977; Robertson & Kandola, 1982; Schmidt et al., 1977). Recent research is characterized by more construct-oriented and theory-driven approaches to the study of applicant reactions. We will discuss two such streams of research. The first consists of construct-oriented studies that focus on the relationship between test reactions and test performance. These studies attempt to understand the nature of reactions by examining their causal relationship with test performance. As we will show later, clarifying the nature of the reactions-performance relationship has important practical implications. The second stream of research consists of studies that employ organizational justice theories to explain applicant fairness perceptions and related reactions. This stream of research is a good example of how theory can form the basis for consideration of implementation and use issues in personnel selection.

Several researchers have argued that reactions to cognitive ability tests are important because they may influence performance on the tests (Arvey, Strickland, Drauden, & Martin, 1990; Cascio, 1987a; Chan et al., 1997; Robertson & Kandola, 1982). These researchers assert that examinees who have negative reactions to a test have low test-taking motivation, and hence will perform poorly on the test. Chan et al. (1997) note that if reactions can influence test performance, then an important practical implication is that it may be possible to increase test performance through interventions (e.g., writing face-valid test items) that will engender more positive reactions. Chan et al. also note that the finding that reactions affect performance on cognitive ability tests does not necessarily change the established validity of cognitive ability tests in predicting job performance. For example, it is possible that test performance may still predict job performance well because it measures both ability and motivational (reaction) differences, and those with low test reactions are also less motivated in the actual job. However, the finding does affect the construct validity of cognitive ability tests insofar as inferences may be made on the basis of test scores about examinees' abilities when a component of the systematic variance in test scores reflects motivational differences.

In the personality area, Schmit, Ryan, Stierwalt, and Powell (1995) report that reframing items on the Conscientiousness scale of the NEO Five Factor Inventory (Costa & McCrae, 1989) led to more positive reactions and to better validity. Items were rewritten to reflect a school context and validity was assessed using grade point average as a criterion. This change in frame of reference and the criterion used was appropriate for their student respondents. A replication of this study in a work-related context would be very useful.

Inferences on causal directions are problematic in the majority of reactions studies because reaction responses are obtained only once and only after examinees have completed the actual test. In such studies, the finding of a significant correlation between test performance and posttest reactions per se is consistent with one or more of the following possibilities: Reactions (developed prior to or during completion of the test) affected performance; performance influenced reactions; reciprocal causation exists between reactions and performance; or some omitted third variable, such as general belief in tests, caused both reactions and performance. In their attempt to clarify the causal relationships between reactions and performance, Chan et al. (1997) had examinees respond to reaction measures (face validity perceptions and test-taking motivation) after they had completed a cognitive ability test but before they proceeded to complete a subsequent parallel test. Results indicated that reactions accounted for unique variance in performance on the second test after the researchers controlled for performance on the first test. Chan et al.'s test of the effect of reactions was highly conservative because they used performance on a parallel test as a control. The correlation between the two parallel tests was .84, and Chan et al. used the contribution of reactions to performance on the second test beyond what would have been predicted on the basis of scores on the first test as the estimate of the effect of reactions on performance.

Because reaction responses were collected only after performance on the first test, Chan et al.'s study does not provide a direct assessment of the effect of pretest reactions on performance or a direct comparison between pretest and posttest reactions. Distinguishing pretest from posttest reactions may be important in studies designed to contribute to our understanding of the reactions-performance relationship. Pretest and posttest reaction responses are likely not interchangeable. For example, given a cognitive ability test, it is possible that relative to posttest reaction responses, pretest reaction responses are more influenced by examinees' general belief in tests and their past experiences with tests, and that posttest reaction responses are influenced by performance on the test. Reactions to the test may be self-serving in the sense that examinees who believe that they did poorly report the test is unfair or irrelevant, whereas those who did well report favorable reactions to the test. Examining the relationships among pretest reactions, test performance, and posttest reactions is important for conceptual, methodological, and practical reasons. Conceptually, such an examination could help clarify the nature of test reactions and the causal relationships between test performance and reactions. Methodologically, if reaction data collected before and after test performance yield different response patterns and have differential associations with external variables (e.g., test performance, general belief in tests), then reaction responses across the two measurement occasions may not be equivalent or directly comparable. When reaction responses from pretest and posttest measurements are combined across studies in a meta-analysis, the results may not be meaningful and may even be misleading.

As noted earlier, test reactions have practical implications because they may influence examinees' attitudes, intentions, and behaviors relevant to the organization. If examinees' pretest and posttest reactions differ as a function of test performance, then inferences based on reactions to selection instruments that underlie important practical recommendations and decisions may vary simply depending on when reaction responses are collected. For instance, in some testing situations (e.g., civil service and police examinations), candidates are typically given sample items prior to actual testing. Test reactions from these candidates could affect their attitudes, intentions, and behaviors toward the organization (e.g., pursuing the job application, recommending the organization to other potential candidates) *prior to actual testing,* but these attitudes, intentions, and behaviors may change *after actual testing* as reactions change after performance on the test.

Recently, we completed a study that directly examined pretest and posttest reactions (Chan, Schmitt, Sacco, & DeShon, 1998). The findings shed some light on the reactions-performance relationship. In the study, we examined the relationships among belief in tests, pretest reactions, test performance, and posttest reactions for cognitive ability and personality tests by using structural equations to model the relationships between test performance and test reactions of 197 undergraduate examinees. On the basis of previous conceptual and empirical work (Arvey et al., 1990; Cascio, 1987a; Chan et al., 1997; Robertson & Kandola, 1982), we predicted that on the cognitive ability test, there would be a reciprocal causal relationship between reactions and performance. That is, pretest reactions would influence performance and performance would influence posttest reactions, even after pretest reactions were controlled for. Neither pretest nor posttest reactions were expected to be related to performance on the personality test, which acted as a quasi-control condition. As hypothesized, we found that on the cognitive ability test, pretest reactions affected test performance and mediated the relationship between belief in tests and test performance. Test performance affected posttest reactions even after the effect of pretest reactions was taken into account. On the personality test, belief in tests affected pretest and posttest reactions, but the three variables were unrelated to test performance (Conscientiousness scores). In addition, we established the generality of these hypothesized relationships across racial groups by demonstrating measurement and structural invariance across Black and White examinees.

Theories of applicant reactions are lacking. At present, organizational justice theories probably constitute the only systematic theoretical framework for examining applicant reactions. There is considerable evidence that perceptions of procedural justice (Leventhal, Karuza, & Fry, 1980)—that is, perceptions about the fairness of the process for distributing rewards regardless of the outcome of the distribution—can influence attitudes about the organization (Folger & Greenberg, 1985; Folger & Konovsky, 1989; Greenberg, 1987, 1990; Kanfer, 1990). For example, studies have shown that fairness or justice perceptions about procedures (e.g., drug testing, grievance resolution, pay raise decisions) are related to citizenship behavior (Moorman, 1991), organizational commitment (McFarlin & Sweeney, 1992), and job satisfaction and performance (Konovsky & Cropanzano, 1991). On the basis of these findings, researchers have argued that applicants who perceive a selection procedure as fair should also be more likely to have positive reactions to and attitudes toward the organization regardless of the selection outcome (e.g., Arvey & Sackett, 1993; Gilliland, 1994; Smither, Millsap, Stoffey, Reilly, & Pearlman, 1996).

Gilliland (1993) defines a number of procedural justice rules specifically for the selection context and classifies these rules into three categories (see Table 7.4). *Formal* rules are determined by the type and content of the specific tests or procedures used in the selection process. Examples of formal rules include job-relatedness of the selection test, opportunity to perform during the selection process, and the consistency of test administration. *Explanation* rules are concerned with the extent to which information derived from the selection process is made known and the decisions made using this information are explained to applicants. Examples include feedback about test results and explanations and justifications regarding how and why selection decisions are made. *Interpersonal treatment* rules concern the actions of test administrators and other human resource personnel encountered by applicants during the selection process; they refer to the extent to which applicants perceived themselves as being treated fairly. Gilliland argues that violations of these rules lead to perceptions of procedural injustice and negative applicant reactions. Findings from studies on reactions are generally consistent with Gilliland's model. For example, Smither et al. (1993) found that applicant perceptions of procedural fairness in civil service examinations were related to their perceptions of job-relatedness of the examinations. In addition, procedural fairness perceptions were related to applicants' willingness to recommend the organization to others.

We believe that studies examining procedural fairness perceptions of selection procedures should also assess, whenever possible, distributive (outcome) fairness perceptions. The organizational justice

Table 7.4   Brief Summary of Gilliland's (1993) Procedural Justice Rules Applied to
             Selection

Formal rules
  Job-relatedness: The selection procedure appears to measure content relevant to the job
    situation.
  Opportunity to perform: Applicants must have the opportunity to demonstrate their KSAOs
    in the testing situation or have control over the information provided.
  Reconsideration opportunity: Examinees must have the opportunity to challenge or modify
    the decision-making evaluation process.
  Consistency: The selection procedures must be used uniformly across people and time in
    making decisions.

Explanation rules
  Feedback: Examinees must receive timely and informative feedback regarding their perfor-
    mance.
  Selection information: Examinees must be provided with an explanation of the employment
    decision as it pertains to them.
  Honesty: Honesty and truthfulness regarding selection information, feedback, and the
    employment process must be upheld.

Interpersonal treatment rules
  Interpersonal effectiveness: Applicants should be treated with warmth and respect.
  Two-way communication: Applicants should have the opportunity to offer input or have
    their views considered.
  Propriety of questions: Questions asked should not reflect personal bias or constitute an
    invasion of privacy.

---

literature suggests that procedural and distributive justice are likely to
have interactive effects on a variety of dependent variables (for a
review, see Brockner & Wiesenfeld, 1996). It also seems likely that
when the outcome of a test (e.g., entry to a job that is highly desirable
or to a graduate program central to the individual's career objectives)
is extremely important to an individual, distributive justice concerns
will be more important in an absolute sense and probably more
important relative to procedural concerns. This interaction has been
studied in the organizational justice literature, but, to our knowledge,
only once in the selection context (Gilliland, 1994). In addition,
studies should also relate fairness perceptions to test performance and
motivational variables. Combining justice theories of reactions (e.g.,
Gilliland, 1994) with accounts of reactions based on applicant motivational and self-serving mechanisms (e.g., Chan et al., 1997) could
provide a better explanation of applicant reactions to selection
systems.

Theory as the Basis for
Consideration of Implementation Issues

We conclude this chapter by emphasizing the relevance and importance of theory as the basis for consideration of implementation and use issues in selection. As we argued earlier in the chapter, the practical usefulness of utility assessments is as dependent on the effectiveness of the assessor in communicating the results to organizational decision makers as it is on the accuracy of assessment. The lack of tests and use of theories of communication and persuasion and innovation adoption and diffusion, as well as theories on how decision makers form judgments and make decisions relating to selection utility, and the knowledge base available in these areas, may explain why selection utility assessments have not received much support from organizations.

We have also noted that selection utility is partly dependent on an applicant's decision to accept a job offer. Motivational theories concerning what drives the applicant to pursue a job application/offer and to make job decisions constitute the basis for variable selection in empirical research on applicant decisions. Applicant decisions are likely to be mediated by organizational attractiveness and applicant reactions to the selection system and related human resource functions (e.g., compensation). Our review of the empirical evidence suggests that organizational justice theories and motivational theories such as equity theory could be used to help design selection systems that would be effectively implemented. We have also noted that the notion of person-organization fit could provide a useful theoretical framework for organizing and designing research concerning the two-way relationship between the applicant and the organization, but that when selection is part of organizational strategy, person-organization fit considerations may not be as relevant or may take a different form.

The effective implementation and use of selection has to take into account the existing constraints on the adoption of selection practices. Johns (1993) argues that the adoption of selection practices (and other psychology-based personnel practices) constitutes an administrative innovation and that such innovation is often not strongly influenced by technical merit (e.g., validity of the selection procedure). We agree with Johns that the implementation of selection can draw valuable lessons from the theory and research on adoption of organizational innovation. In addition to technical merit, the adoption of an organizational innovation (i.e., the proposed selection system) is influenced by a host of factors, including the decision-making frame of managers, the nature of selection theory and research as presented to them, and critical events and players in the environment of the organization. Failure to consider these constraints is likely to result in nonadoption or ineffective implementation and use of the proposed selection system. This view is consistent with our discussions on utility assessment, interactions between human resource systems, external pressures, strategic management, and applicant reactions.

Research Issues

Many of the issues we have discussed in this chapter are underresearched. The following seem most important to us. First, the relationship between selection interventions and subsequent outcomes on the organizational level has only begun to receive attention in the 1990s. Certainly additional research in this area will have practical implications, but it should also result in the infusion of additional organizational-level theory and analytic methods in research on individual differences variables. A second area that has received almost no attention is research on the manner in which selection interventions are introduced in organizations and the manner in which they maintain (or do not maintain) their effectiveness over time. Research in this area could benefit greatly from theory and research on the adoption of innovations and the importance of organization champions when interventions are introduced (Rogers, 1983). We need studies in which the nature of the implementation of selection procedures is assessed across time and related to changes in the organization. Other interventions "decay" or change with time, and there is no reason to expect that selection-based interventions are any different. Third, and related to the concern about the adoption of innovative selection procedures, is a concern about satisfactory ways of communicating the utility of effective selection procedures to management and the general public. One aspect of this research has been reflected in concerns about communicating utility estimates to managers (Latham & Whyte,

1994). Another aspect of communication is reflected in concerns about justice in selection (Gilliland, 1993) and test reactions research. More broadly, more effective methods of communicating with the general public would likely alleviate the social and legal constraints that have been placed on the use of valid selection procedures. A fourth area that should receive additional attention is the impact of increased diversity on organizations and the individuals who work in those organizations. The move toward greater diversity would seem to be in conflict with the notion that organizations (or groups within organizations) should select individuals who fit. We need to understand what produces successful efforts to diversify a workforce and the impacts such diversification may have on organizations, teams, and individuals as well as the society within which the organization is embedded.

8 The Changing Nature
of Work and Implications
for Research on
KSAO-Performance
Relationships

The cover of the September 19, 1994, issue of *Fortune* magazine featured an article titled "The End of the Job." The article's author argues that the familiar well-defined sets of tasks we have traditionally defined as our jobs are disappearing (Bridges, 1994). Employees are now expected to work at different tasks at different times, depending on what demands are being placed on the organization by its customers or the external world. This change is the result of a variety of changes, including advances in technology; the business practice of outsourcing "simple" or routine tasks; the increased use of temporary or part-time workers; organizations' perceived need to downsize, keeping only skeleton forces of personnel who oversee various outsourced projects; a rapidly changing world economy; and the privatization of many government activities, which have always been the source of well-defined jobs. These changes will almost certainly have implications for the ways in which job candidates are selected, what KSAOs are most related to performance in organizations, and the manner in which performance itself is defined.

In this chapter, we describe some of the changes in demands on employees that appear to be occurring and how these may affect selection. We also try to highlight those issues about which more research data would be helpful. Certainly, much of this chapter is speculative; the changes we describe and the impacts we think they will have may or may not develop, but if the field of personnel selection research is to be proactive, rather than reactive, in solving organizational problems, such speculation is necessary. In fact, in many instances, selection researchers are already reacting to these changes. As we argued in Chapter 7, it is obvious that the questions these changes raise will require a coordinated human resource response; that is, recruitment, selection, training, compensation, and career development solutions must reinforce one another if the challenges these changes represent are to be met.

There are five major changes that we believe will affect the ways in which selection is done in organizations. These changes will likely confront individuals who are interested in how people adapt to, and contribute to, the work organizations in which they live. In trying to write about these issues, we realized that all five of these changes are similar, in that we were considering how people would be able to adapt to major change and what questions we, as organizational scientists, should be ready to answer if we are to be of any assistance in meeting the challenges that these changes are and will be presenting.

The first of the five issues we want to address is the *speed of technological change*. We have certainly witnessed rapid changes in the past 100 years in many areas, such as transportation, communications, and the forces of destruction; it is doubtful that anyone but the most imaginative science fiction writer would have anticipated the many changes that have taken place. However, we and our parents could look forward to fairly specific careers or jobs requiring given sets of skills and knowledge. Today, as the *Fortune* article mentioned above argues, this is becoming less and less true, and the demand for adaptability and change is ever increasing. The increasing pace of technological change generates several questions that we think psychologists, including those interested in individual differences in work performance, should be asking and attempting to answer at this point: What is the human capacity for continuous learning? How can organizations identify and select individuals who are willing to learn and adapt and enjoy change continuously throughout their work lives? How can organizations train and appropriately reward individuals for developing attitudes that are consistent with the need for continuous learning and adaptation? Does successful adaptation in one sphere of an individual's life (perhaps indicated in a biodata measure) contribute to that person's capability to adapt in other areas?

A second change that seems to be occurring now and will likely continue is the *use of teams to accomplish work.* The use of coordinated, high-performance teams is often credited with the economic successes of Japan over the past two decades, and many American companies have restructured workplaces so that teams, rather than individuals and supervisors, are responsible for accomplishing work tasks. Teams differ from groups in that the performance of some task is dependent on the contributions of all team members; superior performance by one member of the team often cannot compensate for other members' inferior performance. Teamwork is not an organizational development fad that will soon disappear, because the technological demands of work often require highly developed skills of different types. That the actions of team members must be highly coordinated has become painfully obvious in some highly publicized military accidents (e.g., the downing of an Iranian jetliner by the American military and the friendly fire killing of American soldiers in the Iraqi conflict). The use of teams produces a number of human resource issues in a society in which the focus has always been on individual achievement, as is true in much of the West. How will workers who are used to individual rewards and recognition be happy and motivated working in these situations? How can organizations change reward systems to recognize team performance without producing "social loafers"? Is it possible to select individuals who will work well in teams? What changes in training must be made to develop highly functioning coordinated teams?

Changes in communications technology have also produced many opportunities and new problems in the workplace. Many of us remember marveling at the opportunities that fax transmission of written documents afforded us in our work with colleagues in other organizations or in other parts of the world. That seems like a very long time ago, but it has been less than 10 years since fax transmissions became routine. Today, various computer networks provide instant access to expertise anywhere in the world. Researchers in different organizations and countries can get answers to questions and access to expertise almost instantaneously, simply by requesting it. This communication and cooperative effort should produce an increase in the dissemination of ideas and innovations and increasing interdependence of people throughout the world. In addition, electronic communications and the use of computers have made it possible to decentralize a great deal of work; groups of people can work in their homes or in other geographically separate places and send the products of their efforts back and forth among members of the work group or to members of other organizations. Performance can also be monitored electronically with ease and in great detail. Although all these advancements mean there is greater flexibility in the way work gets done, and when and where it gets done, they may also affect social interaction. The fact that we can videoconference with people in any part of the world, much less with others in our respective countries, means that we do not have to travel to visit people in these disparate locations. This means *less* opportunity to see and appreciate the social and cultural situations in various parts of the world. People who work at home using various electronic communications media to accomplish any required coordination are physically and socially isolated from their coworkers. Under these circumstances, what happens to organizational commitment, organizational citizenship behavior, and social interaction and bonds among coworkers? How does an organization maintain its integrity? What types of people or individual difference variables do organizations need to consider when assigning people to these kinds of work situations? How does the concept of work performance, especially the kind of performance described elsewhere as citizenship behavior, change?

Another significant change is that *most large corporations are now global in nature* and will become increasingly so. Half of Ford Motor Company's employees are outside the United States. Phillips Industries, a Netherlands corporation, has three-fourths of its employees working outside the Netherlands. More than half of the employees of Matsushita Electric of Japan work outside that country. Japanese automakers have been building plants in the United States and employing American workers for more than a decade. Even when a company's products are manufactured at home, a large portion of its sales are likely made to countries and people in the rest of the world. This increased globalization demands that some employees at least become "citizens of the world." This obviously means that employees need to be adaptable and open to cultures other than their own, and to those cultures' work and social customs. When employees' work demands long-term stays in other countries, their family and social lives must be adapted to the local culture. The costs associated with recruiting, selecting, and training workers and their families for work in foreign countries, and the cost of failure in this endeavor, are very large for both individuals and organizations. Research on the impacts of these ventures on individuals, their families, and the organizations that employ them is only beginning to appear in scholarly human resource-oriented journals. Related to the notion of increased globalization and cross-cultural demands are the demographic changes in the workforce caused by immigration and the corresponding demands these changes place on the selection process.

A final change that has been taking place for much of the past two decades is the *increased service orientation* of organizations, along with the increase in the numbers of organizations whose primary product is service (Schneider & Bowen, 1995). Even when service is not a direct product of the organization, the increased concern for competitiveness and quality in a global economy requires that all employees be concerned with and knowledgeable about the organization's customers. Whereas it is necessary that firms concentrate on providing products and services that satisfy customer needs, it is also essential that they develop a customer orientation that recognizes that customers and organizations share interdependencies, values, and strategies over the long term (Schneider & Bowen, 1995). Lengnick-Hall (1996) goes even further and suggests that firms must take steps to optimize the manner in which customers provide input into the ability of the firm to increase its competitiveness and the quality of its product. This customer orientation makes new demands on at least the interpersonal capabilities of the workers in these organizations. We turn now to a more specific discussion of each of these five major developments. Although we emphasize the role of individual differences and the potential contribution of selection in each of these areas, it is obvious that an internally consistent combination of human resource interventions, as described in Chapter 7, is required to address these challenges and opportunities.

Technological Change

Rapid advancements in technology have led to substantial organizational changes in many industries, affecting how work is done as well as the output of work. In the past, organizations could accomplish technological change by selecting people who had the required educational backgrounds and retiring longtime workers or moving them into less-skilled employment. Retraining programs were thought to be expensive and largely unsuccessful because of the degree of new knowledge and different skills required. Today, the focus in many companies is on a constant updating of knowledge and skills, sometimes with no particular immediate organizational needs in mind. With this emphasis on continuous learning, it is necessary to consider whether employees, some of whom are older, can learn as efficiently or in the same ways as was true when they were in school. The willingness of older employees to engage in retraining or relearning their jobs is also a critical factor. If we consider the implications for selection, it might be reasonable to hypothesize that general learning ability, or g, as identified in Chapter 4, rather than specific skills will become increasingly important. A second hypothesis might be that motivational or affective variables will become more important predictors of continuous learning. This second hypothesis would be predicated on the notion that most employees have the cognitive ability to learn new tasks; what differentiates those who learn from those who do not is their willingness or motivation to do so.

Older workers are perceived to be more dependable, cooperative, conscientious, consistent, and knowledgeable, but they are also characterized as harder to train, less able to keep up with technological change, more accident-prone, less promotable, and less motivated (Avolio & Barrett, 1987; Bird & Fisher, 1986; Rosen & Jerdee, 1976a, 1976b; Schwab & Heneman, 1978; Slater & Kingsley, 1976). Further, slightly less positive performance evaluations have been reported for older workers (Cleveland & Landy, 1983; Rosen & Jerdee, 1976b; Schwab & Heneman, 1978). Early attempts to tailor training for older learners emphasized activity, a reduction of descriptions and memorization, and the use of tasks of graded difficulty that would prevent errors by trainees (Belbin & Downs, 1964). Subsequent efforts were designed so that the trainee could discover through doing the principles underlying successful completion of a task (Belbin & Belbin, 1972). Finally, efforts were made to evaluate the trainability of individuals by giving them miniaturized training sessions that mimicked actual training (Robertson & Downs, 1979; Siegel, 1983). Those doing well in these miniaturized sessions were then selected for full-scale retraining efforts.

Occasionally, selection procedures require that applicants learn job-relevant material to perform selection tasks well. An illustration of such an instance is found in Example 3 in Chapter 1. Applicants listened to tape recordings of telephone calls and were asked to record key information about the emergency calls on written forms. The primary purpose of this exercise was to assess the applicants' short-term working memory and clerical-technical skills. The forms they filled out and the emergency telephone conversation examples also served to indicate to the applicants how actual telephone calls needed to be handled and what key information they needed to retrieve from callers. This exercise preceded a telephone call simulation designed to measure applicants' capabilities of handling role-playing callers with emergency messages. The applicants had to obtain information on the nature of the emergency as well as the telephone number, name, and address of the caller, and had to enter this information on the form provided. If applicants had learned from their experience with the first component of this selection process, their performance on the phone call simulation should have been enhanced. Unfortunately, there was no direct measurement of the applicants' learning or improvement across these exercises. If continuous learning is likely to characterize jobs increasingly in the future, then researchers should devote greater attention to the measurement of improvement (i.e., learning) across different and integrated selection components.

There has also been some experimental research that suggests there are differences in the capabilities of older learners, most of which has involved training or retraining workers of different age groups to use computers (e.g., Elias, Elias, Robbins, & Gage, 1987; Gist, Schwoerer, & Rosen, 1988; Hartley, Hartley, & Johnson, 1984). One major conclusion of all of these studies is that older workers can be retrained. However, the older workers in these study samples took longer to learn the new skills and required more personal attention from the trainers in solving problems than did younger workers. One explanation for the longer time it takes older workers to learn new tasks is that they have not had any recent experience in education or training. Thus, their learning strategies are not well practiced. Some research in expertise suggests that practicing experts in a field probably maintain their learning efficiency in that field over their life spans (Poon, 1987; Salthouse, 1984). Poon, Krauss, and Bowles (1984) have argued that if we take into account all the variables that are associated with learning (e.g., intelligence, education, motivation, health), chronological age may have no significant effect on performance. However, the problem remains that some of these other variables are related to age and represent obstacles that must be overcome when older persons attempt retraining. Assessment of the learning capabilities of all workers should contribute to the optimal design of training programs.

There is evidence that attitudinal problems affect the results of retraining efforts. Fossum, Arvey, Paradise, and Robbins (1986) argue that employees' expectations that training will lead to the development of relevant knowledge, skills, and abilities, and that these will lead to valued outcomes, will determine the degree to which they put effort into retraining. Further, these authors maintain that these expectations decrease with job and organizational tenure and, correspondingly, with chronological age. Related to these expectancies, perhaps, is a decline in self-efficacy with respect to learning new tasks among older individuals and, in some cases, a real fear of failure (Sterns & Doverspike, 1989). Self-efficacy has been considered both an important outcome of training and an important determinant of subsequent performance on trained tasks (Kraiger, Ford, & Salas, 1993). Motivation to learn has played a prominent role in models of training outcomes at least since the publication of the Noe and Schmitt (1986) article on trainee attitudes. Research on training and learning in general would indicate that affect should almost certainly be an important factor. How that affect can be measured and used to make valid predictions about the capability to adapt to work changes and continuously learn new tasks has not been explored in any depth.

Some evidence that this "task motivation" is relevant is provided by Miner, Smith, and Bracker (1989, 1994). These authors used the Miner Sentence Completion Scale to assess overall task motivation, a desire for personal achievement, a desire to innovate, a desire to plan and set goals, and a desire to avoid risks. With the exception of the risk avoidance measure, all of these motivational measures were related to the performance of the firms of entrepreneurs in both a concurrent study and a predictive criterion-related study. The firm outcomes included growth in the number of employees, in dollar volume of sales, and in the entrepreneur's yearly income. Although the size of these effects indicates the importance of motivation in growing and managing a high-technology firm, more research on what may have mediated these relationships (e.g., learning new ways of doing things, taking advantage of perceived opportunities more quickly) would be very helpful.

In different parts of the world, assignment to training conveys different messages to workers. In the United States, being assigned to a training group usually conveys a positive message. It tells the trainee that he or she is worth the investment and that the company plans some new role for the trainee in the company's future. In other parts of the world, training is perceived to be remedial and is used only when an employee is perceived to be deficient. Clearly, being asked or ordered to attend training may have very different impacts on the participants' attitudes toward training in these two training climates, and possibly on the effects of training as well. Hence, training researchers should continue to consider the climate for training as one potential moderator of the training-outcome relationship under investigation. Such climate variables will serve to constrain or enhance the role of KSAO-performance relationships.

In some U.S. organizations, the need for a constantly changing and enhanced set of human resources is so important to the organization that skill-based pay systems have been devised. In these systems, employees are paid on the basis of the level and diversity of skills they bring to the workplace. The assumption is that the employee who can perform a wide variety of tasks successfully and knows more is of greater value to the organization and should be paid according to her or his capabilities, not for the performance of a particular job assignment. In industries with rapidly changing technologies, the skills required may also change, and it is critical that the organization have talent that can adapt to these demands. Skill-based pay systems can be tied to either the acquisition of new skills or the level of skill acquired.

Very little academic research has been conducted on the motivational or performance consequences of skill-based pay systems, but one case study found substantial differences on a number of the human resource dimensions and practices in organizations with skill-based systems versus Fortune 1000 companies with more traditional pay-for-performance systems (Tosi & Tosi, 1986). Companies with skill-based pay systems were much more likely to engage in other practices that involved the sharing of power with all employees, such as the use of survey feedback, self-managing teams, participation groups, and quality circle interventions. They also were more likely to share information on the company's business goals and the company's performance and to engage in training job-specific skills as well as cross-training of employees and team-building skills. Finally, and not surprisingly, they were also more likely to experiment with other alternate methods of employee compensation, such as the use of salary systems as opposed to hourly pay and the use of cafeteria systems for fringe benefits.

Clearly, a skill-based pay system ought to stimulate employee reactions that are different from those in performance-based systems, and whether or not they are effective may also be heavily dependent on the expectations and culture of the people in the organization. Something similar to a skill-based system has been used to pay some professionals, such as teachers and university professors. It also seems that a skill-based pay system would be well suited to an organization that must adapt itself to continually changing skill demands and is dependent on a workforce that is willing and capable to engage in continuous learning. Research on the use of these alternate pay systems both within and across cultures would be very useful. Similarly, research on individual differences in workers' reactions to these systems and their performance within these systems would be useful. The latter information might allow organizations to predict how workers would react to various motivational systems and to tailor these systems to individual preferences.

Technological change, then, demands the increased attention of psychologists to a number of human resource issues: the design of training so that it can be delivered effectively and continuously, perhaps in the workplace itself, throughout an individual's career; development of positive motivation and affect among workers toward continuous upgrading of skills; and the development of appropriate reward systems that will stimulate and reinforce continuous skill development combined with the selection of employees who possess the learning skills and attitudes that will result in positive motivation and effective performance in these situations. The success of all these human resource endeavors is likely to be affected by the characteristics and past experiences of the individuals to whom these efforts are directed.

Increased Use of Teams

The second change in the workplace that should affect selection is the increasing importance and use of work teams. Although the importance of teams to organizations has been recognized in industrial and organizational psychology since as early as the 1950s, it is only in recent years that work teams have become a hot topic in both research and practice, as organizations have come to rely on teams to perform complex tasks and improve productivity.

Several factors contribute to the increasing emphasis on and interest in work teams. Complex technology systems adopted by business, military, aerospace, and medical organizations exert demands for effective team functioning. Many complex tasks are assigned to teams because these tasks exceed the capabilities of single individuals. For example, to perform complex surgical procedures, medical teams have to process and act upon specialized information from several expert sources to reach decisions.

In the West, at least in the United States, the perceived decline in the productivity of the workplace, especially in the manufacturing sector, led managers, practitioners, and researchers to look at their international competitors in attempts to discover factors contributing to competitive advantage. A widely held belief in the West was that many organizations in Eastern countries have cultures that emphasize collectivist values over individualism. Collectivist values in the work domain translate into teamwork in the organization.

Although team success has been a source of the increasing interest in research and application of work teams, team failures have also contributed to the perceived importance of teams. In the United States, several civilian airline accidents have been attributed to breakdowns in teamwork among crew members. As indicated earlier, well-publicized military accidents have also been attributed to failures of coordination/communication among members of work teams.

Much of the recent research on teams has focused on the sharing and coordination of information among team members and on the team decision-making process. Information exchange and decision making are primary reasons for the use of teams. As we mentioned earlier, successful performance on complex tasks requires access to multiple expert sources of information, which are seldom available in a single individual. This information needs to be shared, coordinated, and integrated before it can be used effectively to make decisions. These situations define the boundary conditions for much of the recent research on teams, that is, team decision making under conditions of distributed expertise. The types of teams studied are often what Sundstrom, DeMeuse, and Futrell (1990) call action and negotiation teams, where team members with different specialized skills operate together in a dynamic context of high stress and unpredictable events. Examples include military combat units, flight crews, and surgery teams. Research on such teams has been promising. Sophisticated team decision-making models such as the one proposed by Hollenbeck, Ilgen, Phillips, and Hedlund (1994) have been developed and empirically tested.

We believe that one interesting future direction for team research would be the examination of the relationships between these team decision-making models and other models of team functioning developed for understanding the more traditional types of work teams found in business organizations, such as quality circles, production teams, and planning committees. Many of these traditional team models have borrowed heavily from the social psychology of group dynamics. We do know that these teams are no less complex than the action and negotiation teams. What we do not know is how the different organizational contexts of team functioning across the different types of teams affect the applicability of team models and the generalizability of empirical findings from any given team study or the kinds of individual and team characteristics that contribute to successful teams in these different contexts.

Some progress has been made toward the development of taxonomies of teams to provide frameworks for describing the commonalities and uniquenesses associated with different types of teams (e.g., Klimoski & Jones, 1995; Sundstrom et al., 1990). Sundstrom et al.'s (1990) classification differentiates teams in terms of the degree to which members' roles and responsibilities are differentiated, the degree to which the team must integrate its activity with external units, the nature of the work cycle, and the typical outputs produced by the team. These factors identify four different types of teams: (a) advice/involvement, (b) production/service, (c) project development, and (d) action/negotiation. A taxonomy will help us to identify boundary conditions for team research and to develop selection research targeted at the identification of an appropriate complement of team member KSAOs and interventions. For the field of team research to progress, team researchers should at least be cognizant of studies on work teams other than the types they are investigating and should consider how the results of their research apply (or do not apply) to these different types of teams.

From a selection perspective, an important but largely neglected issue in team research is the matching of individuals and teams. The general question of interest is how group composition and the staffing process affect team effectiveness. A team's composition is equivalent to the collection of KSAOs of team members. The staffing process for team effectiveness involves more than simply selecting individuals with the traditional technical KSAOs required for successful job performance, such as cognitive ability and job knowledge. Attention must also be given to team-relevant individual characteristics, including preferences, personalities, and the problem-solving and interaction styles of individuals. Even at the skill level, there has been little research directed to the question of how to compose teams. Questions concerning the effect of variability in team members' skills versus the sum of their skills and the impact on team performance have not been addressed.

Unlike traditional models of job analysis, team staffing needs analysis will have to go beyond the individual level of analysis to consider team-level variables, focusing on the interaction and interdependence among team members and the organizational context of team functioning. For example, in innovative production teams characterized by continuous learning and change, individuals with team-relevant characteristics such as risk-taking propensity and tolerance for ambiguity may be important for effective team performance. However, in other team contexts, these same characteristics may actually hinder effective team performance. In a work team of nuclear plant operators, in which high structure and formal rules are critical for effective team functioning, team members who are high on risk taking are not desir-

Table 8.1 Different Types of Teams and Corresponding Staffing Issues

Team Type	Job Requirements	Recruitment	Assessment/Selection
Command-and-control (e.g., tank crews)	Identifying team KSAOs	Fitting new recruits into established teams	Assessing maximum performance
Production (e.g., automobile manufacturing teams)	Identifying nontraditional individual KSAOs	Establishing right mix of talents	Determining roles of team members
Customer service (e.g., flight attendants)	Identifying team boundaries	Creating team potency	Developing valid measures
Professional/technical	Establishing mission boundaries	Establishing right mix (talent and potential)	Assessment of hidden agendas
Executive	Determining who specifies KSAOs	Establishing right mix (values, experience, and contacts)	Determining who selects

SOURCE: Klimoski and Jones (1995, p. 322). Adapted by permission of Jossey-Bass, Inc.

able. Further, when a specific characteristic is needed on a team, is it enough that one team member has a high level of that characteristic or should all members have at least minimal levels of the trait? In short, in the team staffing process, the search for valid predictors needs to go beyond individual-level variables to consider cross-level individual-by-team interactions. Needs analysis will have to go beyond the traditional task-based job analysis to adopt a process-based and contextual team-level and even organizational-level analysis. Examples of some team staffing issues that arise in different types of teams are provided in Table 8.1, which is adapted from Klimoski and Jones (1995). As those authors emphasize, this table is meant only to be illustrative of the range of issues that become important when an organization attempts to recruit and select team members.

As indicated above, the team staffing process has research and applied implications for the types of selection procedures used. For some time now, it has been widely accepted in industrial and organizational psychology that general cognitive ability, as measured by traditional paper-and-pencil measures, is one of the most efficient predictors of job performance. It is likely that in the case where team member performance is the criterion, noncognitive predictors such as personality characteristics will be even more important than they are in studies of individual performance. In addition, many of the team-relevant KSAOs may be better captured by measures other than traditional paper-and-pencil measures. These alternative measures include assessment center-type exercises and other simulation-based measures, such as the type of situational judgment tests developed by Motowidlo, Dunnette, and Carter (1990). The situational judgment test, mentioned also in Chapter 5, is usually administered as a paper-and-pencil instrument. It consists of situations and action alternatives presented to the job applicant. The applicant's scores on the test are computed on the basis of his or her endorsement of the action alternatives. Endorsement of the action alternatives can be either in a multiple-choice format or in a Likert-type scale format. The scoring key is developed from prior effectiveness ratings of the action alternatives obtained from subject matter experts. The potential use of these situational judgment items in the assessment of team-related concerns is illustrated for several different jobs in Table 8.2. Certainly the most intriguing and challenging possibility is that it may be necessary to consider the characteristics of other team members when selecting an individual team member. Questions regarding the degree to which a particular person "fits in" or complements the capabilities of other team members are important for all four types of teams in the Sundstrom et al. (1990) taxonomy described above and for the teams described in Table 8.1.

An adequate staffing process will not necessarily lead to effective team functioning, because adequate team composition needs to be complemented by appropriate team processes and team member interactions. Hence, team-based interventions to ensure team effectiveness, such as team-building and team-training programs, constitute the other important aspect of team research and practice.

Team building has been a primary technique used in organizational development and change. Team-building techniques are often used in low-structure work teams in which performance goals, tasks, and member roles are not clearly defined. Team building is a process

Table 8.2 Situational Judgment Items Designed to Assess Behavior Relevant to Team Concerns in Different Jobs

---

School administrator

In response to your request, you have a large group of parents who have volunteered to work in the school at various times during the day. You have placed one of your counselors in charge of this volunteer program and she has now informed you that she has more volunteers than she can use. What would you do?

    A. Have the counselor set up a schedule in which all the volunteers can be used, even for just a short time.

    B. Have the teachers create calendars listing activities and how many volunteers are needed, and allow parents to sign up for the activities.

    C. Work with the counselor to identify more avenues for volunteers to assist.

    D. Thank the parents for their generosity, but inform them that you will be using only those parents who can donate the most time to volunteering.

    E. Establish a wait list, and contact volunteers when needed.

Supervisor in an electronics manufacturing plant

You are responsible for setting up electrical equipment for various projects. One of your team members has performed inconsistently in the past. Your six-member team was given 48 hours to complete a project. No other replacement personnel are available and all six members are needed. What would you do?

    A. Meet with the inconsistent team member, specifically discuss what you want him to do, and make sure he understands his responsibilities.

    B. Closely monitor the individual and carefully check over his work after the job is done.

    C. Assign the inconsistent worker the easiest tasks and least amount of responsibility.

    D. Make sure that the inconsistent worker understands how important his role is in completing the work and that you need 100% of his effort on this job.

    E. Divide the group into teams of workers, assigning the weakest member and the strongest member to the same team.

Supervisor in an automobile supply manufacturing plant

An associate has been working only three stations but could perform five if the line were rebalanced to make the stations easier. Rebalancing may cause dissatisfaction among other team members, who would be required to perform additional work responsibilities to maintain production times. What would you do?

    A. Present the proposal to the team to obtain input. If the team does not object, try the new TACT times and then consult the team for a final judgment on the new times.

    B. The needs of one individual should not outweigh the needs of the team. You should not rebalance the line if it means dissatisfying other members of the team.

    C. Investigate the possibility of rebalancing the line. If the changes do not negatively affect quality, make the change.

    D. Discuss the matter with the team. Assuming the change would save money, suggest writing a BEAM and splitting the savings among the team.

    E. Obtain input from the team on whether or not to rebalance the line. Then weigh the costs and benefits prior to making a final decision.

---

intervention that focuses on the management of social conflict within the team and facilitates the building of positive social climate.

In contrast, team training is often applied to high-structure work teams with well-defined performance goals, tasks, and member roles. The focus is on developing task-relevant interaction skills to obtain a coordinated and integrated team in order to enhance team performance. An intriguing series of studies reported by Smith-Jentsch, Salas, and Baker (1996) supports the need for both selection and training interventions as means of increasing appropriate assertiveness by team members. Even these studies, however, focused on individual performance in a team context rather than on the performance of the team. Lorr and More (1980) found that ratings of individuals' team-related assertiveness while working on a computer-based flight simulation were related to self-report measures of independence and directiveness, two of four aspects of assertiveness represented in the Lorr and More measure. In a second study, Smith-Jentsch et al. (1996) found that assertiveness was context dependent. That is, team- and work-based measures of assertiveness were more highly related to peer ratings of performance than were more general measures of assertiveness or measures obtained in a social, as opposed to a work, context. Finally, different types of training in assertive team behavior were provided to groups of individuals participating in the flight control simulation task. Their attitudes toward assertive behavior and their self-reported assertiveness were also measured. Behavioral role modeling was effective in producing higher levels of assertive behavior (as judged by trained raters blind to experimental training condition) relative to a control condition and two versions of lecture-based training. Team- and work-based measures of self-reported independence and directiveness were also related to ratings of assertive behavior ($r = .19$ and $r = .23$), but not at a statistically significant level. These studies, then, point to the importance of both individual differences in attitudes about assertiveness and the capability to be assertive as well as the importance of skill-based training in assertive team skills. In addition, the attitudes that are important are unique to the work and team contexts in which they are relevant.

Although there is a promising research base on training effectiveness at the individual level, very little is known about training at the team level. For example, we know that individuals' perceptions of self-efficacy on a task play an important role in the training of those individuals on that task. Within the team context, the nature of a team member's task is interdependent with that of other members. How will an individual's perceptions of self-efficacy affect team performance? Is there a useful analogous concept of team efficacy? Or consider the process of self-regulation, another important concept in individual-level training that emphasizes the relationships among goals, feedback, and performance. Much is known about goal setting at the individual level of analysis, but what is the relationship between individual and team goals? Are the findings from motivational studies regarding effects of individual feedback generalizable to feedback on team performance?

Consider also the motivational effects of rewards and recognition. At the individual level, the picture is clear. Individual rewards are motivating when they are contingent on the level of performance of individuals. At the team level, things get more complicated. Should rewards be based on individual member performance or team performance? How do different reward allocation strategies relate to justice and fairness perceptions? Justice principles of equity and equality and cross-cultural differences in the values placed on these principles become relevant research issues.

The suggestion that team-level analyses of the effects of training and compensation are necessary is consistent with the notion that there should also be team-level analyses of the effects of various selection procedures. The average of team members' KSAOs may be related to team member performance, but it may also be the pattern of team-related KSAOs across team members that is a critical determinant of team performance. In addition, it is likely that the use of the team as the basis for training and compensation interventions will interact with selection procedures to affect team performance. For example, if we ignore the motivation to work in teams and the type of KSAO mix in teams, it is likely that other human resource interventions will not be as successful as they otherwise might be.

Finally, when team researchers introduce and validate constructs that are team-level analogues (e.g., team efficacy) of established individual-level constructs (e.g., self-efficacy), it is of critical conceptual and methodological importance that these efforts be guided by a consistent multilevel framework. The lack of a multilevel framework for team research is likely to result in fallacious inferences and a proliferation of new team-level constructs that have little, if any, incremental explanatory value (Chan, 1998). In the final chapter of this book, we will elaborate on these important issues concerning levels of analysis in multilevel research.

We have talked about the speed of technological change and the increasing importance of teams. The third challenge to which we want to draw attention is a function of technological changes in communications. Developments in the area of communications have implications for team, group, and organizational functioning.

Increasing Communication Opportunities

Technological advancements have significantly affected the potential for communication among people. These changes have introduced the possibility of nearly immediate communication and transmission of large bodies of information anywhere in the world. We will consider two innovations in communications technology and the changes they have brought to the work lives of people and the individual difference variables that might be important in adapting to these changes. For some types of jobs, it has become possible for workers to work at home and to send the products of their efforts to their "offices" via fax or the electronic transmission of computer files. In January 1996, a blizzard made all forms of travel impossible for 2 days on the East Coast of the United States. The subsequent usage of telephone lines by people trying to perform work at home and send it elsewhere electronically so overloaded the system that it broke down. This is a rather dramatic display of what is possible, though such levels of telecommuting are not yet an everyday practice. A second possibility resulting from increased electronic communications is that of complete or partial monitoring of workers' performance via electronic means. The times at which an individual logs on and off, the number of keystrokes he or she makes in a given period of time, and to whom he or she transmits messages and how often can all be recorded and reported at any level of detail desired.

Shamir (1992) provides useful distinctions among the different types of jobs that are performed at home. The specific type of at-home worker we are concerned with in this chapter is often referred to as a telecommuter. Many jobs in modern society (such as architect, accountant, computer programmer, typist, bank clerk, and system designer) involve the manipulation of symbols, not the direct manipulation of materials or people. The electronic storage, retrieval, manipulation, and communication of work products in jobs such as these by fax, electronic mail, and advanced telephone systems means that these workers' activities need not be concentrated in central workplaces anymore.

Although much of the initial enthusiasm for the decentralization of work that these innovations have made possible has worn off, it remains a possibility, and it is likely that at least a portion of the work done by many people today in centralized workplaces will be done at home. Also possible is that work that used to require travel to other facilities of an organization (often in other countries) will now be done via some electronic means. As Shamir (1992) points out, this decentralization of work has significant implications for the bureaucratic control an organization can wield and potentially the type of people the organization must employ. Unless the organization can and does resort to electronic performance monitoring of the type described above, the workers' efforts are completely invisible to the organization. Clearly, the only means of monitoring work performance lies in the products these people produce. As traditional bureaucratic controls disappear, status and authority relationships in an office change or no longer exist. What, for example, does it mean to supervise a work group whose members never comes to the office? How do supervisory skills change, or do they exist at all in this situation? Which workers work well with this autonomy, and for whom does this independence represent its own challenges?

In addition to the formal controls they institute, organizations also depend on values, norms, and beliefs or organizational culture to regulate workers' behavior and their interactions with each other. The transmission of an organizational culture is difficult when members no longer attend some set of events together or participate in shared experiences. Past research on organizational socialization and such notions as organizational commitment, identification, and loyalty as well as citizenship behavior may be largely irrelevant for workers whose primary work activities never involve their seeing anyone else with whom they work. Can such concepts or notions be transmitted via computer messages or videos or with limited group meetings? Shamir (1992) also points out that with home workers an organization may have a workforce with characteristics (loyalty, commitment, identification, and so on) similar to those assumed to apply to a temporary workforce. Because temporary employees are usually less expensive, it may be tempting for an organization to replace the home worker with a temporary worker. In any event, performance models that include these variables and selection systems developed using these variables as criteria need to be evaluated.

Telecommuting has significant impacts on the individuals who engage in this mode of work as well. Notions about career development almost certainly change, as workers who work at home are unlikely to develop the types of mentoring and political relationships that lead to promotion (Metzger & Von Glinow, 1988). Individuals with professional and entrepreneurial career orientations are likely more suited to working at home than are those whose career orientations are bureaucratic (Kanter, 1989). This is consistent with the work of Miner et al. (1989, 1994), cited above in relation to the task motivation of entrepreneurs.

One major advantage cited by early proponents of work at home was the capability it would give to individuals to meet family responsibilities while also working. However, as indicated above, working at home may result in the marginalization of the worker, making it less likely that he or she will advance in the organization. In addition, some home workers have found that work-family conflict increases when they attempt to accomplish work tasks while also attending to the demands of young children. The conflicts that arise in this situation are well documented by Christensen (1988), and the need for some supplemental child care in these situations is clearly evident. In a review of the relatively small body of literature on this topic, Hall (1990) concludes that individuals with small preschool children at home find this arrangement particularly stressful. Hall also reports that some individuals in this situation will actually construct barriers between family and work in their homes, creating a division similar to the one they were supposedly avoiding by working at home.

Shamir (1992) believes that the home worker faces an identity problem as well in that he or she has a weak or nonexistent linkage to the organization, an unclear or uncertain career path, and ambiguous work-family relationships. The identity problem that results from these ambiguities may lead to ineffective performance in both work and home spheres. Again, a careful examination of the individual's characteristics and the at-home situation would provide useful information to organizations and individuals for whom work at home is an option.

Greater use of electronic technology affords organizations the opportunity to monitor employee performance electronically. More than 10 years ago, the U.S. Congress's Office of Technology Assessment (1987) estimated that the performance of 6 million workers could be electronically monitored. Some companies monitor the work of individual employees (seemingly the preference in the United States), whereas others choose to review performance statistics that have been aggregated to the work group or team level. Monitoring at the group (as opposed to the individual) level seems to result in less worker stress (Aiello & Kolb, 1995; Aiello & Shao, 1993), hence, Norway and Sweden have enacted laws that limit the extent of individual monitoring. Electronic performance monitoring does provide one solution to the problem of the loss of bureaucratic control of home workers noted above, but it clearly raises a host of issues regarding intrusiveness on employee privacy and the health and performance of the individual worker. Whereas employees clearly report greater stress and lowered satisfaction when they are electronically monitored, the relationships of such monitoring to physiological stress and work performance are either quite complex (Aiello & Kolb, 1995) or undocumented. To our knowledge, there has been no research on the characteristics that might determine individuals' capability of functioning successfully and with satisfaction and minimal stress in these situations.

Global Citizenry

As we noted earlier, most large, and many medium and small, organizations have facilities or markets in countries throughout the world. People in these various facilities must communicate with each other and with the home organization. For a variety of reasons, most organizations also feel that it is necessary to locate managerial and, often, technical people from the organization's home country in the foreign facility. These international assignments are usually for a year or more and often necessitate the emigration of the employee and her or his family as well. These moves are extremely expensive; one estimate is that the typical organizational cost associated with an international assignment is four times the employee's annual salary

Table 8.3   Examples of Positive and Negative Reactions to Out-of-Country Work
                 Assignments

Negative Reactions	Positive Reactions
"Weakened long-term commitment because of heavy price paid by family."	"Foreign assign[ment] responsibilities give much broader range of authority and more direct exposure to company senior management and decision makers."
"I am less trusting that my employer will follow through with what they say they are doing to do."	
"Prior to this experience I was . . . looking forward to a continuing relationship with my company. However, . . . I will not remain in this company as a result of the blatant disregard and disrespect that the company shows its expatriates. . . . We have seen the enemy and it is us."	"Enhanced high-level management contacts."
	"Has opened communication channels to more levels of management."
"I am far removed from the strategic core of the company. I was a star performer . . . in the home office. Now I am a forgotten man with no career track. I work more for the money now, rather than blind devotion to the company."	"Raise[d] level of visibility."
	"It has made me a more valuable commodity."
"Removed me from the mainstream and thoroughly reduced promotional opportunities as I am simply not 'available' to be considered."	
"Reduced influence within the company."	
"Employer does not appreciate the increased commitment in hours/stress associated with an overseas assignment vis-à-vis a domestic job."	
"At times I feel recognition for the efforts and results is well below what I expect and have received in previous jobs."	

SOURCE: Material adapted from Guzzo et al. (1994).

(Ronen, 1989). Moreover, estimates of the failure rate (international assignees who return earlier than planned) range from 15% to 75% (Black, Mendenhall, & Oddou, 1991; Ronen, 1989). Beyond the obvious expense associated with these early returns, it is estimated that between 30% and 50% of those who stay are considered ineffective or marginally effective by their employing organizations (Copeland & Griggs, 1985). Finally, the personal costs to the employees can be very high in terms of career and family disruptions. Guzzo, Noonan, and Elron (1994) present some of the reactions of international assignees and the organizational and personal outcomes associated with expatriate adjustment (or lack thereof). Both positive and negative reactions to this experience expressed by members of their sample are shown in Table 8.3. Clearly, these experiences evoke a wide variety of responses. How to predict these reactions and what personal and organizational outcomes are associated with these reactions remain relatively unstudied.

Given the personal and organizational costs associated with international assignments, it is surprising that there are very few research data available regarding the adjustment of expatriates. Black et al. (1991) and Ronen (1989) provide useful reviews of the existing literature, and Black and Mendenhall (1990) have reviewed the results of attempts to train people to work effectively in other cultures. The empirical literature on international adjustment usually points to the importance of one or more of five factors. First, those individuals who have had some previous experience in foreign countries seem to do better and adjust more readily to international assignments. Exactly what types of experience may be helpful and how this experience may facilitate subsequent adjustment have not been studied.

Second, the individual skills of the expatriates play a role in their success. A reasonable number of studies have been directed to this issue, and Kealey and Rubin (1983) provide a list of the characteristics of successful overseas assignees derived from these various studies. Mendenhall and Oddou (1985) provide a useful taxonomy of these skills. Their first dimension, called the *self* dimension, includes skills that help the expatriate maintain her or his own mental health, psychological well-being, and sense of self-efficacy. The *relationship* dimension includes skills that help the expatriate foster relationships with persons in the host country and the headquarters of the organization. The expatriate's ability to perceive and evaluate correctly the behavior of the host country personnel constitutes a *perception* dimension.

The third factor that may contribute to international adjustment is the manner in which organizations select people for these assignments. Even though there seems to be consistent evidence about the importance of a variety of personal and interpersonal factors, organizations usually select individuals based only on technical competence, if they engage in any systematic evaluation of international assignees at all. Tung (1981), for example, found that only 5% of organizations engaged in any evaluation of the cross-cultural skills of the people to whom they gave international assignments. A consulting firm reported in 1987 that only 35% of corporations were selecting from among multiple candidates for overseas assignments and that technical job-related experience and job skills were the most important factors in making these selections. It is certainly possible that the failure rate among international assignees could be reduced if an accurate appraisal of the three skill dimensions outlined in the previous paragraph were developed and undertaken.

The nontechnical aspects of international jobs are probably those that are most different across cultures and are almost certainly those that have the greatest impact on the success of overseas assignees. What few data we have support this hypothesis. For example, Arthur and Bennett (1995) found that the five most important factors cited by international assignees as critical to their success and rank ordered in terms of importance were Family Situation, Flexibility/Adaptability, Job Knowledge and Motivation, Relationship Skills, and Extra-Cultural Openness. These data are complicated further because the types of personality or motivational skills required seem to differ across cultures. Ralston, Gustafson, Elsass, Cheung, and Terpstra (1992) found that managers' values in Hong Kong, the People's Republic of China, and the United States differed on three dimensions: Integration, Confucian Work Dynamics, and Human Heartedness. Clearly, personality variables are important in the success of international workers. It is also the case that an organization may be selecting a family as well as an individual in this situation, more so than in most domestic work assignments.

A fourth set of issues involves the expatriate's nonwork life. Many people return to the United States prior to the completion of overseas assignments simply because their spouses or families cannot adjust (Black & Stephens, 1989; Ronen, 1989). Some organizations interested in the retention of international assignees have developed a variety of programs to address this problem, such as language training, special schools for children of employees, spousal employment, cultural training, and child care. In making international assignments, an organization's failure to consider, and to base selection and training decisions on, the needs of an employee's spouse and children would appear to be a major mistake.

Another nonwork factor is the nature of the host country's culture. A challenging task for any visitor to a foreign country is to learn what are the essential and superficial aspects of the culture. Without knowledge of the local language, it is almost impossible to carry on some relatively simple life tasks. The misinterpretation of nonverbal cues can be devastating in some cultures. It is also necessary for the international assignee to learn something of the host country's geography, demographics, climate, political system, major religious denominations and beliefs, history, and so on. Research on cultural differences has given rise to the notion that cultures vary considerably in their novelty (relative to U.S. culture) and "toughness" (Church, 1982; Mendenhall & Oddou, 1985; Torbiorn, 1982).

Given the very large differences in cultures and the importance that culture plays in the adaptation of individuals in foreign countries, it is perhaps not surprising that cross-cultural training has had positive impacts on individuals' adjustment to cross-cultural situations and on their job performance in other countries (see Black & Mendenhall, 1990, for a review). Black and Mendenhall (1990) tried to contrast training for domestic assignments with training for foreign work by applying social learning theory concepts to these situations. Their comparison highlighted the differences in the novelty of the training material in cross-cultural situations, and they speculate that this may affect attention and retention processes as well as the optimal sequence of various modeling processes.

In presenting their model of cross-cultural training effectiveness and a model of the effectiveness of international assignees in general, Black and his colleagues point to the dearth of theoretically based research (Black & Mendenhall, 1990; Black et al., 1991). In one study that did involve the testing of the importance of a theoretical construct, Guzzo et al. (1994) examined the effectiveness of various inducements and supports provided to expatriates in terms of the degree to which they violated or met the terms of a psychological contract between the employees and the organization. They found that various supports and benefits affected the intent of expatriates to return early or quit, but that these effects were completely mediated by the expatriates' perceptions of the degree to which these supports were sufficient and supportive (these perceptions being the authors' operationalizations of the psychological contract). Guzzo et al. also report the frequencies with which their research participants reported receiving financial inducements, general support (e.g., language training, home leaves, leaves, help in locating homes) and family-oriented support. Interestingly, the participants reported many and varied financial inducements and a wide variety of general support, but relatively little in the way of family-oriented support.

The recruitment, selection, socialization, adjustment (of both expatriates and their families), and work performance of individuals who are assigned to work in foreign countries constitute an area about which we have much to learn. The Black et al. (1991) model incorporating what little is known about adjustment and work performance in different cultures with the domestic socialization literature should provide a useful basis on which to begin the systematic building of a research base. Feldman (1997) also provides a very useful set of hypotheses regarding the socialization of persons who are given international assignments. The U.S. literature contains nothing of which we are aware about the adjustment and performance of persons who come to the United States for work assignments. It would be very interesting to see whether problems of adjustment and the predictors of success are symmetric—that is, if persons going from one culture to another experience the same problems as those asked to migrate in the opposite direction.

Another problem that is beginning to receive some attention is the degree to which expatriates and their families experience adjustment problems upon return to their home countries. The degree to which an international assignment interrupts or enhances an employee's career in an organization and the development of her or his organizationally relevant skills is certainly an important individual and organizational concern. Of equal concern is the ability of the employee and her or his family to reintegrate themselves into the home society and culture and their previous network of family and friends. We know of no research that has examined the prediction of adjustment problems.

We also believe that new challenges for personnel selection researchers are resulting from the increased immigration into the United States of non-English-speaking job applicants with very different cultural backgrounds. The U.S. Census Bureau has projected a net difference between immigration and emigration of 880,000 annually between 1992 and 2005, with about 70% of immigrants expected to be Hispanics and Asian/Pacific Islanders (Fullerton, 1993). Immigrants' participation rate in the labor force is usually high, because immigrants typically come to the United States for economic reasons. Hence, the demographic changes in the U.S. population will be mirrored in the composition in the U.S. workforce.

What are the implications of immigration for personnel selection? At the most fundamental level, effective functioning on virtually all jobs requires workers to have a basic job-relevant proficiency in the English language. Most workers on relatively simple production or service-related jobs need to understand oral and written English to the extent it is used in everyday work contexts. If they are to participate fully in the organization and develop KSAOs that will allow them to be promoted, they will need a much higher level of English proficiency. When a worker lacks basic English proficiency, he or she encounters difficulty in understanding and following directions and in reading memos, manuals, and other written materials. These communication failures are likely to have negative impacts on a worker's job performance and promotability and may result in injury to the worker if he or she does not understand safety instructions.

Recently, we attempted to devise reliable and valid measures of basic English proficiency to be used to predict performance and promotability of entry-level workers in a large food-processing firm (Chan, Schmitt, Jennings, & Sheppard, in press). Using job-relevant material and information obtained from a job analysis that focused on the English requirements of the job, we developed an audio test and a reading test to assess workers' abilities to understand spoken and written English. Examples of items from the reading portion of the tests appear in Table 8.4. We assessed the criterion-related validity of these two instruments by correlating scores on the tests with supervisory ratings (using behaviorally anchored scales) of job incumbents' oral and reading proficiency as it related to the accomplishment of their work tasks and their potential promotability. Both reading and audio portions of the test were valid and each predicted unique portions of the variance in the performance measures. In addition, the tests provided incremental validity beyond assessment of current performance levels in the prediction of promotability.

The assessment of job-relevant English proficiency poses special challenges to selection researchers. Aside from the obvious expansion of the list of relevant KSAOs, selection researchers will often need to collaborate with organizational and community personnel who provide English-language training to ensure the job-relevant nature of such training. In addition, there is the challenge associated with the collection of data from immigrant applicants who may possess some language skills, but are simply unfamiliar with the usual testing situation. Language skills, in fact, may be the easiest to assess. Broader cultural differences may affect motivation and job performance as well. In the example just described above, the organization had considerable difficulty in convincing some workers of the importance of

Table 8.4 Examples of Items From a Job-Relevant Measure of English Proficiency
Developed for Entry-Level Workers in a Food Processing Plant

> NOTICE
> BEYOND THIS POINT
> • HEAD COVERING REQUIRED
> • NO OPEN FOOD OR BEVERAGE
> • NO SMOKING

Circle your answers.

What is required in this area?

   a. can of pop
   b. a hair net
   c. food from the cafeteria
   d. smoking

What is *not* allowed in this area?

   a. a hair net
   b. a helmet
   c. open containers of food
   d. a blue helmet

Circle your answers.

What is this?

   a. glove
   b. pair of boots
   c. helmet
   d. shovel

What does this cover?

   a. hands
   b. feet
   c. head
   d. arms

guidelines related to the use of the bathroom facilities while at work, because these employees' previous living accommodations did not include running water or other indoor facilities.

Customer Service Orientation

Considerable attention has been focused in the professional literature (Peters & Austin, 1987) and in the popular media on the need for organizations to be more sensitive to quality issues and customer satisfaction. In addition, the proportion of the U.S. workforce that is directly involved in service to customers has continued to rise over the past two decades. This increased emphasis on service quality and customer satisfaction has generated some interest in the relationship between employee behavior and attitudes and customer satisfaction. A common notion in this literature is that employees are more likely to deliver excellent service to customers when the organization expects and rewards such behavior and establishes practices that facilitate service delivery (Schneider, Wheeler, & Cox, 1992).

This climate for service was probably first studied empirically by Schneider and his colleagues (Schneider, 1990; Schneider & Bowen, 1985; Schneider, Parkington, & Buxton, 1980). In a recent test of this hypothesis regarding the impact of the organization's service climate, Johnson (1996) found significant relationships between components of a service climate among employees and facets of customer satisfaction as rated by 538 employees and 7,944 customers of 57 branches of a bank. Specifically, information about customers' needs and expectations, training in delivering quality service, and rewarding excellent service were related to overall customer satisfaction and satisfaction with various specific bank services. Most of the correlations between climate and customer satisfaction were in the .30s and .40s.

Another common belief, and one that has received research support, is that employees who are satisfied are likely to produce satisfied customers. Schmit and Allscheid (1995) found that employee satisfaction with management support, monetary support, and support for service were significantly correlated with customer satisfaction in 160 offices of a service organization.

An interesting application of the notions underlying the need to consider customer satisfaction is provided by Heneman, Huett, Lavigna, and Ogsten (1995), who surveyed managers in Wisconsin state government with respect to their satisfaction with staffing services delivered to them by the state's central staffing function. The researchers then used the survey results to develop several initiatives designed to increase quality of the services rendered and, hopefully, the services themselves. The survey itself should be of use to human resource professionals who serve as internal and external consultants to organizations. The trend toward increased outsourcing of these services makes it particularly relevant that customer satisfaction be assessed and considered in this area as well as others.

Hogan, Hogan, and Busch (1984) report on the development and validation of the Service Orientation Index as part of the Hogan Personality Inventory (HPI). The most recent version of the HPI (Hogan & Hogan, 1995) includes a revision of this scale. In the original study reporting the development of this index, validities in four studies against a variety of service criteria and ratings ranged from .20 to .42 (Hogan et al., 1984). Sample sizes in these four studies were quite low (37, 30, 100, and 56), but the results indicate the importance of individual differences in customer or service orientation. The work on effectiveness in sales occupations (Schmitt, Gooding, Noe, & Kirsch, 1984) is also relevant and usually indicates the importance of personality or motivation variables as important determinants of sales success (Ghiselli, 1966, 1973). Certainly, personality dimensions such as sociability and agreeableness ought to predict service orientation. In addition, however, if an individual is going to be oriented toward better serving an organization's clients, he or she must have an interest in the acquisition of information about the customers' needs and the degree to which the employing organization is meeting those needs, as well as the manner in which that individual can contribute to quality and customer service. Cognitive, interest, and affective variables should be related to the development of a customer orientation. The interaction between individual attitudes and personality is also likely to play a role as well (Schneider, 1987). At the most basic level, selection research in customer-oriented organizations must include models and measures of performance in which customer reactions and behavior are an important component.

Summary:
Research Issues for the Future

In this chapter we have described five changes that we think will have impacts on human resource practices, including selection, in organizations. These changes are increased speed of technological change, increased use of work teams, changes in modes of communication, globalization of the economy and many organizations, and greater concern for customer service. Assuming that we are correct about the trends we have identified as well as others described by Howard (1995), there are a number of research issues that should receive greater attention. We have raised many researchable questions in the context of this chapter. The major research concerns that should be addressed are reflected in the following questions:

1. How can organizations select, motivate, and enable individuals to engage in continuous learning?
2. What KSAOs will enable individuals to adapt to a situation in which their work lives are in a constant state of flux? What health or adjustment outcomes will result from this situation, and how can organizations best identify those who are susceptible to these problems so that they can take remedial or preventive action?
3. How do human resource functions (recruitment, selection, training, compensation) change when teams as opposed to individuals become the work unit, and how do these functions interact to affect team performance?
4. How can researchers aggregate team performance and team members' KSAOs to measure KSAO-performance relationships? How do these relationships differ from analogous relationships investigated at the individual level?
5. How do organizations' needs and goals affect the types of teams and team members they need to work effectively?
6. What organizational effects are produced when advancements in communication and technology make it unnecessary for workers to work in a central location? What kinds of KSAOs are predictive of success and adaptation to these circumstances? How do organizations and individuals adapt to decentralized or nonexisting organizational locations?
7. How can organizations best select and train individuals who are likely to adapt and work effectively in other cultures and countries?
8. In the case of immigrant applicants and workers, what are the job-relevant KSAOs and alternate methods of data gathering that researchers should consider in selection and other human resource interventions?
9. How do the important characteristics affecting cross-cultural adaptation vary as a function of the culture in which the individual and the organization are embedded?
10. What are the individual difference and experience determinants of the development of a positive attitude toward customer service? How do these individual difference variables interact with organizational practices and culture to foster a positive customer orientation?
11. All change requires the capacity to adapt. What are the most important aspects of a changing situation as they affect individuals' capacities to perform and their short- and long-term health and work satisfaction? Are these individual differences generalizable across situations that demand adaptation to different circumstances?

9 Programmatic Research
and Theory Development

The Future

_____

In the preceding chapters, we have mentioned areas in which promising research has been conducted and areas and problems about which we have very few data. In this last chapter, we hope to underscore the major research issues as we see them and to describe what we believe to be questions and studies that would be of value in each area. Our discussion is organized into 11 sections, each corresponding to a major set of research issues. In Chapters 2 and 3, we argued that the development of selection procedures should begin with a theory of job performance. In the case of many of the research problems discussed in this chapter, we are suggesting new, or expanding existing, conceptualizations of performance. In the first section, we return to Campbell, McCloy, Oppler, and Sager's (1993) model and discuss some research questions implied by that model and other performance models, including those suggested by cognitive psychology.

That section is followed by a discussion of the issues raised when we expand the domain of work performance beyond the technical aspects of the job, which is suggested by Campbell et al. but made much more explicit by those interested in withdrawal behavior, organizational citizenship behavior, and the like. Proportionally, researchers have spent very little time investigating the manner in which work performance changes over time and what implications any changes in performance might have for selection and other human resource issues. Consequently, in our third section we suggest research related to performance change over time. The fourth set of issues we discuss are those raised when organizations begin to select teams rather than individuals. In the fifth section, we discuss what questions are raised when selection is viewed as an intervention and examine the impact of selection on organizations. The latter involves treating the organization as the unit of analysis rather than the individual, as is customary in most selection research. This raises a number of issues regarding levels of analysis (the sixth section) and how these issues affect the conceptualization and measurement of performance. The changes discussed in Chapter 8 all imply that workers in today's organizations must be prepared to adapt to constant change. This raises questions about the KSAOs required to perform under these conditions as well as the measurement and definition of the performance construct, which we discuss in the seventh section. In Chapter 2, we reviewed literature on KSAO-task taxonomies and indicated the importance of these taxonomies for selection research. We reemphasize the centrality of this concern in the eighth section of this chapter. The long-term and short-term effectiveness of selection interventions may also be the result of applicant reactions. Suggestions for additional research designed to assess the determinants and consequents of such reactions are provided in the ninth section. In Chapters 4 and 5, we mentioned unresolved concerns about the nature of the constructs measured with some predictor instruments. In the tenth section, we discuss future research regarding the constructs measured using different procedures as well as research directed to the assessment and control of various method biases. Finally, concern over subgroup differences in ability and performance continues to be the single most important social and political issue confronting selection researchers. In the last section in this chapter we suggest questions that should be addressed in this area.

Research on Performance Models

Throughout this book, we have emphasized that theory in selection research is essentially a theory of work performance. Our conceptualization of the performance construct is of fundamental importance to selection research because it determines what KSAOs we consider in selecting employees and because this conceptualization determines the measures we use to evaluate the selection process itself. Thus, critical programmatic research should include the development of conceptually adequate and empirically validated performance models.

In Chapters 3 and 4, we discussed several attempts by researchers to model work performance and KSAO-performance relationships. We believe that the Campbell et al. (1993) theory of performance provides a promising direction for future research. As described in Chapter 3, Campbell et al. propose a process-oriented model that emphasizes the multidimensionality of both the KSAO and performance domains. According to the model, there are eight core performance dimensions (e.g., job-specific task proficiency, demonstration of effort), and each component is a function of three categories of performance determinants: declarative knowledge, procedural knowledge and skills, and motivation. These performance determinants constitute the mediating processes between individual difference (KSAOs) and situational variables on the one hand and performance components on the other. Although the model provides a useful framework for conceptualizing the performance construct and KSAO-performance relationships, there is a paucity of empirical research relating directly to the model. A challenge for future researchers will be to translate aspects of Campbell et al.'s model into specific hypotheses and test them in empirical studies. For example, researchers could begin by specifying the substantive nature of the target performance component or components in the KSAO-performance relationship in which they are interested. Different performance components are likely to have different relationships with the same KSAO constructs. These relationships will have to be specified. The substantive content of the domains of knowledge, skill, and choice behavior (i.e., Campbell et al.'s performance determinants) that purportedly mediate the KSAO-performance linkages should be explicated and these mediating hypotheses tested. These mediating processes are important because they shed light on why individuals with certain KSAOs or under certain situations are able to achieve better performance. Identifying these *proximal* causes of performance (i.e., Campbell et al.'s performance determinants) enriches our understanding of KSAO-performance relationships and enables us to specify KSAO-performance linkages that are likely to be replicated in future populations, operations, and settings. Our position is that studies that increase our understanding of work performance and KSAO-performance relationships come about only when researchers carefully think through the potential mediating linkages between KSAO constructs (not KSAO measures) and target performance criterion constructs. A good example of this type of research is provided by the Project A work, especially the paper by McCloy, Campbell, and Cudeck (1994).

When specifying these KSAO-performance linkages and mediating relationships, researchers will have to draw on theories of human behavior and related empirical findings from the relevant psychological literature. For example, the literature on motivation research provides a rich base from which researchers could generate specific hypotheses concerning choice behaviors and specific individual difference constructs (e.g., achievement motivation). From recent training research (e.g., Ford & Kraiger, 1995; Goldsmith & Kraiger, 1997) that is theoretically grounded in cognitive psychology (e.g., Anderson, 1983, 1993; Holyoak, 1991), researchers could specify the substantive structure and content of the relevant domains of knowledge using constructs such as mental models, production systems, strategic knowledge, and metacognition. Based on theory and previous findings relating these knowledge constructs to specific task performance, researchers could map these relationships to Campbell et al.'s core performance components for hypothesis generation and testing. Note that changes in the measures used may also be necessary. As noted by Goldstein and Kraiger (1997), many of the above knowledge or cognitive constructs are unlikely to be assessed adequately by traditional paper-and-pencil measures used in selection research because these measures are unlikely to capture the interrelationships in the knowledge or cognitive structures, that is, the configural properties of knowledge or cognitive representations. Jonassen, Beissner, and Yacci (1993) describe several useful methods for assessing knowledge or cognitive structures. An increasingly popular method among training researchers is the measurement system that employs the Pathfinder scaling algorithm (Schvaneveldt, Durso, & Dearholt, 1985,

1989) as the technique for eliciting and representing structural knowledge. These cognitive methods may play an important complementary role to the traditional ability and performance measures in the testing of performance models.

As stated in Chapter 2, theories of work performance are usually based on an analysis of the job. The focus on cognitive determinants of performance has direct implications for job analysis. Traditional job analysis techniques (see Chapter 2) focus on observable behaviors. To capture the essence of the cognitive requirements of the job defined in terms of cognitive constructs such as mental models and metacognitive activities, the traditional behavioristic job analysis may have to be complemented by some form of cognitive task analysis (CTA). In contrast to traditional job analysis, CTA focuses on the cognitive structures and processes underlying behavior, rather than on the observable behavior itself. For example, in describing the job requirements of an electronic specialist whose primary job duties consist of troubleshooting tasks performed on an electronic system, a CTA may focus on the nature of the mental model that underlies a successful performer's procedural expertise, that is, the performer's cognitive representations of the way the system works. Several CTA techniques exist, including process-tracing methods (e.g., protocol analysis) and structural assessment methods (e.g., eliciting and representing knowledge structures through Pathfinder scaling; see Glaser, Lesgold, & Gott, 1991; Jonassen et al., 1993). Although there has been increasing interest in CTA in training research, there has been a lack of systematic study of CTA and its applications in selection research. Interesting research questions include the following: What are the types of information that a CTA technique could provide that are conceptually meaningful in the context of a performance model and practically useful to selection? Which technique is most appropriate for particular situations? Are CTA techniques capturing critical work-related constructs, some of which are not described in existing KSAO-performance taxonomies? What are the situations in which CTA could supplement or provide clear improvement over traditional job analysis? When specifying and validating CTA techniques, do researchers need validation designs and data-analytic frameworks different from those traditionally used in selection research?

Given that existing CTA methods incur high costs and require highly trained task analysts, a practical approach is to restrict CTA to selection situations in which major investment of effort is appropriate (Glaser et al., 1991). These situations include those jobs or areas in which traditional job analysis has not been able to provide useful information for identifying critical selection KSAOs. Many of these situations are likely to be those that have been strongly affected by modern technology, where the incumbent's work environment involves critical interactions with complex machines (e.g., technical jobs in the military). Our position is that CTA techniques should complement, rather than replace, traditional job-analytic techniques. In selection research, it is often not practical, and indeed not necessary, to perform a CTA at the detailed level typically found in cognitive psychology, which is often concerned with specific tasks. We propose that the focus should be on the specification of the substantive nature of the cognitive processes, type of knowledge domains, and skills required for successful performance. This specification would then guide the identification of the critical selection KSAOs and development of relevant selection instruments. The challenge is to be able to specify conceptually adequate linkages between the target performance components and their cognitive determinants, to employ valid and practical CTA techniques to assess the relevant cognitive determinants, and to match these cognitive determinants to critical selection KSAOs. The important conceptual question concerns the extent to which CTA contributes to our understanding of work performance and KSAO-performance relationships. The important practical question concerns the incremental predictive value that CTA provides over the information that can be obtained with relatively low cost using traditional job analysis.

Another promising direction for research on performance modeling is to examine the relationships between work experience and performance. Work experience is relevant to work performance because individuals differ in work experiences and these experiences provide the "context" or "raw materials" for learning how to perform a task. As described in Chapters 4 and 5, several performance models besides Campbell et al.'s model include work or job experience as a construct affecting performance (e.g., Borman, Hanson, Oppler, Pulakos, & White, 1993; Schmidt, Hunter, Outerbridge, & Goff, 1988). However, inserting a predictor construct in a performance model and labeling it as work experience is not very helpful by itself. Work experience is a multidimensional and multilevel construct (Ford, Quiñones, Sego, &

Sorra, 1992; Quiñones, Ford, & Teachout, 1995). Quiñones et al. (1995) have proposed a useful framework for conceptualizing work experience. In this framework, experience can be measured in three modes (type, amount, and time), and these can be conceptualized at three different levels of specificity (task, job, and organization), producing nine categories of work experience. Job tenure, the most common operationalization of work experience in selection research, is only one of the nine categories of experience. The majority of the other eight categories are underresearched. Our position is that in any performance model, it is of critical importance to specify the precise nature (category) of work experience whenever the construct label *work experience* is used. To assert that work experience is related to performance is not very meaningful unless it is clear to which aspect (category) of work experience one is referring. For example, for a given performance component, one category of work experience may enhance performance, whereas another category may actually inhibit performance (Chan, 1997a). Future research could attempt to map Quiñones et al.'s categories of experience to various performance components and design studies that test how certain categories of experience enhance or inhibit performance.

Expanding Models of Performance

Traditionally, personnel selection research has focused on the prediction and understanding of what Campbell and colleagues have called core technical proficiency (Campbell et al., 1993; Campbell, McHenry, & Wise, 1990). Thus, performance has been defined as proficiency in accomplishing tasks that are more or less directly related to the organization's primary objectives. So, firefighters would be judged on the basis of how well they can perform tasks related to putting out fires and auto mechanics would be judged on the basis of how well they can repair cars. In the past couple of decades, organizational researchers have begun to study aspects of work behavior that are not directly related to these primary tasks (Organ, 1988). These organizational citizenship behaviors (OCBs) have almost always been studied in isolation from core technical proficiency; the work on Project A summarized in Chapter 4 represents an effort in which the measured performance domain included both core technical proficiency and what might be termed citizenship behavior (i.e., effort and leadership, discipline). This expansion of the performance domain has included both some important organizationally relevant measures (e.g., the willingness and capability to mentor less senior colleagues or to serve on special task forces and committees) and some rather mundane activities (e.g., administering the office coffee fund or organizing happy hour activities) and community activities (e.g., leading an effort to clean up a highway or organizing a blood drive) that have no direct relevance to the employing organization. The degree to which these measures are included as criteria in selection research should be a function of the organization's goals, and there are many ways in which these activities can serve such goals. For example, most organizations depend on their local communities for their work-forces and for support in efforts to acquire the infrastructure needed to function (i.e., highways, schools, utilities). Community activities that are identified with the organization can certainly serve to bolster such community support. Related to OCB is the notion that some employees contribute to, or detract from, the smooth functioning of their organizations simply as a function of the interpersonal behavior or interactions they stimulate (Baron, 1996). These activities may contribute to workforce health and organizations' sense of belonging to the community, which in turn may influence their organizational commitment and the length of their tenure.

Perhaps the most comprehensive list of variables that may constitute aspects of contextual performance, of which OCBs are a major component, is provided by Borman and Motowidlo (1997b); their list is reprinted here as Table 9.1. Borman and Motowidlo's article is part of a special issue of *Human Performance* in which various authors raise many of the same questions raised here concerning the nature and importance of contextual performance and the individual difference correlates of such performance (Borman & Motowidlo, 1997a). Borman and Motowidlo (1997b) maintain that personality variables may be the best correlates of contextual performance (see also Motowidlo, Borman, & Schmit, 1997) and that supervisors do consider such elements of performance in making performance ratings. The ways in which OCBs may contribute to organizational effective-ness are listed in Table 9.2, which is reprinted from Podsakoff and MacKenzie (1997). These "examples" represent hypotheses about the processes through which OCBs contribute to organizational effective-

Table 9.1   Borman and Motowidlo's Taxonomy of Contextual Performance

1. Persisting with enthusiasm and extra effort as necessary to complete own task activities
     successfully
     Perseverance and conscientiousness (Borman et al., 1985)
     Extra effort on the job (Brief & Motowidlo, 1986; Katz & Kahn, 1978)
2. Volunteering to carry out task activities that are not formally part of own job
     Suggesting organizational improvements (Brief & Motowidlo, 1986; Katz & Kahn, 1978)
     Initiative and taking on extra responsibility (Borman et al., 1985; Brief & Motowidlo, 1986;
        Katz & Kahn, 1978)
     Making constructive suggestions (George & Brief, 1992)
     Developing oneself (George & Brief, 1992)
3. Helping and cooperating with others
     Assisting/helping coworkers (Borman et al., 1985; Brief & Motowidlo, 1986; Katz & Kahn,
        1978)
     Assisting/helping customers (Brief & Motowidlo, 1986)
     Organizational courtesy (Organ, 1988)
     Sportsmanship (Organ, 1988)
     Altruism (Smith et al., 1983)
     Helping coworkers (George & Brief, 1992)
4. Following organizational rules and procedures
     Following orders and regulations and respect for authority (Borman et al., 1985)
     Complying with organizational values and policies (Brief & Motowidlo, 1986)
     Conscientiousness (Smith et al., 1983)
     Meeting deadlines (Katz & Kahn, 1978)
     Civic virtue (Graham, 1986)
5. Endorsing, supporting, and defending organizational objectives
     Organizational loyalty (Graham, 1986)
     Concern for unit objectives (Borman et al., 1985)
     Staying with the organization during hard times and representing the organization favorably
        to outsiders (Brief & Motowidlo, 1986)
     Protecting the organization (George & Brief, 1992)

SOURCE: From "Task Performance and Contextual Performance: The Meaning for Personnel Selection Research," by W. C. Borman and S. J. Motowidlo, 1997, *Human Performance, 10,* pp. 99-110. Copyright 1997 by Lawrence Erlbaum Associates, Inc. Reprinted by permission.

ness. Data regarding these processes are largely unavailable or indirect; this represents an area in which research might enhance our understanding.

If organizational citizenship concepts are to be measured and used as criteria in the current model of selection research, job analysis methods must be employed that generate information regarding the importance of these activities. In this regard, broad organizational goals must be considered rather than the rather narrow conceptualizations of the job generated in most traditional job analysis efforts

Table 9.2 Summary of Reasons Why OCBs Might Influence Organizational Effectiveness

Potential Reasons Why OCBs Influence Work Group and/or Organizational Performance	Examples
OCBs may enhance coworker productivity.	Employees who help other coworkers to "learn the ropes" may help them to become more productive employees faster. Over time, helping behavior can help to spread "best practices" throughout the work unit or group.
OCBs may enhance managerial productivity.	If employees engage in civic virtue, the manager may receive valuable suggestions and/or feedback on his or her ideas for improving unit effectiveness. Courteous employees, who avoid creating problems for coworkers, allow the manager to avoid falling into a pattern of "crisis" management.
OCBs may free resources up for more productive purposes.	If employees help each other with work-related problems, then the manager doesn't have to; consequently, the manager can spend more time on productive tasks, such as planning. Employees who exhibit conscientiousness require less managerial supervision and permit the manager to delegate more responsibility to them. To the extent that experienced employees help in the training and orienting of new employees, it reduces the need to devote organizational resources to these activities. If employees exhibit sportsmanship, it frees the manager from having to spend too much of his or her time dealing with petty complaints.
OCBs may reduce the need to devote scarce resources to purely maintenance functions.	A natural by-product of helping behavior is that it enhances team spirit, morale, and cohesiveness, thus reducing the need for group members (or managers) to spend energy and time on group maintenance functions. Employees who exhibit courtesy toward others reduce intergroup conflict, thereby diminishing the time spent on conflict management activities.
OCBs may serve as an effective means of coordinating activities between team members and across work groups.	Exhibiting civic virtue by voluntarily attending and actively participating in work unit meetings would help the coordination of effort among team members, thus potentially increasing the group's effectiveness and efficiency. Exhibiting courtesy by "touching base" with other team members or members of other functional groups in the organization reduces the likelihood of the occurrence of problems that would otherwise take time and effort to resolve.

(continued)

Table 9.2   Continued

Potential Reasons Why OCBs Influence Work Group and/or Organizational Performance	Examples
OCBs may enhance the organization's ability to attract and retain the best people by making it a more attractive place to work.	Helping behaviors may enhance morale, group cohesiveness, and the sense of belonging to a team, all of which may enhance performance and help the organization to attract and retain better employees. Demonstrating sportsmanship by being willing to "roll with the punches" and not complaining about trivial matters sets an example for others, and thereby develops a sense of loyalty and commitment to the organization that may enhance employee retention.
OCBs may enhance the stability of organizational performance.	Picking up the slack for others who are absent, or who have heavy workloads, can help to enhance the stability (reduce the variability) of the work unit's performance. Conscientious employees are more likely to maintain a consistently high level of input, thus reducing variability in a work unit's performance.
OCBs may enhance an organization's ability to adapt to environmental changes.	Employees who are in close contact with the marketplace volunteer information about changes in the environment and make suggestions about how to respond to them; this helps an organization to adapt. Employees who attend and actively participate in meetings may aid the dissemination of information in the organization, thus enhancing its responsiveness. Employees who exhibit sportsmanship, by demonstrating a willingness to take on new responsibilities or learn new skills, enhance the organization's ability to adapt to changes in its environment.

SOURCE: From "Impact of Organizational Citizenship Behavior on Organizational Performance: A Review and Suggestions for Future Research," by P. M. Podsakoff and S. B. MacKenzie, 1997, *Human Performance, 10*, pp. 133-152. Copyright 1997 by Lawrence Erlbaum Associates, Inc. Reprinted by permission.

(see Chapter 2). The degree to which these performance aspects are considered important and relevant in comparison to more narrow definitions of job responsibilities represents an interesting research question that has many implications for how organizations are managed. For example, Borman and Motowidlo (1993) question the advisability of rewarding or formalizing OCBs in any way. Their concern is that such formalization may serve to generate undesirable competition, jealousy, and phoniness of purpose among those who engage in these activities.

An interesting, and theoretically and practically important, question related to selection research is whether different sets of KSAOs are associated with performance in these two major work performance domains (i.e., technical proficiency and OCBs). The data from Project A, summarized in Table 4.6 in Chapter 4, suggest some differentiation of individual difference correlates across the different work domains. For example, cognitive ability seemed more highly related to Core Technical Proficiency and General Soldiering Proficiency, whereas personality measures were correlated equally with most domains of performance. However, cognitive predictors were also related to Effort and Leadership, Personal Discipline, and Physical Fitness and Military Bearing, which may be in part a function of behavior similar to OCBs. Likewise, the personality variables were correlated with Core Technical Proficiency and General Soldiering Proficiency. Organ and Konovsky (1989) found that OCBs are determined more by willful cognitive behavior than by simple affective reactions to a work situation. Perhaps those who have the most cognitive ability have the greatest capacity to figure out when and how to engage in OCBs that will most influence raters of their subsequent performance.

Equally interesting is the relationship between engagement in OCBs and the individual's performance of the technical aspects of her or his job. Although the correlation between measures of these different aspects of behavior is often positive (J. P. Campbell et al., 1990; George & Bettenhausen, 1990), it is far from perfect. This suggests that measures of these two broad aspects of work behavior would rank order people differently. One might speculate that those who cannot perform some work tasks make up for these deficiencies by engaging in other work behaviors that impress their peers and supervisors. Alternatively, workers who engage in a great many OCBs simply do not have the time and energy to engage in the tasks that make up the core of their jobs. It is very likely that individuals adopt different roles in organizations and that some engage more effectively in core task behavior and others in OCBs (Ilgen & Hollenbeck, 1991).

An interesting question involves the relationship between OCB and withdrawal. In Chapter 3, we described work by Hulin and his colleagues that supported the view that negative affect toward an organization expressed in low organizational commitment might be a prelude to tardiness, absenteeism, and turnover or sabotage (Hulin, 1991).

It would be interesting if the opposite pole of this continuum were represented by positive organizational commitment and the performance of a variety of OCBs.

If the organization determines that a variety of OCBs contribute in a meaningful way either directly or indirectly to the organization's functioning, it would seem reasonable that those behaviors become part of performance models and that researchers seek to understand what prompts such behavior and what outcomes result. In addition, OCBs may be legitimate criteria of performance (Organ, 1997). This may suggest that researchers should collect performance data from several internal and external organizational informants or constituencies. Supervisors, but also peers and subordinates and customers of the organization, may be informed observers of such behaviors. In addition, community members may actually be the best sources of information on some behaviors; this would be particularly true of police organizations or school principals, for example, in which case there may be no clear distinction between OCBs and behavior related to core task assignments. Although selection researchers have some experience collecting data from peers and subordinates as well as supervisors, they generally gather very few data from customers or community members.

Modeling Changes in Performance Over Time

In Chapter 3, we noted that an individual's performance may change over time and why these changes are important. First, when current job incumbents are employed in criterion-related validation research, their varying levels of job tenure could hide or confound KSAO-performance relationships. Second, if the nature (i.e., dimensionality) of performance changes over time, it is likely that any characteristic associated with performance at one time would not relate to performance at a different point in time. We also noted that changes in performance over time have been studied in a variety of ways, including changes in mean performance, changes in rank order of individuals' performance, and changes in the dimensions (i.e., factor structure) of performance.

As noted in Chapter 4, the KSAO-performance relationships described by Hunter (1983), Schmidt, Hunter, and Outerbridge (1986), Borman, White, Pulakos, and Oppler (1991), Schmit, Motowidlo, DeGroot, Cross, and Kiker (1996), and Schmitt, Pulakos, Nason, and Whitney (1996) are all conceptualized in terms of *static* forms of covariance structure models and tested using cross-sectional data. One of the problems of conceptualizing and testing KSAO-performance relationships as such is that these models are at best a "snapshot" of a dynamic *process* linking KSAO and performance occurring over *time*. To examine changes in performance over time, researchers need to employ longitudinal designs and time-sensitive data-analytic frameworks that can describe, assess, and explain KSAO-performance relationships. There has been some effort to model changes in performance over time. Some examples include models on stability of job performance (e.g., Austin, Humphreys, & Hulin, 1989; Barrett, Caldwell, & Alexander, 1985; Hanges, Schneider, & Niles, 1990; Henry & Hulin, 1987) and models on learning and skills acquisition (e.g., Kanfer & Ackerman, 1989; Snow & Lohman, 1984).

Many of the studies just cited have made significant contributions to the field. Some have sparked interesting debates that remain unresolved to date but are likely to advance the field (e.g., studies on the stability of performance). One of the reasons these contributions and debates have been possible is that conceptualizations and analyses of change over time were made more explicit in the models, which in turn allowed scientific examinations of the complexities involved in the change process. More longitudinal research is needed to examine changes in performance over time. Because in a longitudinal design repeated measurements are obtained from individuals over multiple time waves, such research is well suited for assessing the process of change as it unfolds over time. Repeated time-ordered measurement is the core feature that distinguishes longitudinal design from the cross-sectional design and the pretest-posttest design, which are one snapshot and two snapshots of the change process, respectively.

It is important to note that longitudinal design is not a panacea for all the problems encountered in the assessment of changes in performance over time. For example, because longitudinal studies require repeated measurements over multiple time waves, problems of subject attrition and measurement invariance of responses over time are often exacerbated. Researchers often state in the conclusions of their study reports that they could not make strong causal inferences due to the cross-sectional nature of their study design and that future research should employ longitudinal designs to enable causal inferences to be made. It is true that longitudinal designs, when properly conducted, have many advantages over cross-sectional designs, including the potential for making stronger causal inferences. However, the potential problems and caveats regarding adequate interpretation in longitudinal designs tend to be neglected. One important but often ignored issue in the interpretation of results from longitudinal designs concerns the length of the time interval (i.e., the interval between $Time_t$ and $Time_{t+1}$) in the time-ordered period of study. A change that is in fact continuous and gradual can appear in the results as large in magnitude if the time interval is too large. The converse of this problem can also occur when there is a mismatch between the length of the entire time period in the study and the actual causal interval. A change that is in fact large in magnitude will not be revealed in the results if the time period selected for study is smaller than the causal interval. There is some evidence that the time interval for repeated measurements can have dramatic effects on the results of the analysis performed, including substantial changes in the magnitude of the effect sizes (e.g., Cohen, 1991; Collins & Graham, 1991; Gollob & Reichardt, 1991). The bad news is that we almost never have a good approximation of what the actual causal interval is. Researchers have to make some judgments when selecting time intervals and the time period in the study—educated guesses based on theory and previous research findings.

The validity of inferences from a longitudinal study is no less dependent on the adequacy of the underlying theory of change than is the cross-sectional design. However, an advantage of the longitudinal design is that many fundamental questions concerning the nature of change under study can be explicated and tested within the design. For example, changes in the dimensions (i.e., factor structure) of performance over time can be assessed within a longitudinal design using analytic techniques such as longitudinal covariance structure analysis (e.g., Jöreskog & Sörbom, 1993). In addition, the researcher can test the reversibility of change by tracing the individual growth curve over time. With appropriate measurements and data-analytic models, the longitudinal design also allows an examination of whether change is better characterized as a shared characteristic of a group with no interindividual differences or at the individual level with interindividual differences in intraindividual growth or both.

The notion of *interindividual* differences in *intraindividual* changes is critical in the conceptualization and analysis of changes in performance over time. In the traditional longitudinal research, performance changes over time would be examined at the group or aggregate level (e.g., in terms of mean differences) on data collected from new incumbents at or shortly after entry to the job and at one or more occasions after a period of employment has elapsed. Although this traditional group-level assessment of change may provide some information on the amount of change for a group of job incumbents, it does not provide an adequate conceptualization and analysis of the nature of the *intraindividual* changes over time. Yet intraindividual change over time is the essence of the change phenomenon hypothesized to occur in the individual performance change process. If one focuses exclusively on mean differences over time or within-time interindividual variability, many important issues concerning the nature of intraindividual change over time either are not or cannot be adequately conceptualized and examined empirically. These issues include the following:

1. The form of the intraindividual change trajectory (e.g., linear versus quadratic, increasing versus decreasing)
2. Systematic interindividual differences in initial status at job entry
3. Systematic interindividual differences in the rate of intraindividual change
4. The relationship between initial status and rate of intraindividual change
5. Relationships between person variables (i.e., KSAOs) and initial status and between person variables and rate of change
6. Cross-domain relationships (e.g., between different performance components) with respect to issues 1 through 5
7. The invariance across groups (e.g., gender and ethnic groups) with respect to issues 1 through 6

This list provides a systematic agenda for research on changes in performance over time. Several recent methodological advances, such as hierarchical linear modeling (Bryk & Raudenbush, 1987) and latent growth modeling (McArdle & Epstein, 1987; Meredith & Tisak, 1990; Muthen, 1991; Willett & Sayer, 1994), provide powerful and flexible data-analytic frameworks that structure and assess interindividual differences in intraindividual change over time, providing the opportunity to address directly the changes listed above.

Team Selection

In Chapter 8, we argued that the emphasis on teams and teamwork in organizations is likely to change the manner in which personnel are selected. Perhaps the most important starting point with respect to considering team selection is the development of team performance models. Such models and their implications for selection are almost certainly going to differ as a function of the type of team (Klimoski & Jones, 1995; Sundstrom, DeMeuse, & Futrell, 1990) and the work performed by the team. Following the basic selection test validation model (see Chapter 2), we must begin with a job analysis of teamwork or a good taxonomy of teams, which will serve as the basis of developing team performance criteria and KSAOs at the team level. These job analyses will be complicated by virtue of the fact that we must consider the functions of the team as well as the degree to which individuals and members of the team interact. The focus of the job analyses and the manner in which they are conducted will differ from the traditional analysis, with its focus on individual tasks and responsibilities and the individual KSAOs required to perform them.

Klimoski and Jones (1995) present some preliminary speculation with respect to a meaningful categorization of teams as related to the way staffing would be done. For example, one of their team types (see Table 8.1) is the command and control team, in which it is important that all members of the team be equally and highly expert in the specific tasks for which they are responsible. An example of a command and control team is the military tank crew studied by Tziner and Eden (1985). However, members of a technical or professional team, as defined by Klimoski and Jones, might be chosen so that they represent various important constituencies to whom the product of the team effort may need to be sold. Clearly, one would expect individual and team performance to differ in these two situations.

Cannon-Bowers, Tannenbaum, Salas, and Volpe (1995) analyzed the general and specific competencies required for successful team performance that related to team process and team tasks. They developed a set of competencies that should be transportable to all other teams and a set of competencies that should be transportable to only those teams that have specific characteristics. Their list of team competencies represents an excellent compilation of the literature on group processes, group activities, and group outcomes, and should be a useful starting point for selection research on teams. Their separation of competencies into those related to teams and those related to tasks is reminiscent of Hackman's (1987) model of group effectiveness, in which he distinguishes between process variables and outcome variables. The addition of process variables or team-related competencies means that selection researchers must be prepared to assess and use information with respect to KSAOs related to team process variables as well as specific task-related variables.

In addition to the fact that selecting teams may involve the consideration of additional KSAOs, the staffing professional or researcher must consider the team composition. Klimoski and Jones (1995) believe that the *mix* of abilities, personality/values, and politics in the team must be considered. Two major unresolved issues are whether one team member's capabilities may compensate for another member's lack of capability in a given area, and whether a team can perform better than its best member. As indicated above, the appropriate mix may actually be a function of the type of team and task being considered. Cannon-Bowers et al. (1995) provide some propositions with respect to mix issues, but this is an important area of research about which there have been very few empirical studies.

One problem that has presented significant challenges for work team researchers is referred to as the *level of analysis issue*. This problem is relevant to research on team mix or composition, as well as the use of aggregated individual KSAO or performance indices. When team research is conducted, the unit of analysis should be the team, yet researchers usually measure individual KSAOs and individual performance outcomes. How these data are aggregated, or if and how they should be, is an issue with which all team researchers must deal. The implications of different ways and forms of aggregation for different types of teams constitute an important and complex research issue. We will elaborate on this problem below, in the section on levels of analysis issues.

Finally, an issue that has not been addressed concerns the difference between selecting an entire team for some task and replacing members of an existing team. If an existing team has developed peculiar ways of accomplishing team tasks or the members have developed a special rapport or even language related to team tasks, finding a replacement with the correct mix of skills and the willingness to learn and fit the existing team's culture and values will present challenges different from those that arise in the case in which an entire team is selected. The clear trend toward the increasing use of teams in organizations requires that selection researchers address these and other questions related to the selection of teams.

Selection as an Organizational Intervention and Organizational Effectiveness

In Chapter 7, we briefly reviewed the literature on the use of selection as a corporate strategy or as a means of developing strategy. The evaluation of these ideas requires a very different research approach. At a very basic level, we are asking whether an organization is more effective because it engages in certain selection practices. Answering this question requires that the organization be treated as the unit of analysis and that we confront the very difficult issues of defining and measuring organizational effectiveness (Cameron & Whetton, 1983; Hitt, 1988; Lewin & Minton, 1986; Tsui, 1990). Personnel selection researchers have addressed the utility issue at the individual level, and we reviewed the various utility models in Chapter 5. In these utility formulations, estimates of individuals' contributions to an organization are summed to produce an estimate of the total utility of a selection procedure or other human resource intervention. However, the extent to which these aggregated estimates of utility are recognized by organizations has not been confirmed or disconfirmed at the organizational level. In fact, we are aware of no such research effort. If estimates of utility based on the aggregation of individual indices of utility are not reflected in organizational outcomes, an interesting and practically important question is, Why?

Using organizations as units of analysis will also allow researchers to begin to study the manner in which selection practices can be most effectively introduced and implemented in organizations. To date, most of the research on these questions has produced only anecdotal or case study data (Johns, 1993). Other research on organizational interventions has pointed to the importance of idea champions, the support of upper-level management, the use of similar procedures by other organizations or industry leaders, and the consistency of an intervention with the organization's other practices, climate, and culture, but there are few or no data available on the implementation of successful selection programs.

In addition to the problems and concerns mentioned above, research on selection practices and organizational effectiveness must employ research designs other than correlational, cross-sectional designs. Longitudinal research in which the long-term impact of the introduction of selection practices is assessed will be necessary to address adequately some of the causal issues. Also, the *composition* issue addressed in the next section of this chapter will be important in some of this research. Theories of organizational functioning must be used to formulate hypotheses about the relative importance of specific practices across different types of organizations.

In this section, we have focused on studies of the outcomes of selection practices, but the determinants of the adoption or development of specific practices are obviously important also (Jackson, Schuler, & Rivero, 1989; Schuler & Jackson, 1987). These research data will be useful in our understanding of the role of selection in organizational effectiveness, but they may also be valuable in encouraging managers and practitioners to adopt effective management practices. Frustration with the communication of such results, including the results of the utility analyses outlined in Chapter 5, has been voiced by some researchers (e.g., Latham & Whyte, 1994).

Levels of Analysis Issues

Although it is probably true that most selection researchers agree with the Lewinian dictum that behavior is a function of both person and environment variables, the traditional focus in selection research has been on the *individual* level of conceptualization, measurement, and analysis. Typically, constructs examined in both the predictor and criterion space are individual difference constructs. The person is the unit of theory. However, when we examine team performance or view selection as an intervention and examine its impact on organizations, we treat the team or the organization as the unit of theory rather the individual, as is traditional in selection research. In addition, the adoption of a person-organization (P-O) fit perspective requires the selection researcher to engage in cross-levels theorizing involving multiple levels of analysis. Issues regarding levels of analysis (Rousseau, 1985) have critical impacts on our conceptualization and measurement of performance and KSAO-performance relationships. With the increased interest in multilevel conceptualization and measurement in selection research, levels of analysis issues provide several promising areas for programmatic research and theory development.

Several influential theoretical frameworks for multilevel research have been proposed (e.g., House, Rousseau, & Thomas-Hunt, 1995; Klein, Dansereau, & Hall, 1994; Rousseau, 1985), but a review of these frameworks is beyond the scope of this book. We strongly recommend that readers familiarize themselves with the major issues relating to conceptualization, measurement, and analysis in multilevel research and cross-levels theorizing. Some of these issues include clarification regarding the various types of multilevel models, aggregation biases, and fallacious inferences (e.g., ecological fallacy). In this section, we emphasize the need to specify adequate *composition models,* a critically important but neglected issue in multilevel research and the literature on levels of analysis.

Composition models specify the functional relationships among constructs at different levels of analysis that reference essentially the same content but are qualitatively different at different levels (Rousseau, 1985). *Explicit* composition models are important because they guide the development and validation of newly proposed constructs in multilevel research. For example, a composition model for team efficacy/potency (e.g., Guzzo, Yost, Campbell, & Shea, 1993) would specify how the team-level construct is derived from the established lower-level (i.e., individual-level) construct of self-efficacy (Bandura, 1977) and how this new team-level construct can be empirically validated. Without adequate composition models, there is a danger that the increased interest in multilevel theorizing would lead to a multitude of labels, all of which purportedly refer to scientific constructs but in reality have no incremental explanatory value (Chan, 1998). Chan (1998) has proposed a typology of composition models as a framework for organizing, evaluating, and developing constructs and theories in multilevel research. In Chan's typology there are five basic forms of composition, and each composition model is defined by a particular form of *functional relationship* specified between constructs at different levels. Corresponding to each form of functional relationship is a *typical operational process* by which the lower-level construct is combined to form a higher-level construct. The typology also suggests what *empirical support* constitutes the forms of evidence needed to support the relevant functional relationships and to establish that appropriate combination rules are applied. For example, the *direct consensus composition* model, which is probably the most popular and familiar composition model in multilevel research, specifies that the meaning of the higher-level construct is in the *consensus* among lower-level units. The typical operational combination process is through the use of within-group agreement to index consensus and justify aggregation. The value of some within-group agreement index, such as the r_{wg} (James, Demaree, & Wolf, 1984), could provide the empirical support for the composition. Composing the lower-level construct of psychological climate to the higher-level construct of organizational climate (e.g., James, 1982) is an example of a direct consensus composition.

Composition models have direct implications for the manner in which we conceptualize and measure performance at a level higher than the individual (e.g., team level). Consider the construct of performance at the individual and team levels. Should we adopt an *additive composition* (Chan, 1998) in which the individual team members' performance scores are simply summed or averaged to represent the team's performance? Chan (1998) argues that whether or not the relationship between levels is an additive (or some other composition form) one depends on the definition of the higher-level construct, which is part of the composition theory explicitly specified by the researcher or, more often, implicit in the hypothesized relationships between focal constructs in the study. If by *team performance* we mean the average performance of individual team members, then an additive composition form would be relevant. On the other hand, consider the case in which a researcher is interested in testing the hypothesis that *team performance is positively associated with individuals' perceptions of competitiveness within the team*. The researcher may base this hypothesis on the theory that a high-performing individual will perceive competition when interacting with other high-performing individuals but not when interacting with low-performing individuals, whereas a low-performing individual will not perceive competition when interacting with either high- or low-performing individuals. In this case, by *team performance* the researcher means the average per-formance of a team in which its members have similar performance levels. That is, within-team variance of individual performance becomes relevant because the hypothesis (based on the above theory) refers to teams that are relatively homogeneous in terms of members' performance levels. Additive composition models would be inappro-priate because variances among lower-level units become relevant in composing the lower-level construct to the higher-level construct. Within-group agreement regarding individual performance levels would have to be demonstrated before the average performance score for each team could be used as a measure of team performance. That is, in this case, a *direct consensus composition* model is appropriate.

In some types of multilevel research, both the lower level-construct and the higher-level construct provide the components necessary for the conceptualization and operationalization of the target construct. The researcher begins with two constructs, one at the lower level (e.g., individual) and one at the higher level (e.g., organization). Both constructs may or may not be commensurate constructs. That is, the two constructs may or may not share the same core content dimen-sions. However, each construct must be explicitly defined. The defini-tion of the target construct is then derived from the definitions of these two constructs. The substantive meaning of the target construct is some form of combination of the core elements from *both* the lower- and higher-level constructs. A theory of the target construct specifies the nature and form of the combination. This theory would provide the conceptual basis for the process that specifies how values on the lower- and higher-level constructs should be empirically combined to form values on the target construct.

The focal constructs in person-organization fit research are proto-typical examples of target constructs that are derived from a combi-nation of constructs at different levels. In P-O fit studies, the "fit" construct is a target construct composed from some person-level construct and some organization-level construct. For example, O'Reilly, Chatman, and Caldwell (1991) examined a target (P-O fit) construct that they call *value congruence*, which they define as the match between individuals' values and the organization's culture. These authors used the Q-sort methodology to develop and validate the Organizational Culture Profile (OCP), which is a measure of 54 values. The OCP was used to derive individuals' value profiles and the organization's culture. Value congruence was operationalized in terms of the Q-sort-based profile correlations. O'Reilly et al. demonstrated that value congruence was a valid predictor of satisfaction, commitment, and actual turnover for a 2-year period and that person or organization variables alone were not predictive of these outcomes. Chan's (1996a) study on cognitive misfit of problem-solving style provides another example. Chan began by explicating the construct of *adaptation-innovation problem-solving style,* which is an individual-level construct based on Kirton's (1976) "adaption-innovation" theory. Using Kirton's theory, Chan specified the higher-level construct of *style demands* conceptualized at the work context level. Based on the lower-level construct of problem-solving style and the higher-level construct of style demands, Chan then derived a target construct, *cognitive misfit,* which is the degree of mismatch between an individual's cognitive style of problem solving and the style demands of the work context. Chan operationalized and tested cognitive misfit in terms of a statistical interaction between problem-solving style and style demands. He demonstrated that whereas neither the individual-level construct nor the work context-level construct was associated with turnover probability, the cross-level construct of cognitive misfit provided significant and substantial incremental validity in predicting actual turnover over the predictability provided by performance.

As we have noted in previous chapters, there has been a surge of interest in the study of P-O fit in recent selection research. P-O fit studies are inherently multilevel studies, and the focal constructs in P-O fit research are inherently multilevel in nature. P-O fit researchers should devote more theoretical and empirical effort to specifying and validating multilevel constructs in their studies. Cross-levels theorizing from a P-O fit perspective should begin with a composition theory relating the different forms of P-O fit constructs across different levels.

Adaptability and Selection for Training Capability and Rapid Job Changes

In Chapter 8, we described several changes that we believe are occurring or have occurred in the workplace. What all of these changes seem to have in common are the increased demands they will make on workers to adapt to constant change in the work they do. These constant changes in work demands are likely to demand that workers be able and willing to learn and perform the new tasks required of them. As mentioned in the section on performance change above, the way in which selection research has been conducted in the past assumes a stable set of job tasks and job-relevant KSAOs. The need to take into account a constantly changing job raises important questions about selection research beyond those associated with research design and mode of data analysis. Must a researcher redo a job analysis every time a job changes? How will researchers know when a job changes sufficiently to necessitate a reexamination of the required KSAOs? What KSAOs are required to adapt to change? One of the reasons the U.S. Air Force developed its job analysis inventories was to track task changes that were the result of technological changes in the equipment used (McCormick, 1976), but if these efforts are to be effective in tracking change they must include the new tasks and actually anticipate the changes that are occurring. It may be the case that, even though the job tasks change, the KSAOs that are important for one set of tasks will be those that are important for the new tasks. Certainly the literature on cognitive ability reviewed in Chapter 4 suggests that cognitive ability is an important individual characteristic across a wide variety of different job tasks.

However, selection researchers have not often explicitly considered continuous adaptation to new job circumstances and what that might imply for job performance and the types of abilities required to work effectively in a context that requires constant adaptation to a changing job situation. Recently, Pulakos (1996) attempted to abstract the adaptability requirements of a wide variety of jobs and to consider potential KSAO correlates of these requirements. She analyzed critical incidents related by job incumbents in a wide variety of military and civilian jobs and classified the types of situations that required adaptation, very broadly defined as anything that required a worker to adapt to a new situation. Her final list of adaptive behaviors ranged from "handling crisis situations and work stress" to "learning new work tasks and technologies" and "interpersonal and intercultural sensitivity and adaptability." As one would expect, jobs differed rather substantially with respect to the types of adaptability problems job incumbents reported. The interesting research question is whether the same KSAOs are required in these different situations. It may be that there is a general capacity to adapt (cognitive ability?) and a general positive disposition toward challenging and changing environments that allows some individuals to adapt well to any of these situations. Alternatively, the adaptation may be unique to a given set of circumstances or the result of training and experience.

Chan (1997a) began with a consideration of the nature of adaptation, construing it as the degree of fit between the behaviors exhibited by an individual and the new work demands created by the novel and often ill-defined problems resulting from changing and uncertain situations. In considering both training and individual differences research on adaptability, Chan identified four elements that seem to characterize what researchers describe when they examine the need to be adaptive: (a) Changes and uncertainty in the work situation create novel and ill-defined problems; (b) problems make new work demands on individuals; (c) established and routine behaviors that were successful in the previous work situations become irrelevant, ineffective, suboptimal, or less useful in the new situations; and (d) adaptive behaviors that are in some way qualitatively different from established routines are successful in the new situations.

The literature on adaptability as an individual differences construct most often treats the construct as unitary, but researchers' operationalizations of adaptability clearly indicate that different aspects of the definition and attributes of adaptability as defined above are being used by different researchers, probably because they are dealing with some of the different adaptive situations identified by Pulakos (1996). There is also a training literature that emphasizes the development of adaptive expertise. Holyoak (1991) has identified different phases of research on expertise. Researchers began by defining expertise in terms of general problem-solving skills and the use of search strategies that were applicable across content domains (Newell & Simon, 1972). However, there has been little support for the notion that training on these strategies resulted in transfer across content domains. In addition, research on expert-novice differences revealed that experts' capabilities were at least partly due to their greater knowledge in a specific content domain (Chi, Feltovich, & Glaser, 1981). Novices also appeared to be less able than experts to understand the structural features of a problem and their own capacities to recognize procedures or behaviors that might apply or not apply to the resolution of a problem. The outcome of the research on expert-novice differences was the hypothesis that adaptive experts have developed metacognitive capabilities that are used to monitor and regulate the various cognitive activities involved in matching problems and solutions. Thus, research on training adaptive expertise has focused on trainees' acquisition of appropriate knowledge structures and metacognitive skills. Measurement of both has presented significant challenges (Goldsmith & Kraiger, 1997). From a selection point of view this research has at least two important implications. First, at least some adaptive skills are likely unique to content areas. Second, measures of knowledge structure and metacognitive capabilities might prove useful for predicting performance in situations in which adaptability is required.

To this point, we have discussed the importance of adaptive capability. To anyone who has had to change or convince others to adopt new ways of doing things, it is frequently obvious that the motivation to adapt is also critical. In fact, the greatest attention in the individual differences arena to adaptability has been in the personality area, in which measures of flexibility, rigidity, or adaptability are included in most multiple-scale personality inventories. In fact, one of the Big Five personality dimensions (Digman, 1990) is Openness. To our knowledge, no research has been directed toward ascertaining the relative importance of these "can do" and "will do" dimensions as they relate to adaptive behavior.

Finally, the work of Holyoak (1991) and others regarding the cognitive requirements of adaptability leads to the consideration of the role of previous work experience. Chan (1997a) makes the point that work experience can serve both to enhance and to inhibit adaptive performance. To the extent that work experience results in routinization of specific tasks and procedures, an employee may not expect novel situations or have the knowledge structure or metacognitive skills to perform well in new situations. On the other hand, adaptive experts' greater appreciation for the structural relationships underlying knowledge and the underlying principles involved in problem solution probably is derived from long work experience and familiarization with a variety of problems. In considering the role of work experience, we believe it is important to consider the level (task, job, organization) and type of measure (time, type, and amount) of work experience as discussed above and by Quiñones et al. (1995). These different ways of operationalizing work experience ought to have different implications for the development or inhibition of adaptive expertise and motivation.

Clearly, there are many ambiguities and untested hypotheses and assumptions regarding adaptability. Maximizing the adaptive expertise of workers is almost certainly going to involve the consideration of workers' capabilities and experiences as well as the situation in which they find themselves. If we and others are correct in our speculation that the rate of change in the nature of work tasks will escalate, then research devoted to an understanding and identification of adaptive skills, the aspects of situations that require adaptation, and their interaction is critically important.

KSAO-Task Taxonomies

In Chapter 4, we described several efforts to provide taxonomies of KSAOs and taxonomies of work behavior as well as efforts to link the two taxonomies. Certainly, such taxonomic efforts ought to be one of the goals of every discipline, but the resources necessary to engage in the required research and development are huge. If the effort is not comprehensive, any taxonomy will be incomplete and unlikely to gain any great degree of acceptance. In addition to the resources, then, taxonomic efforts will require the coordinated work of many scientist-practitioners and perhaps various agencies and professional organizations as well. Such efforts should also build on previous similar efforts, described in Chapter 4, and these should include provisions for continuous updating and revision. A generally accepted taxonomy of work behavior, KSAO dimensions, and their linkages could be the stimulant for a great many research programs, perhaps constituting the basis for research in each of the other areas of research interest listed in this chapter and elsewhere in this book.

Applicant Reactions:
Determinants and Outcomes

In Chapter 7, we addressed the practical importance of applicant reactions and how these reactions could affect both the short- and long-term effectiveness of selection interventions. We also noted that recent research on applicant reactions has moved beyond descriptive studies that simply compare reactions to different selection tests to more theory-driven and construct-oriented studies that attempt to identify the determinants of reactions. To identify the determinants of test reactions, it is critical that researchers make a clear distinction between method and content when comparing reactions to different tests. By comparing different test methods with test content (and, hopefully, the constructs assessed) held constant (e.g., Chan & Schmitt, 1997), and by comparing different test content with test method held constant (e.g., Chan, 1997b), researchers should be able to isolate the aspects of tests (method versus constructs) responsible for test reactions.

In Chapter 7, we discussed two streams of research that have adopted theory-driven and construct-oriented approaches to the study of applicant reactions to selection tests. The first focused on the relationship between test reactions and test performance (e.g., Arvey, Strickland, Drauden, & Martin, 1990; Chan, Schmitt, DeShon, Clause, & Delbridge, 1997) and the second focused on the value of organizational justice theories in explaining applicant fairness perceptions and related reactions (e.g., Gilliland, 1993, 1994). Continued research on performance-reactions relationships is likely to shed more light on the role of previous testing-related experiences and self-serving biases and other motivational mechanisms in the development of specific test reactions. The justice research on applicant reactions is likely to increase our understanding concerning what and when violation of specific justice principles will lead to perceptions of unfairness and other related negative reactions. A challenge for future research is to integrate these two streams of research by simultaneously examining the effects of applicant motivational mechanisms and justice principles on reactions. For example, researchers could examine the relative importance of justice rule violation and perceived performance in determining fairness perceptions and related reactions on a selection test (Chan, Schmitt, Jennings, Clause, & Delbridge, in press). Researchers could also employ experimental designs to test the effects of manipulations of different features of the selection process on applicant reactions. Such integrative studies are likely to increase our understanding of applicant reactions and to help in the design and implementation of selection procedures that will engender more positive reactions and hopefully have positive impacts on selection utility (see Chapter 7).

From an organizational perspective, the concern with applicant reactions to selection systems is ultimately a concern with applicant reactions or attitudes toward the organization. An important but neglected issue in applicant reactions research concerns if and how reactions or attitudes toward the organization change over time. These changes are relevant in the contexts of both recruitment and selection. Research is needed to determine how an organization's image changes during recruitment and selection and how this image affects applicant behavior in both the short and the long term. For example, the typical recruit or applicant may begin the process of choosing an organization/ job with little more than a general view (positive or negative) of the organization/job and then gains a more differentiated perception of the organization/job as he or she obtains more information as a function of the recruitment and selection process. The concepts of beta and gamma change (Golembiewski, Billingsley, & Yeager, 1976) provide a useful framework for examining these potential changes in perceptions over time. An interesting research undertaking would be to examine the relationships among the various types of perception changes over time and applicant characteristics. For example, applicants who are more proactive may gather more information about the organization, and their perceptions of the organization may undergo more differentiation over time. Such research has practical value because the results should yield information regarding the effectiveness of various recruiting and selection activities (e.g., giving applicants more information) and how these activities affect the perceptions and behaviors of applicants with differing characteristics. Finally, some organizations are concerned that the selection procedures they use will adversely affect their reputations, and that rejected candidates may no longer buy the organizations' products or services. This was found to be true in the case of selection procedures developed by the first author to select clerical-technical personnel for a large automotive manufacturer (Schmitt, Gilliland, Landis, & Devine, 1993).

Construct Validity
of Predictor Measures

The majority of the research issues described in this chapter relate to the need for greater understanding of the work performance construct. However, a number of the selection instruments described in Chapter 4 are not well understood. Attempts to understand the nature of the constructs underlying biodata continue to be frustrating in spite of several decades of work (Mumford & Stokes, 1992). Part of this frustration may be due to the empirically based keys that traditionally have been used to score biodata forms. Also contributing to the confusion is the fact that some biodata items are relatively factual in nature, whereas others are more like those found in traditional interest or personality measures.

Similarly frustrating have been efforts to understand the nature of constructs measured in assessment centers. In Chapter 5, we described the finding that factor analyses of ratings in assessment centers more frequently identify exercise factors than they do trait or construct factors. More recently, it has proven very difficult to construct highly internally consistent situational judgment items (Motowidlo, Dunnette, & Carter, 1990), and our own factor analyses of these instruments have not produced interpretable factors. It may be that the situations and solutions in these items are inherently multidimensional or have the same situational (or exercise) correlates as do assessment center ratings.

A similar situation exists when job samples are used as part of the selection procedure. A job-relevant work sample should require a complex combination of KSAOs if the job itself makes such requirements. In addition, an interesting question about work samples is raised by the work of Sackett, Zedeck, and Fogli (1988), who posit that these measures are more likely indices of maximum performance (what workers can do) than they are measures of typical performance (what workers will do). In any event, a finding of a substantial relationship between a work sample measure and subsequent job performance shows that this measure is practically useful, but it does not contribute much to our understanding of KSAO-performance relationships.

In the case of all of these measures, it would be useful to have clearly articulated hypotheses about the nature of KSAO-performance relationships prior to the selection or construction of selection proce-

Table 9.3   Examples of Biodata Items Written to Reflect Different KSAO Dimensions

Construct Targeted	Representative Items
Positive image (community involvement)	To how many civic organizations (e.g., school boards, PTA, Kiwanis) do you belong?
	How much time do you volunteer to help service groups in your community?
Effort/motivation (self-comparison)	When working on a team, how much of the final product do you feel is generally attributable to your effort?
	At what pace do you usually work?
Judgment/evaluation (own career)	If you could do it over again, would you still go into your present field?
	About how many times did you change your mind about future vocational plans since the time you entered college?
Adaptability	When there are unexpected changes at work, you . . .
	When things do not go as planned, how would others describe you as acting?
Planning	When buying gifts for friends and/or relatives, how early do you typically make the purchase prior to giving the gift?
	Do you generally use a date book, daily planner, or other scheduling aid?
Willingness to maintain physical ability	How many times a week do you work out in a gym or athletic club?
	How many hours per week of physical exercise did you average during the past 2 or 3 months?

dures. Second, it would also be helpful to devise instruments that on an a priori basis are likely to measure specific KSAOs. For example, it might be useful to write biodata items or situational judgment items that specifically address different KSAOs. In Table 9.3, we present examples of such items that were used to assess KSAOs that the researchers attempted to measure in Example 1 described in Chapter 1. The results of this effort and the correlations of biodata measures with an array of external correlates are presented in Schmitt, Jennings, and Toney (1996). This effort did produce a consistent pattern of relationships with other variables, but the effort was hampered by low internal consistency reliabilities for some dimensions. Third, research on these and similar selection instruments should include the measurement of marker variables. Marker variables are those about which a large body of research exists that provides a reasonable understanding of what is being measured. A pattern of correlations with the new or questionable measures can be used to further understanding of the new measures.

In addition to these studies, selection researchers should spend some time articulating more precisely what they mean by methods variables. In Chapter 5, we mentioned the hypothesized role that social desirability plays in the responses to various measures, in particular personality variables. We believe that additional research should be conducted to ascertain the nature of these methods biases. Such research should include specific measures of the hypothesized methods constructs (Schmitt, 1994), as well as evidence regarding the practical outcomes associated with the use of these measures in the selection context (see Douglas, McDaniel, & Snell, 1996; Hough, Eaton, Dunnette, Kamp, & McCloy, 1990). In addition to direct measurement of response bias, there should be additional research regarding work pioneered by Drasgow using appropriateness fit indices (e.g., Drasgow & Hulin, 1990). Appropriateness fit indices are derived from item response theory (see Chapter 5) and involve the identification of persons whose item responses are inconsistent with their total scores on some KSAO measure. Zickar and Drasgow (1996) report on a study in which these measures were used to detect respondents who were attempting to fake on personality instruments. The results indicated that the item response theory appropriateness fit measure classified a higher number of faking respondents at low rates of misclassification of honest respondents than did a social desirability scale. Schmitt, Chan, Sacco, and McFarland (in press) found that aberrant responses as indicated by appropriateness fit indices adversely affected the criterion-related validity of cognitive ability measures. However, these fit indices based on different tests were relatively uncorrelated, suggesting that the fit indices are specific to a particular measure or highly unreliable. More research is definitely needed to ascertain the meaning and practical utility of the item response theory fit indices.

Minority-Majority Differences
in Ability and Performance

We end our list of future research areas with minority-majority differences in ability and performance. Our position is that theory is no less important in the applied research on subgroup differences than in other research areas. In fact, many of the theoretical issues underlying other research areas are of critical importance in directing future programmatic research on subgroup differences.

Much of the research on subgroup differences is generated by the conflict between the goal of organizational productivity and the goal of equal subgroup representation (see Chapters 6 and 7). The focus in this research has been on attempts to develop valid predictors of performance that have low levels of adverse impact. If a theoretical approach to selection research contributes to the reduction of adverse impact in selection in a specific study, it should be replicable. Most often, research on subgroup differences has been piecemeal and atheoretical, with the result that the only replicable result is that subgroup differences on ability tests remain large. Specifically, we suggest the following three areas of programmatic research.

The first program of research is rooted in the effort to expand models of performance as described in various parts of this book. Traditionally, technical performance has dominated the performance criterion space in selection research, and this has resulted in the adherence to cognitive ability tests as the best predictor of performance. The use of cognitive ability tests in selection produces high levels of adverse impact (see Chapter 6). Instead of proceeding, in an atheoretical fashion, to search for alternate valid predictors that will exhibit low levels of adverse impact, the researcher should begin with a consideration of the organization's goals and the role the organization plays in the community at large when determining what performance criteria to predict. These considerations may result in a performance model in which there are multiple, nonredundant performance criteria. Many of these criteria, such as interpersonal performance dimensions, organizational citizenship behaviors, customer and client satisfaction, and withdrawal behaviors, are not highly related to cognitive ability. That is, a broad range of predictors would be required and the best predictors of these noncognitive criteria are likely to be those other than cognitive ability tests. Our position is that the search for alternate valid predictors with low levels of adverse impact should begin with an expanded model of performance, moving from multiple performance criteria to multiple predictor constructs to the development of measures to assess these predictor constructs. Some may argue that this recommendation represents a method of "gerrymandering" cognitive ability tests out of selection (e.g., see Gottfredson, 1997). On the contrary, *when alternate criteria are demonstrably relevant to an organization's continued viability and success,* the sole consideration of technical proficiency criteria amounts to "gerrymandering" the selection battery so as to produce high adverse impact.

A second area of research that may lead to means of reducing adverse impact originates from the literature on applicant reactions. Several researchers have noted that studies on subgroup differences tend to focus on the ability aspects and ignore the motivational aspects of test performance (e.g., Arvey et al., 1990; Chan et al., 1997, Helms, 1992). Chan et al. (1997) provide some evidence that face validity perceptions affect test-taking motivation, which in turn affects cognitive test performance. Chan et al. also note that the typical Black-White difference in test performance is partially mediated by differences in face validity perceptions and test-taking motivation. Chan et al.'s data are correlational in nature, and strong causal inferences are not possible. Future research should consider experimental designs for manipulating applicant reactions and for examining whether Black-White differences in test performance can be reduced through changes in test reactions and test-taking motivation. Examples of these manipulations include the use of face-valid test items, the use of testing methods that appear job relevant and fair, and variation of the types of selection information presented to applicants. Perhaps even a consideration of cultural differences in writing items and item foils may have an impact on the reactions to items and indirectly on test performance, though an initial attempt in this regard did not produce large effects (Whitney & Schmitt, 1997). The choice of manipulations should be closely guided by some adequate theory of subgroup difference in test-taking beliefs, experiences, and reactions. The recent work by Steele (1997) on the effects of subgroup stereotypic threat on intellectual identity and performance may provide some relevant theoretical bases for such investigations and offer some useful ideas for the design of experimental manipulations.

Another possible means of reducing adverse impact is through the development of new test formats. The multiple-choice paper-and-pencil format remains the most commonly used in the assessment of ability. There is some evidence that a portion of the observed subgroup difference in test scores may be attributable to the format (method) of testing, which is irrelevant to the test content or the constructs intended to be assessed by the test (Chan & Schmitt, 1997). In practice, it may be possible to reduce subgroup differences in performance by simply changing the test format while keeping the test content (and test constructs) constant. As discussed in Chapter 7, changing the test format may also reduce subgroup differences in test reactions. Note that changes in test format need not always involve a redesign of the method of testing. Relatively simple changes in format, including the format of the questions asked and the types of responses required, may be effective in reducing subgroup differences. For example, we found recently that changing the format of the test stimuli and questions asked (i.e., presentation of work-related scenarios and questions on the scenarios) from a paper-and-pencil presentation to a video presentation while keeping the response format (i.e., paper-and-pencil rating scales) unchanged was sufficient to reduce the Black-White standardized mean difference in test performance from .95 to .21 (Chan & Schmitt, 1997). Additional studies designed to examine the efficacy of changes in test format for reducing subgroup differences are certainly required. Future research should be grounded in some "theory of format" specifying clearly the dimensions (e.g., realism, reading requirements) on which different test formats vary and how and why these dimensions have differential effects on different subgroups.

Finally, closely related to changes in test format is the issue of new testing technologies. In recent years, there has been increased interest in the use of new testing technologies, including computer-adaptive testing and multimedia testing (McHenry & Schmitt, 1994). We are not aware of any study that has examined the effects of these new testing technologies on subgroup differences in test performance. These new technologies may produce either smaller or larger subgroup differences in performance compared with those observed in traditional paper-and-pencil testing. With the increased interest in these new testing technologies, research on their relationships to subgroup differences is clearly needed, and our comments on theory-driven approaches to studying the effects of test format apply similarly. Changes in testing formats and technologies, like changes in the criteria against which selection procedures are validated, should always be consistent with job requirements. In addition, selection researchers, users of tests, and policy makers must realize that subgroup differences in measured ability are likely real. Given continued differences in economic and educational opportunity, it might actually be surprising if those differences were not observed.

Concluding Remarks

Now that you have read this entire book, we encourage you to reexamine the four examples provided in Chapter 1. We hope that your understanding of these examples will be greatly enhanced and that your reexamination of them will lead you to think about issues that you did not consider when you first read these descriptions of selection research studies. We also hope that you will be motivated to pursue research that will provide answers to your questions.

In this book, we have presented a summary (sometimes brief) of the majority of the literature on selection. The study of individual differences spans the entire 20th century, and the use of measures of individual differences represents one of the earliest applications of psychological research. Moreover, the use of valid selection instruments can have great impact on organizations' success and can contribute to the adjustment of individuals who are placed in jobs suited to their interests and capabilities. We hope that we have communicated these facts plus some of the technical information necessary for you to engage in selection research. Our major goal, however, has been to impart the notion that the field of selection is not stagnant and that there are many exciting and important research issues that should be addressed. In this respect, the success of our effort should be measured by the degree to which we can stimulate that research and make this book obsolete.

References

Abod, E. T., Gilbert, J. A., & Fleishman, E. A. (1996, April). *A job analysis method to assess the interpersonal requirements of work*. Paper presented at the 11th Annual Conference of the Society for Industrial and Organizational Psychology, San Diego, CA.

Ackerman, P. L. (1989). Within task intercorrelations of skilled performance: Implications of predicting individual differences? *Journal of Applied Psychology, 74,* 360-364.

Adler, S. (1996). Personality and work behavior: Exploring the linkages. *Applied Psychology: An International Perspective, 45,* 207-224.

Age Discrimination in Employment Act of 1967, 29 U.S.C. Sec. 621.

Aiello, J. R., & Kolb, K. J. (1995). Electronic performance monitoring and social context: Impact on productivity and stress. *Journal of Applied Psychology, 80,* 339-353.

Aiello, J. R., & Shao, Y. (1993). Electronic performance monitoring and stress: The role of feedback and goal setting. In M. J. Smith & G. Salvendy (Eds.), *Human-computer interaction: Applications and case studies* (pp. 1011-1016). Amsterdam: Elsevier Science.

Albemarle Paper Company v. Moody, 422 U.S. 405 (1975).

Alderton, D. L., Goldman, S. R., & Pellegrino, J. W. (1985). Individual differences in process outcomes for analogy and classification solution. *Intelligence, 9,* 69-85.

American Educational Research Association, American Psychological Association, & National Council on Measurement in Education (AERA, APA, & NCME). (1998). *Standards for educational and psychological testing.* Washington, DC: American Psychological Association.

Americans with Disabilities Act of 1990, 42 U.S.C. Sec. 933.

Anderson, J. R. (1983). *The architecture of cognition.* Cambridge, MA: Harvard University Press.

Anderson, J. R. (1993). Problem-solving and learning. *American Psychologist, 48,* 35-44.

Andrew, J. D. W. (1967). The achievement motive and advancement in two types of organization. *Journal of Personality and Social Psychology, 6,* 163-168.

Arbuckle, J. L. (1995). *Amos user's guide.* Chicago: Smallwaters Corporation.

Arthur, W., Jr., & Bennett, W., Jr. (1995). The international assignee: The relative importance of factors perceived to contribute to success. *Personnel Psychology, 48,* 99-114.

Arvey, R. D., & Campion, M. E. (1982). The employment interview: A summary and review of recent research. *Personnel Psychology, 35,* 281-322.

Arvey, R. D., Davis, J. A., McGowen, S. L., & Dipboye, R. L. (1982). Potential sources of bias in job analytic processes. *Academy of Management Journal, 25,* 618-629.

Arvey, R. D., Passino, E. M., & Lounsbury, J. N. (1977). Job analysis results as influenced by sex of incumbent and sex of analyst. *Journal of Applied Psychology, 62,* 411-416.

Arvey, R. D., & Sackett, P. R. (1993). Fairness in selection: Current developments and perspectives. In N. Schmitt & W. C. Borman (Eds.), *Personnel selection in organizations* (pp. 171-202). San Francisco: Jossey-Bass.

Arvey, R. D., Strickland, W., Drauden, G., & Martin, C. (1990). Motivational components of test taking. *Personnel Psychology, 43,* 695-716.

Ashworth, S. D., & McHenry, J. J. (1993). *Developing a multimedia in-basket: Lessons learned.* Paper presented at the Eighth Annual Conference of the Society for Industrial and Organizational Psychology, San Francisco.

Atkinson, J. W. (1958). *Motives in fantasy, action, and society.* New York: Van Nostrand.

Atkinson, J. W. (1981). Studying personality in the context of an advanced motivational psychology. *American Psychologist, 36,* 117-128.

Austin, J. T., Humphreys, L. G., & Hulin, C. L. (1989). Another view of dynamic criteria: A critical reanalysis of Barrett, Caldwell, and Alexander. *Personnel Psychology, 42,* 597-612.

Avolio, B. J., & Barrett, G. V. (1987). Effects of age stereotyping in a simulated interview. *Psychology and Aging, 2,* 56-63.

Avolio, B. J., Waldman, D. A., & McDaniel, M. A. (1990). Age and work performance in nonmanagerial jobs: The effects of experience and occupational type. *Academy of Management Journal, 33,* 407-422.

Bachelor, P. A. (1989). Maximum likelihood confirmatory factor-analytic investigation of factors within Guilford's structure of intellect model. *Journal of Applied Psychology, 74,* 797-804.

Bandura, A. (1977). *Social learning theory.* Englewood Cliffs, NJ: Prentice Hall.

Baron, R. A. (1996). Interpersonal relations in organizations. In K. R. Murphy (Ed.), *Individual differences and behavior in organizations* (pp. 334-370). San Francisco: Jossey-Bass.

Barrett, G. V., Caldwell, M. S., & Alexander, R. A. (1985). The concept of dynamic criteria: A critical reanalysis. *Personnel Psychology, 38,* 41-56.

Barrick, M. R., & Mount, M. K. (1991). The Big-Five personality dimensions in job performance: A meta-analysis. *Personnel Psychology, 44,* 1-26.

Bartlett, C. J., Bobko, P., Mosier, S. B., & Hannon, R. (1978). Testing for fairness with a moderated multiple regression strategy: An alternative for differential analysis. *Personnel Psychology, 31,* 233-241.

Bass, A. R., & Ager, J. (1991). Correcting point-biserial turnover correlations for comparative analysis. *Journal of Applied Psychology, 76,* 595-598.

Baughman, W. A., & Mumford, M. D. (1996, April). *Job analysis and clustering.* Paper presented at the 11th Annual Conference of the Society for Industrial and Organizational Psychology, San Diego, CA.

Beauchamp, J. (1994, August 8). Making quality pay. *Business Week,* pp. 54-59.

Becker, B. E. (1989). The influence of labor markets on human resources utility estimates. *Personnel Psychology, 42,* 531-546.

Belbin, E., & Belbin, R. M. (1972). *Problems in adult retraining.* London: Heineman.

Belbin, E., & Downs, S. M. (1964). Activity learning and the older worker. *Ergonomics, 7,* 429-437.

Bentler, P. M. (1985). *Theory and implementation of EQS: A structural equations program.* Los Angeles: BMDP Statistical Software.

Bentler, P. M., & Bonett, D. G. (1980). Significance tests and goodness of fit in the analysis of covariance structures. *Psychological Bulletin, 88,* 588-606.

Berk, R. A. (1983). *Handbook of methods for detecting bias.* Baltimore: Johns Hopkins University Press.

Bernardin, H. J., & Beatty, R. W. (1984). *Performance appraisal: Assessing human behavior at work.* Boston: Kent.

Binet, A., & Simon, T. (1905). Methodes nouvelles pour le diagnostic du niveau intellectuel des anormaux. *Annee Psychologique, 11,* 191-244.

Binning, J. F., & Barrett, G. V. (1989). Validity of personnel decisions: A conceptual analysis of the inferential and evidential bases. *Journal of Applied Psychology, 74,* 478-494.

Bird, C. P., & Fisher, T. D. (1986). Thirty years later: Attitudes toward the employment of older workers. *Journal of Applied Psychology, 71,* 515-517.

Black, J. S., & Mendenhall, M. (1990). Cross-cultural training effectiveness: A review and a theoretical framework for future research. *Academy of Management Review, 15,* 113-136.

Black, J. S., Mendenhall, M., & Oddou, G. (1991). Toward a comprehensive model of international adjustment: An integration of multiple theoretical perspectives. *Academy of Management Review, 16,* 291-317.

Black, J. S., & Stephens, G. K. (1989). The influence of the spouse on American expatriate adjustment in overseas assignments. *Journal of Management, 15,* 529-544.

Bollen, K. A. (1989). *Structural equations with latent variables.* New York: John Wiley.

Bollen, K. A., & Long, J. S. (1993). *Testing structural equation models.* Newbury Park, CA: Sage.

Borman, W. C., & Brush, D. H. (1993). More progress toward a taxonomy of managerial performance requirements. *Human Performance, 6,* 1-21.

Borman, W. C., Hanson, M. A., & Hedge, J. W. (1997). Personnel selection. *Annual Review of Psychology, 48,* 299-337.

Borman, W. C., Hanson, M. A., Oppler, S. H., Pulakos, E. D., & White, L. A. (1993). Role of early supervisory experience in supervisor performance. *Journal of Applied Psychology, 78,* 443-449.

Borman, W. C., & Motowidlo, S. J. (1993). Expanding the criterion domain to include elements of contextual performance. In N. Schmitt & W. C. Borman (Eds.), *Personnel selection in organizations* (pp. 71-98). San Francisco: Jossey-Bass.

Borman, W. C., & Motowidlo, S. J. (Eds.). (1997a). Organizational citizenship behavior and contextual performance [Special issue]. *Human Performance, 10*(2).

Borman, W. C., & Motowidlo, S. J. (1997b). Task performance and contextual performance: The meaning for personnel selection research. *Human Performance, 10,* 99-110.

Borman, W. C., Motowidlo, S. J., Rose, S. R., & Hanser, L. M. (1985). *Development of a model of soldier effectiveness* (Institute Report 95). Minneapolis, MN: Personnel Decisions Research Institute.

Borman, W. C., White, L. A., Pulakos, E. D., & Oppler, S. H. (1991). Models of supervisory job performance ratings. *Journal of Applied Psychology, 76,* 863-872.

Boudreau, J. W. (1984). Decision theory contributions to HRM research and practice. *Industrial Relations, 23,* 198-217.

Boudreau, J. W. (1991). Utility analysis for decisions in human resource management. In M. D. Dunnette & L. M. Hough (Eds.), *Handbook of industrial and organizational psychology* (Vol. 2, pp. 621-746). Palo Alto, CA: Consulting Psychologists Press.

Boudreau, J. W., & Berger, C. J. (1985). Decision theoretic utility analysis applied to external employee movement. *Journal of Applied Psychology, 70,* 581-612.

Bray, D. W., Campbell, R. J., & Grant, D. L. (1974). *Formative years in business.* New York: John Wiley.

Bray, D. W., & Grant, D. L. (1966). The assessment center in the measurement of potential for business management. *Psychological Monographs, 80* (Entire issue, No. 625).

Breaugh, J. A. (1992). *Recruitment: Science and practice.* Boston: PWS-Kent.

Bretz, R. D., Ash, R. A., & Dreher, G. F. (1989). Do the people make the place? An examination of the attraction-selection-attrition hypothesis. *Personnel Psychology, 42,* 561-580.

Bridges, W. (1994, September 19). The end of the job. *Fortune, 130,* 62-74.

Brief, A. P., & Motowidlo, S. J. (1986). Prosocial organizational behaviors. *Academy of Management Review, 11,* 710-725.

Brockner, J., & Wiesenfeld, B. M. (1996). An integrative framework for explaining reactions to decisions: Interactive effects of outcomes and procedures. *Psychological Bulletin, 120,* 189-208.

Brody, E. B., & Brody, N. (1976). *Intelligence: Nature, determinants, and consequences.* New York: Academic Press.

Brogden, H. E. (1946). On the interpretation of the correlation coefficient as a measure of predictive efficiency. *Journal of Educational Psychology, 37,* 65-76.

Brogden, H. E. (1949). When testing pays off. *Personnel Psychology, 3,* 133-154.

Brown, C. W., & Ghiselli, E. E. (1953). Percent increase in proficiency resulting from use of selective devices. *Journal of Applied Psychology, 37,* 341-345.

Brown, S. H. (1981). Validity generalization and situational moderation in the life insurance industry. *Journal of Applied Psychology, 66,* 664-670.

Bryk, A. S., & Raudenbush, S. W. (1987). Application of hierarchical linear models to assessing change. *Psychological Bulletin, 101,* 147-158.

Bureau of National Affairs. (1990). ADA: Americans with Disabilities Act of 1990: Text and analysis. *Labor Relations Reporter, 134*(11), 5-3-5-47 (Suppl.).

Burke, M. J., & Pearlman, K. (1988). Recruiting, selecting, and matching people with jobs. In J. P. Campbell, R. J. Campbell, & Associates (Eds.), *Productivity in organizations* (pp. 97-142). San Francisco: Jossey-Bass.

Butler, J. E., Ferris, G. R., & Napier, N. K. (1991). *Strategy and human resources management.* Cincinnati, OH: South-Western.

Bycio, P., Alvares, K. M., & Hahn, J. (1987). Situational specificity in assessment center ratings: A confirmatory factor analysis. *Journal of Applied Psychology, 72,* 457-462.

Cable, D. M., & Judge, T. A. (1994). Pay preferences and job search decisions: A person-organization fit perspective. *Personnel Psychology, 47,* 317-348.

Callender, J. C., & Osburn, H. G. (1980). Development and test of a new model for validity generalization. *Journal of Applied Psychology, 65,* 543-558.

Cameron, K. S., & Whetton, D. A. (1983). *Organizational effectiveness: A comparison of multiple models.* New York: Academic Press.

Campbell, C. H., Ford, P., Rumsey, M. G., Pulakos, E. D., Borman, W. C., Felker, D. B., de Vera, M. V., & Riegelhaupt, B. J. (1990). Development of multiple job performance measures in a representative sample of jobs. *Personnel Psychology, 43,* 277-300.

Campbell, D. P., Hyne, S. A., & Nilsen, D. L. (1992). *Manual for the Campbell Interest and Skill Survey (CISS).* Minneapolis, MN: National Computer Systems.

Campbell, J. P. (1990). Modeling the performance prediction problem in industrial and organizational psychology. In M. D. Dunnette & L. M. Hough (Eds.), *Handbook of industrial and organizational psychology* (Vol. 1, pp. 687-732). Palo Alto, CA: Consulting Psychologists Press.

Campbell, J. P., Gasser, M. B., & Oswald, F. L. (1996). The substantive nature of job performance variability. In K. R. Murphy (Ed.), *Individual differences and behavior in organizations* (pp. 258-299). San Francisco: Jossey-Bass.

Campbell, J. P., McCloy, R. A., Oppler, S. H., & Sager, C. E. (1993). A theory of performance. In N. Schmitt & W. C. Borman (Eds.), *Personnel selection in organizations* (pp. 35-70). San Francisco: Jossey-Bass.

Campbell, J. P., McHenry, J. J., & Wise, L. L. (1990). Modeling job performance in a population of jobs. *Personnel Psychology, 43,* 313-333.

Campion, M. A. (1983). Personnel selection for physically demanding jobs: Review and recommendations. *Personnel Psychology, 36,* 527-550.

Campion, M. A., Campion, J. E., & Hudson, J. P., Jr. (1994). Structured interviewing: A note on incremental validity and alternative question types. *Journal of Applied Psychology, 79,* 998-1002.

Campion, M. A., Pursell, E. D., & Brown, B. K. (1988). Structured interviewing: Raising the psychometric properties of the employment interview. *Personnel Psychology, 41,* 25-42.

Cannon-Bowers, J. A., Tannenbaum, S. I., Salas, E., & Volpe, C. E. (1995). Defining competencies and establishing team training requirements. In R. A. Guzzo & E. Salas (Eds.), *Team effectiveness and decision making in organizations* (pp. 333-380). San Francisco: Jossey-Bass.

Carpenter, J. B., Giorgia, M. J., & McFarland, B. P. (1975). *Comparative analysis of the relative validity of subjective time rating scales* (Tech. Rep. No. AFHRL-TR-75-63). San Antonio, TX: Air Force Human Resources Laboratory.

Carpenter, P. A., Just, M. A., & Schell, P. (1990). What one intelligence test measures: A theoretical account of the processing in the Raven Progressive Matrices Test. *Psychological Review, 97,* 404-431.

Carroll, J. B. (1968). Review of *The nature of human intelligence* by J. P. Guilford. *American Educational Research Journal, 5,* 249-256.

Carroll, J. B. (1993). *Human cognitive abilities: A survey of factor-analytic studies.* Cambridge: Cambridge University Press.

Carsten, J. M., & Spector, P. E. (1987). Unemployment, job satisfaction and employee turnover: A meta-analytic test of the Muchinsky model. *Journal of Applied Psychology, 72,* 374-381.

Cascio, W. F. (1987a). *Applied psychology in personnel management* (3rd ed.). Englewood Cliffs, NJ: Prentice Hall.

Cascio, W. F. (1987b). *Costing human resources: The financial impact of behavior in organizations.* Boston: Kent.

Cascio, W. F., Goldstein, I. L., Outtz, J., & Zedeck, S. (1995). Twenty issues and answers about sliding bands. *Human Performance, 8,* 227-242.

Cascio, W. F., Outtz, J., Zedeck, S., & Goldstein, I. L. (1991). Statistical implications of six methods of test score use in personnel selection. *Human Performance, 4,* 233-264.

Cattell, R. B. (1966). The scree test for the number of factors. *Multivariate Behavioral Research, 1,* 245-276.

Cattell, R. B. (1971). *Abilities: Their structure, growth, and action.* Boston: Houghton Mifflin.

Cattell, R. B., Eber, H. W., & Tatsuoka, M. M. (1970). *Handbook for the Sixteen Personality Factor Questionnaire.* Champaign, IL: Institute for Personality and Ability Testing.

Cattin, P. (1980). Estimation of the predictive power of a regression model. *Journal of Applied Psychology, 65,* 407-414.

Chan, D. (1996a). Cognitive misfit of problem-solving style at work: A facet of person-organization fit. *Organizational Behavior and Human Decision Processes, 68,* 194-207.

Chan, D. (1996b). Criterion and construct validation of an assessment centre. *Journal of Occupational and Organizational Psychology, 69,* 167-181.

Chan, D. (1997a, August). *Individual difference and learning perspectives on the construct of adaptability: An integrative person-situation interaction approach.* Paper presented at the annual meeting of the Academy of Management, Boston.

Chan, D. (1997b). Racial subgroup differences in predictive validity perceptions on personality and cognitive ability tests. *Journal of Applied Psychology, 82,* 311-320.

Chan, D. (1998). Functional relations among constructs in the same content domain at different levels of analysis: A typology of composition models. *Journal of Applied Psychology, 83*, 234-247.

Chan, D., & Schmitt, N. (1997). Video-based versus paper-and-pencil method of assessment in situational judgment tests: Subgroup differences in test performance and face validity perceptions. *Journal of Applied Psychology, 82*, 143-159.

Chan, D., Schmitt, N., DeShon, R. P., Clause, C., & Delbridge, K. (1997). Reactions to cognitive ability tests: The relationships between race, test performance, face validity perceptions, and test-taking motivation. *Journal of Applied Psychology, 82*, 300-310.

Chan, D., Schmitt, N., Jennings, D., Clause, C., & Delbridge, K. (In press). Applicant perceptions of test fairness: Integrating justice and self-serving bias perspectives. *International Journal of Selection and Assessment.*

Chan, D., Schmitt, N., Jennings, D., & Sheppard, L. (in press). Developing measures of basic job-relevant English proficiency for the prediction of job performance and promotability. *Journal of Business and Psychology.*

Chan, D., Schmitt, N., Sacco, J. M., & DeShon, R. P. (1998). Understanding pretest and posttest reactions to cognitive ability and personality tests: Performance-reactions relationships and their structural invariance across racial groups. *Journal of Applied Psychology, 83*, 471-485.

Chatman, J. A. (1989). Improving interactional organizational research: A model of person-organization fit. *Academy of Management Review, 14*, 333-349.

Chi, M. T. H., Feltovich, P. J., & Glaser, R. (1981). Categorization and representation of physics problems by experts and novices. *Cognitive Science, 5*, 121-152.

Christensen, K. E. (1988). *Women and home-based work: The unspoken contract.* Troy, MO: Holt, Rinehart & Winston.

Church, A. T. (1982). Sojourner adjustment. *Psychological Bulletin, 9*, 540-572.

Civil Rights Act of 1964, 42 U.S.C. Stat. 253 (1964).

Civil Rights Act of 1991, Pub. L. No. 102-166, 105 Stat. 1075 (1991).

Cleary, T. A. (1968). Test bias: Prediction of grades of Negro and white students in integrated colleges. *Journal of Educational Measurement, 5*, 115-124.

Clegg, C. (1983). Psychology of employee lateness, absence, and turnover: A methodological critique and an empirical study. *Journal of Applied Psychology, 68*, 88-101.

Cleveland, J. N., & Landy, F. J. (1983). The effect of person and job stereotypes on two personnel decisions. *Journal of Applied Psychology, 68*, 609-619.

Cleveland, J. N., Murphy, K. R., & Williams, R. E. (1989). Multiple uses of performance appraisal: Prevalence and correlates. *Journal of Applied Psychology, 74*, 130-135.

Cohen, J., & Cohen, P. (1983). *Applied multiple regression/correlation analysis for the behavioral sciences.* Hillsdale, NJ: Lawrence Erlbaum.

Cohen, P. (1991). A source of bias in longitudinal investigations of change. In L. M. Collins & J. L. Horn (Eds.), *Best methods for the analysis of change: Recent advances, unanswered questions, future directions* (pp. 18-25). Washington, DC: American Psychological Association.

Collins, L. M., & Graham, J. W. (1991). Comments on "A source of bias in longitudinal investigations of change." In L. M. Collins & J. L. Horn (Eds.), *Best methods for the analysis of change: Recent advances, unanswered questions, future directions* (pp. 26-30). Washington, DC: American Psychological Association.

Connecticut v. Teal, 457 U.S. 440 (1982).

Cook, T. D., & Campbell, D. T. (1976). *Quasi-experimentation.* Boston: Houghton Mifflin.

Copeland, L., & Griggs, L. (1985). *Going international.* New York: Random House.

Cornelius, E. T., III. (1983). The use of projective techniques in personnel selection. In K. R. Rowland & G. R. Ferris (Eds.), *Research in personnel and human resources management* (pp. 127-168). Greenwich, CT: JAI.

Costa, P. T., Jr., & McCrae, R. R. (1989). *The NEO PI/FFI manual supplement.* Odessa, FL: Psychological Assessment Resources.

Costa, P. T., Jr., & McCrae, R. R. (1992a). Four ways five factors are basic. *Personality and Individual Differences, 13,* 653-665.

Costa, P. T., Jr., & McCrae, R. R. (1992b). *Revised NEO Personality Inventory (NEO PI R) and NEO Five Factor Inventory (FFI) professional manual.* Odessa, FL: Psychological Assessment Resources.

Costa, P. T., Jr., & McCrae, R. R. (1995). Solid grounds in the wetland of personality: A reply to Block. *Psychological Bulletin, 117,* 216-220.

Costanza, D. P., & Threlfall, K. V. (1996, April). *Development of a research-based performance assessment instrument.* Paper presented at the 11th Annual Conference of the Society for Industrial and Organizational Psychology, San Diego, CA.

Coward, W. M., & Sackett, P. R. (1990). Linearity of ability-performance relationships: A reconfirmation. *Journal of Applied Psychology, 75,* 297-300.

Cragun, J. R., & McCormick, E. J. (1967). *Job inventory information: Task reliabilities and scale interrelationships* (PRL-TR-67-15, NTIS No. AD-681-509). Lackland AFB, TX: Personnel Research Laboratory.

Cronbach, L. J. (1957). The two disciplines of psychology. *American Psychologist, 12,* 671-684.

Cronbach, L. J. (1990). *Essentials of psychological testing.* New York: HarperCollins.

Cronbach, L. J., & Gleser, G. C. (1965). *Psychological tests and personnel decisions* (2nd ed.). Urbana: University of Illinois Press.

Cronbach, L. J., Gleser, G. C., & Rajaratnam, N. (1972). *The dependability of behavioral measurements.* New York: John Wiley.

Cronbach, L. J., & Snow, R. E. (1977). *Aptitudes and instructional methods.* New York: Irvington.

Cronbach, L. J., Yalow, E., & Schaeffer, G. A. (1980). A mathematical structure for analyzing fairness in selection. *Personnel Psychology, 33,* 693-704.

Dawis, R. V. (1991). Vocational interests, values, and preferences. In M. D. Dunnette & L. M. Hough (Eds.), *Handbook of industrial organizational psychology* (Vol. 2, pp. 833-872). Palo Alto, CA: Consulting Psychologists Press.

Digman, J. M. (1990). Personality structure: Emergence of the five factor model. *Annual Review of Psychology, 41,* 417-440.

Dipboye, R. L., & Gaugler, B. B. (1993). Cognitive and behavioral processes in the selection interview. In N. Schmitt & W. C. Borman (Eds.), *Personnel selection in organizations* (pp. 135-170). San Francisco: Jossey-Bass.

Dipboye, R. L., Gaugler, B. B., & Hayes, T. (1990). *Individual differences among interviewers in the incremental validity of their judgments.* Paper presented at the Fifth Annual Conference of the Society for Industrial and Organizational Psychology, Miami, FL.

Dodd, W. E. (1977). Attitudes toward assessment center programs. In J. L. Moses & W. C. Byham (Eds.), *Applying the assessment center method* (pp. 161-183). New York: Pergamon.

Dorans, N. J., & Holland, P. W. (1993). DIF detection and description: Mantel-Haenszel and standardization. In P. W. Holland & H. Wainer (Eds.), *Differential item functioning* (pp. 35-66). Hillsdale, NJ: Lawrence Erlbaum.

Dougherty, T. W., Ebert, R. J., & Callender, J. C. (1986). Policy capturing in the employment interview. *Journal of Applied Psychology, 71,* 9-15.

Douglas, E. F., McDaniel, M. A., & Snell, A. F. (1996, August). *The validity of non-cognitive measures decays when applicants fake.* Paper presented at the annual meeting of the Academy of Management, Cincinnati, OH.

Drasgow, F., & Hulin, C. L. (1990). Item response theory. In M. D. Dunnette & L. M. Hough (Eds.), *Handbook of industrial and organizational psychology* (Vol. 1, pp. 577-636). Palo Alto, CA: Consulting Psychologists Press.

Drasgow, F., Olson, J. B., Keenan, P. A., Moberg, P., & Mead, A. D. (1993). Computerized assessment. *Personnel and Human Resources Management, 11,* 163-206.

Dreher, G. F., & Sackett, P. R. (1983). *Perspectives on employee staffing and selection: Readings and commentary.* Homewood, IL: Irwin.

Duncan, S. C., & Duncan, T. E. (1996). A multivariate latent growth curve analysis of adolescent substance use. *Structural Equation Modeling, 3,* 323-347.

Dunnette, M. D. (1966). *Personnel selection and placement.* Belmont, CA: Wadsworth.

Dunnette, M. D. (1976). Aptitudes, abilities, and skills. In M. D. Dunnette (Ed.), *Handbook of industrial and organizational psychology* (pp. 473-520). Chicago: Rand McNally.

Dunnette, M. D., & Borman, W. C. (1979). Personnel selection and classification systems. *Annual Review of Psychology, 30,* 477-525.

Dyer, L. (1983). Bringing human resources into the strategy formulation process. *Human Resource Management, 22,* 257-271.

Dyer, L. (1984). Linking human resource and business strategy. *Human Resource Planning, 7,* 79-84.

Dyer, P. J., Desmarais, L. B., & Midkiff, K. R. (1993). *Multimedia employment testing in IBM: Preliminary results from employees.* Paper presented at the Eighth Annual Conference of the Society for Industrial and Organizational Psychology, San Francisco.

Eberhardt, B. J., & Muchinsky, P. M. (1982). An empirical investigation of the factor stability of Owens' Biographical Questionnaire. *Journal of Applied Psychology, 67,* 138-145.

Edwards, J. R., & Harrison, R. V. (1993). Job demands and worker health: Three dimensional reexamination of the relationship between person-environment fit and strain. *Journal of Applied Psychology, 78,* 628-648.

Elias, P. K., Elias, M. F., Robbins, M. A., & Gage, P. (1987). Acquisition of word processing skills by younger, middle-aged, and older adults. *Psychology and Aging, 2,* 340-348.

Ely, R. J. (1994). The effects of organizational demographics and social identity on relationships among professional women. *Administrative Science Quarterly, 39,* 203-238.

Ely, R. J. (1995). The power in demography: Women's social constructions of gender identity at work. *Academy of Management Journal, 38,* 589-634.

England, G. W. (1971). *Development and use of weighted application blanks.* Minneapolis: University of Minnesota, Industrial Relations Center.

Equal Employment Opportunity Commission, Civil Service Commission, Department of Labor, and Department of Justice (EEOC, CSC, DOL, & DOJ). (1978). Uniform guidelines on employee selection procedures. *Federal Register, 43*(166), 38290-38315.

Erdberg, P., & Exner, J. E., Jr. (1984). Rorschach assessment. In G. Goldstein & M. Hersen (Eds.), *Handbook of psychological assessment* (pp. 332-347). New York: Pergamon.

Feldman, D. C. (1997). Socialization in an international context. *International Journal of Selection and Assessment, 5,* 1-8.

Feldman, J. M. (1981). Beyond attribution theory: Cognitive processes in performance appraisal. *Journal of Applied Psychology, 6,* 127-148.

Ferris, G. R., Fedor, D. B., Rowland, K. R., & Porac, J. F. (1985). Social influence and sex effects on task performance and task perceptions. *Organizational Behavior and Human Performance, 36,* 66-78.

Fierman, J. (1995, December 11). Americans can't get no satisfaction. *Fortune, 132,* 186-191.

Fine, S. A., & Getkate, M. (1995). *Benchmark tasks for job analysis.* Mahwah, NJ: Lawrence Erlbaum.

Fine, S. A., & Wiley, W. W. (1974). An introduction to functional job analysis. In E. A. Fleishman & A. R. Bass (Eds.), *Studies in personnel and industrial psychology* (pp. 6-13). Homewood, IL: Irwin.

Fleishman, E. A. (1964). *Structure and measurement of physical fitness.* Englewood Cliffs: NJ: Prentice Hall.

Fleishman, E. A. (1988). Some new frontiers in personnel selection research. *Personnel Psychology, 41,* 679-702.

Fleishman, E. A., & Hempel, W. E., Jr. (1955). The relationship between abilities and improvement with practice in a visual discrimination task. *Journal of Experimental Psychology, 49,* 301-312.

Fleishman, E. A., & Quaintance, M. K. (1984). *Taxonomies of human performance.* New York: Academic Press.

Fleishman, E. A., & Reilly, M. E. (1992a). *Administrator's guide: Fleishman job analysis survey.* Palo Alto, CA: Consulting Psychologists Press.

Fleishman, E. A., & Reilly, M. E. (1992b). *Handbook of human abilities.* Palo Alto, CA: Consulting Psychologists Press.

Folger, R., & Greenberg, J. (1985). Procedural justice: An interpretive analysis of personnel systems. In K. R. Rowland & G. R. Ferris (Eds.), *Research in personnel and human resources management* (Vol. 3, pp. 141-183). Greenwich, CT: JAI.

Folger, R., & Konovsky, M. A. (1989). Effects of procedural and distributive justice on reactions to pay raise decisions. *Academy of Management Journal, 32,* 115-130.

Ford, J. K., & Kraiger, K. (1995). The application of cognitive constructs and principles to the instructional systems model of training: Implications for needs assessment, design, and transfer. In C. L. Cooper & I. T. Robertson (Eds.), *International review of industrial and organizational psychology* (Vol. 10, pp. 1-48). New York: John Wiley.

Ford, J. K., Kraiger, K., & Schechtman, S. L. (1986). A study of race effects in objective indices and subjective evaluations of performance: A meta-analysis of performance criteria. *Psychological Bulletin, 99,* 330-337.

Ford, J. K., Quiñones, M. A., Sego, D. J., & Sorra, J. (1992). Factors affecting the opportunity to perform trained tasks on the job. *Personnel Psychology, 45,* 511-527.

Ford, J. K., Sego, D. J., Quiñones, M. A., & Sorra, J. (1991). *The construct of experience: A review of the literature and needed research directions.* Paper presented at the Sixth Annual Conference of the Society for Industrial and Organizational Psychology, St. Louis, MO.

Fossum, J. A., Arvey, R. D., Paradise, C. A., & Robbins, N. E. (1986). Modeling the skills obsolescence process: A psychological/economic integration. *Academy of Management Review, 11,* 362-374.

Fuchs, A. H. (1962). The progression-regression hypotheses in perceptual-motor skill learning. *Journal of Experimental Psychology, 63,* 177-182.

Fullerton, H. N., Jr. (1993). Another look at the labor force. *Monthly Labor Review, 116*(11), 31-40.

Gaudet, F. J. (1963). *Solving the problems of employee absence.* New York: American Management Association.

Gaugler, B. B., Rosenthal, D. B., Thornton, G. C., III, & Bentson, C. (1987). Meta-analyses of assessment center validity. *Journal of Applied Psychology, 72,* 493-511.

Gellatly, I. R., Paunomen, S. V., Meyer, J. P., Jackson, D. N., & Goffin, R. D. (1991). Personality, vocational interests, and cognitive predictors of managerial job performance and satisfaction. *Personality and Individual Differences, 12,* 221-331.

George, J. M., & Bettenhausen, K. (1990). Understanding prosocial behavior, sales performance, and turnover: A group-level analysis in a service context. *Journal of Applied Psychology, 75,* 698-709.

George, J. M., & Brief, A. P. (1992). Feeling good-doing good: A conceptual analysis of the mood at work-organizational spontaneity relationship. *Psychological Bulletin, 112,* 310-329.

Gerhart, B. (1992). Employee compensation: Research and practice. In M. D. Dunnette & L. M. Hough (Eds.), *Handbook of industrial and organizational psychology* (Vol. 3, pp. 481-570). Palo Alto, CA: Consulting Psychologists Press.

Gerhart, B., Minkoff, H. B., & Olsen, R. N. (1995). Employee compensation: Theory, practice, and evidence. In G. R. Ferris, S. D. Rosen, & D. T. Barnum (Eds.), *Handbook of human resource management* (pp. 528-547). Cambridge, MA: Blackwell.

Geyer, P. D., Hice, J., Hawk, J., Boese, R., & Brannon, Y. (1989). Reliabilities of ratings available from the *Dictionary of Occupational Titles*. *Personnel Psychology, 42*, 547-560.

Ghiselli, E. E. (1966). *The validity of occupational aptitude tests*. New York: John Wiley.

Ghiselli, E. E. (1973). The validity of aptitude tests in personnel selection. *Personnel Psychology, 26*, 461-478.

Gilliland, S. W. (1993). The perceived fairness of selection systems: An organizational justice perspective. *Academy of Management Review, 18*, 694-734.

Gilliland, S. W. (1994). Effects of procedural and distributive justice on reactions to a selection system. *Journal of Applied Psychology, 79*, 691-701.

Gist, M., Schwoerer, C., & Rosen, B. (1988). The influence of training methods and trainee age on the acquisition of computer skills. *Personnel Psychology, 41*, 255-266.

Glaser, R., Lesgold, A., & Gott, S. (1991). Implications of cognitive psychology for measuring job performance. In A. K. Wigdor & B. F. Green, Jr. (Eds.), *Performance assessment for the workplace* (Vol. 2, pp. 1-26). Washington, DC: National Academy Press.

Goldberg, L. R. (1990). An alternative "description of personality": The Big Five factor structure. *Journal of Personality and Social Psychology, 59*, 1216-1229.

Goldberg, L. R. (1993). The structure of phenotypic personality traits. *American Psychologist, 48*, 26-34.

Goldberg, L. R., & Saucier, G. (1995). So what do you propose we use instead? A reply to Block. *Psychological Bulletin, 117*, 221-225.

Golden, K. A., & Ramanujam, V. (1985). Between a dream and a nightmare: On the integration of the human resource management and strategic business planning processes. *Human Resource Management, 24*, 429-452.

Goldsmith, T. E., & Kraiger, K. (1997). Structural knowledge assessment and training evaluation. In J. K. Ford & Associates (Eds.), *Improving training effectiveness in work organizations* (pp. 73-96). Mahwah, NJ: Lawrence Erlbaum.

Goldstein, I. L. (1991). Training in work organizations. In M. D. Dunnette & L. M. Hough (Eds.), *Handbook of industrial and organizational psychology* (Vol. 2, pp. 507-620). Palo Alto, CA: Consulting Psychologists Press.

Goldstein, I. L., Zedeck, S., & Schneider, B. (1993). An exploration of the job analysis-content validity process. In N. Schmitt & W. C. Borman (Eds.), *Personnel selection in organizations* (pp. 3-32). San Francisco: Jossey-Bass.

Golembiewski, R. T., Billingsley, K., & Yeager, S. (1976). Measuring change and persistence in human affairs: Types of change generated by OD designs. *Journal of Applied Behavioral Science, 12*, 133-157.

Gollob, H. F., & Reichardt, C. S. (1991). Interpreting and estimating indirect effects assuming time lags really matter. In L. M. Collins & J. L. Horn (Eds.), *Best methods for the analysis of change: Recent advances, unanswered questions, future directions* (pp. 243-259). Washington, DC: American Psychological Association.

Gordon, M. E., & Johnson, W. A. (1982). Seniority: A review of its legal and scientific standing. *Personnel Psychology, 35*, 225-280.

Gordon, M. E., & Miller, S. J. (1984). Grievances: A review of research and practice. *Personnel Psychology, 37*, 117-146.

Gottfredson, L. S. (1996a, December 10). New police test will be a disaster. *Wall Street Journal*, p. A23.

Gottfredson, L. S. (1996b, October 24). Racially gerrymandered police tests. *Wall Street Journal*, p. A18.

Gottfredson, L. S. (1997). *The flight from g in employment testing* [On-line]. Available: www. ipmaac.org/nassau

Gough, H. G. (1987). *California Psychological Inventory administrator's guide*. Palo Alto, CA: Consulting Psychologists Press.

Graham, J. W. (1986, August). *Organizational citizenship informed by political theory*. Paper presented at the annual meeting of the Academy of Management, Chicago.

Green, B. F., Jr., & Wigdor, A. K. (1991). Measuring job competency. In A. K. Wigdor & B. F. Green, Jr. (Eds.), *Performance assessment for the workplace* (Vol. 2, pp. 53-74). Washington, DC: National Research Council.

Green, S. B., & Stutzman, T. (1986). An evaluation of methods to select respondents to structured job-analysis questionnaires. *Personnel Psychology, 39*, 543-564.

Greenberg, J. (1987). Reactions to procedural injustice in payment distributions: Do the means justify the ends? *Journal of Applied Psychology, 72*, 55-61.

Greenberg, J. (1990). Organizational justice: Yesterday, today, and tomorrow. *Journal of Management, 16*, 399-432.

Griggs v. Duke Power Co., 401 U.S. 424 (1971).

Guilford, J. P. (1964). Zero intercorrelations among tests of intellectual abilities. *Psychological Bulletin, 61*, 401-404.

Guilford, J. P. (1967). *The nature of human intelligence*. New York: McGraw-Hill.

Guion, R. M. (1988). *Assessment, measurement and prediction for personnel decisions*. Hillsdale, NJ: Lawrence Erlbaum.

Guion, R. M., & Gottier, R. F. (1965). Validity of personality measures in personnel selection. *Personnel Psychology, 18*, 49-65.

Gul, F. A. (1986). Differences between adaptors and innovators attending accountancy courses on their preferences in work and curricula. *Journal of Accounting Education, 4*, 203-209.

Guzzo, R. A., Noonan, K. A., & Elron, E. (1994). Expatriate managers and the psychological contract. *Journal of Applied Psychology, 79*, 617-626.

Guzzo, R. A., Yost, P. R., Campbell, R. J., & Shea, G. P. (1993). Potency in groups: Articulating a construct. *British Journal of Social Psychology, 32*, 87-106.

Hackett, R. D., & Guion, R. M. (1985). A reevaluation of the absenteeism-job satisfaction relationship. *Organizational Behavior and Human Decision Processes, 35*, 340-381.

Hackman, J. R. (1987). The design of work teams. In J. W. Lorsch (Ed.), *Handbook of organizational behavior* (pp. 315-342). Englewood Cliffs, NJ: Prentice Hall.

Hall, D. T. (1990). Telecommuting and the management of work-home boundaries. In *Paradigms revised: Annual review of communications and society* (pp. 177-208). Nashville, TN: Institute for Information Studies, Northern Telecom.

Hambleton, R. K., Swaminathan, H., & Rogers, H. J. (1991). *Fundamentals of item response theory*. Newbury Park, CA: Sage.

Hanges, P. J., Schneider, B., & Niles, K. (1990). Stability of performance: An interactionist perspective. *Journal of Applied Psychology, 75*, 658-667.

Hanisch, K. A., & Hulin, C. L. (1994). Two-stage sequential selection procedures using ability and training performance: Incremental validity of behavioral consistency measures. *Personnel Psychology, 47*, 767-785.

Hansen, J. C., & Campbell, D. P. (1985). *Manual for the SVIB-SCII*. Stanford, CA: Stanford University Press.

Harmon, L. W., Hansen, J. C., Borgen, F. H., & Hammer, A. L. (1994). *Strong Interest Inventory: Applications and technical guide*. Palo Alto, CA: Consulting Psychologists Press.

Harnqvist, K., Gustafsson, J. E., Muthen, B. O., & Nelson, G. (1994). Hierarchical models of ability at individual and class levels. *Intelligence, 18*, 165-187.

Harris, M. M., & Fink, L. S. (1987). A field study of applicant reactions to employment opportunities: Does the recruiter make a difference? *Personnel Psychology, 40,* 765-784.

Harris, M. M., & Schaubroeck, J. (1988). A meta-analysis of self-supervisor, self-peer, and peer-supervisor ratings. *Personnel Psychology, 41,* 43-62.

Harrison, D. A., & Hulin, C. L. (1989). Investigations of absenteeism: Using event history models to study the absence-taking process. *Journal of Applied Psychology, 74,* 300-316.

Hartigan, J. A., & Wigdor, A. K. (1989). *Fairness in employment testing.* Washington, DC: National Academy Press.

Hartley, A. A., Hartley, J. T., & Johnson, S. A. (1984). The older adult as computer user. In P. K. Robinson, J. Livingston, & J. E. Birren (Eds.), *Aging and technological advances* (pp. 347-348). New York: Plenum.

Harvey, R. J. (1990). Incumbent versus supervisor perceptions of job tasks. In K. Kraiger (Chair), *Cognitive representations of work.* Symposium conducted at the Fifth Annual Conference of the Society for Industrial and Organizational Psychology, Miami, FL.

Harvey, R. J. (1991). Job analysis. In M. D. Dunnette & L. M. Hough (Eds.), *Handbook of industrial and organizational psychology* (Vol. 2, pp. 71-164). Palo Alto, CA: Consulting Psychologists Press.

Harvey, R. J., & Lozada-Larsen, S. R. (1988). Influence of amount of job descriptive information on job analysis rating accuracy. *Journal of Applied Psychology, 73,* 457-461.

Hathaway, S. R., & McKinley, J. C. (1943). *The Minnesota Multiphasic Personality Inventory.* Minneapolis: University of Minnesota Press.

Hattrup, K., & Schmitt, N. (1990). Prediction of trades apprentices' performance on job sample criteria. *Personnel Psychology, 43,* 453-464.

Haucke, M. H. P., & Stone, L. A. (1996, April). *Historical review of a personnel research testing branch, restructuring of the Career Qualifications Battery, preliminary findings of the CQB validation project.* Paper presented at the 11th Annual Conference of the Society for Industrial and Organizational Psychology, San Diego, CA.

Hauenstein, N. M. A., & Alexander, R. A. (1991). Rating ability in performance judgments: The joint influence of implicit theories and intelligence. *Organizational Behavior and Human Decision Processes, 50,* 300-323.

Hayduk, L. A. (1996). *LISREL: Issues, debates and strategies.* Baltimore: Johns Hopkins University Press.

Hayward, C., & Everett, C. (1983). Adaptors and innovators: Data from the Kirton Adaption-Innovation Inventory in a local authority setting. *Journal of Occupational Psychology, 56,* 339-342.

Hazel, J. T., Madden, J. M., & Christal, R. E. (1964). Agreement between worker-supervisor descriptions of the worker's job. *Journal of Industrial Psychology, 2,* 71-79.

Heilman, M. E., & Martell, R. F. (1986). Exposure to successful women: Antidote to sex discrimination in applicant screening decisions. *Organizational Behavior and Human Decision Processes, 37,* 376-390.

Heilman, M. E., Martell, R. F., & Simon, R. (1988). The vagaries of sex bias: Conditions regulating the underevaluation, equivaluation, and overevaluation of female job applicants. *Organizational Behavior and Human Decision Processes, 41,* 98-110.

Heilman, M. E., & Saruwatari, L. R. (1979). When beauty is beastly: The effects of appearance and sex on evaluations of job applicants for managerial and nonmanagerial jobs. *Organizational Behavior and Human Decision Processes, 23,* 360-372.

Heilman, M. E., & Stopeck, M. H. (1985a). Attractiveness and corporate success: Different causal attributions for males and females. *Journal of Applied Psychology, 70,* 379-388.

Heilman, M. E., & Stopeck, M. H. (1985b). Being attractive, advantage or disadvantage? Performance based evaluations and recommended personnel actions as a function of appearance, sex, and job type. *Organizational Behavior and Human Decision Processes, 35,* 202-215.

Helms, J. E. (1992). Why is there no study of cultural equivalence in standardized cognitive ability testing? *American Psychologist, 47,* 1083-1101.

Heneman, H. G., III, Huett, D. L., Lavigna, R. J., & Ogsten, D. (1995). Assessing manager's satisfaction with staffing services. *Personnel Psychology, 48,* 163-172.

Henry, E. R. (1966). *Research conference on the use of autobiographical data as psychological predictors.* Greensboro, NC: Creativity Research Institute, Richardson Foundation.

Henry, R. A., & Hulin, C. L. (1987). Stability of skilled performance across time: Some generalizations and limitations on utilities. *Journal of Applied Psychology, 72,* 457-462.

Henry, R. A., & Hulin, C. L. (1989). Changing validities: Ability-performance relations and utilities. *Journal of Applied Psychology, 74,* 365-367.

Hirsh, H. R., Northrop, L. C., & Schmidt, F. L. (1986). Validity generalization results for law enforcement occupations. *Personnel Psychology, 39,* 399-420.

Hitt, E. R., & Barr, S. H. (1989). Managerial selection decision models: Examination of configural cue processing. *Journal of Applied Psychology, 74,* 53-61.

Hitt, M. A. (1988). The measuring of organizational effectiveness: Multiple domains and constituencies. *Management International Review, 28,* 28-40.

Hofmann, D. A., Jacobs, R., & Gerras, S. J. (1992). Mapping individual performance over time. *Journal of Applied Psychology, 77,* 185-195.

Hogan, J. C. (1991). Physical abilities. In M. D. Dunnette & L. M. Hough (Eds.), *Handbook of industrial and organizational psychology* (Vol. 2, pp. 753-831). Palo Alto, CA: Consulting Psychologists Press.

Hogan, J. C., & Hogan, R. (1986). *Manual for the Hogan Personnel Selection System.* Minneapolis, MN: National Computer Systems.

Hogan, J. C., Hogan, R., & Busch, C. M. (1984). How to measure service orientation. *Journal of Applied Psychology, 69,* 167-173.

Hogan, J. C., & Roberts, B. W. (1996). Issues and non-issues in the fidelity/bandwidth tradeoff. *Journal of Organizational Behavior, 17,* 627-638.

Hogan, R., & Blake, R. J. (1996). Vocational interests: Matching self-concept with the work environment. In K. R. Murphy (Ed.), *Individual differences and behavior in organizations* (pp. 89-144). San Francisco: Jossey-Bass.

Hogan, R., & Hogan, J. C. (1995). *Hogan Personality Inventory manual* (2nd ed.). Tulsa, OK: Hogan Assessment System.

Holland, J. L. (1976). Vocational preferences. In M. D. Dunnette (Ed.), *Handbook of industrial and organizational psychology* (pp. 521-570). Chicago: Rand McNally.

Holland, J. L. (1985). *Making vocational choices: A theory of careers* (2nd ed.). Englewood Cliffs, NJ: Prentice Hall.

Holland, P. A. (1987). Adaptors and innovators: Application of the Kirton Adaption-Innovation Inventory to bank employees. *Psychological Reports, 60,* 263-270.

Holland, P. W., & Wainer, H. (1993). *Differential item functioning.* Hillsdale, NJ: Lawrence Erlbaum.

Hollenbeck, J. R., Ilgen, D. R., Phillips, J. M., & Hedlund, J. (1994). Decision risk in dynamic two-stage contexts: Beyond the status quo. *Journal of Applied Psychology, 79,* 592-598.

Holyoak, K. J. (1991). Symbolic connectionism: Toward third-generation theories of expertise. In K. A. Ericsson & J. Smith (Eds.), *Toward a general theory of expertise* (pp. 301-336). Cambridge, UK: Cambridge University Press.

Horn, J. L. (1988). Thinking about human abilities. In J. Nesselroade & R. B. Cattell (Eds.), *Handbook of multivariate experimental psychology* (2nd ed., pp. 645-685). New York: Plenum.

Horn, J. L., & Knapp, J. R. (1973). On the subjective character of the empirical base of Guilford's structure-of-intellect model. *Psychological Bulletin, 80,* 33-43.

Horn, J. L., & Knapp, J. R. (1974). Thirty wrongs do not make a right: Reply to Guilford. *Psychological Bulletin, 81,* 502-504.

Hough, L. M. (1984). Development and evaluation of the "accomplishment record" method of selecting and promoting professionals. *Journal of Applied Psychology, 69,* 135-146.

Hough, L. M. (1992). The "Big Five" personality variables-construct confusion: Description versus prediction. *Human Performance, 5,* 139-155.

Hough, L. M. (1994). *Personality at work.* Paper presented at the Bowling Green Conference on Alternative Selection Procedures, Bowling Green, OH.

Hough, L. M. (1995). Applicant self-description: Evaluating strategies for reducing distortion. In F. L. Schmidt (Chair), *Response distortion and social desirability in personality testing for personnel selection.* Symposium conducted at the 10th Annual Conference of the Society for Industrial and Organizational Psychology, Orlando, FL.

Hough, L. M., Barge, B. N., Houston, J. S., McGue, M. K., & Kamp, J. D. (1985, August). *Problems, issues, and results in the development of temperament, biographical, and interest measures.* Paper presented at the annual meeting of the American Psychological Association, Los Angeles.

Hough, L. M., Eaton, N. K., Dunnette, M. D., Kamp, J. D., & McCloy, R. A. (1990). Criterion-related validities of personality constructs and the effect of response distortion on those validities. *Journal of Applied Psychology, 75,* 581-595.

Hough, L. M., & Schneider, R. J. (1996). Personality traits, taxonomies, and applications in organizations. In K. R. Murphy (Ed.), *Individual differences and behavior in organizations* (pp. 31-88). San Francisco: Jossey-Bass.

Howard, A. (Ed.). (1995). *The changing nature of work.* San Francisco, CA: Jossey-Bass.

House, R., Rousseau, D. M., & Thomas-Hunt, M. (1995). The meso paradigm: A framework for the integration of micro and macro organizational behavior. *Research in Organizational Behavior, 17,* 71-114.

Hulin, C. L. (1991). Adaptation, persistence, and commitment in organizations. In M. D. Dunnette & L. M. Hough (Eds.), *Handbook of industrial and organizational psychology* (Vol. 2, pp. 445-506). Palo Alto, CA: Consulting Psychologists Press.

Hulin, C. L., Roznowski, M., & Hachiya, D. (1985). Alternative opportunities and withdrawal decisions: Empirical and theoretical discrepancies and an integration. *Psychological Bulletin, 97,* 233-250.

Hunter, J. E. (1983). A causal analysis of cognitive ability, job knowledge, job performance, and supervisory ratings. In F. Landy, S. Zedeck, & J. Cleveland (Eds.), *Performance measurement and theory* (pp. 257-266). Hillsdale, NJ: Lawrence Erlbaum.

Hunter, J. E., & Hunter, R. F. (1984). Validity and utility of alternative predictors of job performance. *Psychological Bulletin, 96,* 72-88.

Hunter, J. E., & Schmidt, F. L. (1990a). Dichotomization of continuous variables: The implications for meta-analysis. *Journal of Applied Psychology, 75,* 334-349.

Hunter, J. E., & Schmidt, F. L. (1990b). *Methods of meta-analysis.* Newbury Park, CA: Sage.

Hunter, J. E., Schmidt, F. L., & Coggin, T. D. (1988). Problems and pitfalls in using capital budgeting and financial accounting techniques in assessing the utility of personnel programs. *Journal of Applied Psychology, 73,* 522-528.

Huselid, M. A. (1995). The impact of human resource management practices on turnover, productivity, and corporate financial performance. *Academy of Management Journal, 38,* 635-672.

Huselid, M. A., Jackson, S. E., & Schuler, R. S. (1997). Technical and strategic human resource management effectiveness as determinants of firm performance. *Academy of Management Journal, 40,* 171-188.

Ilgen, D. R., & Hollenbeck, J. R. (1991). The structure of work: Job design and roles. In M. D. Dunnette & L. M. Hough (Eds.), *Handbook of industrial and organizational psychology* (Vol. 2, pp. 165-208). Palo Alto, CA: Consulting Psychologists Press.

Jackson, D. N. (1967). *Personality Research Form manual.* Goshen, NY: Research Psychologists Press.

Jackson, S. E., & Schuler, R. S. (1990). Human resource planning: Challenges for industrial/ organizational psychology. *American Psychologist, 45,* 223-239.

Jackson, S. E., Schuler, R. S., & Rivero, J. C. (1989). Organizational characteristics as predictors of personnel practices. *Personnel Psychology, 42,* 727-786.

Jacobs, R., Hofmann, D. A., & Kriska, S. D. (1990). Performance and seniority. *Human Performance, 3,* 107-121.

James, L. R. (1982). Aggregation bias in estimates of perceptual agreement. *Journal of Applied Psychology, 67,* 219-229.

James, L. R., Demaree, R. G., & Wolf, G. (1984). Estimating within-group interrater reliability with and without response bias. *Journal of Applied Psychology, 69,* 85-98.

Jensen, A. R. (1980). *Bias in mental testing.* New York: Free Press.

John, O. P. (1990). The "Big-Five" factor taxonomy: Dimensions of personality in the natural language and in questionnaires. In L. A. Pervin (Ed.), *Handbook of personality theory and research* (pp. 66-100). New York: Guilford.

Johns, G. (1993). Constraints on the adoption of psychology-based personnel practices: Lessons from organizational innovation. *Personnel Psychology, 46,* 569-592.

Johnson, J., & Ree, M. J. (1994). RANGEJ: A Pascal program to compute the multivariate correction for range restriction. *Educational and Psychological Measurement, 54,* 693-695.

Johnson, J. W. (1996). Linking employee perceptions of service climate to customer satisfaction. *Personnel Psychology, 49,* 831-852.

Jonassen, D. H., Beissner, K., & Yacci, M. (1993). *Structural knowledge: Techniques for representing, conveying, and acquiring structural knowledge.* Hillsdale, NJ: Lawrence Erlbaum.

Jöreskog, K. G., & Sörbom, D. (1979). *Advances in factor analysis and structural equation models.* Cambridge, MA: Abt.

Jöreskog, K. G., & Sörbom, D. (1982). Recent developments in structural equation modeling. *Journal of Marketing Research, 19,* 404-416.

Jöreskog, K. G., & Sörbom, D. (1993). *LISREL 8: Structural equation modeling with the SIMPLIS command language.* Hillsdale, NJ: Lawrence Erlbaum.

Judge, T. A., & Bretz, R. D. (1992). Effects of work values on job choice decisions. *Journal of Applied Psychology, 77,* 261-271.

Kane, J., & Lawler, E. E., III. (1978). Methods of peer assessment. *Psychological Bulletin, 35,* 555-586.

Kanfer, R. (1990). Motivational theory and industrial and organizational psychology. In M. D. Dunnette & L. M. Hough (Eds.), *Handbook of industrial and organizational psychology* (Vol. 1, pp. 75-170). Palo Alto, CA: Consulting Psychologists Press.

Kanfer, R., & Ackerman, P. L. (1989). Motivation and cognitive abilities: An integrative/aptitude-treatment interaction approach to skill acquisition. *Journal of Applied Psychology, 74,* 657-690.

Kanter, R. M. (1989). Careers and the wealth of nations: A macro perspective on the structure and implications of career forms. In M. B. Arthur, D. T. Hall, & B. S. Lawrence (Eds.), *Handbook of career theory* (pp. 506-521). Cambridge, UK: Cambridge University Press.

Katz, D., & Kahn, R. L. (1978). *The social psychology of organizations* (2nd ed.). New York: John Wiley.

Kealey, D. J., & Rubin, B. D. (1983). Cross-cultural personnel selection of criteria, issues and methods. In D. Landis & R. W. Brislin (Eds.), *Handbook of intercultural training* (Vol. 1, pp. 155-175). New York: Pergamon.

Keller, R. T., & Holland, W. E. (1978). A cross-validation study of the Kirton Adaption-Innovation Inventory in three research and development organizations. *Applied Psychological Measurement, 2,* 563-570.

Kenrick, D. T., & Funder, D. C. (1988). Lessons from the person-situation debate. *American Psychologist, 43,* 23-34.

Kinicki, A. J., Lockwood, C. A., Hom, P. W., & Griffeth, R. (1990). Interviewer predictions of applicant qualifications and interviewer validity: Aggregate and individual analyses. *Journal of Applied Psychology, 75,* 477-486.

Kirton, M. J. (1976). Adaptors and innovators: A description and a measure. *Journal of Applied Psychology, 61,* 622-629.

Kirton, M. J. (1977). *Manual for Kirton Adaption-Innovation Inventory.* London: National Foundation for Educational Research.

Kirton, M. J. (1980). Adaptors and innovators in organizations. *Human Relations, 3,* 213-224.

Kirton, M. J., & Pender, S. R. (1982). The adaption-innovation continuum: Occupational type and course selection. *Psychological Reports, 51,* 883-886.

Klein, K. J., Dansereau, R. G., & Hall, R. J. (1994). Levels issues in theory development, data collection, and analysis. *Academy of Management Review, 19,* 195-229.

Klein, K. J., & Kozlowski, S. W. J. (in press). *Multilevel theory, research, and methods in organizations.* San Francisco: Jossey-Bass.

Klimoski, R. J., & Brickner, M. (1987). Why do assessment centers work? The puzzle of assessment center validity. *Personnel Psychology, 40,* 243-260.

Klimoski, R. J., & Jones, R. G. (1995). Staffing for effective group decision making: Key issues in matching people and teams. In R. A. Guzzo & E. Salas (Eds.), *Team effectiveness and decision making in organizations* (pp. 291-332). San Francisco: Jossey-Bass.

Konovsky, M. A., & Cropanzano, R. (1991). Perceived fairness of employee drug testing as a predictor of employee attitudes and job performance. *Journal of Applied Psychology, 76,* 698-707.

Kozlowski, S. W. J., Gully, S. M., Nason, E. R., Ford, J. K., Smith, E. M., Smith, M. R., & Futch, C. J. (1994). *A composition theory of team development: Levels, content, process, and learning outcomes.* Paper presented at the Ninth Annual Conference of the Society for Industrial and Organizational Psychology, Nashville, TN.

Krahe, B. (1989). Faking personality profiles on a standard personality inventory. *Personality and Individual Differences, 10,* 437-443.

Kraiger, K., & Ford, J. K. (1985). A meta-analysis of rater race effects in performance ratings. *Journal of Applied Psychology, 7,* 56-65.

Kraiger, K., Ford, J. K., & Salas, E. (1993). Application of cognitive, skill-based and affective theories of learning outcomes to new methods of training evaluation. *Journal of Applied Psychology, 78,* 311-328.

Kravitz, D. A., Harrison, D. A., Turner, M. E., Levine, E. L., Chaves, W., Brannick, M. T., Denning, D. L., Russell, C. J., & Conrad, M. A. (1997). A review of psychological and behavioral research on affirmative action. *Industrial-Organizational Psychologist, 34*(3), 141-149.

Kristof, A. L. (1996). Person-organization fit: An integrative review of its conceptualizations, measurement, and implications. *Personnel Psychology, 49,* 1-48.

Lance, C. E., LaPointe, J. A., & Stewart, A. M. (1994). A test of the context dependency of three causal models of halo rater error. *Journal of Applied Psychology, 79,* 332-340.

Lance, C. E., Teachout, M. S., & Donnelly, T. M. (1992). Specification of the criterion construct space: An application of hierarchical confirmatory factor analysis. *Journal of Applied Psychology, 77,* 437-452.

Landy, F. J. (1986). Stamp collecting versus science: Validation as hypothesis testing. *American Psychologist, 41,* 1183-1192.

Landy, F. J., & Farr, J. L. (1980). Performance rating. *Psychological Bulletin, 87,* 72-107.

Latham, G. P., Saari, L. M., Purcell, E. D., & Campion, M. A. (1980). The situational interview. *Personnel Psychology, 65,* 422-427.

Latham, G. P., & Sue-Chan, C. (in press). A meta-analysis of the situational interview. In R. W. Eder & M. M. Harris (Eds.), *The employment interview: Theory, research, and practice.* Thousand Oaks, CA: Sage.

Latham, G. P., & Whyte, G. (1994). The futility of utility analysis. *Personnel Psychology, 47,* 31-46.

Lawley, D. N. (1943). A note on Karl Pearson's selection formulae. *Proceedings of the Royal Society of Edinburgh, 62*(Sec. A, Pt. 1), 28-30.

Lawshe, C. H. (1975). A quantitative approach to content validity. *Personnel Psychology, 28,* 563-575.

Lengnick-Hall, C. A. (1996). Customer contributions to quality: A different view of the customer-oriented firm. *Academy of Management Review, 21,* 791-824.

Leventhal, G. S., Karuza, J., & Fry, W. R. (1980). Beyond fairness: A theory of allocation preferences. In G. Mikula (Ed.), *Justice and social interaction* (pp. 167-218). New York: Springer-Verlag.

Levine, E. L. (1983). *Everything you always wanted to know about job analysis.* Tampa, FL: Mariner.

Levine, E. L., Ash, R. A., Hall, H., & Sistrunk, F. (1983). Evaluation of job analysis methods by experienced job analysts. *Academy of Management Journal, 26,* 339-348.

Lewin, A. Y., & Minton, J. W. (1986). Determining organizational effectiveness: Another look and an agenda for research. *Management Science, 32,* 524-538.

Life Insurance Marketing and Research Association. (1979). *Agent selection research questionnaire.* Hartford, CT: Author.

Linn, R. L. (1978). Single group validity, differential validity, and differential prediction. *Journal of Applied Psychology, 63,* 507-512.

Lofquist, L. H., & Dawis, R. V. (1978). Values as second-order needs in the theory of work adjustment. *Journal of Vocational Behavior, 12,* 12-19.

Lorenzo, R. V. (1984). Effects of assessorship on manager's proficiency in acquiring, evaluating, and communicating. *Personnel Psychology, 37,* 617-634.

Lorr, M., & More, W. (1980). Four dimensions of assertiveness. *Multivariate Behavioral Research, 15,* 127-138.

Lowe, E. A., & Taylor, W. G. K. (1986). The management of research in the life sciences: The characteristics of researchers. *Research and Development Management, 16,* 45-61.

Mabe, P. A., & West, S. G. (1982). Validity of self-evaluation of ability: A review and meta-analysis. *Journal of Applied Psychology, 67,* 280-296.

Macan, T. H., Avedon, M. J., Paese, M., & Smith, D. E. (1994). The effects of applicants' reactions to cognitive ability tests and an assessment center. *Personnel Psychology, 47,* 715-738.

MacCallum, R. C., Wegener, D. T., Uchino, B. N., & Fabrigar, L. R. (1993). The problem of equivalent models in applications of covariance structure analysis. *Psychological Bulletin, 114,* 185-199.

Marrs, M. B., Turban, D. B., Dougherty, T. W., & Roberts, R. (1996, April). *Applicant attraction to demographically diverse firms: A person-organization fit perspective.* Paper presented at the 11th Annual Conference of the Society for Industrial and Organizational Psychology, San Diego, CA.

Martin, S. L., & Terris, W. (1991). Predicting infrequent behavior: Clarifying the impact on false-positive rates. *Journal of Applied Psychology, 76,* 484-487.

Maruyama, G. M. (1998). *Basics of structural equation modeling.* Thousand Oaks, CA: Sage.

Mathieu, J. E., & Baratta, J. E. (1989). Turnover type as a moderator of the performance-turnover relationship. *Human Performance, 2,* 61-71.

McArdle, J. J. (1996). Some directions in structural factor analysis. *Current Directions in Psychological Science, 5,* 11-18.

McArdle, J. J., & Epstein, D. (1987). Latent growth curves within developmental structural equation models. *Child Development, 58,* 110-133.

McBride, J. R., & Martin, J. T. (1983). Reliability and validity of adaptive ability tests in a military setting. In D. J. Weiss (Ed.), *New horizons in testing* (pp. 223-236). San Diego, CA: Academic Press.

McCloy, R. A., Campbell, J. P., & Cudeck, R. (1994). A confirmatory test of a model of performance determinants. *Journal of Applied Psychology, 79,* 493-505.

McCormick, E. J. (1976). Job and task analysis. In M. D. Dunnette (Ed.), *Handbook of industrial and organizational psychology* (pp. 651-696). Chicago: Rand McNally.

McCormick, E. J., Jeanneret, P. R., & Mecham, R. C. (1972). A study of job dimensions based on the Position Analysis Questionnaire. *Journal of Applied Psychology, 56,* 347-368.

McCrae, R. R., & John, O. P. (1992). An introduction to the five-factor model and its applications. *Journal of Personality, 60,* 175-215.

McDaniel, M. A., Hirsh, H. R., Schmidt, F. L., Raju, N. S., & Hunter, J. E. (1986). Interpreting the results of meta-analytic research: A comment on Schmitt, Gooding, Noe, and Kirsch (1984). *Personnel Psychology, 39,* 141-148.

McDaniel, M. A., Whetzel, D. L., Schmidt, F. L., & Maurer, S. D. (1994). The validity of the employment interview: A comprehensive review and meta-analysis. *Journal of Applied Psychology, 79,* 599-616.

McEvoy, G. M., & Cascio, W. F. (1985). Strategies for reducing employee turnover: A meta analysis. *Journal of Applied Psychology, 70,* 342-353.

McFarlin, D. B., & Sweeney, P. D. (1992). Distributive and procedural justice as predictors of satisfaction with personal and organizational outcomes. *Academy of Management Journal, 35,* 626-637.

McHenry, J. J., Hough, L. M., Toquam, J. L., Hanson, M. A., & Ashworth, S. D. (1990). Project A validity results: Relationship between predictor and criterion domains. *Personnel Psychology, 43,* 335-354.

McHenry, J. J., & Schmitt, N. (1994). Multimedia testing. In M. G. Rumsey, C. B. Walker, & J. H. Harris (Eds.), *Personnel selection and classification* (pp. 193-232). Hillsdale, NJ: Lawrence Erlbaum.

McIntyre, R., Smith, D., & Hassett, C. (1984). Accuracy of performance ratings as affected by rater training and perceived purpose of appraisal. *Journal of Applied Psychology, 69,* 145-156.

Mead, A. D., & Drasgow, F. (1993). Equivalence of computerized and paper-and-pencil cognitive ability tests: A meta-analysis. *Psychological Bulletin, 114,* 449-458.

Mendenhall, M., & Oddou, G. (1985). The dimensions of expatriate acculturation. *Academy of Management Review, 10,* 39-48.

Meredith, W., & Tisak, J. (1990). Latent curve analysis. *Psychometrika, 55,* 107-122.

Metzger, R. O., & Von Glinow, M. A. (1988). Off-site workers: At home and abroad. *California Management Review, 30,* 101-111.

Meyer, H. H. (1959). Comparison of foremen and general foremen conceptions of the foreman's job responsibility. *Personnel Psychology, 12,* 445-452.

Miles, R. E., & Snow, C. C. (1978). *Organizational strategy, structure, and process.* New York: McGraw-Hill.

Miles, R. E., & Snow, C. C. (1984). Designing strategic human resource systems. *Organizational Dynamics, 13*(1), 36-52.

Millsap, R. E., & Hartog, S. B. (1988). Alpha, beta, and gamma change in evaluation research: A structural equation approach. *Journal of Applied Psychology, 73*, 574-584.

Miner, J. B. (1978). Twenty years of research on role motivation theory of managerial effectiveness. *Personnel Psychology, 31*, 739-760.

Miner, J. B., Smith, N. R., & Bracker, J. S. (1989). Role of entrepreneurial task motivation in the growth of technologically innovative firms. *Journal of Applied Psychology, 74*, 554-560.

Miner, J. B., Smith, N. R., & Bracker, J. S. (1994). Role of entrepreneurial task motivation in the growth of technologically innovative firms: Interpretations from follow-up data. *Journal of Applied Psychology, 79*, 627-630.

Mischel, W. (1968). *Personality and assessment.* New York: John Wiley.

Mitchell, T. W., & Klimoski, R. J. (1982). Is it rational to be empirical? A test of methods for scoring biographical data. *Journal of Applied Psychology, 67*, 411-418.

Mobley, W. H. (1977). Intermediate linkages in the relationship between job satisfaction and employee turnover. *Journal of Applied Psychology, 62*, 237-240.

Moorman, R. H. (1991). Relationship between organizational justice and organizational citizenship behaviors: Do fairness perceptions influence employee citizenship? *Journal of Applied Psychology, 76*, 845-855.

Morita, J. G., Lee, T. W., & Mowday, R. F. (1989). Introducing survival analysis to organizational researchers: A selected application to turnover research. *Journal of Applied Psychology, 74*, 280-292.

Moses, J. L., & Boehm, V. R. (1975). Relationship of assessment center performance to management progress of women. *Journal of Applied Psychology, 60*, 527-529.

Motowidlo, S. J., Borman, W. C., & Schmit, M. J. (1997). A theory of individual differences in task and contextual performance. *Human Performance, 10*, 71-84.

Motowidlo, S. J., Dunnette, M. D., & Carter, G. W. (1990). An alternative selection procedure: The low-fidelity simulation. *Journal of Applied Psychology, 75*, 640-647.

Mullins, W. C., & Kimbrough, W. W. (1988). Group composition as a determinant of job analysis outcomes. *Journal of Applied Psychology, 73*, 657-664.

Mumford, M. D., Baughman, W. A., Threlfall, K. V., Uhlman, C. E., & Costanza, D. P. (1993). Personality, adaptability, and performance: Performance on well-defined and ill-defined problem-solving tasks. *Human Performance, 6*, 241-285.

Mumford, M. D., & Stokes, G. S. (1992). Developmental determinants of individual action: Theory and practice in applying background measures. In M. D. Dunnette & L. M. Hough (Eds.), *Handbook of industrial and organizational psychology* (Vol. 3, pp. 61-138). Palo Alto, CA: Consulting Psychologists Press.

Mumford, M. D., Stokes, G. S., & Owens, W. A. (1990). *Patterns of life adaptation: The ecology of human individuality.* Hillsdale, NJ: Lawrence Erlbaum.

Murphy, K. R. (1983). Fooling yourself with cross-validation: Single-sample designs. *Personnel Psychology, 36*, 111-118.

Murphy, K. R. (1986). When your top choice turns you down: The effect of rejected offers on the utility of selection tests. *Psychological Bulletin, 99*, 133-138.

Murphy, K. R. (1987). Detecting infrequent deception. *Journal of Applied Psychology, 72*, 611-614.

Murphy, K. R. (1996). Individual differences and behavior in organizations. Much more than *g*. In K. R. Murphy (Ed.), *Individual differences and behavior in organizations* (pp. 3-30). San Francisco: Jossey-Bass.

Murphy, K. R., & Lee, S. L. (1994). Personality variables related to integrity test scores: The role of conscientiousness. *Journal of Business and Psychology, 8*, 413-424.

Murray, H. A. (1938). *Explorations in personality.* New York: Oxford University Press.

Muthen, B. O. (1991). Analysis of longitudinal data using latent variable models with varying parameters. In L. M. Collins & J. L. Horn (Eds.), *Best methods for the analysis of change: Recent advances, unanswered questions, future directions* (pp. 1-17). Washington, DC: American Psychological Association.

Newell, A., & Simon, H. A. (1972). *Human problem-solving.* Englewood Cliffs, NJ: Prentice Hall.

Noe, R. A., Hollenbeck, J. R., Gerhart, B., & Wright, P. M. (1994). *Human resource management: Gaining a competitive advantage.* Burr Ridge, IL: Austen/Irwin.

Noe, R. A., & Schmitt, N. (1986). The influence of trainee attitudes on training effectiveness: Test of a model. *Personnel Psychology, 39,* 497-524.

Nunnally, J. C. (1978). *Psychometric theory.* New York: McGraw-Hill.

Nunnally, J. C., & Bernstein, I. H. (1994). *Psychometric theory.* New York: McGraw-Hill.

Offermann, L. R., & Gowing, M. K. (1990). Organizations of the future. *American Psychologist, 45,* 95-108.

Office of Federal Contract Compliance. (1968). Validation of tests by contractors and subcontractors subject to the provisions of Executive Order 11246. *Federal Register, 33*(186), 14392-14394.

Ohmae, K. (1982). *The mind of the strategist.* New York: McGraw-Hill.

Ones, D. S., & Viswesvaran, C. (1996). Bandwidth-fidelity dilemma in personality measurement for personnel selection. *Journal of Organizational Behavior, 17,* 609-626.

Ones, D. S., Viswesvaran, C., & Schmidt, F. L. (1993). Comprehensive meta-analysis of integrity test validities: Findings and implications for personnel selection and theories of job performance. *Journal of Applied Psychology, 78,* 679-703.

Oppler, S. H., Campbell, J. P., Pulakos, E. D., & Borman, W. C. (1992). Three approaches to the investigation of subgroup bias in performance measurement: Review, results, and conclusions. *Journal of Applied Psychology, 77,* 201-217.

O'Reilly, C. A., III, Chatman, J., & Caldwell, D. F. (1991). People and organizational culture: A profile comparison approach to assessing person-organization fit. *Academy of Management Journal, 34,* 487-516.

Organ, D. W. (1988). *Organizational citizenship behavior: The good soldier syndrome.* Lexington, MA: Lexington.

Organ, D. W. (1997). Organizational citizenship behavior: It's construct clean-up time. *Human Performance, 10,* 85-98.

Organ, D. W., & Konovsky, M. (1989). Cognitive versus affective determinants of organizational citizenship behavior. *Journal of Applied Psychology, 74,* 157-164.

Orpen, C. (1971). The fakability of the Edwards Personal Preference Schedule in personnel selection. *Personnel Psychology, 24,* 1-4.

Owens, W. A. (1968). Toward one discipline of scientific psychology. *American Psychologist, 23,* 782-785.

Owens, W. A., & Schoenfeldt, L. F. (1979). Toward a classification of persons. *Journal of Applied Psychology, 64,* 569-607.

Pace, L. A., & Schoenfeldt, L. F. (1977). Legal concerns in the use of weighted application blanks. *Personnel Psychology, 30,* 159-166.

Parsons, C. K., & Liden, R. C. (1984). Interviewer perceptions of applicant qualifications: A multivariate field study of demographic characteristics and nonverbal cues. *Journal of Applied Psychology, 69,* 557-568.

Paulhus, D. L. (1984). Two-component models of socially desirable responding. *Journal of Personality and Social Psychology, 46,* 598-609.

Peters, T., & Austin, N. (1987). *A passion for excellence.* New York: Random House.

Peterson, N. G., & Bownas, D. A. (1982). Skill, task structure, and performance acquisition. In M. D. Dunnette & E. A. Fleishman (Eds.), *Human performance productivity: Human capability assessment* (pp. 49-105). Hillsdale, NJ: Lawrence Erlbaum.

Peterson, N. G., Hough, L. M., Dunnette, M. D., Rosse, R. L., Houston, J. S., Toquam, J. L., & Wing, H. (1990). Project A: Specification of the predictor domain and development of new selection/classification tests. *Personnel Psychology, 43,* 247-276.

Peterson, N. G., Mumford, M. D., Borman, W. C., Jeanneret, P. R., & Fleishman, E. A. (Eds.). (1995). *Development of prototype Occupational Information Network (O*NET)* (Vols. 1-2). Salt Lake City: Utah Department of Employment Security.

Pingitore, R., Dugoni, B. L., Tindale, R. S., & Spring, B. (1994). Bias against overweight job applicants in a simulated employment interview. *Journal of Applied Psychology, 79,* 909-917.

Podsakoff, P. M., & MacKenzie, S. B. (1997). Impact of organizational citizenship behavior on organizational performance: A review and suggestions for future research. *Human Performance, 10,* 133-152.

Poon, L. W. (1987). Learning. In G. L. Maddox (Ed.), *The encyclopedia of aging* (pp. 380-381). New York: Springer.

Poon, L. W., Krauss, I., & Bowles, N. L. (1984). On subject selection in cognitive aging research. *Experimental Aging Research, 10,* 43-49.

Powell, G. N. (1991). Applicant reactions to the initial employment interview: Exploring theoretical and methodological issues. *Personnel Psychology, 44,* 67-83.

Project A: The U.S. Army Selection and Classification Project [Special issue]. (1990). *Personnel Psychology, 43*(2).

Psychological Corporation. (1992). *Differential Aptitude Tests: Technical manual.* New York: Author.

Pucik, V. (1988). Strategic alliances, organizational learning, and competitive advantage: The HRM agenda. *Human Resource Management, 27,* 77-94.

Pulakos, E. D. (1986). The development of a training program to increase accuracy with different rating formats. *Organizational Behavior and Human Decision Processes, 38,* 76-91.

Pulakos, E. D. (1991). Rater training for performance appraisal. In J. W. Jones, B. D. Steffy, & D. W. Bray (Eds.), *Applying psychology in business: The manager's handbook* (pp. 307-313). Lexington, MA: Lexington.

Pulakos, E. D. (1996). *Proposal for the test of a model of adaptability* (Submitted to Department of Defense Small Business Innovation Research Program). Washington, DC: Personnel Decisions Research Institutes.

Pulakos, E. D., Borman, W. C., & Hough, L. M. (1988). Test validation for scientific understanding: Two demonstrations of an approach to studying predictor-criterion linkages. *Personnel Psychology, 41,* 703-716.

Pulakos, E. D., & Schmitt, N. (1995). Experienced and situational interviews: Studies of validity. *Personnel Psychology, 48,* 289-308.

Pulakos, E. D., & Schmitt, N. (1996). An evaluation of two strategies for reducing adverse impact and their effects on criterion-related validity. *Human Performance, 9,* 241-258.

Pulakos, E. D., Schmitt, N., & Chan, D. (1996). Models of job performance ratings: An examination of ratee race, ratee gender, and rater level effects. *Human Performance, 9,* 103-121.

Pulakos, E. D., Schmitt, N., Whitney, D., & Smith, M. (1996). Individual differences in interviewer ratings: The impact of standardization, consensus discussion, and sampling error on the validity of a structured interview. *Personnel Psychology, 49,* 85-102.

Pulakos, E. D., White, L. A., Oppler, S. H., & Borman, W. C. (1989). Examination of race and sex effects on performance ratings. *Journal of Applied Psychology, 74,* 770-780.

Quiñones, M. A., Ford, J. K., & Teachout, M. S. (1995). The relationship between work experience and job performance: A conceptual and meta-analytic review. *Personnel Psychology, 48,* 887-910.

Raju, N. S., Pappas, S., & Williams, C. P. (1989). An empirical Monte Carlo test of the accuracy of the correlation, covariance, and regression slope models for assessing validity generalization. *Journal of Applied Psychology, 74,* 901-911.

Ralston, D. A., Gustafson, D. J., Elsass, P. M., Cheung, F., & Terpstra, R. H. (1992). Eastern values: A comparison of managers in the United States, Hong Kong, and the People's Republic of China. *Journal of Applied Psychology, 77,* 664-771.

Rambo, W. W., Chomiak, A. M., & Price, J. M. (1983). Consistency of performance under stable conditions of work. *Journal of Applied Psychology, 68,* 78-87.

Rauschenberger, J. M., & Schmidt, F. L. (1987). Measuring the economic impact of human resource programs. *Journal of Business and Psychology, 2,* 50-59.

Ree, M. J., Carretta, T. R., Earles, J. A., & Albert, W. (1994). Sign changes when correcting for restriction of range: A note on Pearson's and Lawley's selection formulas. *Journal of Applied Psychology, 79,* 298-301.

Ree, M. J., & Earles, J. A. (1991). Predicting training success: Not much more than g. *Personnel Psychology, 44,* 321-332.

Ree, M. J., & Earles, J. A. (1992). Intelligence is the best predictor of job performance. *Current Directions in Psychological Science, 1,* 86-89.

Ree, M. J., & Earles, J. A. (1993). g is to psychology what carbon is to chemistry: A reply to Sternberg and Wagner, McClelland, and Calfee. *Current Directions in Psychological Science, 2,* 11-12.

Ree, M. J., Earles, J. A., & Teachout, M. S. (1994). Predicting job performance: Not much more than g. *Journal of Applied Psychology, 79,* 518-524.

Regents of the University of California v. Bakke, 438 U.S. 265 (1978).

Reilly, R. R., & Chao, G. T. (1982). Validity and fairness of some alternate selection procedures. *Personnel Psychology, 35,* 1-62.

Robertson, I. T., & Downs, S. (1979). Learning and prediction of performance: Development of trainability testing in the United Kingdom. *Journal of Applied Psychology, 64,* 42-50.

Robertson, I. T., & Kandola, R. S. (1982). Work sample tests: Validity, adverse impact, and applicant reaction. *Journal of Applied Psychology, 55,* 171-183.

Rogers, E. M. (1983). *Diffusion of innovations* (3rd ed.). New York: Free Press.

Ronan, W. W., Talbert, T. S., & Mullett, G. M. (1977). Prediction of job performance dimensions— police officers. *Public Personnel Management, 6,* 173-180.

Ronen, S. (1989). Training the international assignee. In I. L. Goldstein (Ed.), *Training and development in organizations* (pp. 417-454). San Francisco: Jossey-Bass.

Rorschach, H. (1921). *Psychodiagnostics.* Berne: Haber.

Rosen, B., & Jerdee, T. H. (1976a). The influence of age stereotypes on managerial decisions. *Journal of Applied Psychology, 61,* 428-432.

Rosen, B., & Jerdee, T. H. (1976b). The nature of job-related stereotypes. *Journal of Applied Psychology, 61,* 180-183.

Rothe, H. F. (1978). Output rates among industrial employees. *Journal of Applied Psychology, 63,* 40-46.

Rothstein, H. R. (1990). Interrater reliability of job performance ratings: Growth to asymptote level with increasing opportunity to observe. *Journal of Applied Psychology, 75,* 322-327.

Rothstein, H. R., Schmidt, F. L., Erwin, F. W., Owens, W. A., & Sparks, C. P. (1990). Biographical data in employment selection: Can validities be made generalizable? *Journal of Applied Psychology, 75,* 175-184.

Rounds, J. B., Jr., Dawis, R. V., & Lofquist, L. H. (1987). Measurement of person-environment fit and prediction of job satisfaction in the theory of work adjustment. *Journal of Vocational Behavior, 31,* 297-318.

Rousseau, D. M. (1985). Issues of level in organizational research: Multilevel and cross-level perspectives. In L. L. Cummings & B. M. Staw (Eds.), *Research in organizational behavior* (pp. 1-38). Greenwich, CT: JAI.

Roznowski, M. (1987). Use of tests manifesting sex differences as measures of intelligence: Implications for measurement bias. *Journal of Applied Psychology, 72,* 480-483.

Ruch, W. W., Weiner, J. A., McKillip, R. H., & Dye, D. A. (1985). *Technical manual: PSI Basic Skills Tests for business, industry, and government.* Los Angeles: Psychological Services.

Russell, C. J., Colella, A., & Bobko, P. (1993). Expanding the context of utility: The strategic impact of personnel selection. *Personnel Psychology, 46,* 781-801.

Ryan, A. M., & Sackett, P. R. (1987). A survey of individual assessment practices by I/O psychologists. *Personnel Psychology, 40,* 455-488.

Rynes, S. L. (1991). Recruitment, job choice, and post-hire consequences: A call for new research directions. In M. D. Dunnette & L. M. Hough (Eds.), *Handbook of industrial and organizational psychology* (Vol. 2, pp. 399-444). Palo Alto, CA: Consulting Psychologists Press.

Rynes, S. L., Bretz, R. D., & Gerhart, B. (1991). The importance of recruitment in job choice: A different way of looking. *Personnel Psychology, 44,* 487-520.

Rynes, S. L., & Connerly, M. L. (1993). Applicant reactions to alternative selection procedures. *Journal of Business and Psychology, 7,* 261-275.

Saari, L. M., Johnson, T. R., McLaughlin, S. D., & Zimmerle, D. M. (1988). A survey of management training and educational practices in U.S. companies. *Personnel Psychology, 41,* 731-745.

Sackett, P. R., & Dreher, G. F. (1982). Constructs and assessment center dimensions: Some troubling empirical findings. *Journal of Applied Psychology, 67,* 401-410.

Sackett, P. R., Harris, M. M., & Orr, J. M. (1986). On seeking moderator variables in the meta-analysis of correlational data: A Monte Carlo investigation of statistical power and resistance to Type I error. *Journal of Applied Psychology, 71,* 302-310.

Sackett, P. R., & Roth, L. (1991). A Monte Carlo examination of banding and rank order methods of test score use in preemployment testing. *Human Performance, 4,* 279-295.

Sackett, P. R., & Roth, L. (1996). Multi-stage selection strategies: A Monte Carlo investigation of effects on performance and minority hiring. *Personnel Psychology, 49,* 549-572.

Sackett, P. R., & Wanek, J. E. (1996). New developments in the use of measures of honesty, integrity, conscientiousness, dependability, trustworthiness, and reliability for personnel selection. *Personnel Psychology, 49,* 787-830.

Sackett, P. R., & Wilk, S. L. (1994). Within-group norming and other forms of score adjustment in preemployment testing. *American Psychologist, 49,* 929-954.

Sackett, P. R., Zedeck, S., & Fogli, L. (1988). Relations between measures of typical and maximum job performance. *Journal of Applied Psychology, 73,* 482-486.

Salthouse, T. A. (1984). Effects of age and skill in typing. *Journal of Experimental Psychology: General, 113,* 345-371.

Sanchez, J. I. (1990). *The effects of job experience on judgments of task importance.* Paper presented at the Fifth Annual Conference of the Society for Industrial and Organizational Psychology, Miami, FL.

Sanchez, J. I., & Levine, E. L. (1989). Determining important tasks within jobs: A policy capturing approach. *Journal of Applied Psychology, 74,* 336-342.

Schmidt, F. L. (1995). Why all banding procedures in personnel selection are logically flawed. *Human Performance, 8,* 165-178.

Schmidt, F. L., Berner, J. G., & Hunter, J. E. (1973). Racial differences in validity of employment tests: Reality or illusion? *Journal of Applied Psychology, 58,* 5-9.

Schmidt, F. L., Greenthal, A. L., Hunter, J. E., Berner, J. G., & Seaton, F. W. (1977). Job sample vs. paper-and-pencil trades and technical tests: Adverse impact and examinee attitudes. *Personnel Psychology, 30*, 187-197.

Schmidt, F. L., & Hunter, J. E. (1977). Development of a general solution to the problem of validity generalization. *Journal of Applied Psychology, 62*, 529-540.

Schmidt, F. L., & Hunter, J. E. (1981). Employment testing: Old theories and new research findings. *American Psychologist, 36*, 1128-1137.

Schmidt, F. L., & Hunter, J. E. (1996). Measurement error in psychological research: Lessons from 26 research scenarios. *Psychological Methods, 1*, 199-223.

Schmidt, F. L., Hunter, J. E., McKenzie, R. C., & Muldrow, T. W. (1979). Impact of valid selection procedures on work-force productivity. *Journal of Applied Psychology, 64*, 609-626.

Schmidt, F. L., Hunter, J. E., & Outerbridge, A. N. (1986). Impact of job experience and ability on job knowledge, work sample of performance, and supervisory ratings of job performance. *Journal of Applied Psychology, 71*, 432-439.

Schmidt, F. L., Hunter, J. E., Outerbridge, A. N., & Goff, S. (1988). Joint relation of experience and ability with job performance: Test of three hypotheses. *Journal of Applied Psychology, 73*, 46-57.

Schmidt, F. L., Hunter, J. E., & Pearlman, K. (1981). Task differences as moderators of aptitude test validity in selection: A red herring. *Journal of Applied Psychology, 66*, 166-185.

Schmidt, F. L., Hunter, J. E., & Pearlman, K. (1982). Assessing the economic impact of personnel programs on work-force productivity. *Personnel Psychology, 35*, 333-347.

Schmidt, F. L., Hunter, J. E., Pearlman, K., & Hirsh, H. R. (1985). Forty questions about validity generalization and meta-analysis. *Personnel Psychology, 38*, 697-798.

Schmidt, F. L., Hunter, J. E., Pearlman, K., & Shane, G. S. (1979). Further tests of the Schmidt-Hunter Bayesian validity generalization procedure. *Personnel Psychology, 32*, 259-282.

Schmidt, F. L., Hunter, J. E., & Urry, V. W. (1976). Statistical power in criterion-related validation studies. *Journal of Applied Psychology, 61*, 473-485.

Schmidt, F. L., & Kaplan, L. B. (1971). Composite vs. multiple criteria: A review and resolution of the controversy. *Personnel Psychology, 24*, 419-434.

Schmidt, F. L., & Ones, D. S. (1992). Personnel selection. *Annual Review of Psychology, 43*, 627-670.

Schmidt, F. L., Pearlman, K., & Hunter, J. E. (1980). The validity and fairness of employment and educational tests for Hispanic Americans: A review and analysis. *Personnel Psychology, 33*, 705-724.

Schmit, M. J., & Allscheid, S. P. (1995). Employee attitudes and customer satisfaction: Making theoretical and empirical connections. *Personnel Psychology, 48*, 521-536.

Schmit, M. J., Motowidlo, S. J., DeGroot, T. G., Cross, T. C., & Kiker, D. S. (1996, April). *Explaining the relationship between personality and job performance.* Paper presented at the 11th Annual Conference of the Society for Industrial and Organizational Psychology, San Diego, CA.

Schmit, M. J., Ryan, A. M., Stierwalt, S. L., & Powell, A. B. (1995). Frame-of-reference effects on personality scale scores and criterion-related validity. *Journal of Applied Psychology, 80*, 607-620.

Schmitt, N. (1976). Social and situational determinants of interview decisions: Implications for the employment interview. *Personnel Psychology, 29*, 79-101.

Schmitt, N. (1993). Group composition, gender and race effects on assessment center ratings. In H. Schuler, J. Farr, & M. Smith (Eds.), *Personnel selection in industrial research and development* (pp. 315-332). Hillsdale, NJ: Lawrence Erlbaum.

Schmitt, N. (1994). Method bias: The importance of theory and measurement. *Journal of Organizational Behavior, 15*, 393-398.

Schmitt, N. (1997). Assessment without adverse impact. In A. Lesgold, M. J. Feuer, & A. M. Black (Eds.), *Transitions in work and learning: Implications for assessment* (pp. 215-234). Washington, DC: National Academy Press.

Schmitt, N., Chan, D., Sacco, J. M., & McFarland, L. (in press). Relationships between appropriateness fit, test reactions, test-taking motivation, conscientiousness, subgroup differences and test validity. *Applied Psychological Measurement.*

Schmitt, N., Clause, C. S., & Pulakos, E. D. (1996). Subgroup differences associated with different measures of some common job-relevant constructs. In C. R. Cooper & I. T. Robertson (Eds.), *International review of industrial and organizational psychology* (Vol. 11, pp. 115-140). New York: John Wiley.

Schmitt, N., & Cohen, S. A. (1989). Internal analysis of task ratings by job incumbents. *Journal of Applied Psychology, 74,* 96-104.

Schmitt, N., & Coyle, B. W. (1976). Applicant decisions in the employment interview. *Journal of Applied Psychology, 63,* 184-192.

Schmitt, N., Coyle, B. W., & Rauschenberger, J. (1977). A Monte Carlo evaluation of three formula estimates of cross-validated multiple correlation. *Psychological Bulletin, 84,* 751-758.

Schmitt, N., & Fine, S. A. (1983). Inter-rater reliability of judgements of functional levels and skill requirements of jobs based on written task statements. *Journal of Occupational Psychology, 56,* 121-127.

Schmitt, N., & Gilliland, S. W. (1992). Beyond differential prediction: Fairness in selection. In D. Saunders (Ed.), *Human rights and employment: Interdisciplinary perspectives* (pp. 21-46). Greenwich, CT: JAI.

Schmitt, N., Gilliland, S. W., Landis, R. S., & Devine, D. (1993). Computer-based testing applied to selection of secretarial applicants. *Personnel Psychology, 46,* 149-165.

Schmitt, N., Gooding, R. Z., Noe, R. A., & Kirsch, M. P. (1984). Meta-analyses of validity studies published between 1964 and 1982 and the investigation of study characteristics. *Personnel Psychology, 37,* 407-422.

Schmitt, N., Hattrup, K., & Landis, R. S. (1993). Item bias indices based on total test scores and job performance estimates of ability. *Personnel Psychology, 46,* 593-611.

Schmitt, N., Jennings, D., & Toney, R. J. (1996). Can we develop biodata measures of hypothetical constructs. In R. A. Stennett, A. G. Parisi, & G. S. Stokes (Eds.), *A compendium: Papers presented to the First Biennial Biodata Conference* (pp. 37-71). Athens: University of Georgia.

Schmitt, N., & Klimoski, R. (1991). *Research methods in human resources management.* Cincinnati, OH: South-Western.

Schmitt, N., & Noe, R. A. (1986). Personnel selection and equal employment opportunity. In C. L. Cooper & I. T. Robertson (Eds.), *International review of industrial and organizational psychology.* New York: John Wiley.

Schmitt, N., Noe, R. A., Meritt, R., & Fitzgerald, M. P. (1984). Validity of assessment center ratings for the prediction of performance ratings and school climate of school administrators. *Journal of Applied Psychology, 69,* 207-213.

Schmitt, N., & Ostroff, C. (1986). Operationalizing the "behavioral consistency" approach: Selection test development based on a content-oriented strategy. *Personnel Psychology, 39,* 91-108.

Schmitt, N., Pulakos, E. D., Nason, E., & Whitney, D. J. (1996). Likability and similarity as potential sources of predictor-related criterion bias in validation research. *Organizational Behavior and Human Decision Processes, 68,* 272-286.

Schmitt, N., Rogers, W., Chan, D., Sheppard, L., & Jennings, D. (1997). Adverse impact and predictive efficiency using various predictor combinations. *Journal of Applied Psychology, 82,* 719-730.

Schmitt, N., & Schneider, B. (1983). Current issues in personnel selection. In K. R. Rowland & G. R. Ferris (Eds.), *Research in personnel and human resources management* (pp. 85-126). Greenwich, CT: JAI.

Schmitt, N., Toney, R. J., & Ree, M. J. (1997). *Illustrating the benefits of a multivariate approach to correcting for range restriction.* Paper presented at the 50th Anniversary of the Psychology Department, Michigan State University, East Lansing.

Schneider, B. (1972). Organizational climate: Individual perceptions and organizational realities revisited. *Journal of Applied Psychology, 61,* 459-465.

Schneider, B. (1987). The people make the place. *Personnel Psychology, 40,* 437-453.

Schneider, B. (1990). The climate for service: Application of the construct. In B. Schneider (Ed.), *Organizational climate and culture* (pp. 383-412). San Francisco: Jossey-Bass.

Schneider, B., & Bowen, D. E. (1985). Employee and customer perceptions of service in banks: Replication and extension. *Journal of Applied Psychology, 70,* 423-433.

Schneider, B., & Bowen, D. E. (1995). *Winning the service game.* Boston: Harvard Business School Press.

Schneider, B., & Konz, A. M. (1989). Strategic job analysis. *Human Resource Management, 28,* 51-64.

Schneider, B., Parkington, J. J., & Buxton, V. M. (1980). Employee and customer perceptions of service in banks. *Administrative Science Quarterly, 25,* 252-267.

Schneider, B., & Schmitt, N. (1986). *Staffing organizations.* Pacific Palisades, CA: Scott, Foresman.

Schneider, B., Wheeler, J. K., & Cox, J. F. (1992). A passion for service: Using content analysis to explicate service climate themes. *Journal of Applied Psychology, 77,* 705-716.

Schneider, J., & Schmitt, N. (1992). An exercise design approach to understanding assessment center dimension and exercise constructs. *Journal of Applied Psychology, 77,* 298-308.

Schneider, R. J., Hough, L. M., & Dunnette, M. D. (1996). Broadsided by broad traits: How to sink science in five dimensions or less. *Journal of Organizational Behavior, 17,* 639-658.

Schuler, H., & Fruhner, R. (1993). Effects of assessment center participation on self esteem and on evaluation of the selection situation. In H. Schuler, J. L. Farr, & M. Smith (Eds.), *Personnel selection and assessment: Individual and organizational perspectives* (pp. 109-124). Hillsdale, NJ: Lawrence Erlbaum.

Schuler, R. S., & Jackson, S. E. (1987). Organizational strategy and organizational level as determinants of human resource management practices. *Human Resource Planning, 10,* 125-141.

Schuler, R. S., & MacMillan, I. C. (1984). Gaining competitive advantage through human resource management practices. *Human Resource Management, 23,* 241-255.

Schumacker, R. E., & Lomax, R. G. (1996). *A beginner's guide to structural equation modeling.* Mahwah, NJ: Lawrence Erlbaum.

Schvaneveldt, R. W., Durso, F. T., & Dearholt, D. W. (1985). *Pathfinder: Scaling with network structures* (Memorandum in Computer and Cognitive Science, MCCS-85-9, Computing Research Laboratory). Las Cruces: New Mexico State University.

Schvaneveldt, R. W., Durso, F. T., & Dearholt, D. W. (1989). Network structures in proximity data. In G. G. Bower (Ed.), *The psychology of learning and motivation* (Vol. 24, pp. 249-284). New York: Academic Press.

Schwab, D. P., & Heneman, H. G., III. (1978). Age stereotyping in performance appraisal. *Journal of Applied Psychology, 63,* 573-578.

Scott, W. D. (1911). *Increasing human efficiency in business.* New York: Macmillan.

Seaburg, D. J., Rounds, J. B., Jr., Dawis, R. V., & Lofquist, L. H. (1976, August). *Values as second order needs.* Paper presented at the annual meeting of the American Psychological Association, Washington, DC.

Shamir, B. (1992). Home: The perfect workplace. In S. Zedeck (Ed.), *Work, families, and organizations* (pp. 272-311). San Francisco: Jossey-Bass.

Shavelson, R. J. (1991). Generalizability of military performance measurements: I. Individual performance. In A. K. Wigdor & B. F. Green, Jr. (Eds.), *Performance assessment for the workplace* (Vol. 2, pp. 207-257). Washington, DC: National Academy Press.

Siegel, A. I. (1983). The miniature job training and evaluation approach: Additional findings. *Personnel Psychology, 36,* 41-56.

Slater, R., & Kingsley, S. (1976). Predicting age-prejudiced employers: A British pilot study. *Industrial Gerontology, 3,* 121-128.

Smith, C. A., Organ, D. W., & Near, J. P. (1983). Organizational citizenship behavior: Its nature and antecedents. *Journal of Applied Psychology, 68,* 653-663.

Smith, J., & Hakel, M. D. (1979). Convergence among data sources, response bias, and reliability and validity of a structured job analysis questionnaire. *Personnel Psychology, 32,* 677-692.

Smith, P. C., & Kendall, L. M. (1963). Retranslation of expectations: An approach to the construction of unambiguous anchors for rating scales. *Journal of Applied Psychology, 47,* 149-155.

Smith-Jentsch, K. A., Salas, E., & Baker, D. P. (1996). Training team performance-related assertiveness. *Personnel Psychology, 49,* 909-936.

Smither, J. W., Millsap, R. E., Stoffey, R. W., Reilly, R. R., & Pearlman, K. (1996). An experimental test of the influence of selection procedures on fairness perceptions, attitudes about the organization, and job pursuit intentions. *Journal of Business and Psychology, 10,* 297-318.

Smither, J. W., Reilly, R. R., Millsap, R. E., Pearlman, K., & Stoffey, R. W. (1993). Applicant reactions to selection procedures. *Personnel Psychology, 46,* 49-76.

Snow, C. C., & Snell, S. A. (1993). Staffing as strategy. In N. Schmitt & W. C. Borman (Eds.), *Personnel selection in organizations* (pp. 448-480). San Francisco: Jossey-Bass.

Snow, R. E., & Lohman, D. L. (1984). Toward a theory of cognitive aptitude for learning from instruction. *Journal of Educational Psychology, 76,* 347-376.

Snyder, M., & Ickes, W. (1985). Personality and social behavior. In G. Lindzey & E. Aronson (Eds.), *The handbook of social psychology* (pp. 883-947). New York: Random House.

Society for Industrial and Organizational Psychology. (1987). *Principles for the validation and use of personnel selection procedures.* College Park, MD: Author.

Spearman, C. (1904). General intelligence objectively determined and measured. *American Journal of Sociology, 15,* 201-293.

Spearman, C. (1927). *The abilities of man.* New York: Macmillan.

Steele, C. M. (1997). A threat in the air: How stereotypes shape intellectual identity and performance. *American Psychologist, 52,* 613-629.

Steers, R. M., & Rhodes, S. R. (1984). Knowledge and speculation about absenteeism. In P. S. Goodman & R. S. Atkin (Eds.), *Absenteeism: New approaches to understanding, managing, and measuring employee absence* (pp. 229-275). San Francisco: Jossey-Bass.

Steiger, J. H. (1990). Structural model evaluation and modification: An interval estimation approach. *Multivariate Behavioral Research, 25,* 173-180.

Sternberg, R. J. (1977). *Intelligence, information processing and analogical reasoning: The componential analysis of human abilities.* Hillsdale, NJ: Lawrence Erlbaum.

Sternberg, R. J. (1979). The nature of human abilities. *American Psychologist, 34,* 214-230.

Sternberg, R. J. (1988). *The triarchic mind: A new theory of human intelligence.* New York: Cambridge University Press.

Sternberg, R. J., & Gardner, M. K. (1983). Unities in inductive reasoning. *Journal of Experimental Psychology: General, 112,* 80-116.

Sterns, H. L., & Doverspike, D. (1989). Aging and the training and learning process. In I. L. Goldstein & Associates (Eds.), *Training and development in organizations* (pp. 299-332). San Francisco: Jossey-Bass.

Stokes, G. S., Mumford, M. D., & Owens, W. A. (1989). Life history prototypes in the study of human individuality. *Journal of Personality, 57,* 509-545.

Stone, D. L., Stone-Romero, E. F., & Hyatt, D. E. (1994). *Some potential determinants of individuals' reactions to personnel selection procedures.* Paper presented at the Ninth Annual Conference of the Society for Industrial and Organizational Psychology, Nashville, TN.

Sulsky, L., & Balzer, W. K. (1988). Meaning and measurement of performance rating accuracy: Some methodological and theoretical concerns. *Journal of Applied Psychology, 73,* 497-506.

Sundstrom, E., DeMeuse, K. P., & Futrell, D. (1990). Work teams: Applications and effectiveness. *American Psychologist, 45,* 120-133.

Sussmann, M., & Robertson, D. U. (1986). The validity of validity: An analysis of validation study designs. *Journal of Applied Psychology, 71,* 461-468.

Taylor, H. C., & Russell, J. T. (1939). The relationship of validity coefficients to the practical effectiveness of tests in selections: Discussion and tables. *Journal of Applied Psychology, 23,* 565-578.

Terman, L. M. (1916). *The measurement of intelligence.* Boston: Houghton Mifflin.

Terpstra, D. E., & Rozell, E. J. (1993). The relationship of staffing practices to organizational level measures of performance. *Personnel Psychology, 46,* 27-48.

Tett, R. P., Jackson, D. N., & Rothstein, M. (1991). Personality measures as predictors of job performance: A meta-analytic review. *Personnel Psychology, 44,* 703-742.

Thissen, D., Steinberg, L., & Wainer, H. (1993). Detection of differential item functioning using the parameters of item response models. In P. W. Holland & H. Wainer (Eds.), *Differential item functioning* (pp. 67-114). Hillsdale, NJ: Lawrence Erlbaum.

Thomson, D. (1980). Adaptors and innovators: A replication study on managers in Singapore and Malaysia. *Psychological Reports, 47,* 383-387.

Thorndike, R. L. (1949). *Personnel selection.* New York: John Wiley.

Thurstone, L. L. (1938). Primary mental abilities. *Psychometric Monographs, 1.*

Thurstone, L. L. (1941). Primary mental abilities of children. *Educational and Psychological Measurement, 1,* 105-116.

Torbiorn, I. (1982). *Living abroad.* New York: John Wiley.

Tosi, H., & Tosi, L. (1986). What managers need to know about knowledge-based pay. *Organizational Dynamics, 14*(3), 52-64.

Tracey, T. J., & Rounds, J. B. (1993). Evaluating Holland's and Gati's vocational interest models: A structural meta-analysis. *Psychological Bulletin, 113,* 229-246.

Tracey, T. J., & Rounds, J. B. (1996). The spherical representation of vocational interests. *Journal of Vocational Behavior, 48,* 3-41.

Tsui, A. S. (1990). A multiple-constituency model of effectiveness: An empirical examination of the human resource subunit level. *Administrative Science Quarterly, 35,* 458-483.

Tsui, A. S., Egan, T. D., & O'Reilly, C. A., III. (1992). Being different: Relational demography and organizational attachment. *Administrative Science Quarterly, 37,* 549-579.

Tucker, L. R., & Lewis, C. (1973). A reliability coefficient for maximum likelihood factor analysis. *Psychometrika, 38,* 1-10.

Tung, R. L. (1981). Selection and training of personnel for overseas assignments. *Columbia Journal of World Business, 16,* 68-71.

Turban, D. B., & Keon, T. L. (1993). Organizational attractiveness: An interactionist perspective. *Journal of Applied Psychology, 78,* 184-193.

Tziner, A., & Eden, D. (1985). Effects of crew composition on crew performance: Does the whole equal the sum of its parts? *Journal of Applied Psychology, 70,* 85-93.

Ulrich, L., & Trumbo, D. (1965). The selection interview since 1949. *Psychological Bulletin, 63,* 100-116.

Undheim, O. J., & Horn, J. L. (1977). Critical evaluation of Guilford's structure-of-intellect theory. *Intelligence, 1,* 65-81.

U.S. Congress, Office of Technology Assessment. (1987). *The electronic supervisor: New technology, new tensions* (OTA-CIT-333). Washington, DC: Government Printing Office.

Vance, R. J., Coovert, M. D., MacCallum, R. C., & Hedge, J. W. (1989). Construct models of task performance. *Journal of Applied Psychology, 74,* 447-455.

Vance, R. J., MacCallum, R. C., Coovert, M. D., & Hedge, J. W. (1988). Construct validity of multiple job performance measures using confirmatory factor analysis. *Journal of Applied Psychology, 73,* 74-80.

Vinchur, A. J., Schippmann, J. S., Smalley, M. D., & Rothe, H. F. (1991). Productivity consistency of foundry chippers and grinders: A 6-year field study. *Journal of Applied Psychology, 76,* 134-136.

Viswesvaran, C. (1996, April). *Modeling job performance: Is there a general factor?* Paper presented at the 11th Annual Conference of the Society for Industrial and Organizational Psychology, San Diego, CA.

Wagner, R. (1949). The employment interview: A critical summary. *Personnel Psychology, 2,* 279-294.

Wanous, J. P. (1992). *Organizational entry: Recruitment, selection, orientation, and socialization.* Reading, MA: Addison-Wesley.

Wards Cove Packing Co., Inc., v. Atonio, 490 U.S. 642 (1989).

Watson v. Fort Worth Bank & Trust, 487 U.S. 977 (1988).

Webster, E. C. (1964). *Decision making in the interview.* Montreal: Eagle.

Weiss, H. M., & Adler, S. (1984). Personality and organizational behavior. In B. M. Staw & L. L. Cummings (Eds.), *Research in organizational behavior* (Vol. 6, pp. 1-50). Greenwich, CT: JAI.

Wexley, K. N., Alexander, R. A., Greenawalt, J. P., & Couch, M. A. (1980). Attitudinal congruence and similarity as related to interpersonal evaluations in manager-subordinate dyads. *Academy of Management Journal, 23,* 320-330.

Wexley, K. N., & Silverman, S. B. (1978). An examination of the difference between managerial effectiveness and response patterns on a structured job analysis questionnaire. *Journal of Applied Psychology, 63,* 646-649.

Whitener, E. M. (1990). Confusion of confidence intervals and credibility intervals in meta-analysis. *Journal of Applied Psychology, 75,* 315-321.

Whitney, D. J., & Schmitt, N. (1997). Relationship between culture and responses to biodata employment items. *Journal of Applied Psychology, 82,* 113-129.

Wigdor, A. K., & Green, B. F., Jr. (Eds.). (1991). *Performance assessment for the workplace* (Vol. 1). Washington, DC: National Academy Press.

Willett, J. B., & Sayer, A. G. (1994). Using covariance structure analysis to detect correlates and predictors of individual change over time. *Psychological Bulletin, 116,* 363-380.

Williams, C. R. (1990). Deciding when, how, and if to correct turnover correlations. *Journal of Applied Psychology, 75,* 732-737.

Wilson, M. A. (1990). *Respondent estimates of task inventory validity.* Unpublished manuscript.

Wilson, M. A., Harvey, R. J., & Macy, B. (1990). Repeating items to estimate the test-retest reliability of task inventory ratings. *Journal of Applied Psychology, 75,* 158-163.

Wonderlic, E. F. (1984). *Wonderlic Personnel Test manual.* Northfield, IL: Author.

Wright, P., Ferris, S. P., Hiller, J. S., & Kroll, M. (1995). Competitiveness through management of diversity: Effects on stock price evaluation. *Academy of Management Journal, 38,* 272-287.

Yerkes, R. M. (1921). Psychological examining in the United States Army. In *Memoirs of the National Academy of Sciences* (Vol. 15). Washington, DC: Government Printing Office.

Youndt, M. A., Snell, S. A., Dean, J. W., Jr., & Lepak, D. P. (1996). Human resource management, manufacturing strategy, and firm performance. *Academy of Management Journal, 39,* 836-866.

Zickar, M. J., & Drasgow, F. (1996). Detecting faking on a personality instrument using appropriateness measurement. *Applied Psychological Measurement, 20,* 71-87.

Author Index

Subject Index

About the Authors

Neal Schmitt is University Distinguished Professor of Psychology and Management at Michigan State University. From 1989 to 1994, he served as editor of the *Journal of Applied Psychology,* and he was President of the Society for Industrial and Organizational Psychology from 1989 to 1990. He was a Fulbright Scholar at the Manchester Institute of Science and Technology in 1987. He has coauthored two textbooks, *Staffing Organizations,* with Ben Schneider, and *Research Methods in Human Resource Management,* with Richard Klimoski. He coedited *Personnel Selection in Organizations,* with Walter Borman, and has published more than 100 articles in selection and measurement topics in a variety of journals. He has also worked with many public and private organizations in the development and validation of selection systems and has served as an expert witness in legal cases involving allegations of unfair employment practices. He received his Ph.D. in industrial/organizational psychology from Purdue University in 1972.

David Chan is Lecturer in Psychology at National University of Singapore. From 1990 to 1992, he designed the Singapore Police Force (SPF) Assessment Center and served as its Chief Administrator. He also developed the concept plan for the SPF's Police Psychological Unit, which became operational in 1993, and served on the SPF's advisory panel of psychologists in 1992. He was an Overseas Graduate Scholar at Michigan State University from 1993 to 1998. In 1998, he received the Edwin Ghiselli Research Design Award from the Society for Industrial and Organizational Psychology as well as the American Psychological Association Dissertation Research Award. He has published research on selection and applied cognitive measurement in several journals, including the *Journal of Applied Psychology, Cognition, Organizational Behavior and Human Decision Processes, Applied Psychological Measurement, International Journal of Selection and Assessment, Journal of Occupational and Organizational Psychology, Intelligence, Journal of Business and Psychology,* and *Human Performance.* He has also worked with a variety of public and private organizations on selection-related projects. He received his Ph.D. in industrial/organizational psychology from Michigan State University in 1998.